1972, his activities as choreographer, teacher, performer, and impresario illuminate as well the struggles against current sexual and cultural prejudices made by all early modern American dancers as they fought to take their rightful place on the concert stage of the world.

Part Two of this book describes fourteen dances representative of that struggle. "They were pioneering works for their day," Mumaw observes, "and I therefore believe they merit the attention of those who wish to trace the stream of American dance back to one of its most important sources."

Encompassing sixty years of his creative life, Barton Mumaw's autobiography unfolds like a novel. Anyone who is intrigued by the varied aspects of human character will be richly rewarded by reading it.

*Barton
Mumaw,
Dancer*

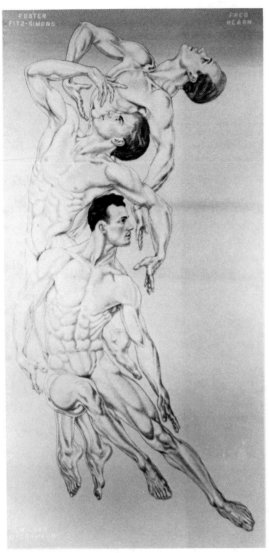 

Fred Hearn

Foster Fitz-Simons

Wilbur McCormack

Ted Shawn

Frank Overlees

Dennis Landers

Barton Mumaw

Barton Mumaw, Dancer

From
Denishawn
to
Jacob's Pillow
and Beyond

by
Jane Sherman
and
Barton Mumaw

Dance Horizons
New York

ACKNOWLEDGMENTS

The conventional acknowledgment seems to the authors a
feeble means by which to express our gratitude to each of
those who generously shared with us their assistance, their
memories, their material, their loving encouragement, or a
combination of all these. We prefer, therefore, simply to say
"Thank you" again to William Como, Kitty and Francis
Cunningham, Anne Douglas Doucet, George Dorris,
Stephan Driscoll, Ambrose du Bek, Stanley Faulkner, Sarah
Jeter, Etta Mumaw Klee, Ruth Koch, Ann and Jack
Kolodny, Ned Lehac, Joseph E. Marks III, Jess Meeker,
Esther Miller, Marvin Morgenstern, Norton Owen, Patsie
Padula, Barbara Palfy, Richard Philp, Viola E. Purvis,
Edith Royal, Christena L. Schlundt, Gertrude Shurr,
Beatrice Siegel, Louise Smith, Grace Mumaw Snyder, John
W. Stoakley, Walter Terry, and Kathryn E. Williams.

Copyright © 1986 by Jane Sherman and Barton Mumaw

ISBN 0-87127-138-9

Library of Congress Catalog Card Number 83-71538

Printed in the United States of America

Dance Horizons, 1801 East 26th Street, Brooklyn, N.Y. 11229

TO THE MEMORY OF TED SHAWN

AND TO HIS "BAND OF EXPERT DANCERS ALL

IN THE FIRST BLOOM OF YOUTH."

—Homer, *The Odyssey*, trans. by E.V. Rieu

Contents

LIST OF ILLUSTRATIONS

All photographs are from the collection of Barton Mumaw
unless otherwise indicated.

Title page: Ted Shawn and six of his Men Dancers, tryptich
painted by dancer-artist Hubert Stowitts.

Page vii: Invitation to Jane Sherman from Ted Shawn, 1941.

Part-title pages: Photograph by John Lindquist of the
weathervane on top of the Ted Shawn Theatre at Jacob's
Pillow, a pose from Barton Mumaw's solo, *Bourrée.*

Ruth St. Denis and Ted Shawn in *Siddhas of the Upper Air,* 1964. (Collection of Jane Sherman)

Barton Mumaw and Ted Shawn teaching, Jacob's Pillow, 1971. (Photo by John Van Lund)

Reunion at Jacob's Pillow, 1971. (Photo by John Van Lund)

Last studio portrait of Ted Shawn, 1971. (Photo by Jack Mitchell)

Last photograph of Ruth St. Denis, 1968.

Last photograph taken of Ted Shawn and Barton Mumaw together, 1971. (Collection of Edith Royal)

Barton Mumaw in performance at Jacob's Pillow, Ted Shawn memorial season, 1972; in *Mevlevi Dervish.* (Photo by John Van Lund)

Ted Shawn in *Mevlevi Dervish.* (Collection of Jane Sherman)

Barton Mumaw in performance, Ted Shawn memorial season; in *Divine Idiot, Four American Dances,* and *Negro Spirituals.* (Photos by John Lindquist)

Barton Mumaw in *O Brother Sun and Sister Moon,* 1981. (Photo by Stephan Driscoll)

Men Dancers, Jacob's Pillow, 1934.

Men Dancers, Jacob's Pillow, 1982. (Photo by Stephan Driscoll)

Barton Mumaw demonstrating for students during "Denishawn Week," April, 1984, at The Florida State University, Tallahassee.

Nancy Smith Award plaque, June 1984.

PART TWO

PAGE 248:

Ted Shawn and Ruth St. Denis in *Idyll.* (Collection of Walter Terry)

PAGE 250:

Ted Shawn in *Gnossienne.* (Collection of Jane Sherman)

Barton Mumaw in *Gnossienne.* (Photo by Forbes)

PAGE 254:

Barton Mumaw in *The French Sailor.* (Photo by Shapiro)

PAGE 258:

Barton Mumaw in *Fetish.* (Photo by Barret Gallagher)

Miss Fern Helscher
Mr. Ted Shawn
Mr. Barton Mumaw

Friday, March twenty first
from four to seven

cocktails

R.S.V.P.   (over)   Hotel Sevillia
117 W. 58th St.

Invitation to Jane Sherman from Ted Shawn, 1941.

Dear Jane,
     I was thrilled to get
your personal note on the
postcard – I do hope
you can come Friday so I
can refresh my eyes with
your beauty once more!
Papa Denishawn   T S.

Preface by Jane Sherman

The year was 1941. Since I could not attend the party, I did not meet Barton Mumaw until 1976—our rapport was instantaneous. Stimulated by our shared Denishawn experience (albeit at different periods), by our shared respect, admiration, and affection for Ruth St. Denis and Ted Shawn (albeit to different degrees), we determined to write Barton's story as we relived it together through his spoken and written memories—his choreographic notes, books, letters, tapes, programs, interviews, clippings, photographs, and music.

When we began the exploration of this jungle of material, we soon perceived a goal more significant to dance history than the recording of the life of a single dancer. Inevitably, our adventure would lead us to follow the hitherto untold story of Shawn and Barton, of Shawn after the dissolution of Denishawn, of Shawn when he and his Men Dancers built Jacob's Pillow from a ramshackle farm into a world-renowned teaching and performing institution, of Shawn when his tours cleared the path for the male dancers who enrich American dance today.

Shortly after we started work on this book, I visited Barton's home in Florida on a balmy Christmas night. He led me outdoors to show me a patio he had just fenced and a little fish pond he had just completed, both built with the strong, square hands that remembered the boulders and timber of the Berkshires. From the cupped fingers of a stone cherub, a stream of water splashed down on cement waterlily pads artfully spaced in the pool. Along one patio wall stretched a scarlet silk dragontail banner, its serrated edges vivid with green, its large black Chinese characters spelling out RUTH ST. DENIS, TED SHAWN AND THEIR DENISHAWN DANCERS—a gift to Barton from Shawn. It was a souvenir of the Tokyo Imperial Theatre engagement during the famous 1925–26 Orient tour, of which I had been a part. Around the pool flickered lighted votive candles, each enclosed in a small paper bag standing upright on a base of sand.

This miniature stage set typified the labor, the persistence, the taste, and the creativity of Mumaw, man and dancer. As the candlelight on dark water reflected the bright and somber thoughts he was entrusting to me, so I have tried to reflect in these pages that gentle yet determined glow.

Introduction by Barton Mumaw

"Barton Mumaw is Ted Shawn's son by a Javanese princess," it was whispered.

"Barton Mumaw is a full-blooded American Indian," wrote a Boston critic as late as July 31, 1969.

"Barton Mumaw's mother and father begged Mr. Shawn on bended knees to take their son as a protégé," went the gossip.

All my professional life I have been plagued by such scraps of misinformation cut from the whole cloth of fiction. I am not Ted Shawn's son, by princess or by commoner. I cannot claim the distinction of having Indian blood, as the strange sound of my last name made many think. Mumaw is Dutch, and my stiff-necked, beloved Pennsylvania Dutch parents never bent knee to beg anything of anyone.

The mundane truth is that I left my middle-class, small-town home to enter the dance world on my own two feet, just at the time when Denishawn was disintegrating. For years, that institution had introduced new dance to thousands across our land and around the world with a theatrical color that was as important to the future development of American dance as were the innovations of Diaghilev's Ballets Russes to classical ballet. I made my modest debut in the Denishawn concerts of August 24, 26, and 28, 1931, at New York's Lewisohn Stadium. I little suspected then that these concerts marked the end of the seventeen-year-old partnership of Ruth St. Denis and Ted Shawn, and that the beautiful Denishawn House where I was studying was soon to close. Miss Ruth would depart for

California, and Ted Shawn would begin his arduous battle to advance serious dance as an acceptable art form for men.

It is a curious fact that women, although they had to struggle as hard to earn recognition in painting, writing, and music as in science, medicine, or business, nevertheless reigned supreme in dance. Until Shawn leaped upon the scene, no American male dancer equalled the fame and the originality of Isadora Duncan, Ruth St. Denis, Loie Fuller, or Maud Allan in the early days of what was to become modern dance. Shawn's fight for the right of men to participate in creative dance in the United States was as difficult as the fight of the suffragettes for the right of women to vote, and ultimately as successful. But the effort and the cost in personal conflict were enormous, as I know all too well. For I had the good—and sometimes the bad—fortune to have lived through the seven years of touring by the Men Dancers and to have contributed to the creation of the Theatre and School of Dance now known as Jacob's Pillow.

I look back in wonder at this painful, yet joyous, period of dance growth. As I try to recapture its excitement on paper, I wish I had been blessed with Ted Shawn's phenomenal memory. He had an unusual ability to recall the times and places, the details and circumstances, of his life. He lived with an immediate sense of the past, the present, and the future, while I concentrated on doing my best each day in order to do better on the next. This, unfortunately, often prevented me from paying close attention to what was going on right under my nose.

Somewhere, Virginia Woolf wrote a marvelous prescription for a successful biography: "To record on two levels of existence the rapid passage of events and actions, the slow opening up of single and solemn moments of concentrated emotion." It is a prescription I would love to be able to fill, but this is a most exasperating form of writing. In an autobiography where total revelation might unintentionally hurt others or seem to take advantage of those who can no longer speak for themselves, the author might appear unfeeling. Yet if he chooses to refine his ingredients to the point that most of the seasoning is omitted, the result can only lack flavor.

As I wrote this book, I followed as closely as possible a correct sequence of those events which are the most meaningful to me and will, I believe, shed the clearest light on this period of Shawn and the American dance. Some dates may not be precise and some significant persons or happenings may have been omitted. My memories are selective, as are the memories of most of us, and that is why this is perforce a personal rather than a historical document. Its claim to validity is based on my recollections of how a group of male dancers won recognition at a particular stage of our country's artistic development, and of my relationship to Ted Shawn.

By any standards, he was a titan—an American Renaissance man famous not only as dancer-choreographer, but as a compelling dance writer, lecturer, and raconteur whose every public appearance was a stunning performance; an innovator in education; a manager of dance companies, dance schools, and a dance theatre in an era when each had to pay its own way without help from government or corporations.

At the end of his long, honorable career of struggle and heartache, of accomplishments and honors, Ted Shawn was living in his Florida home-studio surrounded by the wood sculpture he called his "avocation." He was beset by the exigencies of age, illness, financial insecurity, and preparing for the fortieth season at Jacob's Pillow. Nevertheless, with characteristic fervor, he confirmed his faith in his life's work by writing and publishing *Credo*,* part of which I quote:

> I believe that dance is the oldest, noblest, and most cogent of the arts.
> I believe that dance has the power to heal, mentally and physically.
> I believe true education in the art of dance is education of the whole man—his physical, mental, and emotional natures are disciplined and nourished simultaneously in the dance.
> I believe that dance is the universal language, and, as such, has the power to promote One World. Dance can replace misunderstandings due to verbalization which distorts communication between the nations and races of mankind.
> I believe that dance is a way of life, which will lead humanity into continually higher and greater dimensions of existence.

This was the creed of the man in whose shadow and sunshine I lived most of my life.

---

*Ted Shawn, *Credo* (Privately printed ca. 1970).

PART ONE:
LIFE IN TIME

1

(1912–1930)

"The Day's At the Morn"

In essence, my life began in 1927, when I took my first dancing lesson in Eustis, Florida, and ended in 1972 when Ted Shawn died there. In fact, I was born in Hazleton, Pennsylvania, on August 20, 1912, and still function as a teacher, lecturer, and reconstructor of Shawn works. It will become clear, however, why the most significant years of my professional and personal life were bounded by the small southern town where my family settled around the end of World War I.

I was blessed with Margaret May, always known as Mazie, for mother, and Barton for father. Even as a child, I called them by their first names. They maintained their youthful sweetheart relationship, their "God's in his Heaven, all's right with the world" attitude, throughout their lives. This may sound syrupy, but syrup had been totally omitted from the recipe that determined their characters. Rather, the chief ingredient was a tough courage that enabled them to survive many hardships.

A team from their childhood days, they both had had to go to work for a living right after they graduated from high school. And, by coincidence, they both had studied voice with a pupil of the famous Mme. Mathilde Marchesi, who had taught Nellie Melba, Emma Eames, and other noted singers. Mazie and Barton married young and began their life together in Hazleton, a community in the heart of an anthracite coal region. Its location at the highest altitude of any town in the state was responsible for my parents' decision to move south when the mountain winters proved too rigorous for Barton. His job as a master moulder in a foundry was important and well-paying, particularly during the 1914–18 war. But he hated the hard physical labor and the harsh climate, both of which he blamed for the supposedly weak lungs and heart he had developed.

The only contacts we had in Florida were my aunt Kathryn and my uncle Clarence, who was Secretary of the Eustis Chamber of Commerce. Eustis, therefore, seemed the logical place to begin a new and presumably more healthful life. As a child, I could not know my family's financial situation, but, during my year in kindergarten, I learned that my mother worked part-time as a saleslady in the Hazleton Bon Ton Department Store (considered a "tony" position for a woman). There is little doubt that she and my father had accumulated some extremely modest savings toward this fresh start.

Mazie, believing every word she had heard, read, or been told about Florida's sunny climate, gave all our winter clothing to needy neighbors. Since the train coaches were heated and we would be in the tropics after a few days travel, there was no sense burdening ourselves with clothes we would no longer need. She then proceeded to deck the three of us out in raiment she considered appropriate for a journey into the southland. I can still see her fine figure and noble posture in her beige shantung silk suit, with a broad-brimmed hat to match which she had made herself. For my father she bought a lightweight, light-colored suit and a flat straw boater that he had to jam firmly on his head against the February breezes. I was garbed in short tan pongee pants, mini-socks with open-toed sandals, and a shirt on which Mazie had embroidered brown bears. Relatives who assembled to see us off at the railroad station reported in shocked tones that my legs were blue with cold.

Even at the tender age of five or six, I did not complain. My parents had taught me, by example and by discipline, that one's inner feelings must not be allowed to surface—a lesson that determines my reactions to this day. As I grew older, Dad often tried to see how much I could take without "showing," not in a malevolent way, but to train me how to be strong and stoic and thus able to face the world according to his beliefs. For example, when still very young, I was sent down into town all alone to have my hair cut at the nearest barber (unknown to me, my father followed at a distance to be sure I came to no harm). During the first few summers after we settled in Eustis, I was even shipped on my own by train to aunts in Pennsylvania because Mazie and Barton were convinced that the unrelenting heat would injure my health. These and similar independent experiences should have made me an outgoing person, but, except on certain occasions and with certain people, I have remained reticent, if not close to inarticulate.

Eustis, we discovered, was situated on the shore of one of the many large, crystalline lakes in central Florida. We were ecstatic with our new home that was set smack in the middle of citrus groves. As I was to learn in my teens, the scent of their flowering trees was devastatingly romantic, especially when a full moon shimmered on the mirror lake.

The town attracted regular seasonal visitors, who arrived from the north by train or by motorcar each December to stay at the Ocklawaha Hotel and spend their vacations boating or fishing or shuffleboarding or even trying their hand at the newfangled game of golf. Later, the fountain pen manufacturer, Frank D. Waterman, who made his winter home in Eustis, built the Fountain Inn. It was a model of taste and imagination for its day. I remember that palmetto stalks manipulated like rattan had been used to make the furniture, which was then painted pale green or yellow. Over the enormous lobby fireplace hung an equally enormous painting of De Soto first setting foot on Florida sands as he majestically acknowledged the "welcome" of an Indian who knelt before him, head bowed. The cuisine served in the elaborate dining room was excellent, but too expensive for most local pocketbooks.

The biggest treat for us was to take Sunday dinner at the Grand View. This white clapboard hotel sprawled like an overgrown private home, its wide verandahs shaded by luxuriant trees and bougainvillea vines. To my youthful eyes, the dim, cool dining room seemed vast and inviting, its tables gleaming with snowy napery and bright silver. And I pronounced the food super.

I must have loved to eat because I grew into a roly-poly grammar-school youngster with round cheeks and noticeably sturdy legs. I never walked, I ran: to school and back, to the store and back, and up and down stairs. I lengthened into a slim, firmly muscled adolescent with an erect carriage inherited from Mazie, all of whose relatives stood straight as flagpoles. Somehow I was made aware that, with my brown eyes, my high cheekbones, my dark hair, I was considered good-looking. This realization gave me neither a swelled head nor an outsize ego; I simply accepted it as a fact. By the time I entered high school, I had outgrown the vanity of plastering my locks into an imitation of Rudolph Valentino's patent leather hairdo, although I continued to think him beautiful.

Movies were a regular and an important part of our lives. The Busby Berkley musicals thrilled with their dance formations, "Tip-

toe Through the Tulips" was an unforgettable song, and Jeanette
McDonald's blonde loveliness turned my heart to jelly every time I
saw her on the screen. Yet, probably because that glamorous world
was too remote, I never yearned to be in pictures. Instead, since
both parents were musicians, music drew me like a magnet. I was
fascinated by our hand-wind Victrola, even when I was still so small
that I had to climb up on the chair next to it to reach the controls. I
danced to whatever record was played. When I was only four, I well
remember my grandmother's announcement that I would have to
buy her a new rug because I had worn a threadbare patch right in
front of the "talking machine."

My taste in classical and operatic works was formed by the
RCA Victor Red Seal records in the family's extensive collection, to
which I was given free access. The coloratura soprano voice especially entranced me: the "Jewel Song" from *Faust,* the "Bell Song"
from *Lakmé,* the *"Caro Nome"* from *Rigoletto,* all were favorites. It was
only later that I graduated to Beethoven or Tchaikovsky, and still
later to hours of Wagner.

Amateur singers though they were, Mother and Dad always
conducted themselves as true professionals whenever they appeared
in public. It was from their example that I acquired the discipline of
keeping one's word, of responsibility toward one's audience, of absolute self-dependence. None of these principles was pounded into
me; they simply constituted the fabric of our lives as Pennsylvania
Dutchmen. Barton had a light tenor voice, while Mazie's contralto
wrapped one in warmth. Together they made music, mostly celestial
because they sang a great deal in churches where Dad was an excellent, self-taught choral director. They always took me along to choir
rehearsals, during which I sat quietly (I am told) in a pew. I soon
learned that the music contingent was the war department of a
church of any denomination—the goings-on in the vestry were every
bit as explosive and temperamental as those I later witnessed backstage at Broadway musicals or ballet concerts.

Dad was also a very good violinist. He insisted upon giving me
lessons on his fiddle. But after a year of practice that sounded more
like a carpenter's rasp on glass than a horsehair bow on gut, I finally
confessed that the instrument and I would never be in tune. No
doubt delighted to be relieved of the daily torture I had inflicted on
their sensitive ears, Barton and Mazie readily agreed to get me the
piano for which I asked.

We had moved from the house in the citrus groves to an apartment at the center of town, the third home we had occupied since

coming to Eustis. (I was learning to adjust quickly to different habitations, an ability for which I would be grateful in future years of one-night stands.) The huge square piano, which took up most of the living room, had cost $50, representing a sizable expense. My parents never made me feel guilty about this, nor did they force me to take the lessons I soon began with Mrs. Cecil Strong. No one had to urge me to practice; I took to the keyboard like the proverbial duck to water. It was not long before I was playing accompaniments for Mazie and Barton on the frequent occasions they were asked to perform. Strictly in private, we called ourselves "The Unholy Three," after a popular horror movie of the day.

This close relationship, together with our standards of behavior and our many musical activities, tended to separate me from my contemporaries. In truth, the stigma of being "different" had been stamped upon the Mumaws from the day we arrived in Eustis. We had been taken aback upon first meeting our southern neighbors to hear them boast that they had been grown men or women before they knew that "damnyankee" was two words. Despite the handicap of being a northerner, however, from the moment I entered school I never lacked companionship. Girls and boys, teachers and other grownups became my good friends. Not all the boys accepted me into their circle of activities, and there were times when I felt this ostracism keenly. Yet the hurt did not prevent my work at the piano or my appearance in school plays. By the time I began to take dancing lessons, I think my peers had become so reconciled to my differentness that they took my weird new interest in stride.

I had moved easily and without self-consciousness for as long as I could remember, but I had never done anything that could remotely be called dancing. In my early teens, I made my debut on the streets of Eustis, doing a minuet with my classmates. I wore a wig, made of cotton batting, and knee britches of sateen, when I stepped with pointed toe and bowed with serious grace among the other young citizens who had been roped into a celebration of Washington's Birthday (Lincoln's was, of course, ignored). I was enchanted by the costume and by the formal movements that transformed me into a character who was no longer Barton Mumaw, Jr. I think it was then I knew that I had to learn more about this magic.

Around 1927, I found my way to a local teacher who gave me my first lessons in "classical ballet." Next, I came to the attention of Berte Rita Lipton, whose parents owned the Eustis Bargain Store and were friends of ours. During a brief New York visit, she had picked up a smattering of what she called "modern dance" and, with the super-enthusiasm of a convert, she urged, she demanded that I study with her. I cannot imagine what technique she taught me during the few lessons I had, but I do remember that she would take hold of my arms, my legs, my back, and actually mould my body into the positions she wanted it to assume. I also remember with gratitude her tremendous vitality and her insistence that I become a dancer. Hers was one of several influences—remarkable for a town the size of Eustis—that determined my future.

When I was fifteen, I was taken to see two gentle, graceful, elegant young women give a dance recital in the lobby of the Grand View Hotel. The audience sat in a semicircle of white wicker chairs ranked between potted palms. It was in this straitlaced, "genteel" atmosphere that I first saw free, expressive dance movement. One dancer, dressed in long, pale chiffon garments that reminded me of the robes worn by Greek goddesses in textbook pictures, moved on bare feet to lines of poetry recited by the other, who was identically robed. They were serious, original, full of unsophisticated sweetness and light. They bewitched me. I had read so little about Ruth St. Denis and Isadora Duncan that I failed to recognize the influence of those two great innovators of American dance. Why these young ladies were performing in a small-town hotel lobby is a question that intrigues me to this day. I suspect that they were dancing for their supper, something Ted Shawn and his Men Dancers often had to do in later years.

I took my next step into the world of dance by enrolling in a correspondence course given by the Veronine Vestoff Academie de Danse. Because its advertisement had appeared in my "bible," *Dance Magazine,* I saw nothing extraordinary about attempting to learn ballet by mail. Every seventh day I ran to the postbox to seize upon the envelope that contained a pamphlet describing in detail the progressively more difficult step-of-the-week. Each exercise came with appropriate sheet music and an ingenious instructional aid—a small flip-book with photographs of a dancer who seemed to move, as the pages were rapidly flipped, in a series of steps or combination of steps.

On the strength of these lessons, my father built a *barre* for me on our back porch and hung a shelf that held a record player and a stack of records. There, every day after school, rain or shine, I followed my texts and imitated my "motion pictures" as I learned to dance by long-distance. Having no ballet shoes, I wore soft slippers; having no practice costume, I wore my one-piece wool knit bathing

suit. I did not know that hundreds of Denishawn pupils were similarly garbed for their classes.

Neither did I know, in my enthusiasm and ignorance, that men
never danced *en pointe*. In answer to another *Dance Magazine* advertisement, I ordered by mail the largest size box-toe slippers listed. When
they arrived, I ran to put on my bathing suit and to fasten, with heavy
rubber bands, the beautiful pink satin slippers on my bare feet. Calling Mazie to bring our Kodak and record the momentous event, I
clumped out to the *barre*. Gripping it with my left hand, I assumed
fifth position and arched my right arm overhead. When Mother assured me she had me in focus, I took a deep breath and rose to the tips
of my toes. Immediately, my shoulders hunched up to my ears in
reaction to the unexpected, intolerable pain. I managed to hold the
awkward pose one unique instant as the shutter clicked. Then, with
exquisite relief, I brought my heels down, never again to wear the
treacherous slippers. No one had told me of lamb's-wool cups.

On flat foot and half-toe and sometimes in bare feet, I persisted
in my back-porch practice. Every week, I filled out and returned to
the correspondence school the question-and-answer tests sent to me.
I never received any marks, however, and, alas for posterity, no
record of my "graduation" from the Academie de Danse exists.

Disillusioned, but far from disheartened, I discovered Professor
Ebsen (father of the dancer-actor Buddy Ebsen). This good and distinguished gray-haired man ran a ballet school in Orlando. Much
like an old-time circuit preacher, he gave lessons in nearby towns on
a regular schedule. Leesburg on Mondays, Mt. Dora on Tuesdays,
and so on. With great excitement, I learned that he taught each
Wednesday in neighboring Tavares. These classes were held in a
lake-front mansion whose owner donated the ballroom on the top
floor of her home for Prof. Ebsen's weekly visits. Although I barely
knew the meaning of the word, I recognized that he was extremely
courtly. I was impressed by his teaching costume of black silk knee
britches, white shirt with full Lord Byron sleeves, white silk stock-
ings, and black slippers. I responded respectfully to the touch of the
long wand with which he corrected our positions. Perhaps he did not
give me much basic ballet training, but I loved every minute of the
discipline. I was later to be grateful for a bravura Brahms *Hungarian
Dance No. 5* that he taught my class.

Good fortune next directed me to the garage-studio of Ada
McLean, a beautifully trained ballet dancer, who had lost her opportunity for a professional career when both her ankles were broken in

an automobile accident. She gave me a first-rate technical foundation, for which I was always to be thankful.

It is curious that, despite all my dance activity, I had no burning desire to perform. Subliminally, I must have heard the siren song of the theatre, but before I succumbed to its lure I had an adventure that raised more than a few eyebrows in town. The summer of 1928, following my junior term in high school, I went to Paris with my language teacher.

Ruth Swinson had taught me French for two years, but I was not a particularly brilliant linguist and I had had no encounter with her outside the classroom. She was middle-aged, with an attractive figure, and hair the color people then called "titian"; I found her charming. What prompted her to invite me to accompany her abroad remains a puzzle, as does what prompted Mazie and Barton to let me go. They calmly accepted the invitation as a rare chance for me "to see something of the world" and "to improve your French." With the egotism of youth, I chose to ignore the obvious fact that they could not afford to give me such a trip, although neither of them indicated by so much as a flicker of an eyelash that paying for it might mean a sacrifice.

Years later, I learned how this episode in my cultural education had been financed. Most of the surrounding citrus groves were owned by our neighbors. We never had to buy oranges or lemons or grapefruit because these small growers designated certain cherished trees for themselves and their friends. The Keiths' distinctive oranges and the enormous, seed-free grapefruit and sweet lemons raised by Harry Day were always ours for the picking. The summer my parents sent me to Europe, they survived on a diet of this fruit, with bread, butter, and coffee. True to character, they never told me this, knowing that if they had, I would have refused to go.

It seemed that neither Mother nor Dad imagined that a sexual relationship might develop between the respectable teacher and their wet-behind-the-ears son during the weeks we would be together. *I* never imagined such a possibility because I was still at the stage when kissing and necking with a girl was as far as I dared to go—as far as I knew how to go.

I had made only one serious effort to learn more. Bewildered by hints of deeper sexual mysteries that I had heard from older boys, I confessed my puzzlement to a classmate, Sanford Horstman. Since he was equally puzzled, we concocted the idea of pooling our month's allowances to order a certain "book of sexual knowledge," which Sanford had seen advertised in the back pages of Physical Culture *magazine. We decided this should be mailed (in a plain wrapper, of course) to me, care of General Delivery. While awaiting its arrival, we nearly*

*exploded with anticipation. I ran to the post office every afternoon right after school
to ask for a package. The employees must have thought it peculiar for a postman's
son to expect mail at General Delivery. (Barton had passed Civil Service examination to become a mail carrier. He thought being out in the sun and fresh air every
day would build up his health. He was right. He lived to be eighty-five.) When
the book at long last arrived, I gave it to Sanford for safekeeping until we could find
a chance to read it together. Before we could turn a page, his mother, having been
informed of our nefarious partnership, confiscated the volume.*

*My parents never mentioned this incident to me. But not long after, Barton,
in his role as "Father," led me one Sunday morning to a small wooden pier on the
shore of the lake, where we sat with our feet dangling over the water. He pointed to
the schools of tiny fish we could clearly see swimming below us, and began to talk.
I listened to every word as he quietly, factually, and quite beautifully explained the
miracle of bringing new life into the world. Try as I would, however, I could find
no relation between the procreational activities of the silver minnows and the immediate questions that were so disturbing me. But I did not have the heart to tell
Barton this.*

Dad must still have wondered if I were really prepared for an
adult encounter with a person of the female gender while I was far
from home. On the eve of my departure for Europe, he approached
one of his cronies at the post office. This man apparently had told
Barton lurid tales of the hot times he had had as a doughboy in
France during World War I. My father, appreciating the value of
experiences far beyond his ken, asked his friend to pass this superior
knowledge on to me. It is impossible to tell which of us was more
embarrassed when the poor guy and I sat on the stoop of our house
on a warm June evening while he mumbled ways to avoid the temptations of Gay Paree.

Sure enough, I was tempted, almost the moment we reached
France! After dinner with Miss Swinson, I went out alone for a
walk—what red-blooded adolescent could endure sitting by himself
on his first night in Paris in a room containing a *bidet* (its use I only
instinctively guessed, but it fired my imagination)? As I had been
warned, a woman approached me before I had gone a half-block
from the hotel. I knew exactly what she was up to, even though I
could not understand a syllable of her whispered French. In the
damp gloom, I gained an impression of soft, drifting fabric and a
heady perfume before I turned hastily back, resisting temptation.
Exhilarated by this romantic, if abortive, adventure, I scurried up to
my solitary room, where I promptly pulled the flimsy white cotton
screen around the *bidet* and just as promptly sat down to write a
poem which I entitled, "The Painted Women." Now that I knew

Paris was indeed the evil city I had been told it was, I penned my sorrow at the plight of those whom one "saw" but could never "meet." The next morning, I mailed this opus to my parents.

Miss Swinson and I made a companionable, if incongruous, pair as we traveled around France. Only once in our weeks of journeying did we share a moment that hinted of sex. She was lying down in her room to rest from a day's sightseeing and I was sitting on the bed beside her, chatting. I do not remember what subtle sign she may have given me, but I suddenly felt the flare of a magnetic force between us. It expired as swiftly as a Fourth-of-July rocket, as far as I was concerned, because the powerful attraction so frightened me that I stumbled at once to my feet and escaped to my own room. No such incident ever occurred again. I remain as astounded by this as by the fact that no one back home ever questioned my parents about the propriety of lady teacher and male pupil traveling together unchaperoned on the wicked Continent.

I was much more fascinated by that continent than I was by dear Miss Swinson. I particularly enjoyed exploring Paris on my own, taking extensive, inexpensive bus tours of the city. This led to another "first" in my sexual education. One sunny afternoon, on a ride out to the Porte de Versailles, I became aware that a man in the seat opposite was staring at me with an oddly fixed expression. To my bewilderment, when my eyes met his, I experienced a strong physical reaction. Confused, yet at the same time intrigued, I jumped off the bus at the next stop. To my further confusion, the man followed me. There began a deliberate chase through many narrow, unfamiliar streets, during which I became thoroughly lost. When at last I succeeded in eluding my pursuer and found myself back at the hotel, I was (as in my encounter with the Lady of the Streets) not sadder or wiser, but I was certainly puzzled. Neither Barton's minnows nor his post-office buddy had alerted me to the possibility of this strange happening or of the conflicting emotions it had aroused in me.

For the rest of our tour, Miss Swinson and I followed the tourist route through cultural and historical treasures. She was so fluent and I so bashful in speaking the language that, by the end of the summer, all I achieved was the ability to read French aloud with an accurate Parisian accent (I have a good ear) but with only the vaguest idea of what the words meant.

I did, however, increase my dance education when I saw my second live professional performance. My first had occurred in New York before we set sail. Miss Swinson had taken me to the Roxy, *the* foremost movie palace of the day. The prologue preceding the film included a ballet sequence that left me spellbound. It was the first "toe dancing" I had ever seen on stage. I must, subconsciously, have been impressed by the structure, clarity, and apparent ease of that dancing because, when I saw the ballet in *Faust* at the Paris Opéra a little later, I was acutely critical of the dancers' awkwardness and lack of discipline. I later learned that my amateur reaction to the performance had been correct; the quality of the Opéra ballet in that period had deteriorated badly. It was also August, which meant that anybody who was anybody had left Paris and I had not seen the top dancers.

After I returned to home and school, I put aside my growing interest in dance to resume musical and theatrical activities, one of which left an indelible scar, but taught an invaluable lesson. I appeared as the leading man in the high-school senior class production of *The Last Mile*. The role of the priest who accompanied me from the death cell to the electric chair had been assigned, for an unfathomable reason, to a boy who was well known throughout the town as a comedian. When I entered to walk my "last mile," he followed me at a respectful distance, hands properly folded over his white surplice, a properly sanctimonious expression on his face. The audience burst into laughter the moment they saw him. Having no idea what they found funny in this tragic situation, I was mortified, but managed to keep in character. By the time I exited into the spotlight's glare, declaiming, "The valiant never taste of death but once" (or words to that effect), I had some members of that laughing audience in tears. As well as myself. Inconsolable, I ran weeping to the dressing room, convinced that I had ruined my best scene. I learned from this painful humiliation a professional rule I was never to forget: Carry on no matter what.

I have always been glad that I grew up in a community in which we all knew one another. Thanks to Barton and Mazie, I was never infected by any sex, race, class, color, or religious prejudices— a unique parental achievement in the South of the twenties. Members of the town's two Jewish families were among our friends, and we took it for granted that blacks were equal to everyone else.

Recalling this healthy attitude of my parents, I responded wholeheartedly to something Ted Shawn once said to me: "To know a man's actions is more revealing than to know his church affiliation or what he does in bed. His inner ethics interest me, not the labels our culture applies to outward appearances."

There were, of course, divisions of opinion and behavior among the residents of Eustis, but in general they were closely knit. I remember the time I ate ten doughnuts at a single sitting in the school cafeteria and the woman who had baked them telephoned Mother to warn her that she might have a sick'un on her hands. She was right, but to this day I have never tasted equally delicious doughnuts. A development much more serious than an upset stomach was handled with such wisdom by my high-school teachers that I still marvel at it.

Before I describe this, I should emphasize that homosexuality in the United States of that era was an unmentionable subject. I am positive, for example, that my father only vaguely understood the meaning of the word, even in those years to come when the topic began to be openly discussed. As for me, the bus incident in Paris had made no dent in my total innocence. From the time I could toddle, girls as well as boys had been my playmates. In Hazleton, I had grown up with numerous female cousins. In Eustis, especially after I had reached that arcane age when boys allow themselves to notice the opposite sex, I had many girls for friends as well as many girlfriends. I was as eager as any male contemporary to take my date to a secluded spot on the lake beach where the citrus-scented air was as intoxicating as forbidden wine and where I learned to "pet." I thoroughly enjoyed these fumblings, although I lacked the courage, the expertise, and the opportunity to go beyond them.

Even as I was happily participating with girls in these delightful explorations, I was also fantasizing about boys. Yet it was not precisely fantasizing because that implies the possibility of reality, whereas I had not the slightest idea what boys might do together sexually. In fact, sex of any kind remained nebulous to me right up to the day when I began to realize that my mathematics teacher filled my every waking thought.

This seemed mysterious and compelling, but hardly a serious problem. All I wanted was to be with Vernon Steen and to have him know what I felt for him. So, one day after class, I asked him to come to my house. I cannot now imagine what reason I fabricated for this invitation, but it must have been a convincing one because he arrived when my parents were not home, as I had planned. Since I had had no sensual experience with boys beyond the usual tentative touchings during swimming or when staying overnight with a current best friend, what could I possibly have said to the dumb-struck Mr. Steen? What went through the man's mind when he grasped the meaning of my naive mumbling? Well, I do not remember what he said, but I do remember what he *did*—he got out of the house as fast as his legs could carry him. We were never alone together again and, to my surprise, I quickly recovered from my strange emotional crisis.

I now see that this recovery was due, in great part, to the tact and understanding of my teachers. Suddenly, the physical education coach began urging me to try out for the basketball team, a ploy that failed, but I did play soccer for some time. Suddenly, other suggestions were made, aimed at helping me to "grow out of it." I was not for an instant made aware of being guided or guarded, an awareness that could have done me harm at that vulnerable time of my life.

All these perceptive teachers knew and respected my parents. They had no doubt decided among themselves to "cure" me of my "aberration" without alarming Mazie or Barton, for which I am still grateful. Their unusual concern for me may also have been caused by their belief that I was somehow special. I had won music memory contests and spelling bees in grammar school. I had written a "poem" that had been printed in the local paper when I was only ten years old:

> When ice cream grows on macaroon trees,
> When Sahara's sands are muddy,
> When dogs and cats wear overshoes—
> That's when I'd like to study.

In addition to this sign of literary talent, I had performed as Little Prince Sunshine in a children's musical and later had acted Eugene O'Neill heroes in several high-school productions of his plays.

I suffered a few more fantasy-yearnings after my experience with Mr. Steen but when I started "going around" with Mary Kinser, they vanished over my horizon like clouds before a strong wind. Mary's mother and father, who was a scientist-biologist, had given their daughter a very advanced education; she was much more exciting to talk to than the more conventional girls in my senior class. She had Rapunzel hair, one eye more green than gray, one eye more blue than gray, a mind as keen and frank as those eyes, and a physical attractiveness that I found irresistible. On many a moonlit night, our esoteric explorations of ideas ended in kisses that led to explorations of another kind more daring than any I had yet ventured—but never to complete discovery. If this puzzled Mary, I did not notice it.

Truth to tell, my limited sexual experience did not trouble me because I was champing at the bit to race into my future, although I had no idea what that future would be. It was the cultural activity of the town that persistently pointed me in the direction I would ultimately take. The self-proclaimed leader of that activity was an ample, redheaded steamroller named Anna Schumacher.

Mrs. Schumacher generally made life miserable for a lot of people who later came to be thankful to her, myself included. President of the Women's Club, active in the Eastern Star, the Garden Club, and the Episcopal Church choir, and an officer of the Florida State Federation of Music Clubs, she, among other things, also brought Chautauqua to Eustis. For those too young to remember it, Chautauqua was the great American cultural traveling institution that carried concerts and lectures into the hinterlands. It still exists in western New York State, but no longer travels. Watching the Chautauqua tent go up on a vacant lot in town was as exciting as the arrival of the Ringling Brothers Circus. Everyone bought season tickets long in advance to be sure not to miss this variety show under canvas that introduced us to noted speakers, singers, actors, actresses, and musicians.

A wonderful hostess, in a down-to-earth way, Mrs. Schumacher entertained these visiting celebrities whether they wished to be entertained or not. This was nice for my parents who, as the local artists, were always invited to whatever luncheon, tea, or dinner the indomitable Mrs. S. had arranged. It was very nice for me, too, because I was always invited as companion to the Schumacher daughter, Catherine, who was in my class at Ada McLean's ballet school. Dr. Schumacher made a gruff if charming host. He was a somewhat unorthodox osteopath, who had been trained in Germany. This placed him even further outside the Eustis pale than if he had been a Yankee, but the townspeople grudgingly appreciated his enthusiastic support of their artistic events.

Mazie, Barton, and I unfailingly participated in local presentations of *An Evening of Gilbert and Sullivan, Excerpts from Grand Opera,* and various annual outdoor pageants, as did most Eustis residents. Our town was too far off the main line to attract professional touring productions. The Mumaws and all their friends had to drive the twenty-eight miles to Sanford to hear Sergei Rachmaninov at the local high school, where he played to a packed audience. We were deeply impressed by the advance publicity that claimed this great man transported his own piano to every performance. Rich and rare fare, indeed! And the round trip to the concert over a single-lane road of brick paving was an adventure in itself.

I would have traveled over shattered glass to see theatre of any kind. The day Barton bought us tickets for *The Student Prince,* playing in Orlando thirty miles away, I was so excited that I raced my parents on my bike as they drove the car home to get ready for the trip. My front wheel hit a hole in the road, turning me 360 degrees over

the handlebars to land on my right hip. Dad and Mother rushed me
to Dr. Schumacher. He treated my spectacular bruises but found no
broken bones. He did inform us, however, that as a result of my
severe fall, I would probably have to walk with a cane by the time I
was forty years old.

But we had tickets for *The Student Prince*! In spite of the pain and
the dire prognosis for my future, Barton cushioned me with pillows
in the back seat of the car next to Mazie and off we went to Orlando
as if nothing had happened. I hopped into the theatre by clinging to
Dad and Mother as to a pair of crutches and collapsed into my seat
on my left buttock, my right leg stretched straight out into the aisle.
Immobile throughout, I enjoyed to the utmost what must at best
have been a third-rate performance of the indestructible musical. To
this day, the singing of "Overhead the moon is beaming" creates
nostalgia too strong for comfort, and a twinge in my right hip socket.

For less exciting entertainment, we attended private musical
evenings presented by community talent, or we listened to the symphonies and operas that issued from the "magic box" of radio. This
miraculous invention had recently become an essential piece of furniture in every home that could afford it. It was treated with such
respect that we made advance plans to go to a neighbor's house to
hear special programs. Once seated in the parlor, everyone behaved
as if in a real theatre, attending a real concert. Talk and refreshments
were reserved for after the performance.

The Bohemian Girl, staged at our movie house, had been the first
full-length professional production I had seen. The opera company
that put it on had been brought to town by Mrs. Jessie Mae Brown,
who owned the theatre. Originally from a large northern city, she felt
that all Florida was a cultural wasteland. To fill the void, she would
occasionally book a touring attraction if it met her high standards
and her low budget. Because we could not afford better seats, Mazie, Barton, and I sat in the balcony. From there, I glimpsed a perspective of bodies moving through three-dimensional space in a predetermined pattern, a choreographic problem that was to command
a great deal of my attention.

The director of *The Bohemian Girl* on this occasion was May
Valentine, renowned for being the first woman orchestra conductor
to tour the country. She produced, directed, and conducted the production, but I had no yardstick against which to measure the quality
of her accomplishments. To me, it was all wonderful. Years later, I
noticed her name in a program which listed her as director of the
chorus. I went backstage to pay her my belated respects. Before me

stood a tiny, aged woman with an expression in her eyes that could still snap to attention the most egotistic tenor or the flightiest prima donna. Madame Valentine smiled regally as she held out her hand to be kissed when we were introduced.

But this was in the future, and that future was undecided when I graduated from high school in 1929. I envied my classmates, all of whom, it seemed to me, were smugly assured of either going to college or entering their fathers' businesses. College was a financial impossibility for me, and I was not burning to follow Barton's footsteps on a mail-delivery route. I sought consolation for my unhappiness in dating a ravishing beauty named Dorothy Smoak. She was a year older than I, which lent me a certain badly needed cachet among my contemporaries. She was also the niece of Mrs. Will Goin. Mrs. Goin, familiarly known as Gillie, was a leader of the town's musical faction. She had long been a friend of Mazie and Barton. We often gathered at her large, beautiful home to hear newly-issued Red Seal records, played on her large, beautiful Victrola, or to sing together on Sunday evenings. In truth, the relationship between the ravishing Dorothy and me was based more upon her lovely soprano voice and my piano accompaniments than upon romance, a fact I carefully kept hidden from my envious classmates.

Mrs. Goin remained somewhat of an enigma to us. She was more than generous with time and money in her musical and religious activities, but all of us recognized that she was a mite miserly when it came to what she considered "unnecessary" expense. Thus, hungry as we might be, we always scrupulously refused "another" delicate Sunday-supper waffle, proffered though it was on the finest china; we always took care to assure her that we preferred to walk home, rather than oblige her to offer the use of the big motorcar parked under the porte-cochere. When it was her pleasure, however, she could and did open the purse strings which, in turn, opened influential doors. She was very ambitious for Dorothy to become a professional singer and underwrote her tuition at Rollins Conservatory of Music in nearby Winter Park. I was a favorite of Mrs. Goin. She frequently talked of helping me obtain a scholarship at the Conservatory for the coming fall term—talk that was music to my ears.

But Anna Schumacher, Gillie's rival as commander of the town's cultural forces, had other ideas for me. Madame Anna (as I always called her, much to her delight) was sending Catherine that summer to the Denishawn School of the Dance in New York City's Van Cortlandt Park. Denishawn House, she explained, was a kind of finishing school, where girls lived in a dormitory, studied dance and its related arts, were conscientiously chaperoned, and guided *en masse* through the city's museums as part of their training. The school also took nonboarding male students, and Mrs. S. thought I should be one of these.

I knew little about Ruth St. Denis and Ted Shawn, but Madame Anna described their ideas in such rapturous detail that I immediately began to dream of going north. It was a thoroughly impractical dream, of course, because I could not afford the trip to New York, let alone my living expenses and my lesson fees if I got there. Nevertheless, I will never forget that it was Mrs. Schumacher who gave me that dream, and who took a group of "artistic" young people from Eustis to see a Denishawn concert in Tampa. She did not know it. I did not know it. But that concert changed my life.

Above: Barton Mumaw and his mother Mazie, Hazleton, Pennsylvania, 1913.

Below: Mazie, Barton, Jr., and Barton, Sr., shortly before departure for Florida.

Right: A studio portrait of Barton Mumaw as "Little Prince Sunshine," his first stage appearance, grammar school in Eustis, Florida.

Lower right: Barton Mumaw in costume for his first dance, a minuet to celebrate Washington's Birthday, Eustis, Florida.

Barton Mumaw, Jr.
with great faith
in his future
from
Ted Shawn
Sept
1930

Ruth St. Denis on the roof terrace of Denishawn House, New York, 1930.

Opposite page, top left: Mary Kinser.

Opposite page, top right: With his parents, Barton Mumaw, age 14, in his first long pants.

Left: Ted Shawn as Jurgen in his ballet of the same name. Inscribed "To Barton Mumaw, Jr. with great faith in his future, from Ted Shawn. Sept. 1930".

Denishawn House, Van Cortlandt Park, New York, 1927.

The great studio at Denishawn House.

Ted Shawn in his *Flamenco Dances,* 1931.

Above: Ted Shawn as Satan in dress rehearsal of his ballet, *Job,* Lewisohn Stadium, New York, 1931. Barton Mumaw second from right in backbend.

Left: Barton Mumaw and Ada McLean in Shawn's *Idyll,* Eustis, Florida, 1931.

Below: Ted Shawn in *Frohsinn,* Germany, 1930.

2

(Summer 1930)

The Way Is Clear

A truly ecstatic experience is both unforgettable and impossible to recall. Of that most important dance performance by Ted Shawn and the Denishawn Dancers, I saw only a golden body that radiated intense energy. I knew then and there that I would be a dancer.

When the concert ended in a blur of color and music and the thrilling explosion of clapping hands, I automatically followed Madame Anna and her little band backstage to meet Ted Shawn. In my euphoria, I did not connect this ordinary mortal in a white robe with the supernal figure I had seen across the footlights. It was only during the drive home that fragments of the sights and smells and voices of that dressing-room scene merged into a clear mosaic in my mind: the brilliant electric bulbs encircling the large mirror; the makeup shelf cluttered with mysterious jars and gadgets; the odd, alluring odor of cosmetics mingled with perspiration; and Madame Anna relentlessly extolling the gifts of Catherine, the soon-to-be Denishawn pupil. With consternation, I realized that Mrs. Schumacher had also praised my own dancing talent to the no doubt exhausted but patient man. And then, I finally heard Ted Shawn telling me, "If you can come to New York this summer, I might include you in the ensemble for the two Lewisohn Stadium concerts." (I would not have been so overcome had I realized that, even if I had had two left feet, Denishawn would have accepted me; *any* male dancer at that time was a *rara avis* to be eagerly netted.)

I returned home determined to get to New York come hell or high water. Mazie and Barton had no savings at all—everything they had accumulated had been swept away in the whirlwind of that October's infamous stock market crash. The whole town had been hit by the same disaster, so the Mumaws felt no special shame at their situation: Mazie had lost to bankruptcy the Ladies Fashion Shoppe she had opened the previous year and Barton had cashed in his life insurance policy to pay the debts. How was I to go to, and stay in, New York? That I was going to dance on the same stage with Ted Shawn if I had to beg my way every step of the 1,100 miles that separated us was not a question.

I have always believed that our lives are more or less predetermined by a plan for each of us. This belief was soon justified for the first of many times. Just when I despaired of ever reaching New York, my teacher and friend, Antoinette Mulliken, told me that she and two other teachers had rented an apartment near Columbia University, where they planned to take courses that summer. A hall bedroom in the same apartment was available; she suggested that I might live there with them. (Tony was repeating her role as *dea ex machina:* it was she who had taught me the minuet for the Washington Birthday celebration, she who had directed me in many high-school plays.) With the prospect of reasonable and respectable shelter for their ambitious son, Mazie and Barton assured me they would, somehow, scrape together $10 a week for my living expenses. I was saying goodbye to them, ready to set out on my odyssey by foot, when, like Cinderella's coach, a truck stopped at our door. The driver, a family friend, was headed north to deliver some goods. He offered to take me as far as Charleston.

It may seem strange that such a callow teen-ager could leave parents, home, and familiar surroundings without a qualm. But my lack of fear for the morrow was one of the many gifts my parents had bequeathed me. Furthermore, in those days, no one was apprehensive about hitchhiking because this was a principal method of travel in the desperate search for jobs during the Great Depression. With the compassion that common misfortune always seems to evoke, people lucky enough to own a car shared it with the less fortunate. The thumber and picker-upper were equally safe.

Long before I was taught the gesture theories of François Delsarte, I learned the power of the thumb—it was my passport to glory. After my truck lift to South Carolina, I had no trouble getting rides that carried me into New York in only three days, sleeping the nights through in whatever vehicle was transporting my weary body. The two-lane main roads passed through the heart of every town and I was beguiled by their individuality.

Once settled in my shoebox of a room, I went right out to explore Manhattan. I was not intimidated by its enormity or confusion because I walked its avenues with the confidence of one who had an assured income. After paying my rent of $6, I was certain I could stretch the remaining $4 to cover the week's food and transportation. Fortunately, I was often invited to have dinner with my three teacher-Graces; otherwise, I would have gone to bed hungry many a night. Fortunately, the subway fare was only five cents; otherwise, I would have had to walk long distances. My first ride on the IRT was, of course, a pilgrimage up to Van Cortlandt Park, where Denishawn House perched on the brink of a reservoir, its Moorish architecture an island in a sea of red brick Bronx apartment houses.

Mrs. Schumacher had told me that this glamorous establishment had been built with the money earned from the forty-week tour of the 1927–28 *Ziegfeld Follies,* of which Ruth St. Denis, Ted Shawn, and their Denishawn Dancers had been the stars. She had also said that at its dedication Miss St. Denis, placing one hand on a wall, had exclaimed to the distinguished guests, "Every brick a one-night stand!" So, on this July morning, I was prepared for my initial sight of the beautiful building where I hoped to study. But I certainly was not prepared to meet either the fabulous St. Denis or the golden Shawn. Fearing such an encounter, I had to force myself to knock on a door marked "Office." It was opened by a tall, gauntly handsome man who introduced himself as Fred Beckman. (I later learned that he was an escapee from Kankakee, Illinois, who had joined the Denishawn Company as personal representative after Ted Shawn met him in Corpus Christi, Texas, during the *Follies* tour.) Seating me in a chair near his desk, he charmingly put me at ease by asking all the right questions in his strong midwestern accent. I must have given all the right answers because the next thing I knew, I was rehearsing for the ballet, *Angkor Vat,* in the Denishawn House studio.

This room rose a full two stories and, to my dazzled eyes, appeared to be at least a block long. The walls were hung with soft green draperies which, I was to discover, concealed the *barres* and the tremendous mirrors until they were needed for classes. An ebony concert grand piano stood in the right front corner at the foot of a life-size Buddha, whose gold-leafed image was reflected in the surface of the polished wood floor. With his reassuring, enigmatic smile, he was to become, for me, the guardian spirit of the school.

I was to discover that a flat roof invited sunbathing or afternoon tea and that a large outdoor patio, paved with tile and surrounded by high plaster walls, served for social functions, special classes, and countless publicity photographs. But at the moment, I had eyes only for the first bona fide dance studio I had ever seen, a memorable introduction to those other studios in which I was to spend much of my subsequent life.

Despite the beauties of the room, I was apprehensive about participating in the rehearsal. I looked in vain for the familiar face of Catherine Schumacher among the dancers who were filing into the studio. Although the night was warm, I shivered in my bare feet and my old bathing suit (which I had been instructed was de rigueur), isolated among the many similarly clad young girls and a sprinkling of young men, all of whom seemed to know one another. The more animated their talk, the more I felt totally alone.

We were rehearsing at night for a simple economic reason: most of the extras chosen by Miss St. Denis and Mr. Shawn for the up-coming August 12 and 14 appearances had to hold on to their mediocre daytime jobs in order to indulge in the art of dancing after dark. These pupils and outside dancers were brought in to fill the gap in the professional Denishawn Company, which was far too small for the elaborate productions planned for the great stage of the Stadium.

The blackness beyond the tall studio windows created an illusion of boundless spaciousness within. I was not the least surprised to see that when Ruth St. Denis and Ted Shawn finally entered this space, they seemed to loom above the rest of us like two giants from another world. I stood wooden with awe at my first sight of the white-haired goddess who drifted by in pale, floating chiffon. She smiled with gentle firmness as she began to place one dancer "Here, dear" and another "There, dear" and the rest wherever her whims directed. But the figure in his stark, black silk leotard truly riveted my attention.

To my disappointment, Mr. Shawn disappeared after having assisted at the rehearsal only a brief time. When he returned, he was unexpectedly costumed in tight black tapered pants, frilled white shirt, cummerbund under short black jacket, broad-brimmed black Andalusian hat, and the heeled boots that could and did become musical instruments. He stood before us tall, silent, tense, almost menacing until, without a word from him, we sat down on the floor to watch what I presumed was a new number he wished to try out before an audience. Instead, he began the same stunning Flamenco dances I had seen in the Tampa concert. Perhaps he intended, by this unusual studio performance, to stimulate a more enthusiastic spirit in his dancers. If this were his intention, it worked, at least for me. Excited by the brilliant technique—the deft, intricate footwork, the snapping fingers, the physical sensuality, the arrogant pose at the end—I leaped to my feet, applauding madly. A pupil tried to pull me down, but I shook him off, crying, "Get up, all of you! Get up!" When Mr. Shawn ignored my standing ovation, I sank back to the floor, thoroughly convinced that I had made an idiot of myself. (He was not to tell me until many months later how much my spontaneous homage had pleased him.)

The Ted Shawn of 1930 was at the peak of his maturity as man and as artist, handsome and confident in a full-bodied, authoritative, masculine way. Small wonder that he commanded the respect of those who saw him on the lecture platform as well as on the stage; that he was able to change the attitude of an entire country toward men in the dance; that I responded unselfconsciously when he first danced so close to me that I could hear his breathing, feel his powerful heel-beats reverberate up my spine from the gleaming floor to the top of my head.

I came down to earth after a few weeks of rehearsals when I realized that I would have to find some way to eke out my meager allowance if I were to continue with Denishawn beyond the summer. Recalling my "success" as the lead in the play, *Jazz and Minuet,* for which our high school had won a State award, I decided that the theatre was the logical place to seek a job. I began to knock at the stage door of theatres up and down the alleys off the side streets near Broadway. (On the eve of our first tour, Shawn instructed his inexperienced Men Dancers how they could always be sure to locate the stage door at any theatre they were to play: "Just go down an alley and up a drain and there it will be," he told us.) Most of the formidable iron barriers I approached remained locked. On the rare occasion when a doorman answered my knock, he gaped at me as if I were crazy when I asked him for work, then slammed the door in my face. No one troubled to tell me that this was not the way an aspiring actor breaks into the theatre.

In the end, it was a way. One day I passed the open door of the Cherry Lane Theatre in Greenwich Village. Men and women walked in and out; voices declaimed from the barren stage I glimpsed inside. Grasping my courage in both fists, I followed another young man into the theatre and presented myself to the stage manager. He took one look at us, muttered, "You'll do," and handed us each a script to study before reading for the director. My co-actor and I went to a corner of the stage to rehearse our scene. As we started to feed each other lines, it dawned upon me that we were supposed to enact the roles of lovers. This was a great shock to one

who had declaimed the words of O'Neill's rugged heroes and long
dreamed of playing Romeo. Why had I been so quickly chosen to
try out for such a part? I dropped my script to the floor and ran from
the backstage gloom into the sunlight.

Disillusioned and discouraged, I scoured my brains for some
other way to make money. I remembered that, shortly before I left
Eustis, Mazie had wanted a portrait of me, so we had gone to a
photographer who was new in town. When he looked over the
proofs, he asked permission to use my pictures in his window display, casually remarking that I might make a good model. This was
a word that meant nothing to me at the time, but now it did. I
dashed to the first agency I could find where, of course, "May I see
your photographs?" was the first question I was asked. I had none.
In my innocence, I had supposed that they would do the picture-
taking. Some days later, armed with the glossy prints Mazie had sent
in response to my telegram, I returned to the same agency. This
time, instead of examining my proffered pictures, the interviewer
eyed me up and down. "Is *that*," he asked, pointing disdainfully at
my best suit, "the only outfit you own?" Well, yes. It was. Back
home, that one "good" suit was all I had needed. Now it looked
much the worse for wear in the hellish heat of a New York summer
and, since I could not afford to increase my wardrobe, my modeling
ambitions came to as abrupt an end as had my acting career.

Squeezing by on my $10 a week, I went every night to
Denishawn House where, in the fascination of rehearsals, I forgot
the problems of humdrum daily life. It was on a subway trip up
there that I first met Jack Cole. One look at my bag of practice
clothes and he knew we were both bound for the same destination.
Jack was a member of the Denishawn Company, and I looked up to
him with admiration. As we talked over the subway's rumble during
the long trip, I saw he was amused by my naiveté.

That year, I was a Denishawn "new one" among the dancers
who had appeared in previous Stadium concerts. It was always a
problem to discover enough men for the ensembles demanded by the
progressively larger productions. Arthur Moore, a young dancer
and upstate-New York college professor, helped St. Denis and
Shawn recruit—from physical education departments, from the
Y.M.C.A., from friends of friends—any male who could be persuaded to participate in this questionable activity. Arthur must have
pointed me out to Shawn as a rookie who might merit watching
because, at an afternoon party for the company, the Great Man

singled me out for a brief chat about dancing. That was as close as I got to him all summer.

Shawn had no role in the St. Denis ballet, *Angkor Vat,* but he came often to help "Ruthie" with her choreography of group movement. We overheard frequent exchanges of "Teddy, don't you think that . . ." and "I know, dear, but . . ." and much laughter as they experimented with ways of manipulating us into a semblance of the famous sculptures. At one point, after everyone had been assigned places in a certain scene, two dancers remained on the sidelines. One of them timidly asked Miss St. Denis what they should do. She frowned down at them from her private reverie, pursed her lips like a schoolteacher, and replied, "Oh, just go over there, dears, and make an elephant." They did.

This faith in the ability of the human body to be anything was typical of St. Denis. Shawn once told me that, when she was working out her famous solo, The Legend of the Peacock, *a friend who had been watching her peculiar strutting movements turned to Ted in bewilderment. He reassured the puzzled man with a grin, saying, "That's all right. Ruthie believes she's a peacock. Just agree with her and she won't become violent."*

I soon learned that while St. Denis and Shawn handled the difficulties of their craft with humor, both conscious and unconscious, they had different standards for rehearsals. She loved to put on a show for the distinguished visitors who often dropped in to watch our progress: real work came to a halt as rehearsing was immediately transformed into performing. He banned all spectators when he was choreographing in the belief that "outside" vibrations interfered with his concentration.

I also learned that one could feel solitary even when surrounded by many people. I made no new friends, and Catherine Schumacher might just as well have still been in Eustis as far as I was concerned. She studied in the school by day and, each night after rehearsal, she and the other girl-boarders were led by a chaperone back to the dormitory to see that they got their proper rest, it was said. I suspect it was to ensure that they did not get involved with the male pupils.

If it had not been for my deep involvement in the dance work, I might have been very lonely. The technique, although different from anything I had been taught, was engrossing. I slipped into it as if I had studied it for years, to find that I could do anything I was asked to do. Working in bare feet did not seem strange because I had frequently done my back-porch *barre* without slippers, and more than once I had spontaneously danced barefoot on the lawn of a warm evening to recorded music that came through the open living-room windows. Perhaps I was a born Denishawner, for to me all dancing was dance—from Ada McLean's formal ballet to the Burne-Jones "Grecian" ladies in the Grand View Hotel lobby to Professor Ebsen's Hungarian romp. I saw no reason why one style should exclude another, nor why, for that matter, dance should not encompass music, poetry, and drama.

As work progressed to the conclusion of *Angkor Vat*, I sensed that this would be a remarkable recreation in dance of those fantastic ruins. St. Denis choreographed steps and movements based upon the ancient carvings with which the temple walls were covered. Her vision was realized through the skill and artistry of Pearl Wheeler, her close companion and long the invaluable costume designer for Denishawn. In a setting painted the sand and earth colors of the structure in its jungle setting, the dancers wore costumes of the same shades, their bodies tinted with brown paint. Under expert lighting, each intricate, crumbling sculpture came to breathing life.

It was inexpressibly thrilling to be even a minor part of such a work. But as the weeks passed, I began to worry about what I would do after the Stadium performances. I had made no progress at all in finding that essential self-supporting job or discovering any help that might advance my career as a dancer. I feared I would have to go back to Eustis after my modest debut, when Fate intervened to deprive me even of that achievement.

I was returning from a delicatessen with supplies for a dinner with my three teachers, when I stepped off a curb and was knocked flat by a taxi. Embarrassed by my stupidity, I gathered up the spilled groceries, assured the cab driver I was all right, walked two blocks, climbed up the stairs to the apartment, opened the door, and collapsed. My old don't-let-it-show training got me through that little performance, but I was left with an ankle so severely twisted that all immediate hopes of dancing were blasted.

With the deepest despair, I forced myself to make the trip up to Denishawn House the next morning to report what had happened. I limped painfully into the office, showed Fred Beckman my injury, and, assuming a mask I hoped disguised my real feelings, held out my hand to say goodbye. To my surprise, Mr. Beckman suggested that I might want to see Ted Shawn before I left. He led me into the dining room, which was deserted at that hour, and told me to wait until Mr. Shawn had finished teaching a class. When he came into the room, he was wiping his face with a towel. A long white cotton kimono hung open over his black suit and perspiring body. Although he looked to me like a sun god, his first words were as down-to-earth as a chiropractor's. Examining my ankle, he told me in stern, businesslike tones, to go home and apply alternate hot and cold cloths, followed by manipulation and short periods of walking. As he took my arm to help me hobble to the door, he said, "You know, Barton, our temporal plans often do not work out, but our dreams sometimes do."

I have remembered each word, not only because they lifted my spirits at a time when they badly needed a hoist, but because they were so characteristic of the way Shawn always combined the practical with the philosophic. I was to hear him repeat this same observation in similar "therapy" situations throughout the coming years.

When I thanked him and mumbled a goodbye that I was sure would be forever, I committed the ultimate *gaucherie:* I asked him for an autographed picture. With grave courtesy hiding his amusement, he promised to send one to my home.

At the Stadium on the night of August 12, I sat, aching in ankle and heart, at the highest level of the enormous stone semicircle that formed a Grecian amphitheatre. There, I could lean back against one of the columns and stretch out my injured leg. I watched every seat begin to fill as the sky darkened. The lights above me dimmed. The huge audience fell silent after the conductor took his place before the New York Philharmonic Orchestra. I clutched my program in both hands to keep from crying. It was no consolation that my name was listed in that program.

Of the concert, I remember only the St. Denis *Brahms Waltz-Liebestraum,* my first experience of this ineffably poignant solo. It reflected my own sense of loss so accurately that I remained sunk in self-pity until the bittersweet evening came to an end.

I spent the next days contemplating my wretched ankle, sulky with frustration and disappointment. By the time my week's rent came due, I had rationalized my accident as a sign that I was destined to return to my first love, music. If Mrs. Goin could still get me a scholarship to Rollins, maybe it would not be too late to make something of myself after all. When I packed my bag and headed south, I felt as I would years later in England. On the June dawn of D-Day, a soldier pointed to the hundreds of ships in the bay before us and exclaimed, "Now, *that's* a step in the right direction!"

This time, my thumb was my passport to reality.

3

(1930–1931)

I Search — I am Found

Afoot and light-hearted I take to the open road,
Healthy, free, the world before me,
The long, long road before me,
Leading wherever I choose. . . .
(Walt Whitman. Leaves of Grass: Song of the Open Road)

With the Men Dancers in later years, I was to sing-shout these words as accompaniment to a Shawn solo. Now, they were sadly inappropriate to the feelings of the solitary figure who limped along the open road leading south. I was very happy to reach home, and Barton and Mazie were happy to have me there. Gillie Goin saw in my defeat as a dancer her opportunity for a victory over Mrs. Schumacher. She at once started to pull strings for a scholarship at Rollins Conservatory of Music for the coming term and quickly succeeded in getting it, without my even having to audition. This came about so easily that I did not realize how lucky I was. I simply experienced great relief at having my immediate future promptly settled.

Mother and Dad, in view of their straitened circumstances, had accepted Mr. and Mrs. Kinser's offer to stay in their home rent free while the Kinser family took their annual Canadian vacation. When I returned, it was to move into Mary's bedroom. Surrounded by her books, her paintings—and inadvertently coming upon some of her writings and poems—I formed a new concept of my friend with the Rapunzel hair and the sea-change eyes. Until then, I had seen her as frolicky as a colt, tanned from head to toe from daily swimming,

31

more tomboy than romantic girl. When she came home to pack for her sophomore year at Rollins (and the Mumaws moved as house-sitters to another place across the lake), I sought her out for the sensitive qualities I had discovered.

In the few weeks before we both left for Winter Park, Mary and I constructed a fresh, vital relationship in which we confided our secret dreams for the future. We discussed the poems we read, the music we heard, confident that we were two isolated art sophisticates in a world of Philistines. We grew so close that we even planned in detail the décor of the New York skyline-view apartment we would one day share. Our intense mental rapport often and inevitably became urgently physical, but, as in the past, I did not bring this to fulfillment. Mary's perceptive eyes began to haunt me with a question for which I had no answer.

I knew by now, however, that I was faced with a puzzle that must be solved, although I did not know to whom I could turn to seek its solution. Some instinct kept me from approaching Dad or Dr. Schumacher or any of my male relatives or former teachers, as if I sensed that that would be futile. It was Mary who finally guided me with kindness and insight and precocious knowledge to an understanding of my true nature. Little by little, she led our conversations to an examination of the cultures of other civilizations. She gave me the *Dialogues* of Plato to read. She helped me to recognize my feelings for what they were and counseled me to be at peace with them. She directed my mind to discover the truth my body had yet to verify.

Suddenly I felt whole and content and exceptionally competent. I was certain I could handle the future, whatever it held. As a first essential step, I set out to find a way to earn my living expenses at Rollins. When the organist of the Eustis Presbyterian Church died, what I called Fate again intervened to help me. My father, with his considerable influence as choir director and his infinite trust in his son's abilities, urged the music department of the church to let me take her place, since I could easily return from college for weekend services. The nearest I had ever come to a pipe organ was when, as a child, I had sometimes been allowed to sit next to the organist at choir rehearsals and watch the quadruple manipulations of pedals, manuals, and stops. Once the pastor agreed to take me on, I could not refuse merely because I was ignorant of the subtleties of the instrument. I would, I promised myself, learn as I went along. So I was off to Rollins with a new job, a new contentment, and a new confidence that I would become something meaningful.

Rollins was then considered a school for the sons and daughters of the well-to-do. As a scholarship student, with no car of my own, I naturally failed to receive a bid from a fraternity. I soon found myself among a group of other outcasts who had decided that they possessed qualifications of greater value than money, social position, or athletic ability. When they set up their own fraternity, I became a charter member. I was proud to be among these elect because, although I had no ambitions to be a "frat man," I was snob enough to enjoy the exclusivity of "our sort" and "that sort." I appreciated the brotherly bonding which, in my innocence, I was sure would last a lifetime. My infinite trust in human beings often led me to commit *faux pas.* I long ago reached the conclusion that I must be plain dumb: no really smart person could have been so naive for so long and on so many occasions.

Soon disillusioned, I dropped out of fraternity life to concentrate on my music. The Conservatory practice rooms were housed in a vintage Victorian building. There I learned, perforce, to concentrate on my scales and *arpeggios,* my Czerny and Chopin, without being distracted by the Ivesian dissonance of voices, strings, and woodwinds that echoed through the halls. I often pretended I was the soloist in this cacophonous concerto, a fantasy more challenging than if I had been practicing in an odorless, colorless, soundproofed studio. In our resonating white clapboard ark, each student could keep track of the others' progress with approbation or envy.

My Sunday organ playing in Eustis was also fun, much as I may have shocked churchgoing friends by the selections I chose to play. Since I had no time to learn new pieces, I performed solos I had learned to play on the piano. Thus, the weekly Prelude, Offertory, and Postlude might consist of opera arias such as Azucena's "Home to Our Mountains," Mignon's *"Connais-tu le Pays?,"* Delilah's "My Heart At Thy Sweet Voice," or even a popular song like "The Rosary." (I suspect I escaped condemnation for *that* note of papacy either because the congregation failed to recognize my rendition or because they loved me and therefore tolerated my whims.)

When I had my first organ lesson at Rollins, I overconfidently confessed that I was already playing in a church. The professor almost blew a pipe in the Conservatory's venerable instrument. Once he calmed down, to his great credit, he began at once to instruct me how to play the simplest hymn accompaniments. Sunday by Sunday thereafter, my playing improved and my choice of music became more orthodox.

I danced once in this period, when I was inveigled into contrib-

uting a number to some college affair. For the only solo I knew,
Professor Ebsen's *Brahms Hungarian Dance,* I scrambled together everything needed as a costume. Everything except the footwear. I
solved this problem when I remembered that I had often seen a
young woman, dressed in shirt and jodhpurs, who regularly exer-
cised her horse on the college bridle path. When I appealed to her, as
a fellow student, she very kindly loaned me a pair of ankle-high
riding boots. They looked magnificent; they pinched infernally. Still,
the Mumaw show must go on. After rehearsing in full costume the
afternoon of the performance, I could not wait to remove the boots.
But my feet had swollen so much that I realized once off, never again
on. I wore them until that evening when I *kazatskied* and stamped
and leaped to the fiery hussar's final arrogant bow. The applause
compensated for the suffering I had endured, but I have no idea how
I ever removed the boots.

Involved as I was with new friends, music, my churchly duties,
my precious if platonic dates with Mary Kinser, I had almost succeeded in forgetting the pain of my Denishawn disappointment.
Then, as if it were a ticking bomb, I held in my hands a photograph
of "Himself." He had remembered! He had inscribed it, "To Barton Mumaw, Jr., with great faith in his future from Ted Shawn"!
He stood costumed for *Jurgen,* the ballet I knew he had created to
Deems Taylor music, based on James Branch Cabell's then notorious novel. Like Sir Galahad, he looked directly into my eyes with a
steadfastness that left me limp. How could I not be a dancer when he
had faith in my future? When he had remembered me? (Fortunately, I did not know then that theatrical personalities often inscribed their photographs with extravagant phrases nor that Shawn
had remembered me only because, to him, every promise was an
obligation to be kept.)

As if the unexpected gift were a portent of more significant
events, I learned that Ted Shawn and the Denishawn Dancers were
actually to appear at Rollins. My anticipation was unbearable. On
the day that the troupe was to arrive at the only hotel in town appropriate for visiting dignitaries, I kept its switchboard alight and abuzz
with telephone calls as I tried to get through to Mr. Shawn. At last, I
reached Margerie Lyon, whom I had known at Denishawn House
in her role as personal secretary to Ruth St. Denis and Ted Shawn.
Now a guardian knight protecting her liege lord before a performance, she would not let me talk to Shawn, but did promise to thank
him for the photograph and to tell him I was coming to the concert.
Some instinct prompted me to leave my telephone number. Soon

thereafter, Miss Lyon called: "Mr. Shawn would like to know if you want to see the performance from backstage." I was waiting at the stage door long before the earliest ticket holders began to enter the theatre lobby that night.

When the program began, I was completely oblivious of the fact that, at my assigned standing room in the wings near the switchboard, I was a confounded nuisance to stagehands and performers alike. Mesmerized by my privileged closeup view of the beauty and strength of the dancers, I nearly inched my way right out among them on the stage. I was brought to my senses only when I got the "hook" from the irate stage manager.

I wish today's dance generation could have seen that concert. It demonstrated, even in the absence of St. Denis, the essence of the unfettered Denishawn choreography that developed into our modern dance.* For the period, Ted Shawn's *Four Dances Based on American Folk Music* were rare in intent, movement, and design. His *Divine Idiot* presaged the era when he would cease to be "Papa Denishawn" and become, uniquely, Shawn. I was enraptured by the love duet, *Man and Woman Dancing,* which he performed with Ernestine Day. I greatly admired the technique and characterizations of Jack Cole and Campbell Griggs in *Camel Boys,* a duo from an East Indian Suite. Shawn's *Mevlevi Dervish* had me whirling with him in an empathy of religious ecstasy, but I hardly saw the rest of the program as, with thumping heart, I awaited its finale—his *Flamenco Dances.*

The audience went as wild as I did. Encore followed encore until, in the sweltering night, under the searing lights, Shawn discarded first the *sombrero de caballero,* then the brief bolero jacket. At the final encore, he opened the studs of his high-collared shirt and tore off the narrow black tie. Against clamorous shouts of "Bravo!," the curtains at last closed. But for me, a world was opening—one for which I had been preparing, one into which I was now ready to enter.

Mr. Shawn opened the door to that world by inviting me to his dressing room. Jack Cole, who was acting as his dresser, greeted me with his customary sardonic smile. After signing autographs and saying goodbye to the last of the visitors, Shawn sank down on a chair so heavily I feared it might collapse beneath his weight. When he gave a deep sigh, I instinctively understood his relief at being free to return to himself. Throughout the routine of removing boots, costume, and facial makeup, he teased me with questions as to what

*Many of the Denishawn dances mentioned in this book are fully described in Jane Sherman's *The Drama of Denishawn Dance,* Middletown, Conn.: Wesleyan University Press, 1979.

I thought of such a life and whether I believed I could endure it. I can still see his eyes crinkling in the special way they always did when he joked about a subject in order to cover his true feelings about it. Dressed at last in his street clothes, he emerged from the room looking more like a successful stockbroker than a dancer. He said goodnight to Jack and led me out of the theatre as if it were only natural that I should accompany him through the arches of live oaks that lined the deserted campus walks I knew so well.

Supper was already laid out in his hotel room. Inviting me to sit at the table, Shawn went first into the bathroom to shower. Through the open door, we talked as companionably as if we were old and equal friends. While the theatrical illusion of tan paint was being washed away, I suddenly realized that it was this very illusion I had been in love with, that this was the closest I had ever been to the person who was emerging, that I might be on the brink of a deep and terrible disappointment. I watched in apprehension as, with the final cleansing, the god retreated, the dancer made his exit, the teacher retired, and at last only the man stood there.

I rose to meet him when he approached, his white robe open above his naked body, his hands outstretched to take mine. He looked at me with an expression of such tenderness that I felt enfolded by warmth and understanding as never before in my life. Then all was clear—pure—radiant—everything I had expected, knowing yet not knowing what to expect, but with no shame, no fear, no hesitancy.

I was not sad when I discovered that Shawn had left early the next morning. That, too, I had expected. I went as usual to my classes, but the change that had occurred in my life's direction did not go undetected by my most perceptive teachers. When my theory professor passed me the day after the Denishawn concert, he paused a moment to look at me with a cool, appraising glow in his eyes. He remarked impersonally, "Don't let it happen again, Barton," as he continued on his way. I did not understand what he meant until I encountered the patrician lady who taught History of Music. She smiled as I held the classroom door open for her, and said, "I can tell by looking at you, Barton, how much you enjoyed last night." By the time my distinguished piano teacher stopped in the middle of a lesson to discuss my future, I was prepared to admit that I really did not want to be the pianist of my original ambitions. I wanted to be a dancer.

When, therefore, Ada McLean asked me if I would dance with her in a program at the Eustis Women's Club, I agreed at once. I immediately decided to recreate the *Man and Woman Dancing** that I had seen Shawn do with Ernestine Day. Fortunately, G. Schirmer had published the R.S. Stoughton music (which Shawn had specially commissioned) with explicit choreographic notes and photographs of St. Denis and Shawn posed in costume. Then called *Idyll*, the work had first been performed by them in 1929.

Ada and I copied the costumes, worked out the steps, and finally performed in a style that approximated the original. The clubwomen applauded the duet with touching enthusiasm, perhaps seeing reflected in it their adolescent dreams of the perfect romance. Ada danced beautifully. As for me, I found an added dimension in the dance as I sublimated the memory of my emotional and physical experience with Ted Shawn in the quiet movements that expressed the sensual feelings of a man and a woman for each other.

Not long after this, I received a letter addressed in handwriting that I instinctively recognized. Mr. Shawn was inviting me to meet him in New York when he returned from a spring concert tour of Switzerland and Germany. He offered me tuition, housing, and meals, in return for which I would dance in the ensemble of the Denishawn company and act as his chauffeur and dresser. I do not know how I lived through the following weeks because, of course, I was going to be on that pier to meet his ship.

I cannot recall what plausible explanation for my sudden change in careers I gave Mazie and Barton, my teachers, or helpful Gillie Goin, but they all accepted my decision without inflicting upon me the pain of having to justify it. For this, I silently blessed them as I said goodbye. I kissed Madame Anna, Tony Mulliken, Ada, and my beloved, wise Mary as if I would never in the future see them with the same eyes. In May 1931, I set forth like Dick Whittington to seek my fortune.

This time I traveled to New York in relative splendor. Theodore Dreier, a Rollins professor, had asked me to come along to spell him at the wheel when he drove north. We had not known each other well, but we found common ground when he casually mentioned that his aunt knew Ted Shawn. Surely, Fate decreed that I would ride through the warm spring landscape with the nephew of Katherine S. Dreier, one of the prime movers of the modern art awakening in the United States and a devoted Shawn patron. The good professor was a sensitive man whose conversation enlivened the long trip. It was a journey upon which I had embarked with total, blind confidence, but as it progressed I suffered from an in-

*A full description appears in Part Two.

creasing sense of inferiority. Unresponsive, moody, almost sullen,
when it was my turn to drive my foot pressed down with reluctance
on the accelerator. How could I have ventured so unthinkingly into
the unknown that lay ahead of me?

On our last night out, a trivial incident raised my self-esteem.
After we had turned into our separate motel beds and put out the
lights, I propped myself against the pillows and rather ostentatiously
lighted a cigarette. Smoking, I had learned from my fraternity
brothers, was the *sine qua non* of sophistication, and I badly needed at
that late hour to assure myself that I was sophisticated. I had assumed that Mr. Dreier was asleep, but, just as I snubbed out the
cigarette in the ashtray, his voice spoke softly from across the room:
"What an extraordinary picture, Barton, to watch you smoking in
the half dark. Your face one moment is the mask of Tragedy, the next
moment the mask of Comedy, floating, disembodied." My spirits
soared. What more perfect accolade of maturity could a nineteen-
year-old desire?

Once in New York, I hastened to the Hudson River docks on
the day Shawn's ship was due to arrive. I ran through the enormous,
chilly, gray structure of the pier just as the liner was nosed by tugs
into its slip. As I neared the gangplank placed in readiness at the oily
water's edge, I knew instantly that I would have to improvise the
poetic words of welcome I had memorized. Standing there with
Margerie Lyon was Ruth St. Denis.

I was torn between hoping she would recognize me and hoping
she would not. She did. She smiled at me in the same gracious,
aloof, impersonal way she always had, as if I were an insignificant
fragment of a vast undertaking. I smiled back from a respectful distance when Miss Lyon mouthed "Hello," glad to remain apart as I
stared up at the ship's rail. We must all have seen Shawn at the same
moment because three hands waved simultaneously. From the corner of my eye, I saw Miss St. Denis turn to regard me with sudden
interest. I blushed under her scrutiny.

Then there was a flurry of hugs and kisses, of effusive greetings,
of "Dears" and "Darlings," of "Teddys" and "Ruthies," during
which I was totally ignored, if not actually pushed like a puppy from
underfoot. I had to be content with a brief handshake from Mr.
Shawn when he introduced me to his accompanist, Mary Campbell.
After we left the pier, however—all baggage at last cleared of customs and collected—I found myself in a cab with Shawn, Miss
Lyon, and Miss Campbell. Still smiling, white head erect, Ruth St.
Denis rode off in another cab, alone.

4

The Learning Begins

When the taxi stopped at the Buckingham Hotel on West 57th Street, I emerged from it like a duckling from its nest into what was then New York's artistic mainstream. Carrying Shawn's attaché case, I followed the tall, erect figure who would teach me how to swim in these turbulent waters. I knew I had reached the end of my bucolic boyhood, had forever forsworn my small-town security.

In the few steps from curb to hotel entrance, I could swear that above the traffic I heard violins and French horns at practice, that above the stench of gasoline I sniffed an artist's turpentine and the special perfumed sweat of dance studios. Close by, I glimpsed Carnegie Hall, where Denishawn had had its greatest triumph. Later, as I came to know the street as well as the Main Street of Eustis, I discovered the Art Students League and the little art galleries sandwiched between the little dress shops, the incredible delicatessen that supplied us with exotic nourishment and the Russian Tea Room where we dined when sufficiently flush, the newsstand that displayed every known musical, art, and dance publication as well as papers in several languages, Steinway Hall with its show window featuring grand pianos that made my mouth water, the two-storied, north-facing windows of painters' and sculptors' ateliers, and the corner drugstore that specialized in theatrical makeup.

Just as there are ear-minded or eye-minded people, I am convinced that there are nose-minded people for whom the mere whiff of a certain odor takes them back to a scene complete with sound effects and color. For me, this has remained a heavy Parisian scent

39

called "Amber" that still returns me to the day when I first unpacked for Shawn. In my new role of dresser-valet, I began to empty
the drawers of his wardrobe trunk which, with its band of faded
blue-and-yellow identifying Denishawn stripes, had been around the
world. A hint of Amber rose from every piece of clothing I touched,
overpowering the dry newspaper smell with accents of mold that
permeates all luggage which has spent years in ships' holds, railroad
baggage cars, and trucks.

Country boy that I was, I ogled the piles of creamy undershirts
made of a unique soft and springy weave that could cling wondrously to the body. They had been purchased in Switzerland, I noted. I
noted, too, that the percale shorts were designed with movable but-
tons to accommodate a contracting or an expanding waistline.
(Shawn was plagued all his life by weight problems. Like Isadora
Duncan and the Greeks, he considered the middle area of the body
"the seat of the soul" and was never comfortable with any constric-
tion about his waist.) I discovered that all Shawn's socks were seam-
less, to preclude the possibility of blisters, and that he wore none but
Arnold's Glove-Grip shoes because, he maintained, they provided
the only last that did not deform the toes.

*Feet, obviously, are of utmost importance to a dancer. Shawn was delighted
to see that each of my big toes grew straight out from the ball of the foot, with a
noticeable separation between it and the second toe. "Now," he exclaimed,
"that's the way a foot should look!" His admiration may have helped to wing
my feet with the lightness, swiftness, and dexterity upon which critics were later to
comment. Needless to say, his own hard-working pedal extremities were strong and
shapely. Shawn was to insist that in the donning of footwear—dancers' boots,
ballet slippers, bedroom scuffs, or street shoes—the right foot must be shod first.
This rigid habit did not arise from a neurotic compulsion but from the practical
necessity of thousands of quick changes when a fumbled foot meant a missed cue.*

After I succeeded in unpacking the trunk without his specific
instructions, Shawn taught me the procedure he wished me to follow
for breakfast the next day—and for hundreds of days to come, never
to vary except during the exigencies of touring or when he was a
house guest. Two slices of wholewheat toast, buttered from crust to
crust and served warm with strawberry preserves. Light cream and
sugar for the coffee, which had to be freshly brewed, the preferred
brand changing over the years as one kind after another altered in
flavor. Whenever possible, breakfast was served in bed. It was eaten
slowly in the absolute silence Shawn required so that he might gather
his forces to face the world. This suited me perfectly, since I have
never been one to spring from bed to "challenge the day."

Ablutions were then performed, each motion and prop identically choreographed. Shawn would use nothing but Sayman's Soap, claiming its frothy suds were the only kind that cut through theatrical body makeup. He shaved with a straight razor, as his father had taught him. In spite of elegant gifts of silver or gold safety razors, he could not be persuaded to use them, protesting that his beard was too heavy for such light machinery. The one time he did succumb to the pressures of new inventions, he deigned to try an electric razor, but he immediately discarded it with the disdainful assertion: "Most modern conveniences are not truly improvements."

In the first few days of this new life, my proud Dutch heritage rebelled against my servitude. But rebellion subsided as soon as I realized that Shawn had a deep respect for honorable work honorably done, whether it was the Sistine Chapel ceiling or a good beef stew. I began to follow his routines as much for my own satisfaction in doing them well as for the pleasure of a lord and master. He himself gave the chores of daily life the same scrupulous attention he gave the chores of creation, believing all contributed equally to the whole. If necessity dictated that he cook the meals in the absence of help, or paint a room when there was no money to pay a professional, he cooked with the dignity of an Escoffier and painted with the integrity of a Raphael. This made him a demanding and knowledgeable employer because whatever he asked one to do he had probably also done—and well. He therefore expected as much perfection from the studio scrubwomen, the house manager, or the publicity person as he did from his dancers. This meticulous attention to detail was only one of the many attributes he had to have in order to head a company and a school.

Jack Cole and I were settled into a small apartment-*cum*-studio on West 55th Street, where Shawn began blocking out his ballet, *Job*, one of the three large works scheduled for that season's Lewisohn Stadium concerts. My days of dilettantism came to an abrupt end. Like a stonecutter apprenticed to Michelangelo, I began to learn my craft while at the same time learning how to live. Master-servant, teacher-pupil, confessor-confessee, sophisticate-neophyte—these aspects of my relationship to Shawn were now almost entirely dominated by the work at hand.

The reality Shawn shared with me proved far more exciting than my romantic fantasy of an "artist's life." I discovered that his every thought and act was determined by dance. Food was valued not only for its taste but for the strength and energy it contributed to physical endurance; books, not simply for their literary pleasure or

information but for the inspiration they might provide for dance
scenarios; music, as much to stimulate choreographic fancies and
movement ideas as for enjoyment. Every cultural and social influence to which he was exposed became grist for Shawn's mill. He
would sometimes quote Diotima from Plato's *Symposium*: "Every
one of us, no matter what he does, is longing for the endless fame,
the incomparable glory that is his, and the nobler he is, the greater
his ambition, because he is in love with the eternal." Ted Shawn
lived by that precept.

Alas for *my* "longing for the endless fame": the first task I was
assigned as a member of the company had nothing to do with dancing. Jack and I had to go out each dawn to search the deserted
Manhattan streets and collect empty cardboard cartons before they
were picked up by the garbage trucks. We were not to learn the
reason for our mysterious scavenging until we saw the sets for *Job*.

Just before he returned from his German-Swiss tour, Shawn
had stopped over in London to confer with Ralph Vaughan Williams, who had recently completed his composition, *Job, a Masque for
Dancing*. From its title, Shawn envisioned the orchestral work as the
accompaniment for a ballet. The piano score was played for him by
Constant Lambert (then Vaughan Williams's student and a promising young composer). It was a disappointment. Shawn found the
music so thin and dull that he changed his mind about using it.

Throughout the summer I was fascinated by the parade of people through Shawn's hotel room, his 55th Street studio, and his
Steinway Hall studio, which housed the Denishawn School that
year. He had appointments by the hundreds, it seemed, with reporters, photographers, business managers, costumers, wigmakers,
lighting experts, students, financial supporters, close friends, and
famous personalities like Hans Lange, who was to conduct the Stadium concerts. Yet he remained hypnotized by his vision of Job.
Reconsidering the Vaughan Williams music, he cabled London his
decision to mount the production in August. When the score arrived, Shawn, Mary Campbell, and I gathered in the 55th Street
studio to hear Mr. Lange play it on the piano, muttering all the
while, "Ach, zo Ainglish! Zo Ainglish!" The *Job* music was, indeed,
"Ainglish," since Vaughan Williams had based his themes on old
English dance forms. Hardly inspirational to begin with, they
sounded singularly unsuited for a powerful Biblical story. But when
we eventually heard the score played by the New York Philharmonic
Orchestra, it proved stimulating enough to carry both message and
choreography.

Shawn had long been enamored of the William Blake illustrations for the Book of Job. He took great care to reproduce their exact shades in the settings he helped to design. His choreography as faithfully evoked the flowing dynamics of Blake's compositions. To achieve an accurate whole, however, also demanded accurate costumes. This presented problems. Shawn could not afford to order a distinguished theatrical supply firm like Dazian's to bring swatches of material to his studio. Instead, he had to follow the Denishawn tradition of allowing necessity to dictate invention. In search of desirable fabrics, he sent his dancers out to department stores, manufacturers' outlets, and little yard-goods shops hidden away on side streets. He had determined, for example, that his Angels must be garbed in golden material that was diaphanous, yet drapeable. One of us finally located bolts of a very wide, gauzy ribbon that was interwoven with metallic thread. It was difficult to piece this together into floor-length robes to cover the six-foot men destined to portray heavenly beings, but it worked. Because they were thin enough to reveal musculature, Shawn's own form-fitting Swiss undershirts were dyed tan and thus became leotards that matched the body paint of the Sons of Job.

At last, Cole and Mumaw discovered the secret of the cartons they had so unwillingly but diligently collected: they had been cut, glued into block forms, and painted to make Job's sacrificial altar. Forced to use similar ingenuity to complete the rest of the set, Shawn fell back on one of his favorite Delsarte tenets, the Law of Trinity. Because there was no way to hang scenery on the open Stadium stage, he created three levels from a series of platforms and stairs to represent Heaven, Earth, and Hell. Flats, painted to resemble clouds, had been fashioned so as to slide toward each other from opposite sides of the stage to change a scene, or to pull apart to reveal Heaven.

Shawn was to dance the leading role of Satan. For the part of Job's son, he had especially engaged Paul Haakon, who was then at the height of his career as a popular performer in musicals. I was cast as one of Job's Three Comforters, while Jack Cole played Elihu. Since the Blake drawings show Elihu with a shock of golden hair, Shawn insisted that Jack let his own locks grow long and peroxide them. This disfigurement so disgusted Cole that right after the final Stadium performance, with his intractable sense of mischief, he gleefully shaved his head. He knew this act of lese majesty would enrage Shawn because there was a strong possibility that *Job* might be presented on Broadway in the immediate future (a possibility that was never realized, thanks to the Great Depression).

Everything, then, was ready for opening night—except the cos-

tume for Satan. Blake reproductions give no hint as to the color
intended, showing only a black-and-white nude figure with scales
covering the lower torso and thighs. Shawn was positive that Blake
had not created the conventional red devil, so we made a trip to the
Boston Public Library to beg a glimpse of the original watercolors.
These were kept under lock and key to protect the delicate tints from
light, but we were permitted to examine them long enough to determine that the artist had conceived Satan as an acrid green reptile, in
vivid contrast to God's golden being with his streaming silver hair
and beard. We were so moved to see and touch these precious pages
that we found ourselves whispering, as if we feared to disturb Job
and his sons and daughters.

When we came down to earth, we realized that the Satan
makeup would be fiendishly complicated. That did not faze Shawn.
He had a wig made of green rope. He designed and had made a
G-string of flesh-colored silk, on which were sewn large green se-
quins that resembled shiny scales. He and I concealed his body beneath a coat of special green paint, which we applied by hand. Over
that, we painstakingly drew with a black liner pencil one reptilian
scale overlapping another, until we had covered both legs back and
front. We blacked out the second toe on each foot to achieve the
effect of cloven hooves. By outlining in black the major muscles of
his upper body and drawing a hideously evil face, we completed a
terrifying image. It took both of us more than a hour to transform
the handsome man into this repellent saurian figure.

Miss St. Denis was choreographing her two full-length works,
Unfinished Symphony and *The Prophetess,* up at Denishawn House, while
Shawn kept busy creating *Job* in the 55th Street studio. Somehow, he
also found the time and energy to teach the enlarged summer classes
at Steinway Hall, where I had my first real lessons in Denishawn
technique.*

What with classes and rehearsals, valeting and costume making, I was tuned to such a high mental, physical, and emotional
pitch that I was unaware of dissonance in the orchestrated activity
around me. I only began to hear the forte clash of loyalties and
tempers and ambitions when Jack Cole expressed his concern about
the discord in Denishawn harmony. Neither St. Denis nor Shawn
was infallible, he pointed out to me, and their covert disagreements
were separating them as widely as the distance from 57th Street to
Van Cortlandt Park. Even while I chided him for his incorrigible

*See pages 315-317.

cynicism, I had to admit to myself that he was right.

When I joined the company, I learned just how shrewd and independent Jack could be. He could also be recalcitrant. In the middle of one tour, he went into a terrible rage because he disliked wearing a certain costume. He tore it to shreds. Such an act in the theatre is the churchly equivalent of a sin against the Holy Ghost. Costumes cost money and there was rarely a duplicate ready for the next performance. Shawn's explosion sent Jack crawling for needle and thread with which to sew together the patchwork outfit he was condemned to wear for the balance of the tour. In truth, the electric energy both men possessed created not only sparks between them but a close bond. Each respected the other. Jack was one of the few people I ever heard Shawn ask for criticism or advice during the choreographing of a dance.

Shawn did not discuss with me the personal disintegration that must have been troubling him. Because of the unrelenting work, our discreet private moments were treasured as an escape from stress. It was then that Shawn revealed the poetic, sensitive nature hidden within the practical daytime man. It was then that he expressed the most beautiful, the most meaningful ideas about sex as a physical manifestation of Divinity and as a powerful natural force which, like lightning, must be handled with the greatest respect, caution, and understanding. Eros, he maintained, leads the philosopher to goodness through an ascent in pursuit of beauty. As did the Greeks, he believed the homosexual mode of life filled a need for personal relationships of an intensity not commonly found either within marriage or between parents and children. His personal credo of the body was rooted in Havelock Ellis's *Studies in the Psychology of Sex* and in *Love's Coming of Age*, by Edward Carpenter (the friend of Walt Whitman), yet was uniquely his own. As with all else in his life, dance was an integral part of it.

Now that I had seen firsthand the strenuous labor he expended, I asked him, "Is it worth all you have to do before you can step out on that stage?"

"It is worth it!" he answered vehemently. Then he lay back, hands clasped behind his head, and continued quietly, "You see, Barton, dancing is like making love, and how often do we experience *that* kind of perfect fulfillment? When it does happen, there is no sensation to compare with it, unless perhaps what a saint experiences at the instant of illumination." He sighed with great weariness. "That is what keeps us slaving—the hope for the instant of illumination in a rare perfect performance."

"Which would you choose," I wondered aloud, "a perfect love act or a heavenly dance moment?"

"The dance! The dance! Always the dance!" he replied, sitting up and throwing wide his arms as if to embrace the universe. "Because it alone can strengthen those qualities that will sustain a dancer through all the other experiences of his life."

I believed. I was also uneasy because I sensed that neither of us was ready for a permanent relationship. I was too young and inexperienced, he was too preoccupied with earlier commitments and responsibilities, which he could not honorably shirk. Although I already knew I would be in the company he was taking out on tour the next season, he had given no hint of what might follow after that. But I lacked the courage and self-confidence to confess my anxieties to him.

Job was to be my first experience as a professional, both as performer and as Shawn's dresser. I was justifiably nervous, even though I was to appear only in the one ballet. The Stadium had been built as an athletic arena for track events of the City College of New York, not for theatrical presentations. A temporary stage had been erected for the summer outdoor performances of the New York Philharmonic Orchestra. It was placed midfield and had no proper lighting equipment, no flies from which to hang scenery, and no backstage facilities. Performers had to rough it in tents behind this makeshift structure, out of view of the audience.

From St. Denis and Shawn to the lowliest member of the ensemble, everyone sat on wobbly planks before tables similarly constructed of planks that were precariously balanced on sawhorses. Bare bulbs, strung on wire looped over small, cheap mirrors, provided light so the dancers could make up. There was no plumbing. We washed in cold water that filled buckets set around the tents and we used other buckets for other human needs. The regular Denishawn Dancers, accustomed to the rigors of one-night stands in small towns, took these conditions in stride: the fifty or more student novices—their heads filled with the glamor of The Theatre—were bewildered. In the confusion, they barely managed to slather their bodies with paint and fasten their costumes right side front. Luckily, they had to make no quick changes between numbers or there would have been utter chaos.

The Denishawn management had had only sufficient funds to allow one dress rehearsal with the orchestra. Despite their five summers' experience playing in the pit, the musicians still considered it demeaning to have to accompany mere dancers. They would therefore stop playing in the middle of a bar the instant overtime was clocked. In the few hours permitted us, we had to learn the tricks of making our entrances on cue. Since there were no wings or curtained crossover, we climbed up rickety stairs to reach the stage and then exited down the stairs to the ground, where we ran to the other side to make another entrance. Old pros and young amateurs alike did the best they could with a maximum of good humor and a minimum of temperament.

In fact, the crowded tents, the bare earth under our bare feet, the bustle and excitement all created a carnival atmosphere that was fun. Shawn, however, did not find it at all amusing to sit naked and shivering in a galvanized washtub as I poured a bucketful of cold water over him in order to scrub off the green Satan paint. This had to be done swiftly to give him time to make up for his next dance. I was so involved in the process on the first night that I forgot until much later that I had just made my debut before an audience of thousands, and that *Job* had been received with great enthusiasm.

Once I had helped Shawn through the changes for his solos, I was free to sneak out front to watch Ruth St. Denis's "synchoric orchestra" of forty girl-dancers perform to Schubert's *Unfinished Symphony*. Then, for the first time, I saw her as Shawn's partner in "my" duo, *Idyll*. This was the only work on the program in which they appeared together, a fact so unusual it should have been significant. Audiences since 1914 had romanticized them as the ideal married dancing couple. Now their adoring public saw Ruth St. Denis and Ted Shawn move as affectionately in this most explicit of their love duets as they had throughout the previous eighteen years of their partnership. Even if no one in that Stadium audience suspected it, those two—who had lived and worked with one another so sensitively for so long—must have known that this was the last time they would appear together as Denis-Shawn.

5

(1931–1932)

The End of Denishawn

Exhausted by the strain of the performances and the debilitating heat of New York, a small band of Stadium survivors set out to seek relief up at what Shawn called the "Farm." Located near the highest point in the Berkshires, he had bought the 150-acre property as a hideaway where he might some day go to create, undistracted by classes, business or social demands, and the artificialities of urban life. With the same aim in mind, a few years earlier he had invested an unexpected $1,000 legacy in an acre of land on the Saugerties River in Westport, Connecticut. There, with his savings from the *Follies* tour, he had built a Japanese pavilion which served as a summer Denishawn camp-school and his home. As the area became suburbanized, he discovered that he could find neither the space nor the privacy he needed, so he sold the property to buy the Farm.

I am sure he never suspected that this refuge in the Berkshires would serve as anything but a retreat from the intrusions of civilization. The eighteenth-century house, with its columned, two-story front porch in the style of old Natchez, had been closed for five years. Named "Jacob's Pillow" by the Carter family, who had owned it for over a century, it had been a self-sufficient working farm and noted as a station on the underground slave railway to Canada before and during the Civil War. Now a disused summer home, its buildings badly needed painting and repairs. Its surrounding grounds were overgrown with wild shrubs, knee-high grasses, and tangled vines.

But our weary group, drunk on the pine-scented mountain air, was not discouraged by its bleak appearance. Margerie Lyon and

49

Mary Campbell donned slacks and men's shirts and got to work in the house. Jack Cole and I, together with Harry Joyce and Don Moreno (both of whom had danced in *Job*) cleared a path from back door to outhouse. Shawn went straight to the largest of the barns.

When he had first seen this structure, the giant sliding door was off its track, the loft was overflowing with musty hay, and the stalls were cluttered with bridles, bits, reins, and horse collars that still emitted a sweetish leather-and-animal odor. The enormous floor space was a layer of packed earth and flat slabs of granite. Shawn had decided to transform the barn into a dance studio. This required ordering the installation of new doors, large plate-glass windows, sheetrock walls, and, most importantly, a splinter-proof hard maple floor laid over the ground. He planned to move mirrors and *barres* from the Westport studio and, when a patron contributed her grand piano, all would be ready for our first class. Pleased as he was to see how many improvements had been completed, he also knew that before we could concentrate on perfecting our dance space, we had to secure a roof over our heads.

We worked in uniforms of navy-blue sweat shirts with baggy pants of the same material. Long before this outfit was adopted by joggers, Shawn had admired the style and fabric in Germany and had brought back to the States a dozen sets in different sizes. Dressed thus alike, canvas espadrilles on our feet, we five men grabbed brooms to sweep out the living quarters from attic to cellar. I am sure that it was only during this process that Shawn fully discovered the imperfections of the property whose beauty had seduced him into buying it.

We found a rusty coal furnace crammed into a tiny, stone-walled cellar that had originally served in winter to store apples, potatoes, carrots, turnips, and onions. At the far end of the upstairs hall, which divided the four small bedrooms, we inspected a so-called bathroom that had been squeezed into an impossibly small space. The shower stall, wash bowl, and flush toilet met in such close proximity that it was impossible for a large person to do a deep *plié* when necessity demanded. The men, therefore, preferred to use an edifice that Jack Cole immediately christened "The Boocherie Pooch," Miss Lyon more delicately referred to as the Japanese *benjo*, and some later wag named "The New Yorker" because its walls were papered with covers from that magazine. I have forgotten who provided the unique dispenser that played *The Blue Danube* as toilet paper was unrolled. When innocent, distinguished guests came to the Farm, their reactions to this gadget were so interestingly unpredictable that we often lurked nearby when a first visit was made.

Because the house heating and plumbing were unreliable, only the Misses Lyon and Campbell risked the uncertainties of the indoor shower. The rest of us lined up every day at the pump outside the kitchen door, lathered lavishly, then sluiced one another with bucketsful of the icy well water (always forewarning our proper ladies in order to spare them the sight of our naked bodies). I never became inured to this chilling experience, although Shawn assured me it was invigoratingly Spartan.

That backyard well (which still functions) also supplied delicious pure water for cooking. A wood stove in the kitchen, abutting a small pantry, guaranteed hot meals (and hotter cooks), while a fireplace in each of the ground-floor rooms provided warmth as the nights grew colder. Despite these back-to-nature inconveniences, we were a relaxed and companionable little crew. The hills in their autumn colors, the country silence filled with country sounds, the gathering of blueberries on hot, sunny afternoons, the starlit nights, the walks with Shawn through the woods—these, for me, merged into a halcyon entity. We enjoyed exercising new muscles when we yanked up armloads of brambles, cleared a vegetable garden patch of its gross weeds, or hauled ancient farm machinery from barns to junk pile. Since we also had to ready the house for occupancy by the regular company members, who would soon be joining us to rehearse, we scrubbed floors and washed windows (supervised by Miss Lyon), painted exterior and interior walls and woodwork (instructed by Shawn), repaired roof leaks, and replaced rotting porch floorboards (under our own steam, with many a thumb smacked by many a hammer).

In the equality of shared labor, in the freedom from professional and emotional responsibilities, I discovered a new Shawn. He grew tanned and lean, full of high spirits, encouraging Jack's practical jokes and sometimes going him one better. I was delighted by this change, which suddenly brought us closer in age. (I also realized that the man was living those years he had missed when, at seventeen, he had been bedridden following a siege of diphtheria. The serum prescribed had saved his life but left him paralyzed from the hips down. It is now part of American dance lore how he had, by sheer guts, taught himself to walk again.) His joie de vivre, his vitality, his sense of fun also enlivened those moments when we two could be alone and behave like adolescents on their first adventure away from parental supervision. I still remained so much in awe of him that I habitually called him "Shawn," but there were a few times when I felt confident enough to whisper "Ted" as we talked late at night after a day of good, hard work.

The barn-studio was at last finished and the living quarters were more or less habitable. Shawn had made his bedroom handsome with Japanese prints on its walls, a collection of bronze Siva statuettes, and Javanese batik curtains with matching bedspread for the walnut double bed he had brought with the rest of the furniture from his Grandmother Booth's family home in Kentucky.

A poignant entry in Ruth St. Denis's journal notes:

September 5, 1931. Just now stopped a moment by Teddy's open door [in Denishawn House]—the room is empty—he has sent for all his furniture to take up to his farm in Mass.—It looked so deserted—and my heart asked and I thought again—"What does this cruel and stupid thing mean?"

Soon, the rest of the company arrived to prepare for the 1931–32 tour of Ted Shawn and His Dancers. (The Denishawn named had been dropped.) Campbell Griggs and Lester Shafer joined Jack and me in a hayloft dormitory in one of the smaller barns, while the six girls occupied the house bedrooms. Mary Campbell was to be both rehearsal and performance pianist for a program that would include several ensemble dances and one outstanding new solo for Shawn. Here, again, I met a different man.

This was my first opportunity to observe Shawn, the choreographer, at work on a complete program. I have no idea where he found the hours or the strength to plan the music, steps, costumes, and lighting for ten new numbers. But from first company get-together to final dress rehearsal, he knew precisely what he wanted each of us to do. And when I, alone, was permitted to watch him choreograph his solo, *O Brother Sun and Sister Moon,* I saw how he struggled through trial and error to reveal in movement the message and the emotion he was determined to express. He told me then that, for nearly a decade, he had studied the life of St. Francis of Assisi in writings, paintings, statues, and woodcuts. This accumulated contemplation inspired each step he set to the Respighi music. His integrity was as patent as his effort.

Shawn kept this solo in his repertory to the end of his performing days. In 1963, he referred to it as "a dance closer to my heart than anything I have ever done." When he was seventy-five years old, he danced it at Jacob's Pillow—the last time he appeared in a concert.

A word to those who were too young to have seen Shawn or his works during the Denishawn heyday or the period of his Men Dancers: between 1914 and

1931, he choreographed 185 dances and nine major ballets for Denishawn, co-creating with St. Denis another three ballets. Between 1933 and 1940, he choreographed for his Men Dancers fifty-seven group or solo dances and six full-scale numbers that could be called "ballets." He danced in many if not most of these works that were performed to critical acclaim around the world.

Among the familiar Denishawn dances Shawn programmed for our upcoming tour, I had the thrill of performing Charles Weidman's role in *Boston Fancy: 1854*, staged for four couples. Most significantly for the future, however, the concert with which we opened the tour in December at the Pittsburgh Syria Mosque featured three numbers for men alone: *Brahms Rhapsody, Workers' Songs of Middle Europe,* and *Osage-Pawnee Dance of Greeting.*

The latter marked a humiliation I cannot forget. As Shawn's dresser, within all too few minutes I not only had to help him change for the next dance but also zip out of my mid-Victorian *Boston Fancy* trappings into the nearly nude outfit of an American Indian. Even moving as fast as I could, it was more than I could manage. I ran from Shawn's dressing room to the wings, a breathless warrior brave, only to see three Osage-Pawnees toe-heeling and gourd-rattling to center stage. Tailpiece between my legs, I stood there imagining my immediate dismissal from the company. (Only after many similar emergencies did I learn to slip unobserved by the audience into a work-in-progress.)

Lester Shafer, who doubled as stage manager and was inured to disasters far worse than a missed entrance, clapped me on the bare back and said, "Better luck next time, Barton." I was grateful that he did not report my horrendous sin, but when Shawn read the next day's newspaper reviews, he could hardly have failed to notice that one critic had written, "The Indian dance was enjoyable although only three paleskins [sic] appeared instead of the programmed four." I was truly touched that Shawn never spoke to me about this.

Dressing the star for his many dances in a concert would have been a tough job even if I were not also dancing myself. Our race against time was as strictly choreographed as any duet, because the audience must not be kept waiting. After my first missed cue, I very quickly learned that every item of each of our costumes had to be laid out in precise order in precisely the same spot for every performance. Shawn and I used to rehearse particularly difficult changes to be sure they could be made within the minutes allotted. And always on hand in case of ripped seams, snapped elastic, loosened hooks and eyes, or a stuck zipper was a kit of scissors, pins, threaded needles, razor blades, makeup pencils, and similar tools of the trade.

I was usually so busy with backstage chores that I had few opportunities to see Shawn perform. One season, when I did watch his solo concert from out front, I sensed with what skill he built the response of the audience, dance by dance, relentlessly, until, almost as at a religious revival meeting, he had them on their feet, shouting, at the end. I no longer doubted the story that, in Germany, Shawn had once received forty-seven curtain calls for his solo Frohsinn.

Our tour was to be one of the few that ventured into the "sticks" for some years after the Depression had closed the road as abruptly as a slammed door. Although we had assurances of fifty bookings—from New York to St. Petersburg, Florida, from Minneapolis to Middletown, Connecticut—it was a challenge to reach each stop on the way because so many trains had been taken out of service. We often had to catch a local at five in the morning in order to arrive at the next town in time to put on that night's performance. This meant we sometimes sat in station waiting rooms for endless hours before we could make a connection. It meant no dining cars, and that meant we had nothing to eat but cold, practically inedible box-lunches for many hours on many journeys.

From December 4 to March 1—in rain, sunshine, snow, hail, or sleet—our lives were determined by timetables, second-rate hotel rooms, greasy-spoon cafeterias, and concerts danced in every kind of structure, from Philadelphia's Garrick Theatre to Terre Haute's State Teachers College Gymnasium. We even appeared at the Nicholas Roerich Museum in New York where, as she recorded in her journal, Miss St. Denis came to see us:

> December 16, 1931. Tonight down at Roerich's Museum, Teddy gave his American program. It was superb—I was as proud as I could be—went back [stage] afterwards and told him how splendid it all was—we spoke again—deeply of Denishawn and what it stands for—that there is a destiny for us to fulfill.

[It now seems sad that she was still thinking of a future with Shawn, in their work, in their life.] They spent that Christmas together, and she wrote of their parting:

> Teddy has been here to say goodbye before he goes on his tour of nine weeks. We had a sweet and harmonious visit. He said as he left—that we had the center—what happened on the circumference did not matter.

But, of course, it did matter.
After weeks of living off the lean of the land, it was pure syba-

ritic pleasure to have ·dinner and then perform, by invitation, at Miami's luxurious Surf Club. By the time the show was over and we removed costumes and makeup, saw the women dancers off to their hotel, and packed our gear, we five men were the only ones left in the building. Shawn, Jack, Campbell, Lester, and I took one look at that dark, deserted beach with its white line of breakers and, without a word, we tore off our clothes to run like pagans through the hot night into the ocean. Although I had lived most of my life in a near-tropical climate close to water, this was my introduction to nude bathing. I was instantly converted to its joys.

Three nights later, we closed the tour with the Triumphant Return of the Dancer, Barton Mumaw, to his home town, Eustis. My father, as a member of the Kiwanis Club and its Leader of Songs, had persuaded that organization to sponsor Ted Shawn and His Dancers as the main attraction for its annual community fund-raising effort. We were to play one concert in the Municipal Auditorium. Needless to say, it was sold out weeks in advance.

The Mumaws were once again house-sitting, now in a plantation-style home set in the middle of orange groves. Shawn and I were billeted there with the young women members of the company, while the boys were guests of family friends. I was overjoyed to see Mazie and Barton after my long absence. I was also apprehensive. Would my unsophisticated parents know how to provide suitable hospitality for my worldly theatrical companions? I should have known the answer to that snobbish question. My father was a natural-born host who could put anyone at instant ease; Mazie was a natural-born charmer. I should have foreseen that they would fall in love with the members of the company and, most particularly, with Shawn, who could also be a charmer in his own inimitable way when he put his mind to it. My mother was a fabulous cook who wooed and won all hearts with meals that made those train box-lunches almost worth enduring. We ate like starving Okies.

I never learned what my parents knew about my relationship to Shawn. My father was nine-tenths a saint, but he was no fool. Although he never indicated the slightest censure or even curiosity when my visits to Eustis with Shawn became regular occurrences, I suspect he may have been patiently waiting for me to make some disclosure. The occasion never arose.

I do believe that Mazie recognized the relationship for what it was and accepted it without distress. The only hint I ever had of this was when a neighbor lady once asked me, in my mother's presence, when I intended to marry. Before I could fumble a reply, Mazie briskly interjected that I was married—to my career. And that was that.

Of course, everybody who was anybody in Eustis attended our performance, after which I had my first heady experience of holding court backstage for a line of well-wishers. Madame Anna and daughter Catherine followed Gillie Goin and niece Dorothy Smoak. Tony Mulliken came with a group of my other high-school teachers, accompanied by most of my former classmates. I treasured a hug and a kiss from my dear Mary Kinser as we exchanged knowing smiles. I was a very happy young man that night.

I was not so happy when Shawn announced that he was leaving with the company the next day to take a coastwise steamer from Jacksonville to New York. I was to remain in Eustis because he "needed to be alone" to straighten out some business and personal "chores." I was astonished and deeply hurt by this rejection, little knowing that the Eustis concert had signaled the end of a significant chapter in Shawn's life. I clung to the reassurance that he would send for me to help him ready the Farm for rehearsals of the company he planned to take out on a brief summer tour of New England. I sought comfort in sleeping late into sunny mornings, in swimming, sunbathing, and taking trips to Wekiva or Rock Springs with Mary, where my brilliant friend identified by its Latin name every weed and crittur below the crystal waters. These lazy days soothed the pain of my parting from Shawn, and, with Mazie's soul-satisfying food, cured the battle fatigue caused by three months on the road.

All was not paradise in my haven. One night, for the first time, I became the target of that harpoon of prejudice which society then aimed at a male dancer. I had taken Mary to a roadside "juke joint," where we anticipated dancing to the latest hits. A prominent Eustis businessman was lounging at the bar and, as soon as we sat down at a nearby table, began to heckle me in a loud, drunken voice. I felt my neck redden as I turned on him, prepared for a bloody confrontation. More quickly than I could, Mary hurried to the man's side. To my amazement, I heard her ask him to dance with her, which he did. When she returned to our table, Mary winked at me and giggled at the tactful denouement she had created. I fear its humor was wasted on the two antagonists. There were no more such traumatic experiences during the rest of my stay at home.

As the days of separation from Shawn continued into weeks, I was hit by the realization that my entire life was magnetized around this single human being, a man who, while certainly of this earth, was to me divine. Over and over during sleepless nights, I relived the coldness he had deliberately placed between us—his reluctance to confide—his reticence that I had found disturbing yet, in the excitement and demands of the theatre, I had had no time to weigh. Now rested and removed from distractions, I forced myself to face the truth that I needed a deeper response from the Master. I wanted him to look at me with eyes more penetrating than those he fixed upon his devoted apprentice. I wanted him to speak words more revealing than any he had yet shared with his ardent emotional partner. I wanted, in short, to be a permanent part of his life as well as of his work. I had little reason to hope that this desire could or would be fulfilled.

Shawn had sent a long, charming thank-you letter to Mazie and Barton. I could clearly picture him at what he called his daily "stint," typing it and answers to other communications pulled from the overflowing briefcase which was his constant companion and which he had nicknamed "The Poisoned Pup." Why had I not received so much as a postcard from him since his return to New York?

I was rescued from despair by an invitation to dance at a charity dinner to be held at The Fountain Inn. Since I had not yet been taught a solo by Shawn, I had no idea what to do. I turned to music for my inspiration, and went through my collection of *Étude* magazines. In one issue, I found a Japanese poem around which I could create a dance. It had been set to a composition that was probably as "Japanese" as anything written by Puccini or Sir Arthur Sullivan. With my equally inauthentic technique, I thought it would be the perfect accompaniment. My knowledge of Japanese costuming was sketchy, but I assumed that a kimono-souvenir of the Denishawn Orient tour would be appropriate. Shawn had given me one of white cotton with a brilliant, bold design in blue. I had used it as a theatre dressing gown because its short sleeves did not interfere with the application of makeup.

After the kimono had been spotlessly washed and creaselessly ironed by Mazie, I wrapped it about me with a blue belt and fashioned a headband of the same fabric. I applied a heavy coat of tan greasepaint and powder and slanted my eyes and eyebrows with a black liner. Then I combed my dark hair down over my forehead, fastening it there by means of a fillet under the headband to make a straight line across the brow—a trick Shawn used for his solo, *Gnossienne*.

I rehearsed in the writing room of the hotel, which was seldom used by guests and contained, unaccountably, a piano. My accompanist was Mrs. Cecil Strong, my first piano teacher. Our positions were now reversed as I dogmatically instructed her how I wanted my tempos, rubatos, and crescendos played. Mrs. Strong managed, with wonderful control, not to chuckle. I think I even paid her the munificent sum of $5.

My performance was a great success, as it would have been no matter what I danced. No one in the audience had any clearer idea of what I was doing than I had. Ignorance was indeed bliss. Only much later, when describing my creation to Shawn, did I learn that a "Gentleman of Japan" would prefer to commit hara-kiri than to appear in public in his bathrobe and bare feet. Nevertheless, when I later studied Japanese technique, I discovered to my surprise that my naive little dance had not been too incorrect.

I was packed and ready to leave home long before the telegram finally arrived to summon me north. Because my first two journeys to New York had been prosaic, I determined that this third—and perhaps most fateful—would be as glamorous as I could afford. I booked a single cabin on the same steamer Shawn and Company had taken earlier. Each time I made my entrance into the dining salon, I imagined myself a famous actor on an Atlantic liner. My gourmet persona chose from the menu only those dishes with the most recherché names, many of which proved to be boiled fish smothered in cream sauce or stuffed with a flavorless mush. I soon learned to avoid the soupe du jour at all costs, but I could not resist a Pêche Melba—half a slimy canned peach filled with a dollop of vanilla ice cream.

A straight-backed, smouldering Valentino, I would order a Manhattan at the bar, more for the maraschino cherry than the bourbon, then light a cigarette. I sat in a corner of the lounge like a man of mystery concealing a secret sorrow, while I read books from the ship's library. When a storm off Cape Hatteras sent most of the passengers to their bunks, I weaved my way in solitary glory to eat the inedible meals, or tramped the deserted, heaving decks with a sure-footed stride—Joseph Conrad facing whatever future loomed beyond the black horizon. When I was at last cornered by fellow passengers, who asked what my occupation was, I fell from the high wire of fantasy into the net of reality. To my shame, I mumbled that I was a student.

I arrived at the Farm in the fresh, green New England spring. I was apprehensive about my reunion with Shawn, but I need not have been afraid. He greeted me simply, warmly. His mood was somber, yet it seemed to me he had made some peace with himself. We walked our favorite path through the woods several times during the next few days, while he explained, with the frankness for which I had longed, the problems that troubled him.

Now I began to understand the reason for past behavior that had seemed heartless: Ted Shawn could not allow himself to unbend while struggling against the emotional, financial, and professional bonds that still tied him to Ruth St. Denis. Only now that he had freed himself from the most pressing of these obligations could he confide in me. I shared his very real sadness at the dissolution of the partnership that had produced Denishawn, even though I felt a guilty joy at being permitted, at last, to glimpse the whole man.

According to Shawn, and contrary to public belief, his marriage to St. Denis had been in jeopardy from the beginning, primarily because each had a different vision of dance. They shared the ideals that made it possible for them to study, create, perform, and live in harmonious, if temperamental, tandem, but at heart their differences were irreconcilable and caused continual conflict. To realize his vision, Shawn relied on organization, emphasized the importance of the school, and recognized the necessity for many dull, difficult tours if Denishawn were to survive financially. Miss Ruth, for her part, was driven to explore mystical, metaphysical, and religious areas as sources of her inspiration and fulfillment.

Many years later, I learned from St. Denis's dairy what her reactions had been to some of the same events Shawn had described to me. She believed that their personal crisis had begun during the 1927–28 Follies *tour, when Shawn, to escape the tensions that had built between them, first suggested separate rooms. She believed the beginning of the end of Denishawn was signaled by the departure in 1925 of Louis Horst, their musical director for ten years, and culminated in the departure of Doris Humphrey, Charles Weidman, and Pauline Lawrence in 1928. As her relationship with Shawn disintegrated, Miss Ruth wrote: "It [Denishawn] has existed because of the good and true in our marriage." Without that, it could no longer exist.*

Even if the reasons for it were not always openly acknowledged by the two combatants, a final battle became inevitable.

March 8, 1932. BB [Best Beloved, one of her private names for Shawn] came last night after a terrible boat trip from Florida. We sat up in my room and I talked first . . . I only want to unfold my latent capacities, my own being, and I want him to do the same. I want what he can do to adjust with what I can do, but it must seem to him quite otherwise. For a little while it seemed as though our whole attempt to live and work together had been worse than a failure . . . that it had been quite futile. Will he always feel that I am standing in his light? Will he always feel that I interfere with him? How awful it is. What are we doing to each other that is so wrong—I wish I knew.

At times, Shawn told me "Ruthie" felt he imposed upon her such a stultifying life that she separated herself from it completely to create programs for solo concerts or for a tour with an ensemble of girls. Shawn then carried on the teaching and occasional tours with a group of his own, until Miss Ruth returned to reassume her inspirational role in his life and the lives of their students. Throughout the Golden Era of Denishawn—the three Daniel Mayer tours of the United States, the Orient tour, the Arthur Judson American tour of 1926-27—the irresistible force partnered the immovable object, a miracle, it seemed, in view of all that Shawn was revealing to me.

> October 1931. Teddy called and asked me not to call him Teddy! as I lowered his dignity in his own eyes! . . . It was pathetic—horrid— emotional. In spite of himself—*he* wept a little too.

> March 20, 1932. Teddy [she still referred to him by the name] came this afternoon and we talked about my catalogue [for lessons at Denishawn House] and Teddy pointed out, very truly and strongly, that I had no right to give the impression to the public that I was continuing the Denishawn School—I was astonished and hurt deeply and terribly by the way he did it. I cried and grew quite needlessly hysterical and said, "This is indeed the end. I have made all the overtures that were possible to me. You have not met me in any real spirit of reconciliation, so we had better, indeed, agree to disagree as quietly and decently as possible."

The separation was equally painful for Shawn. He had seen his dream of Denishawn House as a great American school and theatre of the dance fall victim to the Depression. He had paid off the current mortgage debts on that dream, even knowing it was doomed. He had had the foresight to purchase a sizable annuity for Miss Ruth from their earnings of the *Follies* tour, so that she, at least, would always have enough money on which to live. Because he still felt the love for her that he would express to the end of his days, her security gave him great peace of mind.

> April "13," 1932. Those little marks always mean 'versary [she and Shawn were married on August 13, 1914]. Teddy came to our business meeting this morning with his arms full of Gladioli. It did give me a little thrill, a warm feeling around the heart after these last

dreadful inner days. I am grateful for this simple expression of love. . . .

When Miss Ruth's mother died that spring of 1932, Shawn wrote a long letter of sympathy to his "Darling Ruthie," which ended:

> I don't know just when I will be down in New York again—but if you *want* me—even for just the comfort of my presence—let me know and I will come.
> It has been snowing here [at the Pillow] for three days . . . I figured I could live here more cheaply than anywhere else. But chopping wood—pouring boiling water down the frozen pump—cooking over a fireplace—practically takes up [all] one's time . . . I am still scrabbling for money for this spring and summer . . . As soon as I *do* come down to New York I will come to see you immediately.

As Shawn continued to confide in me, we drew closer than I had dared hope. With a new ease between us and a certain resolute cheerfulness, we rolled up our sleeves to go back to work. It was, as always, invigorating and companionable physical labor expended mostly on improving the Farm. We did little dancing beyond a brief daily *barre* because Shawn had, as yet, no definite plans for rehearsals or performances. In spite of his own precarious financial situation, when that of Denishawn House worsened, he invited Miss Ruth to come to the Farm that summer to work on her own things. I was amazed to see how naturally this great lady fit into our simple life.

I was to observe then, as through all the years Miss Ruth visited the Pillow, how she and Shawn, supreme egotists both, achieved an almost astral relationship that was to endure until her death in 1968. She came to the Berkshires from as far away as California, not only to perform, but, as she said, "for a talk with Teddy," or to see his new works, or to be with "the boys." At the end of one of her early visits, I was elected to drive her back to New York. She was so natural, so relaxed, during the trip that I found myself describing an idea for a dance which, in my inexperience, I thought very original. Miss Ruth listened, straight-faced, as if my inspiration really were unique, then encouraged me to get right to work to realize it.

That summer, I began to know Miss Ruth as a person, and she to know us.

June 12, 1932.   Teddy's farm—We have all sat around the supper table. Jack Cole, Campbell Griggs, a new boy [me] and Ted and I.

The boys cooked a lovely supper and Teddy read Whitman. We talked and discussed while the boys listened. What else could they do? . . . It still seems all strange, though no longer am I suffering. There is no hint of any home together, and I am puzzled to know what is Truth and Love in reality, and what is still illusion. "Lose him and let him go" . . . Oh Beloved.

June 13.   I am now sitting by a table in front of a blazing wood fire. Teddy and Mrs. MacDowal [Alice Dudley's mother] and Duds and the boys are playing cards. A curious scene—a sort of "domestic" art scene: a feeling of warmth and home, and yet no core to this hustle. Or am I quite wrong, and has Teddy really found his home spirit with one of these boys? If he is really happy inside, if he has really finished the long trek with me, not as fellow artist, but as lover and a wife, then will it not be wise for me to take up the dropped divorce question as soon as is practical?

It never did become practical. Miss Ruth returned to Denishawn House and her emotional involvements there. Shawn worked on new dances in the barn-studio on the Farm to develop his ideas for an all-male company. But they remained in contact, and I was sometimes invited to dine with them in the city when they met to discuss business problems. On those occasions, even as I recognized the harmonious modus vivendi they had established, I also sensed tensions close beneath the surface. Shawn hid his worries under a mask of confidence that no longer deceived me; St. Denis smothered hers with charm. One evening Shawn praised me for the proficient way I was handling my duties. Considerably embarrassed, I protested that it was always easier to look out for another than for one's self. Miss Ruth turned the spotlight of her smile on me. "Ah!" she exclaimed, "there speaks the young philosopher." I realized then that her power of enchantment was more than the by-product of theatrical magic.

I was amused to notice that, in their dialogue, they assumed the characters they believed themselves to be with an intensity neither seemed to find to the same degree with any other person. In a social environment, both were extremely engaging. Shawn's vocabulary varied from colloquial to scholarly and his interests from ancient cultures to current events. He was a superb story-teller, with such an innate sense of drama that he seldom hesitated to improve upon facts when a compelling point was to be made. Miss Ruth equaled him in this, but with a subtlety that often concealed sharp thrusts. She could give the impression that she was withholding certain facts, that she did not wish to commit herself in words to the conclusion she implied. When they were in a room together with other people, they permitted little chance for general conversation. Everyone present had to listen to *their* views of, *their* aims for, and *their* theories about the development of that "American culture" which they wished to "give to humanity." Of course, neither Miss Ruth nor Shawn saw their attitudes in quotation marks. They were, rather, the vertebrae that made up the backbone of their lives.

On September 29, 1932, Miss Ruth reported, "A blessed, blessed evening with my beloved. . . . He was inspired in a long talk on what his vision of dance meant to him. I listened entranced. It was a new Teddy." But by the end of October, when she came up to the Farm to celebrate Shawn's birthday with us, she saw that the severance was complete: "A peaceful but quite fruitless time—I shall not go again."

There remained the painful question of what to do with the Denishawn properties they owned in common. One fall day, Shawn asked me to drive him to New York and help him through an unpleasant task. His face wore the grim expression of one who dreads what lies ahead. He explained that, in the course of previous meetings, he and Miss Ruth had amicably, if sadly, divided between them the most precious of their personal costume items: to Siva went the forty pounds of silver chains, bracelets, and belts Shawn had bought in India for his *Cosmic Dance*; to the Nautch Dancer, her green satin, gold-bordered circular skirt, belled anklets and jewelry; to the Emperor Tepancáltzin, the enormous cape of orange feathers he had worn when partnering the young Martha Graham in *Xochitl*. Each also kept those costumes in which they would perform in years to come: her *White Jade* draperies, her *Black and Gold* sari; his *Gnossienne,* his *Thunderbird*; their *Tillers of the Soil*.

Stored at Denishawn House, however, a vast accumulation of scenery, backdrops, screens, props, and ensemble costumes awaited its fate. These could not remain on the property and no other company or theatre would accept them, even when freely offered. There seemed no likelihood that the Denishawn ballets would ever be resurrected, even if dead-storage bills on the historical hoard could be paid. Miss Ruth and Shawn alone could decide what was to be done with it. That was the purpose of our drive down from the Farm.

When we arrived at Van Cortlandt Park, we found that the division of theatrical spoils had already begun under the supervision of Pearl Wheeler. (The "keeper of many keys," Shawn called Denishawn's brilliant costume designer, who was also Miss Ruth's confidante and dresser. Although he valued Pearl's indispensable talents, he had too often found her a thorn in his side because she guarded St. Denis with ferocious devotion.) Several outsize blue-and-yellow-banded wardrobe trunks stood open in the studio. Under the eyes of the household Buddha, Miss Ruth and Pearl were sorting the contents of the trunks on one side of the mirrored room. Shawn and I stood waiting on the other. As each costume, each wig, each trinket was unpacked, the two women—one tall, white-haired, graceful and the other short, heavy, gray-haired, dour—signaled one another if they wanted it. Those things they rejected were relinquished to Shawn. I added them to the collection we would take back to the Farm.

Not one of the four of us spoke a word during this dismal process. When the trunks had been emptied, Miss Ruth suddenly called out, almost gaily, "Here, Teddy!" With a final dramatic gesture, she tossed a large, pale-green square of silk in our direction—the veil around which she and Doris Humphrey had choreographed *Soaring*, one of Denishawn's most beloved dances. I reverently folded the yards of shimmering fabric and placed it with our pile of costumes, while Shawn watched, frowning. Then he looked across the room and held out his hand. "Ruthie, please—Come with me?" he asked quietly. She went to him at once and they left the studio together.

A silent, sullen Pearl and a very dejected Barton continued to stack the varicolored, varishaped materials. We looked up from our work in surprise when a student came from another part of the building to tell us that Miss St. Denis and Mr. Shawn were asking us to join them outside. Puzzled but obedient, Pearl and I followed him to the street entrance of the storage area, where two other male students had already pushed apart the double doors, exposing to the light of day the mysteries of a theatrical warehouse. Shawn spoke to us with dignity, his face expressionless, his voice steady. "Miss Ruth and I have agreed that there is only one way we can bear to bring Denishawn to an end—with fire—with a cleansing fire that will free our spirits from material encumbrances so we may each go on to achieve what we can, alone."

I heard a gasp from the students. I saw Miss Ruth reach for Pearl's hand. I stared at Shawn in disbelief. When and how had they reached this terrible decision? Before anyone could protest, Shawn seized the first roll of canvas on which he could lay his hands, hoisted it to one shoulder, and carried it to the middle of the large vacant lot adjoining the Denishawn land. Reluctantly following his lead, we men brought to him, piece by piece, fragments of the epochal Denishawn sets: the thirty-foot-high flats representing Babylonian gods from *Ishtar of the Seven Gates*, the Hopi adobe house from *The Feather of the Dawn*, the *Spirit of the Sea* rock and fishing net and green-blue backdrop, the *Cuadro Flamenco* baskets of flowers, *Job*'s altar made of cartons, animal silhouettes from *Angkor Vat*. We came with armloads of shoes and wigs, of scarves and garlands, of leotards and gauzy nautch skirts, of Egyptian masks and Viennese ball dresses. The sun had set by the time we had placed everything flammable in the center of the bare ground. There, like a surrealist tower of weird angles and jutting corners, it glittered in the dim light.

Ruth St. Denis and Ted Shawn stood facing this grotesque monument to their life's work. Then she turned to him and he nodded. As in the ritual of an Indian burning ghat, where the closest relative lights the cremation fire of a loved one, he paced around the periphery of the edifice, pouring kerosene from a container. He hesitated only an instant before he picked up a makeshift torch, lighted it, and flung it into the pile.

Pearl and I stood mute and motionless and apart when Miss Ruth ran to Shawn's side as the flames crackled high around the pyre. I turned away, unwilling and unable to witness their grief. Were they listening to the *Radetsky March* while the *Straussiana* linden trees burned? Could they see Martha and Doris and all the other Denishawn Dancers rise in their Grecian tunics to vanish into the grey smoke? Would they scent remembered sandalwood and incense of the Orient beneath the stench of scorched canvas? Did they bow one last time together to the roar of applause in the roar of the flames?

Through the spark-filled dusk, I saw a figure with white hair flee toward the house. A figure with bowed head walked with wooden steps toward me.

Denishawn had ended.

The Farm (Jacob's Pillow). The original house, more
or less as Barton Mumaw first saw it in 1931.

Barton Mumaw sweeping out the studio at Jacob's Pillow, 1933.

Ted Shawn teaching in an early open studio at Jacob's Pillow, 1934.

Ted Shawn and Barton Mumaw, Jacob's Pillow, 1932.

Above: Barton Mumaw at Jacob's Pillow, ca. 1935.

Above right: Margerie Lyon in California, ca. 1935.

Right: Fern Helscher in one of her "crazy" hats.

Below: Ted Shawn's Company rehearsing his *Boston Fancy: 1854* at Jacob's Pillow, 1931. Jack Cole far right, Barton Mumaw second from right.

Ted Shawn in *Osage-Pawnee Dance of Greeting,*, choreographed in 1930.

6

(1932–1933)

A Phoenix Rises

Shawn returned to the Farm a free but poor man. For one of the rare times in his long career, he had no prospect of performing. In an ill-advised moment months earlier, he had signed a disastrous contract, which was in the process of litigation. Until and unless he extricated himself from this control over tours of his company, the only way he could earn a living was to teach. The phoenix destined to rise from the ashes of Denishawn was to have an indefinite period of incubation.

Young and untested as I was, I could do little to help him. But I could perfect my craft, discipline myself to adapt to a man possessed of an egocentricity that often tried my admiration, and learn the strengths and weaknesses of an artist who was *muy hombre*. As I began to understand this person closest to me in the world, I might, perhaps, come to understand myself.

Leaving Denishawn House the day after the cremation, Shawn and I did not speak a word as I drove out of the city. After the enormous finality of what had happened, I could only guess at his thoughts. But my own reactions, with their undercurrent of guilt, appalled me. Was it conceivable that I—an insignificant, twenty-year-old student—had caused the rift between Ruth St. Denis and Ted Shawn? The question hinted at a responsibility that I had neither the wish nor the courage to accept. After many miles of brooding silence, I forced myself to ask Shawn if my fear had any basis in reality. He turned to me with such immediate shock and such concern for my feelings that I could not doubt the honesty of his "No!"

67

For the next hour, he talked to me with a frankness that stripped his complicated character to the bone. He told me that his emotional break from Miss Ruth had begun some years before he had met me, when he had been drawn into a serious relationship outside his marriage. To my intense relief, I learned that it was this earlier involvement that had shattered the partnership which had withstood all previous personal strains. I had had nothing to do with his separation from Miss Ruth or with his subsequent separation from the man.

Never, at any time, did Shawn hint to me of Ruth St. Denis's extramarital affairs, recounted by her biographers and by Miss Ruth herself in her autobiography, An Unfinished Life. * *Only after that book appeared did he once refer to her story about a lover in India: "You know, Barton," I remember his saying with a smile, "I think Ruthie must have made that up. I don't recall any such thing happening, but I well know that she was inclined to romanticize her friendships into affairs." He did frequently mention Miss Ruth's "menials, worshipers, and servitors" (of whom there were, in truth, many), but never to suggest physical attachments. He, who had once aspired to the ministry, indulged in gossip no more than he did in profanity.*

In fact, during our years together, Shawn and I were so complete in ourselves and in our work that neither of us ever again mentioned earlier amours, *male or female. Shawn was an ethical man. Never promiscuous, never driven by sex for its own sake, he dedicated his whole heart to a relationship. This remained true throughout his mature life, even though he was always surrounded by temptations and had every opportunity to surrender to them had he so chosen. Yet, during the half-century that Shawn was my friend, to my knowledge he responded only to four great loves in his life, of which Miss Ruth was one and I am profoundly thankful to have been another.*

By the time we reached our russet and gold hills, everything had been said. Our mood was relaxed; we were at ease with one another and happy to be home. I steered the old Ford with the skill of long practice up our winding road, avoiding the rocks and ruts as best I could. (In March and April, this dry, flinty single lane turned into a river of mire, fed by a mountain spring bubbling up right in the middle of it. Often, we had to walk to our neighbor's farm, beg him to bring his team of horses, and tow the car up to the house.) Because Margerie Lyon had stayed in New York to wind up Denishawn business matters and Mary Campbell was vacationing at her home in Maine, Shawn and I would be blessedly alone for a few

*New York: Harper and Bros., 1939.

weeks before we had to buckle down to what we knew would be a hard winter.

We got out of the car in front of the house and stood inhaling the sharp, resinous air. Then we opened the door on the spiders and the silence and the clammy chill. I collected the groceries we had bought in Lee and stashed them away in the kitchen. One look around made it obvious that the furniture Shawn had ordered from Bloomingdale's had not been delivered. We were too content, though, to let minor inconveniences upset us. I soon had a fire going in the range and another in the living-room fireplace, while Shawn began to prepare our dinner: potatoes baked in their jackets in the coals and his own special lamb chops—thick-cut, wrapped in bacon with garlic, speared like kebabs on long toasting forks and broiled over the flames. We drank sherry and ate chunks of Vermont Cheddar cheese, turned the potatoes occasionally and watched the meat char while we sniffed the good smells that filled the room. Then we ate with the hearty appetite of those whose boat has reached harbor after weathering a storm.

By the time we had finished our coffee and a drop of brandy, we were too sleepy to think of making beds. On impulse, we piled blankets into a makeshift mattress on the floor before the fireplace and wrapped ourselves in additional blankets against the cold. I remember murmuring vaguely that a spark might set us and the whole house ablaze. But we were too lost in the euphoria of what Ted called "a new chapter in both our lives" to fear the flames which signaled that beginning.

The next morning, we put on our worn sweat shirts, pants, sweaters, and espadrilles and went right to work after breakfast. We stored the props and costumes we had salvaged from Denishawn House. We chopped and sawed wood to replenish our supply against the coming winter months. When the furniture finally arrived, we placed a modern mini-fourposter into my narrow room under the stairs (in future years to be Shawn's office), Miss Lyon's double bed in her room on the ground floor, and twin beds in the company rooms upstairs. We folded linens, stacked them in their proper closets, and aired blankets and pillows. Ted continued to do all the cooking; I navigated the Ford down to the village store to buy fresh meat and vegetables and to make any necessary telephone calls.

There was no telephone at the Farm, no radio, no delivery of daily newspapers. Only an occasional car lurching past our driveway reminded us that, beyond our mountains, a world did exist into which, sooner or later, we must once again venture. Our sole visitors were two neighbors, who proved all too generous with gifts for the body and for the mind. This husband and wife would appear unannounced at odd hours to proffer fresh-baked bread and a discourse on another freshly discovered panacea to cure the ills of society. Oblivious to the fact that we were very busy, they would settle down for a long chat which, much as we appreciated their kindnesses, often tried our patience to the limit. From the unwelcome sound of their approaching automobile originated the cry that Ted and I used for years when we wanted to alert one another secretly that something dire was about to happen: "Here come the Talbots!" (Not their real name.) We had many occasions to utter this warning.

As always in the work-and-nature environment of the Farm, Shawn slimmed down and became less tense. He tackled rough jobs with gusto, actually seeking them out if the chores around house and barns were not vigorous enough to challenge his energy. We began to remove boulders that studded the surrounding fields, dragging them up hillock and down on a wooden stoneboat, as the old-timers had. One by one, we placed them in the walls that had collapsed around the boundaries of the property. We, too, collapsed after an early dinner and a game of Russian Bank or a two-handed solitaire called Blue Moon.

I was always amazed at how well Ted could sleep, no matter what his physical, mental, or emotional problems. This ability stemmed, I think, from his strong will, from the necessity to function under all kinds of circumstances, and from a faith in his destiny that compelled him to discipline himself to a degree that would have driven a more self-indulgent person to nervous prostration. I came to learn these facets of the man while we worked side by side through the days. I also learned to be more assertive as Shawn grew more pliable. The master-servant relationship had imperceptibly but definitely altered to become a partnership. Although Ted would always remain my teacher, I was now less the unquestioning disciple. We exchanged ideas about the dance, about the world, about human beings as they relate to one another, and about sex as a force for constructive good as well as destructive evil. He examined my thoughts as respectfully as I did his.

Nowhere was I more aware of my new maturity than when Shawn and I discussed choreography. I quickly discovered that when he asked for suggestions about his work, he was really asking for approbation. Armed with this insight, I learned to present my reactions in such a way that, if my ideas were later incorporated into a dance, they appeared to be his own. If I asked him for advice on my choreographic attempts, he responded with such impersonal, helpful interest that I experienced none of the nervousness I had anticipated. When he evaluated the efforts of another dancer, I cannot recall that Shawn ever insisted upon his own way of doing something. His sole concern was to help shape the material into an effective whole by trimming or enlarging it. I find it hard to understand why he could not maintain this same professional attitude when his own dances were criticized by someone else.

Despite our very real worry about the lack of performing prospects and our financial insecurity, we planned programs together and shared many moments of laughter. Shawn had such a marvelous sense of humor that he could even laugh at himself—at least when we were alone. He also took daily delight in surprising me with culinary masterpieces, such as his East Indian kedgeree made of fish and served with rice flecked with currants and almonds. Our life was as rich as our food, and we dreaded the return of the others with the inevitable impingement on our privacy.

Knowing this might be the last chance to be alone together for some time, we set out on our favorite walk the day before Miss Lyon and Miss Campbell were to arrive. We climbed slowly up the familiar overgrown road that had been used by woodcutters long ago. It led high into the hills through a thinning forest of hardwoods and conifers, whose decayed leaves and needles covered the earth with a sweet, thick mulch. As if it shone through immense Gothic windows, the setting sun painted elongated patterns on this ochre carpet. The churchly silence was broken only by the whisper of our footsteps, a bluejay's cry, or the whoosh of a startled partridge. Then I was startled by the sudden sound of Shawn's voice.

"Are you certain you want to dance beyond all things in this life, Barton? You know there are pleasanter and easier ways of making a living."

I knew the answer, but I sensed something more portentous in the question. I hesitated before replying, "Yes. I would rather be the last dancer in the last row of the chorus and *dance* than do anything else." I felt my face redden as I went on with the overly emphatic words and gestures of an adolescent. "I tell you on my *honor* that I will scrub floors. I will dig ditches. I will do whatever I must. But I *will* dance."

Shawn nodded gravely and moved ahead. I followed him until he stopped at the flat rock ledge we called "our box seats at Nature's show," where we had often rested. When we sat down, the man next to me began to talk as if he had just escaped from years of solitary confinement. I listened apprehensively, not knowing what to expect. Shawn repeated his relief at being released from the falsities, the obligations, the anguish, the indecisions of his earlier life. He brooded a moment, then added, with a gentleness that verged on timidity, that his heart and mind were no longer in bondage to the past. He was totally free to pledge himself to another human being in an enduring relationship—if that being, too, were ready.

I looked at him through tears caused as much by his pain as by my joy. He grinned at me and I grinned back. Simultaneously, we began a dialogue with each interrupting the other. "Don't you think so?" and "Why, that's exactly how *I* see it!" and "But isn't *this* the most important thing?" as Ted outlined a future in which we would both find fulfillment through our dedication to dance and to one another. We promised solemnly to share equal responsibility in all things that might affect us.

But we laughed aloud when I asked, "How do we manage in public?"

"Perfectly naturally, of course," he answered, with a defiant tilt to his chin. "Except that I do think you should not call me Ted when others are around. After all, I am still your teacher, and old enough to be your father as well."

"Okay, Papa," I teased. It was the first and last time I called him by his Denishawn nickname.

I rose and held out my hand to pull him to his feet. We stood a moment staring at a sunset that seemed exceptionally radiant. Then we turned to go back to the Farm. I was carried along down the hill on a spate of talk as Ted expressed his pent-up thoughts. I floundered in hyperbole when he declaimed his ideas of the metaphysical, of the Divine Being, which he and I together, in our works and in ourselves, would discover. In my state of emotional turmoil, I finally could grasp no more; I challenged Ted to race me home. Light-footed, fleet, we sped down from the heights of intellect to our earthbound hearth. There we toasted our pledge in domestic sherry that now tasted like vintage champagne. While we savored this unique moment, Shawn took down his well-worn copy of Plato and read aloud from the *Symposium* words that movingly described our relationship:

> The whole soul, stung in every part, rages with pain; and then again remembering the beautiful one, it rejoices. . . . It is perplexed and maddened, and in its madness it cannot sleep at night or stay in any one place by day, but is filled with longing and hastens wherever it

hopes to see the beautiful one. And when it sees him and is bathed with the waters of yearning, the passages that were sealed are opened, the soul has respite from the stings and is eased of its pain, and this pleasure which it enjoys is the sweetest of pleasures at the time.

Therefore the soul will not if it can help it, be left alone by the beautiful one, but esteems him above all others, forgets for him mother and brothers and all friends, neglects property and cares not for its loss, and despising all the customs and proprieties in which it formerly took pride, it is ready to be a slave and to sleep wherever it is allowed, as near as possible to the beloved; for it not only reveres him who possesses beauty, but finds in him the only healer of its greatest woes. Now this condition, fair boy, about which I am speaking is called Love by men.

In 1977, I read Joseph Mazo's fine book, Prime Movers, * *in which he mentioned the period in Shawn's life after the end of Denishawn:*
Shawn, a man who was an incurable teacher, could well have been seeking a protégé. . . . He needed assurance, praise, and a center on which to balance himself. St. Denis, great as she was, did not fit those requirements.

Although I could not foresee it at the time, I was for eighteen years to be that protégé, that center. Ted, in one of his frequent Biblical moods, had once embarrassed me dreadfully when he announced to a roomful of friends that he felt he was John the Baptist proclaiming the coming of the Lord of the Dance (meaning me!). I was even more distressed when he added that I was the dancer he would have liked to have been.

One by one, some of Shawn's "children" began to return to the Farm. Tall, dignified Margerie Lyon—a stage manager with no productions to manage, a secretary with no school to supervise—resumed her role as "house mother." She was pleased with the way we had prepared her room (on the first floor near mine) and lost little time closeting herself there with Shawn to report on the windup of Denishawn House finances.

It has always intrigued me that she chose to cast her lot with Ted rather than with Miss Ruth since she had for years been equally devoted to them both. I suspect that this proper spinster had an unacknowledged romantic attachment to Shawn.

Mary Campbell arrived and headed straight for the studio to limber her fingers and test how badly the piano needed tuning. To be ready for chore assignments, Jack Cole and Campbell Griggs donned their work clothes in the old barn quarters Shawn had nicknamed "Number Nine." (This structure was later to house the first Men Dancers, who slept, bunkhouse style, in its upper reaches redo-

*New York: Wm. Morrow, p. 94.

lent of bygone years of haying. Still later, it served as a library, music room, and retreat for students.) It was good to have their trusted, friendly hands to help with the many tasks that remained to be done, good to hear music floating through the open doors of the studio. Ted, Jack, Campbell, and I soon joined Mary there to stretch our neglected muscles at the *barre,* then try the new floor with the strenuous leaps, jumps, and stomping steps we called "Primitive Beats."

Even though we all knew we could not perform until Shawn was freed from his contract, we worked as hard as if he had a tour booked. He started to teach us his famous solo, *Gnossienne,** as a classroom exercise. He must have been surprised at how quickly I learned the tricky, angular movements because he took me aside to coach me in the subtleties and humor of the dance. Sometimes, after our practice classes, we were in a nostalgic mood. Ted might then ask me to do *Pierrot in the Dead City** for him alone. (This was the first dance he had choreographed specifically for me, but I had yet to perform it in public.) If he felt especially lighthearted, he would work out on me parts of the satirical mini-ballet he planned to create, using Milhaud's music for *Le Train Bleu,* in which I was to play a French sailor.*

With all our dance activity, we also continued to work hard on the many improvements that had to be made on both house and studio. After supper, we still managed to find the energy to play our favorite card games in front of the living-room fire. Some fine afternoons, we would simply take off on long hikes together or gather to have tea on the front porch while we admired the foliage—quite like the Maple-leaf Viewing Party in Shawn's 1926 Japanese ballet, *Momiji-Gari.* Often Ted would declare a twenty-four-hour holiday after we had been laboring over some particularly dull jobs. At hot noontime, we would drop everything to troop down to Greenwater Pond for a swim. Now and then, fed up with our own home cooking, we would treat ourselves to dinner at The Log Cabin, a roadside diner whose proprietors were fans of Shawn. Best of all, once in a while we would pile into the car and drive to Pittsfield to the movies. We seldom bothered to find out what was playing. Just to go was a pleasure in itself.

The gathering of the clan for a sip of sherry became a daily ritual before dinner. On Sundays, we ate this meal at midday. Ted would prepare one of his special dishes and always make a Pink Lady for our two ladies. These blushing cocktails, despite their in-

*A full description appears in Part Two.

nocuous appearance, had such a relaxing effect that our Sunday dinners were always happy events.

It was a wonder, in such a tightly knit community, that Ted and I never became neurotic about our personal involvement, even though we felt honor-bound to keep it secret from the others. This was not from any sense of shame that might compel dissimulation, but from a deep desire for dignity that demanded privacy. Our discretion could not help but cause a certain strain in our otherwise open and warm relationships with the boys, Mary, and, especially, Margerie Lyon, if only because it inhibited complete frankness.

I can never forget one night when I was tiptoeing from my room up to Ted's. (We seldom shared a room because each of us was too self-centered to endure sleeping in the same space with another.) All at once, the door to Miss Lyon's room was flung open. There she stood, like Hera confronting Zeus *in flagrante delicto*. I froze in the beam of bright light until, without a word having been spoken, she backed away and closed her door. Dreading his anger, I crept on to Ted's room and whispered that Miss Lyon had just seen me going upstairs in pyjamas and robe. To my amazement and relief, Ted's response was a cool, "Oh, Barton, it had to happen sooner or later. Might as well get into bed, now that she knows you're here."

Miss Lyon, of course, never alluded to the incident. Shortly thereafter, she entered the studio by chance while I was working by myself to the only melody I could recognize in a recording of Stravinsky's *Firebird*. Embarrassed by this first meeting alone after our nocturnal encounter, I admitted that I was too shy to show my choreography to Shawn. She asked me to show her the dance. When I had finished the brief piece, she remarked only that I had "a nice quality of movement," from which I clearly understood that I was not to bother "Teddo" (her name for Shawn) with my attempt.

Some days later, Ted asked me to drive her into Lee on errands. I made uneasy small talk as we bumped down our rocky road until she interrupted by asking, "Why don't you call me Marge, Barton?" I was so exhilarated by this signal of acceptance that, involuntarily, I stamped my foot down on the gas pedal and the car fairly leaped ahead. To celebrate my new status, I offered "Marge" a cigarette and took one myself, lighting both with the car's lighter. With a debonair, absent-minded gesture, I then tossed the gadget out the open window, as if it had been a match. We collapsed in laughter, cementing a friendship that endured for the rest of her life.

Much later, I saw this exact incident reenacted in the film, A Letter to Three Wives. *Its screenwriter was Vera Caspary, who had formerly been an editor of the fledgling* Dance Magazine. *It amused me to imagine that Marge-rie, then working in the California William Morris Agency office, might have described the scene to Caspary.*

As our little work force continued to button up the Farm against the coming winter, an opportunity to reenter the world of dance presented itself. To understand how this came about requires a flashback:

In May, Shawn had been invited to present a program at Springfield College, thirty-six miles from the Farm. Under its official title of International Young Men's Christian Association College, this was the leading school in the United States for physical education teachers, playground directors, and athletic coaches. Its graduates filled more than half the positions in the country in those fields. With Mary as accompanist, Shawn planned to use Jack Cole, Campbell Griggs, Lester Shafer, and me to demonstrate his lecture with two of the all-male dances we had done during the 1931–32 tour: *Brahms Rhapsody* and *Workers' Songs of Middle Europe.* Since this would be the first time we were to appear before an audience made up entirely of young male athletes, I was filled with trepidation. If Shawn were apprehensive, no one could have guessed it.

As might be expected, we danced in the gymnasium, bare of scenery and nearly as bare of costume. We were astonished by the enthusiastic reception given our work by the athletes who filled that enormous room. As a result of this single performance, the head of the college, Dr. L.L. Doggett, asked Shawn if he would teach a dance semester some time. Ted agreed on the spot: This would present a new opportunity to spread the gospel of male dancers as artists and be a chance to make the money that would be sorely needed in the nonperforming near future. Sadly, Dr. Doggett had to admit that his budget did not permit these classes to be scheduled until a later date. Shawn, even though he had no idea how he would manage to live, offered to teach for no payment if he could begin the first of the year. His offer was gratefully accepted.

A college spokesman announced in the *Springfield Union* of November 10, 1932, that our demonstration had been " '. . . so revolutionary in quality and so unusual in its work for men that the faculty of the college, particularly in the physical department, was deeply interested in Shawn's proposed dance courses.' " The article went on:

> It is significant that Springfield is the first college ever to invite a great artist-dancer to join the faculty, and while there has been an

increasing amount of interesting material offered to women in this field, *there is almost nothing but folk or tap dancing available for men.* [My emphasis] It is to fill this need that Mr. Shawn's course is being given.

As we began to prepare Shawn's courses, which would start in January 1933, he asked me to be his co-teacher and co-demonstrator. I had proven I could demonstrate adequately, but teach? When I was only just beginning to conquer the problems of my own technique?

"Yes!" Ted exclaimed. "You learn by teaching, you teach by learning. I need you and I know you will do well." With which, he pushed me into unfamiliar waters—as he was to do time and again.

Between us we devised exercises, steps, and formations that could be taught to muscle-bound physical education students. We decided to include a group dance that would not threaten their self-image as he-men—our old *Osage-Pawnee Dance of Greeting* with the number of braves increased from the original four to a whole class. We were confident that the primitive rhythms and choreography of the work would be simple enough for them to master.

Unfortunately, this otherwise rewarding labor would not put food in our mouths or costumes on our backs, so the indomitable Shawn also made an arrangement to teach on a percentage basis at Miriam Winslow's School of Dance. (Miriam Winslow, whose father owned the *Boston Herald*, had been an advanced pupil of Shawn. When the beautiful Braggiotti sisters gave up their school, Mimi took it over.) Shawn was not in the least perturbed by the prospect of our having to drive over icy, snowy roads one day a week, round trip between Boston and Springfield, through ten weeks of winter. The logistics of existence demanded that this was what had to be done.

After Christmas on the Farm, Jack and Campbell returned to New York to await a hypothetical call to rehearse for a hypothetical tour. Shawn collected and typed up his teaching materials. We mended and laundered our leotards and dance trunks. Margerie and Mary assembled clothing, portable typewriter, and musical scores like the troupers they were. I packed Ted's bags and my own, stowed everything in the car, locked those doors and windows that had locks, and the four of us were off to Springfield before deep snowfall could trap us on our mountaintop.

The living quarters assigned to us near the college proved to be the home of the noted naturalist, Ernest Thompson Seton, who was away on safari. Although the house was new and comfortable, it had been Mr. Seton's whim, to superimpose an ancient appearance: a roofline that sagged and rough stonework that supported the statue of a brown bear climbing up the chimney and the painting of a green snake slithering down. Margerie and Mary became hysterical at their first sight of that snake, much to the amusement of the cockney housekeeper we had inherited. (She did not live in the house but came occasionally to help out. We were to do our own cooking and cleaning, as usual.) When Shawn asked her to pack away the many realistic artifacts that lurked in every corner of every room, she admitted she was delighted to be rid of "them dust 'arborers."

Ted had the master bedroom on the second floor, where Margerie, Mary, and I each had a single room. Nothing in our household arrangements struck us amiss; they were simply a continuation of the way we had been living. On those occasions when we entertained faculty members, however, we were to discover from their oblique questions that our foursome was a matter of considerable curiosity to town and campus. This amused more than disturbed us. Mary and I often found it hard to contain our giggles when, on the lakefront before the house, we ice-skated as an affectionate pair under the stares of inquisitive public eyes.

We were far more concerned about the reception our classes would have. With wisdom and foresight, Shawn had insisted that his course be compulsory for every student to preclude the possibility that those men who elected to take it would be called "sissies" by those who chose not to. Dr. Doggett agreed with this strategy. He also arranged for Shawn to address the entire staff and the 500 members of the student body on opening day of the semester. Ted explained his theory of dance as an ingredient essential to total education, threw in a bit of history of male dancing in other cultures, and stressed the value of dance discipline to the physique of an athlete. Delivered with his customary charm, fluency, and enthusiasm, his talk was so dignified and so patently sincere that it was greeted with respect rather than the hostility we had feared.

Nevertheless, we deliberately made the first lessons tough. We suspected that few of the students had ever seen any real dancing, and, either through ignorance or prejudice, would resent having to attend our classes. We knew others were skeptical and a handful downright antagonistic, especially when they learned that they would have to dress only in gym trunks, with bare upper torsos and feet. To overcome their reluctance, Shawn and I first demonstrated without music the vigorous, straightforward movements of running, stretching, leaping, turning, and bending in all directions. Then we asked the men to follow us in a large circle around the slippery gymnasium floor, repeating what we had done. We could tell from their puzzled expressions that the movements were proving harder than they had expected, even without the extra effort needed to point toes or straighten knees. When footballers began to huff and puff as violently as if they were doing pushups on the practice field, we hid our smiles.

Subsequently, we sympathized when they limped into class complaining of sore muscles they had never before used in such ways. Little by little, we lured each group from exercises into steps, from defiance into participation, from sullen obedience into competition with one another. To reach this point, Ted and I created choreography based on activities with which the men would surely be familiar: rowing a boat, using a scythe, chopping down a tree, sawing a plank, sowing grain. As they repeated these "steps" over and over again, we noticed that they no longer sneered at this classwork as "effeminate."

Mary played Indian drum music, folk tunes, and Negro spirituals whose rhythms could be easily identified. It was fascinating to watch as these sports-conditioned men came to respond unselfconsciously to the different moods of the music. Came, in short, to dance. Their movements were far from polished, but they were done with a strength and clarity that needed no interpretation. To see a group of young American males of that time move together in communicative patterns was to glimpse a new development in the ancient art of dance. Once I learned that I could teach with authority, I took pride in my contribution to this development.

At the end of the course, each student was required to write an evaluation paper. The reactions were nearly unanimous. At first, they had believed dancing to be easy, unmasculine, and a bore. As the term progressed, they experienced real enjoyment in the release they found in this dance experience. They hoped that similar courses would be included in all future physical education curricula.

On the day we taught at the Winslow School, Ted and I got up in the black of night in order to arrive in time for morning classes. I drove over treacherous two-lane roads, through drizzle, sleet, and snow. The old car leaked wind and wet through every joint, and had no heater. We wore our heaviest clothing, our thickest gloves, wrapped ourselves in blankets, and placed at our feet hot-water bottles that chilled to ice long before we even reached Worcester.

When we arrived at the school, Ted taught his special class for teachers, while I put younger students through their Denishawn

paces. After our lessons, we stowed our blanketed selves back into
our refrigerated automobile and returned to Springfield through the
freezing dusk. Miserable, nerve-wracking routine though it was, we
enjoyed the weekly opportunity to be alone together. Through chat-
tering teeth, we filled the hours of the journey with good talk about
things dear to our hearts. I was especially pleased if Shawn praised
my progress as a dancer.

For we had (the good Lord alone knows how or when) found
the time and energy to rehearse my solos. We had also, just for the
hell of it, started to coach eight of the most promising Springfield
students in the stage version of the Osage-Pawnee dance. In this
ceremony of friendship, the dancers carried a rattling gourd in each
hand, which they shook to accent the steps throughout the dance.
Although the beat was simple to follow and the characterization was
obvious, the steps and formations were more complicated than any
we had earlier taught the men. After some weeks of work, however,
Ted and I were confident that when they were properly costumed
and lighted, they could appear on stage without shaming us.

As if in response to our confidence in the future, Shawn was
suddenly released from the onerous contract that had prevented his
performing. As if in response to *that* piece of good fortune, he received an invitation to give nine matinee and evening concerts with
a mixed group of girls and boys. These were to be presented at the
end of March, in Boston, under the unlikely auspices of the Florence
Crittenton League for the benefit of its Welcome Home (established
for the "protection and care of delinquent and wayward girls").

Elated by this chance to appear in public again, Shawn accepted the offer without the slightest idea when he could find time to
rehearse, what numbers he could schedule, or where he could assemble a company. Once again, something had to be done and Ted,
always unflappable, solved every problem before it arose. He sum-
moned Regenia Beck and Alice Dudley, of the 1931–32 tour, to rehearse in her school with Mimi Winslow and two gifted young
dancers, Virginia Kyle and Miriam Catheron. Jack Cole was called
to Springfield to help me break in three talented students for those
numbers that required more than two male dancers. Because the
program Shawn put together was made up mainly of dances Jack
and I knew well, he was free to complete his new Milhaud work,
Kankakee at Cannes, while the girls rehearsed their own solos and ensemble dances. We got the necessary old costumes down from the
Farm and the necessary new ones made.

We decided to add the eight Springfield men to the last of our group of Negro Spirituals, and taught them how to "distress" the costumes they were to wear. These consisted of work pants and cotton work shirts, bought to size and all bright and new. In order to give them the worn appearance Shawn demanded, he showed each man how to drag the pants through mud, let them dry, then drag them and dry them again and again until they looked thoroughly beat up. Despite some grumbles, he also insisted that they rip the hems of their shirt sleeves into ragged edges, then dip the shirts in a strong solution of tea to give them the correct work-stained shade. Turning a deaf ear to the complaints about this "sissy" activity, he made the men continue with the process until he was satisfied with the results.

Against all odds, we were finally ready for our opening concert on March 20, but not before we had lived through some hilarious moments. One Sunday, for example, we were rehearsing in the Springfield studio of Anatole Bourman (the ballet teacher and author of a biography of Nijinsky). Everyone froze in mid-leap at the sudden sound of loud knocking and the shouted command, "Open up! Police!" Sure that an escaped thief or murderer must be hiding on the premises, I ran to open the door on a pair of bluecoats.

"You're all under arrest," one of them announced.

"What for?" Shawn demanded, as he hastened to place himself between his startled brood and this unexpected menace.

"For dancing on the Sabbath, *that's* what for," he was told in no uncertain tones. "And *that's* breaking the Blue Laws of the Commonwealth, it is."

Ted protested fiercely that we were only perfecting our Art, an argument that fell on deaf ears. He then exerted his full powers of persuasion to plead ignorance and innocence and to promise to "reform." At that, the officers agreed to let us off with a warning if we stopped the rehearsal at once. We needed no further word of encouragement to scurry off to the dressing rooms and get into our street clothes. We heaved a collective sigh of relief when we reassembled, thankful that we had been spared the humiliation of being hauled away in the paddy wagon in our bathing suits. Locking the studio door behind us, Ted walked down the street with me. He was outraged and furious; he kept muttering imprecations against Bourman who, he firmly believed, had set the cops on us. (This suspicion was not as paranoid as it might now seem because those were the days when proponents of The Ballet and of The Modern Dance had been known to assault one another physically in theatre lobbies.)

Then came the comical hour when our eight new additions to

the company were introduced to their costumes for the Osage-Pawnee dance. Since I had been left in charge of these details, it was up to me to get each of them into a chamois-cloth cap Ted and I had made to imitate a shaven skull, each cap sprouting a topknot of feathers. There was a lot of horseplay and war whoops in the locker room when the men first looked at themselves in the mirror. It took some time before I could calm them down sufficiently to dress them in an outfit that was made up only of two panels of decorated buckskin hanging fore and aft over a minimal tan G-string, leaving the bottoms mostly uncovered. My warriors reacted with collective shock when it dawned upon them that, in the course of their dance, the exposure would be considerable.

Having made my own professional debut in this very number, I understood their apprehension. I therefore hastened to assure them that everything would be most respectable because the orange-red lighting would be dim and their bodies would be entirely covered with a deep red-brown paint. The howls of rage that greeted this piece of news would have made an Iroquois enemy shiver with terror. Before I completely lost my courage, I blurted out that they would also have to shave.

"You mean we have to shave *there*, for Christ's sake?" one of the more hirsute yelled.

I swallowed an impulse to chide him for using profanity on Christian territory as I explained in a shaky voice that Massachusetts law did not permit the showing of pubic hair in public. From the expression of their faces, I was no longer sure we would have eight Indians to perform our opening number. I have no idea how I got them shaved, painted, costumed, and on stage for their history-making debut at the Boston Repertory Theatre. But I did.

The day of the first concert, a conventional Denishawn program featuring the five girls and the five men of the regular company, turned out to be a day of double disaster: President Roosevelt closed the banks and Shawn dislocated his sacroiliac. Because of the unexpected Depression-induced bank holiday, the average person was left with just the cash in his pocket. This was hardly money that one would dare spend on theatre tickets. Because of his injury, it was feared that Ted could not dance. Nevertheless, he was determined that our show must go on. He announced that scrip would be accepted at the box office in lieu of coin of the realm. (This decision put him no more than $10 in the red at the end of the engagement, a Pyrrhic victory if ever there was one.) He also informed his physician that he absolutely *would* dance.

Faced with granite stubbornness, the doctor reluctantly strapped his patient into a "corset" of wide, heavy adhesive tape that was hidden beneath Shawn's briefest costume. Although it was supportive when first applied, this brace weakened under the strain and sweat of dancing. It therefore became my dreaded duty after every performance to rip off the old tape in order to put on the new. Ted's screams during this operation could be heard as far away as the Old North Church. By the end of the week, that entire area of his body was a mass of torn skin and blisters.

Our program on Tuesday, March 21, 1933, made up for pain and panic. Purely as an experiment, Shawn had scheduled for that single night dances done only by males—the first such program in the modern world. Since I was to perform his solo, *Gnossienne,* in this unique venture, I was unforgettably nervous. I must have danced it well because there was a cloudburst of applause after I exited. Ted was standing in the wings. I was so exultant that I could have hugged him right then and there, had I dared. But he remained aloof and businesslike as he calculated the strength of the continuing applause. He told me to take another bow. Then another. Finally, he signaled Mary at the piano on stage down right, gave me a push on the shoulder, and with a big smile whispered, "Give it to them again, Barton! Give it to them again!" I did. And that, too, was unforgettable.

Our Springfield men had been astonishingly effective in their opening number. Furthermore, considering that they had never had a chance to rehearse with the full company, they were very good in *Calvary,* which concluded the program. In this, the ensemble of thirteen men, led by Shawn, was somberly lighted from opposite wings of the stage, their shadows adding dark patterns to the slow, marchlike formations of the work. As a critic for the *Montreal Star* was later to write, "The religious dances which brought the program to a close were in some respects the best of all. . . . All the Negro Spirituals were danced perfectly, alike as to rhythm and to emotional values." We felt it was a real triumph that eight amateurs could convincingly project the intensity of those of us who were professionals.

The audience reaction at the end of the concert was memorable. There had never been anything in our experience to equal such applause for concerts that had included girl dancers. Ted, Jack, and I were stunned. Our student-dancers, grinning as if they did not know what had hit them, took the countless bows with us, shuffling from one bare foot to the other. When at last the houselights were brought up to disperse the audience, we left the stage together like a football team that had just scored the winning touchdown.

In his dressing room—after the many well-wishers had greeted him, been greeted by him, and departed—Ted stood in a daze. He did not so much as wince when I ripped the adhesive from his raw flesh. We were both close to tears that had nothing to do with physical suffering.

Then, matter-of-factly, he put on his robe, sat down at his dressing table, and began to remove his makeup. He paused, towel in hand, just long enough to look up at my reflection in the mirror and say, "This means the time has come. The time has really come."

7

(Summer 1933)

Jacob's Pillow Is a Rock

That the time had indeed come for an all-male company was also recognized by Lucien Price, a distinguished editor of the *Boston Globe* and a man of rich musical and literary culture. He wrote to Shawn on April 2, 1933, thus beginning a lifelong friendship with him and with his Men Dancers:

> You have hit upon a powerful idea and, given the requisite years of hard work, I do not see how anything can stop it or you. . . . The dancing of the young men was boldly original [and] in your company for the first time, it seemed to me, I saw young Americans dancing *as* Americans and dancing in an art form. . . . In the *Rhapsody* of Brahms, you succeeded in translating the music into abstractions expressed in motion. It was made visible—Life Leaping!

But the "powerful idea" to which Price referred had not been conceived on that March night of 1933. As far back as 1917, Bernarr MacFadden's magazine, *Physical Culture,* had featured Shawn with a cover photograph and his profusely illustrated article entitled *Dancing for Men.* In it the twenty-five-year-old Shawn emphasized that the dancing is done by men in all primitive tribes and countries. He outlined practical beginning dance exercises for the modern American male. And he described how he had presented, in the 1916 appearance with Ruth St. Denis and the Denishawn Dancers at the University of California's Greek Theatre at Berkeley:

> . . . a group of [himself and seven of] my men pupils, all American

boys who had had no training but what I had given them, and that only a few months, in the *Pyrrhic Dance*. In a performance lasting over two hours, with solos and group dances and many beautiful and skilled girls, this dance by a group of men received the largest amount of applause from an audience of nearly ten thousand people.

Throughout the Denishawn era, Shawn had continued to choreograph ensemble numbers for men, in addition to solos for himself and Charles Weidman. The question now was, would the American public support entire concerts of serious dance performed only by men? It would take great courage to find the answer, even though Shawn, at age forty-two, was still a big draw. Without a company, adequate housing for a company, complete programs, bookings, or much money in this fourth year of the Great Depression, he was nevertheless determined to try.

——The Company

Before Shawn could dream of assembling a company, he had to acquire enough money to support one. As one source of funds, he accepted an engagement to dance at the annual festival presented by the Order of the Alamo in San Antonio, Texas. With this fee, the income from teaching he scheduled to do en route, and a borrowed $1,500, he figured he could maintain a small group of men through the summer of rehearsals that would prepare them for a tour.

The theme of the 1933 festival was India. Ted decided to perform his *Cosmic Dance of Siva* that had been such a hit all over Texas when he had danced it on the *Ziegfeld Follies* program. As part of the planned festivities, a local beauty-contest winner was to be crowned Queen of the Court. When Shawn arrived at the San Antonio city limits (with Mary as accompanist and me as chauffeur, co-teacher, and dresser), the first thing he saw, arched over the street, was an enormous banner that read, THE CROWNING OF THE QUEEN with TED SHAWN. We laughed so hard I almost drove the car off the road.

This appearance proved far more fortuitous than the money it brought in. We broke our long drive west to stay with Ernestine ("Teenie") Day, who had been a longtime Denishawn Dancer. Now married, she taught dance in her hometown of Arkansas City, Kansas. She was producing a church pageant for which a young composer named Jess Meeker had written the music. Shawn and I were impressed both by his composition and by his sensitive piano playing. When Jess told us he was on his way to Dallas for a convention of pipe organists, we invited him to join our caravan. We also planned to stop in Dallas to teach some advanced classes for Edith James, another former Denishawn Dancer, and the leading dance teacher in that city.

Edith's classes were held in a hotel ballroom that doubled as a conservatory. It was entirely roofed with glass. One day, Jess and I were leaving an organ recital when a sudden rain of hailstones, seemingly as large as baseballs, descended upon us. "The glass roof!" I yelled. With visions of Ted lying bleeding and unconscious, I raced to the hotel, Jess at my heels. In the ballroom, the floor was indeed covered with shards of glass but, to my intense relief, no bodies lay among the splinters. Everyone, by some miracle, had escaped without a scratch. This frightening shared experience, coupled with our common love of music, forged a strong bond between Jess and me. Before we drove on to San Antonio, I promised to keep in touch with him.

When we were back at the Farm, Ted repeated his admiration for Meeker's talents. Mary Campbell then admitted that she felt uncomfortable at the prospect of accompanying an all-male group. She feared she could not compose the kind of music that would be essential for our new dances, and furthermore she wanted to accept a permanent position with the Winslow School. She urged Shawn to ask Jess to take her place. He did. With Meeker's prompt arrival in the Berkshires began his enduring association with Shawn, the members of the Men Dancers, and the many Jacob's Pillow students and performers who later came to know and love him. From his first day with us, he slipped into our routine as into a pair of well-worn overalls. No doubt his childhood on a Kansas farm had prepared him for our hardscrabble life. Although we missed our dear Mary, we welcomed him as the invaluable *compañero* and co-creator he immediately became.

Shawn selected six dancers to coalesce around this indispensible musical core: Wilbur McCormack, Frank Overlees, Dennis Landers, George Horn, Fred Hearn, and me. I was the only one who had had more than a minimum of dance training. We all knew our work was cut out for us if we were to be integrated into a professional ensemble prepared to go out on tour in a mere six months.

Wilbur McCormack had been in Shawn's class at Springfield College and had appeared in the memorable Boston Repertory Theatre concert. A high-school letterman in football, basketball, baseball, and track, he had also been captain of the college wrestling team. With his muscular body, he was to develop a commanding stage presence. Because we were similar in size and build, Shawn

often used us together in compositions. Mac became the closest to
me of all the men in the company.

Frank Overlees, a champion swimmer, was also a veteran of the
original all-male concert. His grandmother was a full-blooded
American Indian, from whom he had inherited an exceptional physique. From his father's Dutch ancestry, he had inherited an inscru-
table personality with unexpected flashes of humor.

Dennis Landers had studied with Teenie Day in his hometown
of Arkansas City. For a long time, he had held the high-school pole
vault record and had been a member of the team that won the state
basketball tournament. Dark and very good-looking, he had the taut
body of a runner with the high-strung disposition to match.

George Horn, a little older than the rest of us, had had just
enough dance schooling to earn him a job or two in musical comedies. His was an outstanding ability to design and execute costumes
and to devise everything from props to headdresses out of scraps.

*He was also a natural born clown whose inventive tricks cheered us through
many a depressing moment. I think, indeed, he may have saved the group from
dissolution when the grind of class, rehearsals, and house-and-field work tempted
us to throw the whole idea of men dancers into the ashcan.*

*I particularly remember one occasion: after a day's strenuous activities, we
were sitting around the dining-room table sewing beads on costumes by the light of
two kerosene lamps. As gray-green, grim, and dispirited as Van Gogh's* Potato
Eaters, *we were as bone-weary as we looked. Suddenly, George disappeared. Just
as suddenly he reappeared, draped in an outlandish outfit of kitchen towels, a scrub
brush dangling from the buckle of his belt and a mop held above his head in both
hands like a spear. Stomping, turning, hissing, posing, he staged a great burlesque
of Shawn's famous* Japanese Spear Dance *as he whined an off-key accompaniment. He caricatured Ted's gestures with outrageous exaggeration and ended in
the familiar pose with knees bent in a deep* plié *over flat feet turned out in second
position, the mop-spear held upright at arm's length. We whooped and hollered
and applauded loud enough to startle the dead sleeping down in Becket cemetery,
thanking George for the relief of laughter. He was one of the few people I knew
who could tease Shawn and get away with it, which he did, he claimed, to keep us
from being so "god damned arty."*

Fred Hearn had auditioned for Shawn when we played
Asheville, North Carolina. He was blonde and lean, and his sunny
nature masked a responsible attitude toward life that I came to trust
and admire. Later, when the group spent winters in Eustis, Freddy
met a school friend of mine whom he married. I well remember
holding in my arms the younger of his two infant sons, when I was
on leave from the Army.

George Gloss was to play an important nondancing role in the early company. He had a Master's in Physical Education, had been in the chorus of *Job* at the Stadium, and was obsessed with the idea of establishing dance in the physical education departments of the nation's schools. Although he was handsome and personable, he was too big-boned to be a dancer. I was relieved when he resigned himself to this reality; had he ever performed with us, I was certain no one in the audience would have seen any dancer but George.

Because he could not dance with us, he determined to help in any other way he could. He offered to try to book dates for the as yet unknown, untried Men Dancers. Shawn sent him out on the road with a tentative schedule and his blessing. He recognized that George's missionary enthusiasm could charm both the hearts of female sponsors and the minds of male physical education directors.

As had Mary Campbell, Margerie Lyon decided that she would be out of place in an all-male company; she preferred to return to Los Angeles. Ted and I knew just how much we would miss her when she promised to seek engagements for the group as she traveled westward, thereby dutifully, if sadly, terminating a twelve-year association with Shawn. Her dignified carriage and her British accent so impressed club ladies and university heads with her "respectability" and her devotion to "culture" that Margerie secured many bookings for us, while George proved as successful with society leaders and the chairmen of athletic departments. Thanks to their efforts, we played one hundred and eleven performances on our very first tour—"A feat," as Shawn never tired of boasting, "not equalled by any touring American dance company since the Denishawn days!"

Long before that first tour, however, Ted and I were left alone on the Farm with six comparative strangers. We felt vaguely threatened by their presence until we observed how well they complemented one another at physical labor, during the course of daily life, and in the studio. Each went about his tasks of improving and running the Farm and submitted to Shawn's tough dance discipline as if he were competing for a place on his school team and Shawn was the coach, with Meeker following the plays from the sidelines. As assistant trainer, I was the only one to be given solos that first year. It must have been apparent from this, if nothing else, that Ted and I were close. But no one of the six showed a sign of envy or jealousy.

I recently read Timothy Findley's novel The Wars* *which, although writ-*

*New York: Delacorte, 1978, pp. 114–115.

*ten in another context, shed for me some light on the unique relationship that
developed among the members of the Men Dancers. A character is speaking:*
  I think the fact is that extremely physical men . . .
  *are often extremely sensitive men as well. Not your local football players, mind
  you! They're more apt to be maudlin and sentimental. But the true athletes—the
  ones who seek beauty through perfection. I think they seek out poets and artists just
  as poets and artists seek them out. Maybe not always as lovers—though "love"
  has so many ways of expressing itself outside the physical. I certainly don't want to
  paint a picture of a lot of poets and athletes lusting after one another's bodies! But
  love—yes.*

I believe Shawn's strict impartiality was responsible for good
group spirit and morale. He treated me exactly as he did the others,
whether I was mixing cement or taking class. When he thought I
deserved criticism in my dance work or my communal duties, he
gave it to me straight from the shoulder and in front of the other
company members. (I died a thousand deaths whenever this happened because a born Leo cannot tolerate the slightest threat to his
concept of himself as perfect, a not very laudable fact.) Despite this
scrupulously fair treatment of me and despite our increased discretion, everyone soon recognized my emotional involvement with Ted.
Although I have no idea what they may have discussed among themselves, not one man hinted at this involvement either to me or to
him. Relatively unsophisticated though they were, they honored
with public silence our privacy. We, in turn, honored them for their
sensitivity.

Remarkable as it may seem, this reciprocal loyalty remained
unbroken for seven years. Shawn never interfered with those
amours that came to his attention unless he feared they might disrupt the company or affect the work. In that case, he could be, and
was, severe, but there was seldom any cause for him to be. The men
respected his standards. They handled with taste those few affairs in
which they could be involved—few, because of the restrictions imposed by touring, the ceaseless work, the isolation from outsiders for
long periods of time, and the rigorous schedule of classes, rehearsals,
and performances. Under such conditions, it is small wonder that
Mac, George Gloss, Freddy, Foster Fitz-Simons, Frank, and Denny
all postponed marriage until after the group disbanded in 1940.

When girl students came to live at Jacob's Pillow during summer school, all social contact between them and male students or
company members was supposed to be supervised. Chaperones
Carol Lynn and Eugenia Dozier—gentle, charming women both—

could be fearsome duennas who would actually beat the bushes if need be.

Lucien Price told me one of my favorite stories about Mac. After a Pillow concert, he was approached by a woman who asked him, "Tell me, young man, what do you do sexually?" To which Mac replied with hauteur, "There are avenues of exit from the Farm, Madame. We all have feet by which we can get out, and we have wheels."

It was also remarkable how rarely serious clashes, quarrels, or even differences of opinion arose among us. I can recall only one actual fight. I do not know what caused the shouting match that flared between Denny Landers and Wilbur McCormack. Denny was known to have a short fuse; Mac, although slower to anger, could spit fire when aroused. Since both were in peak condition, all hands converged when their shouting stopped and a swinging of lethal fists began. In terror, I jumped between them. I grabbed Denny in a bear hug with a force I did not dream I possessed, yelling, "You can't do this to each other! You can't do this!"

Others had seized Mac, and we all stood transfixed in a silence broken only by the grunt of heavy breathing. Then Denny swiveled his head to look into my tear-filled eyes, going limp in my arms. Mac, ever the good sport, pulled out of the grip in which Frank and Freddy held him. He offered his hand to Denny. Denny shook it. That was the beginning of a long, firm friendship.

Through the coming years, others would join the group to make their special contributions as friends and co-workers: Foster Fitz-Simons, member of the swimming and fencing teams at Emory University in Georgia, a writer and composer as well as dancer; William Howell, football and track letterman from Knoxville, Tennessee; Ned Coupland from Dallas, a youngster who finished his last two years of high school while he was with the Men Dancers; the striking Delmar twins, John and Frank, from Chicago, both outstanding athletes and huntsmen; Johnny Schubert, our baby, destined to be killed in the war; Harry Coble, Sammy Steen. . . .

As the company changed, so, too, did the Farm. Year by year it was being transformed into the school and festival which is now known as Jacob's Pillow.

—Building The Base

Those who visit the Pillow today find the mighty rock from which it got its name diminished by the trees that have soared above it in the past half century. One of them is a blue spruce that Margerie Lyon and I splurged to buy for a long-ago Shawn birthday, a beautiful sturdy sapling that pleased him enormously. Those who now see the unique Ted Shawn Theatre, well-kept lawns, landscaping, parking lot, tastefully decorated main house with offices and staff quarters, dining rooms and modern kitchen, three spacious studios, and cabin accommodations for at least seventy students—these visitors will find it impossible to picture what the property was like in 1933. Every spring and summer thereafter until his death, Shawn, with his own hands, whatever volunteer labor he could round up, and whatever professional help he could afford, created beauty from nonentity.

One of the earliest tasks he and I tackled together was thoroughly unnecessary in light of the many fundamental repairs then crying out to be made. Somehow, Shawn had learned that the town of Lee contained one of the oldest marble quarries in New England, and that they sold broken pieces of the stone at giveaway prices. Never able to resist a bargain, he ordered a ton of odd-shaped, vari-colored slabs to be delivered to our doorstep. When they arrived, we had not the faintest idea what to do with them until one of us suggested we might enlarge the living room of the house by constructing a terrace beyond its door. We could entertain guests there in a style and a space befitting the Father of American Dance.

By first digging, then carting thousands of wheelbarrow-loads of earth from field to site, Ted and I raised the level of the surrounding land that sloped down from the front porch. This gave us a fine, flat area with a view of the road and the distant hills. The reward for our toil was the exquisite pleasure of paving that area with cement into which we fitted fragments of marble. When we had placed the final piece of our colorful mosaic, we straightened up to contemplate it with pride and with loud, competitive complaints about whose back was more broken, whose fingers more severely cracked. Then Shawn bellowed for everyone to stop what he was doing and come at once to admire his (sic) handiwork.

Ted always expected to be complimented on his achievements, whether as bartender, cook, or choreographer. He took particular pride in his cement work and house-painting. A treasured snapshot shows him perched on a homemade ladder at second-story height, where he is applying a coat of white paint to the side of the house. Like a statue by Praxiteles with a brush in hand, he poses in a broad-brimmed hat and costume G-string.

The first construction job assigned the new men was to convert one of the sturdier barns into a bunkhouse. Ted and I were already all-round architects and handymen, but the others were inexperienced in such fields. It was interesting to see how quickly they learned and how the chores divided to suit their different temperaments, although all had to share equally in digging roads, clearing the land, maintaining the garden, and making costumes. Ted and I continued to do the stonework at which we had become proficient. Dennis built his own cabin in the woods. Mac and Frank eventually did the same, showing an aptitude for carpentry that placed them in charge of all hammer-and-nail projects. Frank also drove daily into Lee for mail and supplies. Mac later taught in the school and supervised the parking of cars for the visitors who began to come to our weekly lecture-demonstrations.

Freddy had a green thumb and a strong back. He willingly became head gardener and filled our table with fresh vegetables, cared for the lawns, and planted flower beds. Because he also had a head for figures, he kept our accounts. George Horn, in time off from his seemingly ceaseless sawing of wood, was then responsible for costume designing and fabricating. After Foster Fitz-Simons joined us, he became boss of the kitchen crew when he was not keeping our tax records straight. The Delmar twins built miles of walks and walls of native fieldstone, and gunned down the critters that invaded garden and house alike. (Shawn was to recall that porcupines had eaten the supporting stringers of a floor.)

The ideal that creative artists should live close to the land, work with their hands, and be isolated from urban influences sometimes met with resistance from Shawn's followers. He would not permit us even to have a radio on the place. And it was not until we built a cabin for Fern Helscher, who became our press representative, that he allowed a telephone to be installed for her—albeit six-hundred feet distant from the rest of us. Some of the men railed against certain of Ted's edicts. There is no doubt that his pursuit of his ideal was extreme.

The group was saved from despair and eventually disciplined into a respectable working unit by Shawn's "Daily Routine":

7–8 A.M.	Breakfast.
8–10 A.M.	Studio. Warming-up exercises, on floor and upright, to stretch and strengthen muscles and achieve fluidity [these varied as Shawn invented new ones]. Fundamental *barre* to develop technique, dexterity, and body line. Open floor for single steps, then a combination of these steps into dance phrases [called in ballet terms

	enchaînements]. Accompanied by piano music, recited poetry, singing, chanting, percussion, and/or no accompaniment at all [these echoed my infant dancing to the Victrola]. Class ended with a repetition of sections of works in progress.
10 A.M.–NOON	Group rehearsal led by Shawn of current repertory.
NOON–2 P.M.	Gathering on platform outside studio (if sun shone): lunch in the nude; Shawn reading aloud to us. [Some of this was heavy going—Gilbert Murray on Greek poetry, Ouspensky's *Tertium Organum,* Havelock Ellis, Aristophanes, Goethe—but also news from the morning paper, selections from *archie and mehitabel,* a Robert Benchley humorous essay, or even quips from Groucho Marx on the theory, I suppose, that all thought and no laughter make a dull dancer.]
2–3 P.M.	Studio. Review of repertory and work on new compositions, under my supervision.
3–5 P.M.	Outside chores to maintain and improve property.
5–6 P.M.	Shower, rest, and social hour for those not involved in preparing dinner.
6–7 P.M.	Dinner.
7 P.M.–BEDTIME	Work on costumes, props, addressing and folding circulars, preparing press material, or whatever other sit-down chores had to be done.

Many a night, I left the others to their chores and returned to the studio alone to work on my own choreography or polish a new solo Shawn had created for me. As dancers will, I often repeated one phrase many, many times. (Later, working with Jack Cole in Hollywood, I remember his struggle with a single eight-bar passage for an entire day.) One night very late, a guest at the Pillow heard a brief section of my music played over and over on the gramophone as I labored with rhythm and line. He was so impressed by my industry that, instead of being angry at having been kept awake, he left $75 with Ted as a present for me.

Shawn also demanded that we obey one rule which, he felt, would hold us together in harmony: whenever a difficulty arose with which we could not cope—personal or communal—we must come to him at once. He believed that a problem sooner faced was sooner solved with least damage to the welfare of the company. While this was an admirable aim, it was not always realized. Ted could be so dictatorial and opinionated that one was often reluctant to divulge certain matters on which he had taken a stand. What is more, his charm, which seldom failed with women, had an equally persuasive effect on men. He could frequently talk one into a change of attitude or behavior that might later be regretted.

It was a constant battle to stick to the routine through aches, pains, blisters, injuries, minor illnesses, and the urgent menial tasks that might demand instant attention. We tried, however, and discovered that to some who did not share its vicissitudes our life seemed idyllic. In one of Lucien Price's earliest letters to Shawn, he wrote:

> The ones I do envy are those young fellows whom you are training. Lucky cusses! They have an art form through which to express themselves—a thing that not one young American in ten thousand ever has—and they have an ideal purpose to live for and work for. . . . I congratulate them on having to cook and chop wood and put up with hardscrabble. It is a wonderful experience, and really nothing in your letter struck me as so picturesque and pioneering (in the genuine old spirit) as the thought of you fellows living on a farm in the Berkshires, boiling your own coffee, cutting your own firewood, and then coming down to the Repertory Theatre [in Boston] and putting on a performance as thoroughly artistic as yours was. If that isn't romance, I don't know the meaning of the word.
>
> [After a later concert, he wrote:] Whether you [Shawn] and the boys are aware of it or not the special quality which comes through your performances is . . . such a kind of moral beauty as seldom comes from the stage. It is American, it is typical of American youth and . . . it is brand new and unexampled. I do not believe it would be possible for your performances to give me the sort of glow they do if you were not personally fine fellows.
>
> [And still later, he wrote:] I have to thank you for a satisfaction of mind which I never expected to enjoy in the modern world. The sight of life devoted to the practice of a fine art being lived by a confraternity of young men is the Periclean ideal: "We Athenians are lovers of the beautiful. We are simple in our tastes and we cultivate our minds without a loss of manliness."

Well, we did not quite fulfill the "Periclean ideal," but even as Shawn equipped us with admirable standards that would help shape our future lives, we were never free from mundane responsibilities. For one thing, early facilities were plagued by lack of sufficient water. When the number of students and the size of the audiences increased, a probe had to be sunk through the granite mountaintop in search of a more abundant supply. As Shawn was to report in 1950:

> On the day of the first performance, they reached 200 feet. I was in my room dressing to greet the first audience of the season when one of the boys came in and said "Shawn, I don't want to get you needlessly excited, but the well diggers have sent for you!" I went out. We all stood about praying that they had hit *enough* water—and they had! So I went on stage trembling, to tell the first audience that from now on they could flush the toilets with impunity!

Such was this artist who, with equal aplomb, could take curtain calls in the best theatres in the world and also announce in his own theatre that the toilets were functioning!

Busy and distracted as we always seemed to be, Ted and I were nevertheless closer than we had ever been. He masterminded everything. I was a "sorcerer's apprentice" deluged by more duties than I should reasonably have assumed. Somewhere, somehow, we found time each day to be alone for a walk, a talk, a shared evaluation of the progress of each group member, a mutual plan to improve faults we had observed. In its activities, its anticipation of performing, its common faith in Shawn's plans for the future, the group little by little was shaped into an effective performing band.

One example perhaps best illustrates the men's basic attitude toward Shawn and toward the building of Jacob's Pillow. In 1935, we voted unanimously to open the summer school to men students who would live on the premises. (Until then, there had been classes only for girls, who were housed and chaperoned in nearby local homes.) This decision entailed the enlargement of existing dormitories and the construction of a decent-sized dining room. After Shawn borrowed money to buy an adjoining fifty-five acres of land on which were several rickety edifices, he reluctantly permitted the first electric line to be strung to the property. We discussed where it would be most practical to put the dining room. We even staked out the space we estimated it would need, placing card tables on the ground near the kitchen to measure the area. But nothing definite had been done to start this project before Ted and I had to leave the Farm for several weeks to teach at Peabody College in Nashville, Tennessee.

Every one of those weeks away from home, Ted fretted because letters from the boys contained no word of the work they were supposed to be completing.

"What in God's name are they *doing*?" he once exploded.

"Having a high old time while you and I are getting up at the crack of dawn and sweating like bulls every day to support them?"

He was enraged when his direct questions remained unanswered. He wrote to Mac sarcastically, "I do hope you are all enjoying this beautiful Spring in the Berkshires."

On our journey home from Peabody, Shawn kept urging me to drive faster, urging I did not need because I knew that lack of money determined that we had to avoid the expense of hotel bills. It was already black night when we reached the Farm. The meticulous Ted had written Mac our expected arrival time, and when we turned into our unlighted driveway, he was livid with anger because there was no sign of welcome or even of life.

We drove slowly past the kitchen, staring out at the area where we hoped to glimpse the framework of the new dining room. We saw little as I stopped the car and switched off the ignition. Then, from the opposite barn, a brilliant floodlight illuminated a stone structure that looked as if it had grown right out of the New England soil. Set with multipaned windows, its boulder walls rose to a peaked roof, at one end of which loomed a solid chimney. We gaped when the plank door rolled open on its hinges, inside lights flashed on, and six figures ran out shouting, "Surprise! Surprise!"

For one of the few times in all the years I knew him, Ted could find no words. We let the boys lead us around the exterior of the little building, then into its interior. There, each man boastfully pointed out his individual contribution to the construction. Never having been any good at work that demanded this kind of expertise, I was as flabbergasted as Shawn.

Mac and Denny explained how they had managed to fit windows into stone walls. George and Freddy exhibited the details of the huge fireplace they had built. Frank showed off the enormous table he had made (in use every season since), while Jess stood by, beaming. We were served hot food and cold drink to christen the refectory, and when we had finished eating, Ted rose, glass in hand. With a brevity that bespoke deep emotion, he toasted his dancers in words of gratitude, of admiration for the quality of their work, and of pride in their character, initiative, and accomplishment.

That dining room became the setting for decision-making sessions, for end-of-season parties, for confrontations and consultations, for happiness and grief. It was a place where I shared many memorable meals with world-famous artists, devoted workers, fellow teachers and performers, and young students. But I will never forget the brotherliness we eight men experienced seated around that table on that first night in the summer of 1935.

—*Cooks and Cooking*

In *Remembering Poets,* Donald Hall has written, "Domesticity pre-
cedes ideology, for all men and women."* Indeed, many aspects of
domesticity penetrated life at the Farm, not the least of which was
food and its preparation. Shawn saw to it that we were all well fed,
but he took the budgetary precaution of buying outsize dinner
plates, theorizing that, with large first helpings, we would not go
back for seconds. Gross miscalculation: we were dancing and laboring furnaces that had to be properly fueled if we were to function, so
we simply filled those plates twice at a sitting.

In the earliest days of the company, we did our own cooking.
This resulted in very plain fare except when Ted took over. It also
disrupted rehearsals and classes when men assigned to KP duty for
that day had to leave early. This conflict soon impelled Shawn to
employ a chef. It was not easy to find someone who would accept the
position, however, because no self-respecting cook would consent to
operate in our primitive kitchen with its ancient wood- and coal-
burning range, old-fashioned icebox, tiny storage pantry, nonexistent counter space, and zinc sink with a hand pump that supplied
only cold water. Those hashslingers who did sign up were usually
itinerants down on their luck, several of whom would have to be
fired and replaced during a single summer.

Shawn could afford to hire any kind of cook only during the
school and performance season. After that, we were again on our
own. From his experience with interminable one-night stands and
their indigestible food, Ted especially respected healthful nutrition. He
frequently subjected us to weird diets, even though it was always difficult for *him* to stick to any diet because he was too fond of sweets. (He
described so often a favorite confection of his youth that I remember it
to this day: a pistachio filling sandwiched between two pecan halves,
the whole dipped in dark chocolate. As an adult, he read in bed many
a night while feasting on cashew nuts and milk.)

How could I forget the Hay Diet (which contained no hay)? It
was based on the theory that only one category of food should be
consumed at a time. We all good-humoredly swallowed meals designed along these restrictive lines until the morning we served Ted a
dish of peeled Bartlett pears in hot grape juice as his entire breakfast.
That ended the Hay Diet. After surviving sliced raw cabbage with
crushed pineapple for lunches, and a dinner dish called Rink-Tum-
Ditty—melted cheese poured over slices of toast—our menus re-

*New York: Harper & Row, 1977, p. 102.

turned to the conventional: breakfasts that consisted of orange juice, eggs with bacon or sausage, cereals, milk, coffee, toast; lunches of different kinds of salads with crackers and fruit; and dinners of soup, a meat or fish dish, vegetables, breads, and desserts that varied from pie to custard to ice cream.

Whenever sufficient funds were available, we added a modern improvement to the prehistoric kitchen. (It was not properly enlarged and equipped until the sixties). Our seasonal cooks improved accordingly. In 1936, we acquired the first of several jewels, each of whom proved to be much more than a cook. Wally Dittberner descended upon us like an angel from a German culinary heaven. She was small, cuddly, cheerful, and had bright eyes that missed nothing. Beneath this deceptively girlish exterior, she was a mature woman who ran a no-nonsense kitchen. She quite soon came to adore Shawn (recognizing, no doubt, a fellow gourmet) and was not long in finding her way to the boys' beds. Since nothing happened to endanger the rapport of the group (and since we loved Wally and her wonderful cooking), Ted and I stopped trying to avert these liaisons. Despite the camaraderie, not to say familiarity, that developed between Wally and certain company members, she maintained her dignity as a lady.

This was made especially clear to us on one occasion. Through Ted's close friendship with Tanglewood founder, Gertrude Robinson-Smith, we were all invited to attend the opening performance of the Boston Symphony the year the famous Shed was completed. Ted invited Wally to come with us. She accepted with delight because she had precious few opportunities for entertainment beyond the confines of the Farm.

The company had just returned from our London tour, so fortunately each of us owned the black-tie outfit that was de rigueur for the event. But one day Ted consulted me with a worried frown.

"Do you suppose Wally has anything appropriate to wear to the concert?" he whispered fearing she might overhear him and be hurt.

"I don't know," I whispered back. "I've never seen her wear anything but white shirts and skirts and aprons."

"Do you think I should ask her if I might buy her a gown as a present? I'd hate to insult her, but at the same time I don't want her to feel uncomfortable among all the dressed-up ladies there."

We discussed the pros and cons and finally decided that it was too delicate a subject to broach. Since we were not snobs, we would protect our Wally from possible snobbish stares or remarks, whatever she chose to wear.

The men assembled in tuxedoes outside her cabin early on the night of the concert. Ted called, "Are you ready, Wally? We must leave now if we aren't to be late."

The door opened. There stood our little cook in a long evening gown, a matching stole around her shoulders, high-heeled sandals on her feet. In her upswept hair, usually covered by a bandanna, she had placed a suggestion of a tiara. Passing before nine pairs of astounded eyes, she grinned at the gasps from nine pairs of lungs as she led the way to one of the cars.

When we arrived at the beautiful new Shed, we were ushered to the guest-of-honor box, where we placed Wally in the middle of the front row of chairs. To each of the many friends who came to our box in the intermission to ask Shawn, sotto voce, "Who *is* that attractive woman?" Ted answered with casual pride and a broad smile, "Why, that's our cook."

Everyone missed Wally in his own way when she returned to Germany at the end of that season.

The wonderful Esther Miller arrived in 1942. Pennsylvania Dutch, energetic, intelligent, and independent, she was one of my mother's few close women friends. Through Mazie, she had become interested in Shawn's work. She was also a superb cook, and I suspect it was my mother who engineered the mutually delightful plan that Esther should serve as Pillow chef that summer.

I had prepared her for inadequate cooking facilities, but not for the cultural shock of the typical Jacob's Pillow activities that greeted her when she arrived: Prussian commands of "Up de legs! Up de legs!" boomed from behind a hedge where Joseph Pilates was shaping dancers' muscles; strains of a Viennese waltz interrupted by what sounded like four-letter words in Russian as Bronislava Nijinska scolded her ballet class in a nearby studio; drumming and a tinkling of bells in the woods where La Meri illustrated ethnic movement in relation to nature; and everywhere boys and girls in a state of considerable undress.

Esther's first sight of her kitchen gave her an even greater shock. Although we had at last graduated to running water and electricity, the huge secondhand refrigerator listed tipsily against one wall, and the sink's faucet arrangement was pure Rube Goldberg. She gaped at our four-burner kerosene stove "Without an oven, yet!" She swore there was not enough room "A cat to swing!" But once she became accustomed to our puzzling goings-on, and adjusted to the limitations of her work space, she managed to prepare delicious meals for the lot of us throughout a busy season.

The students loved her as much as we did. Esther knew which of them worked hard because they truly wanted to dance and which put on a show of effort only when Shawn was around to notice. "Ach, the way they try to catch that man's attention!" she once exclaimed scornfully. "He told me yesterday a beautiful thing: 'When you dance with a woman, she should be like a thought in your arms.' Well, now, Barton, I could tell you one big name who is like a three-column editorial, more!"

Esther disciplined renowned artists as strictly as teen-age pupils. Fame meant nothing to her, and that summer there were several famous dancers at the Pillow when Shawn presented a historic program: *"First Generation of American Concert and Theatre Dance—Anna Duncan, Ruth St. Denis and Ted Shawn."* Esther protested to me in private, "All hours of the day and night people were bringing *her* [Miss Ruth] cups of tea! Now, when I leave a kitchen at the end of a day, I have it set up all ready for breakfast. I'd be switched if I was going to clean up after *her* cohorts had messed it all up. So the next night, I locked the door and crawled out the back window, and nobody could get into the kitchen and nobody could find me. *She* got the message!"

The following excerpt from her diary shows why she was missed even more as a person than as a cook at the end of "Esther's Summer":

> Sept. 25th, 1942.   My last day on the Pillow. We had the first frost this morning. I spent the whole day baking bread and a pie for Frank [Overlees]. Thoroly cleaned the pantry—carefully packed the 36 large glasses of jelly I made—hope the rats don't get them. Gave the kitchen a final cleaning—and put the last kitchen utensils away. I am very tired.
>
> The Pillow rests calm and serene tonight. Under the full moon, the theatre roof shimmers like silver. I seem to hear the beat of bare feet, and faint strains of music, and the throb of Asadata's [Dafora] drums. The echo of happy laughter hangs over the place, and peace, like a blanket is over all. A real farewell to the Pillow. I love it. Thank heaven we have our memories and dreams—good and bad. And most times we remember best the good times.

——*The Teas*

Shawn had the great gift of creating and teaching movement that was original, yet immediately understood by an audience, powerful and athletic, yet expressive. His intuition told him that men's dancing should be based on familiarity with male physical limitations and abilities as well as with the work and ideals considered "masculine" at the time. (He believed, for example, that strong, harsh, broad movements corresponded to the lower, or masculine, section of the musical scale, whereas softer, more lyrical feminine movements corresponded to the scale above middle C. He later conceded that there was a discrepancy in this rigid differentiation, but he never entirely abandoned his belief.) He was daily gaining confidence in his crusade on behalf of male dancers, but he was also growing impatient. Public approbation was needed to confirm his theories.

The opportunity to perform before an audience for the first time since we had become a group came about by accident and resulted in what were known as "The Teas." We could not then imagine that these events marked the beginning of the Men Dancers and of Jacob's Pillow as a teaching and performing center.

One day, F. Cowles Strickland dropped in to watch Shawn teach a class. "Strick" was the director of the Berkshire Playhouse at nearby Stockbridge and a good friend of Ted. He had often before been welcome to observe our work, but this time he began to ask questions about it. Shawn answered him first with words, then by dancing with the group. Strick was so intrigued by this improvised lecture-demonstration that he urged Shawn to plan similar, once-a-week programs in the studio for other interested friends. Ted was reluctant, fearing that no more than a handful would come. It was when Strick suggested we might charge as much as seventy-five cents a person that Shawn's ears perked up.

Strick's idea was that Ted should talk for twenty minutes or so about the work to be shown, then demonstrate twenty minutes of classwork with the men, and conclude with two ensemble dances and two solos by Shawn. I do not know whose idea it was to make this also a social occasion and serve a high tea complete with sandwiches and cakes before the program. It could, logically, have been Ted's because the serving of food and drink on any pretext seems to have been a long-standing Denishawn tradition.

Shawn wrote to Lucien Price about our new venture:

He [Strick] offered gratis the use of his publicity man—and would announce it [the lecture] in his program at the [Berkshire] Playhouse. The boys rose to the idea—and yesterday [July 14, 1933] was our first one, and we took in $39.00. Of course we had to buy cheap cups, saucers, spoons, table covers, etc. But if this attendance keeps up it will contribute considerable to the grocery bill. It gives the boys an incentive to concentrate on the two dances they are to do next, and try to have them as perfect as possible by Friday—and gives them audience experience and stimulus. Everyone was enchanted with yesterday's program—no costumes, makeup or theatrical effects—just as if the audience were attending a rehearsal . . . all very informal including my talk which was interspersed throughout the whole period. I think it also provides the opportunity to spread the gospel and let the people know what is back of the program which they will finally see completed. It does break into our isolation somewhat. The world begins to make the path to our door, which has its drawbacks. But it seemed to be a legitimate thing to do.

[Two years later he was writing:] The barn has two new additions to show you. . . . They were necessitated in order to get additional seating space for the Friday teas. Even the additional forty seats thus provided are sold out each week, and standing room at a premium, and so for the coming three weeks, we are announcing a Saturday afternoon as well as Friday afternoon, hoping to switch enough Friday people to Saturday to make both the audience and ourselves more comfortable.

For that first tea, we set up enough seats for twenty-five guests at the rear of the studio. Fifty-seven people showed up, after an announcement of the event appeared in the society pages of *The Berkshire Evening Eagle*. Ted made sure that chairs in the front row were reserved for those local dowagers who were intent on supporting the area's cultural activities, among them Gertrude Robinson-Smith. (I regret to report that she and the other good ladies were baptized into the world of dance by the beads of perspiration that sprayed from us.) Those of the audience who could not find chairs sat on the floor, and those who could not squeeze into the studio at all looked and listened through the open windows. When we saw standees, we knew we had a hit.

To cash in on this unexpected bonanza, we first had to clear a parking lot. That done, we centered every Friday's routine around The Tea. Everyone shared the sweeping of the studio and the setting of rows of camp chairs in place. Then Frank drove off to Lee with the list of required groceries. Ted and Foster planned the menu and, when Frank returned, sorted the cakes and made the sandwiches. Freddy raided his garden for tomatoes, cucumbers, and lettuce. He arranged his flowers around the studio and the "Tea Garden" just outside its doors, and joined the rest of the team to set the small tables with white cloths, china, and silver [sic]. As the hour of four approached, we went down to help Mac direct the parking of cars in the new lot.

We soon decided that, since we were to be serving the public as well as performing for it, we should wear a distinctive uniform in which to greet the audience. We voted that our "school colors" should be white and gold. Knowing that the outfits must be washable, durable, and cheap, we settled on white duck trousers with an open-collared, short-sleeved cotton sport shirt of bright yellow. It was my unenviable responsibility to see that these uniforms were always spotless. Every Friday morning, therefore, I raised my plaintive voice: "*Please,* fellas, don't set up the studio in your *tea* clothes!" I resorted to much stronger language and a much louder command if that first plea was not obeyed.

In an attempt to put a few more dollars in the till, I rigged up a miniature bazaar on a counter under a rustic roof, where I displayed for sale batiks, saris, those East Indian headsheets called chuddars, brass objects, and other treasures from the collection Ted had brought back from the Orient as well as some very good pieces of American Indian turquoise-and-silver jewelry. While Shawn greeted the guests and Fern Helscher extracted the admission fee from them as tactfully as possible and the boys served them tea, I offered my wares in a polite, subdued manner. When the gong signaled the start of the program, Ted led the audience into the studio and the rest of us made a dash to the nearest barn or bushes to change into our performing costumes.

These we called our "tea trunks." They were made of sturdy, skintight silk that had been dyed suntan to match the shade of our bodies. This permitted an uncluttered line that would best demonstrate Shawn's movement design. The effect was startlingly bare. Ted donned similar trunks to wear under the long, white, silk, Chinese dressing gown in which he appeared for his preliminary talk. Huddled out of sight near the rear studio door, we awaited his cue to come on stage.

Later, we treated ourselves to white terry-cloth robes in which we could make our entrance with greater dignity, like gladiators into the arena or boxers into the ring. The impact was truly theatrical when we stripped off our robes. Today's audiences would take the sudden sight of our near nudity without blinking an eye, but in the thirties, with the front row of spectators less than three feet away, the shock was real. Even though our lady patrons may have been attracted by this unconventional closeup of well-muscled young male bodies, it was the avant garde spirit they showed in attending our Teas that merited respect.

After we had performed our group dances, we dashed again to barn or bushes, resumed our pants and sport shirts, and were ready to unpark the cars by the time the first members of the audience emerged. Once everyone had left, we put on our old work duds to wash the dishes, stack away the chairs and tables, and clean up the studio in readiness for the next day's classes and rehearsals. Shawn did not permit the unexpected success of The Teas to sidetrack him from his prime objective, particularly since word from Margerie and George indicated definite bookings for a fall and winter tour. This meant we had to prepare and perfect the program.

—— *The Program*

Now began the process of becoming professionals, of rehearsals during which each man learned not only his own faults and talents but those of the group as a whole. They were hours in which we came to know Shawn, the choreographer—he used us as raw material to shape his visions, and heaven help the dancer who was recalcitrant or lazy! He became the immediate target of a memorable tongue-lashing, which was forgotten by Ted as soon as we left the studio. There was nothing personal in his rages. They were the bare bones of an art experience that came straight out of our lives and our labor together—something that only a few fortunate ones can ever enjoy.

Learning new roles and perfecting old ones, we knew that Shawn had created a style of movement that audiences could respect, which gave us the confidence we needed to venture into a prejudiced world. As we worked to improve this style, we may have been competitive in the studio but we were never allowed to be competitive on the stage. This gave our ensemble a unique quality of unity that those who later tried to revive our dances found impossible to duplicate.

Ted taught us the fine points of makeup, which included one of the most exasperating chores ever required of a performer: the weekly all-over shave. A smooth body under tan paint, he explained, would clothe even our nudest dances with a sexless impersonality, thus permitting the most squeamish members of the audience to enjoy our program without offending their sense of modesty. We recognized the need, but how we loathed the deed!

Ted and George Horn, designers of most of our costumes, taught us to make and repair our outfits, accessories, and headdresses. Because they were often contrived of odd materials, we had to have strong hands and feet with which to operate our old-fashioned treadle Singer sewing-machine. We nicknamed this the "ziggurat," and it accomplished feats no later models could equal. However, we were not up to fine seams or tailoring. For this, Shawn brought Hattie Sherman from Harlem, where she had retired after having worked for Denishawn under Pearl Wheeler's direction.

Hattie knew all about the strain that dancing places upon fabrics that must nevertheless keep their shape. We welcomed her into the family. I doubt if she had ever been out of New York before, but she showed no disdain for the primitive living conditions of the Farm, or any fear of the open spaces that surrounded it. Professional though she was in her craft, Hattie drew the line at one thing: she insisted that George do the fitting of our costume G-strings.

By the time the leaves began to turn, all costumes had been completed and we had held several dress rehearsals. Our program was ambitious, original, exhausting, and exhilarating.

The opening group of "Music Dances" was based on St. Denis's music visualization theories. The *Polonaise* was a rugged and aggressive dance that depicted the idealistic battles of youth. The two Bach numbers (danced by Frank, Mac, Denny, and me, dressed in dark blue trousers with torsos bare) were abstract and contrapuntal. Shawn joined us for the Brahms *Rhapsody*, in which our five figures spiraled into Laocoön-like formations. As if the dance were a piano concerto, Ted established the melody and the rest of us responded to and supported him. According to his program notes, "It might be the story of the leader, the prophet, the visionary of all times struggling through the misunderstanding of his environment to rise, in the end, with his vision triumphant over all."

In *Japanese Rickshaw Coolies,* Denny, Mac, and I portrayed these characters at play—gambling, imitating the poses of Kabuki actors, racing after one another—and at work, when tourists appear to command their services. For this, we wore short cotton *haori* coats over breech clouts, and flat, round straw hats. Frank, Denny, Mac, and George did the Osage-Pawnee dance, and then I replaced George for the *Workers' Songs* and *Cutting the Sugar Cane.** In the last section of the program, I had the opportunity to perform my first self-choreographed solo, *Fetish.**

The second section was devoted to Shawn's epic seventeen-minute solo, *John Brown Sees the Glory,* for which Jess Meeker had written stirring music. Dressed in rough, work-soiled denims, Shawn danced out the great Kansan's life: The young man walks alone into the plains, where the spirit of God descends upon him. In a vision, he sees a procession of all the slaves in the world. He accepts his destiny to be the instrument to set them free and calls together his little band of volunteers to attack Harper's Ferry. The dance proceeds through his defeat, imprisonment, hanging, and fu-

---

*A full description appears in Part Two.

neral, when he sees his soul rise from the grave to lead the forces of freedom to ultimate victory. A truly remarkable work, it was the longest solo dance in modern times up to then, a tour de force of endurance and imagination.

As we packed in readiness for the tour, our excitement was tinged with apprehension because we knew we had confirmed bookings only from the end of October through November, with just a hope that more might follow. Our summer income had been spent on food. Our small savings had been invested in costumes. Shawn was in debt for the down payment on a Ford panel truck, in which we would transport costumes, lighting equipment, floorcloth, backdrop, and props. Some of us would travel in this truck; the rest, including Shawn, would be chauffeured by me in Ted's ancient Buick (nicknamed Juno because of its voluptuously bulging rear).

Since we had no way of knowing if box-office receipts would cover our living and traveling expenses, we decided that whatever cash we earned must first pay for food, lodging, and gas. Only if there was a surplus would money be shared equally as salaries.

So it was that, on October 23, 1933, we locked the Pillow doors and drove off into the vivid autumn early morning to start our pioneer adventure at the Strong Theatre in Burlington, Vermont.

Above: The first company of
Men Dancers, 1933, in "Swing
Low, Sweet Chariot" from *Negro
Spirituals.* L to R: George Gloss,
Ted Shawn, George Horn
(hidden), Wilbur McCormack,
Frank Overlees (hidden), Dennis
Landers, Barton Mumaw.

Right: Barton Mumaw with the
Men Dancers in *Polonaise,*
choreographed in 1930.

SHAWN
AND HIS ENSEMBLE OF
MEN DANCERS
Barton Mumaw, Frank Overlees, Wilbur McCormack, Dennis Landers, George Gloss, George Horn
JESS MEEKER at the Piano

Program

I. MUSIC DANCES:
1. Polonaise (*Edward MacDowell*) . . . . . Ensemble of Six
2. March Wind (*Edward MacDowell*) . . . . . SHAWN
3. VI Prelude from the Well-tempered Clavichord (*Bach*)
   and Two Part Invention, No. 4 (*Bach*) . . . Ensemble of Four
4. Rhapsody, Op. 119, No. 4 (*Brahms*) . . . SHAWN and Ensemble

II. JOHN BROWN SEES THE GLORY—An American Epic . . SHAWN
(Music especially composed by Jess Meeker)

III. PRIMITIVE THEMES, RHYTHMS OF LABOR AND PLAY
1. Japanese Rickshaw Coolies (*Ganne*) . . Mumaw, Landers, McCormack
2. Invocation to the Thunderbird (*Sousa*) . . . . SHAWN
3. Osage-Pawnee Dance of Greeting (*Grunn*) . . . Ensemble of Four
4. The French Sailor (*Milhaud*) . . . . . Barton Mumaw
5. Flamenco (*Spanish*) Dances (*MSS*) . . . . . SHAWN
6. Workers' Songs of Middle Europe (*Reinitz*) . . . Ensemble of Four
   (a) March of the Proletariat, (b) Vagabond's Song, (c) Millers' Song
7. Frohsinn (*Lincke*) . . . . SHAWN
8. Cutting the Sugar Cane (*Lecuona*)
   Messrs. Mumaw, Overlees, Landers and McCormack

IV. RELIGIOUS DANCES
1. "O Brother Sun and Sister Moon"
   A Study of St. Francis of Assisi (*Respighi*) . . . SHAWN
2. Fetish (*Meeker*) Inspired by Primitive African sculpture . . Barton Mumaw
3. Three Negro Spirituals:
   (a) "Nobody Knows de Trouble I've Seen" . . . SHAWN
   (b) "Go Down, Moses" . . . . SHAWN and Three Men
   (c) "Swing Low, Sweet Chariot" . . . SHAWN and Six Men

Program presented at the Rome Free Academy Auditorium, Rome, New York
on January 25, 1934.

Below: The Men Dancers in rehearsal of
Kinetic Molpai, Jacob's Pillow. Ted Shawn
holding hand of Barton Mumaw.

Above: Jacob's Pillow,
1935. Ted Shawn in
*O Brother Sun and Sister Moon
(A Study of St. Francis),*
choreographed in 1931.

Jacob's Pillow, 1937. L to R: Foster Fitz-Simons, Barton Mumaw,
Paolo D'Anna, Ted Shawn, and Johnny Schubert.

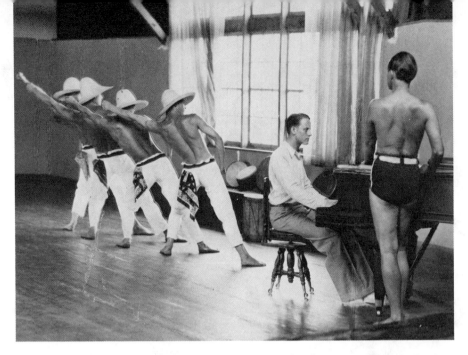

Above: In the studio at Jacob's Pillow, 1933. Ted Shawn teaching *Cutting the Sugar Cane* to four Men Dancers, Jess Meeker at the piano.

Below: Barton Mumaw, Leader of the Chorus in Aeschylus' *The Persians*, sung and danced by the augmented men's group, Jacob's Pillow, 1939.

Men Dancers in the "Basketball" section of *Olympiad*. Barton Mumaw center.

Men Dancers in a dramatic moment from *Kinetic Molpai*. Dennis Landers in the air. Barton Mumaw right rear, looking up.

The Men Dancers, at their new winter headquarters of Eustis, Florida, 1936. Ted Shawn center. Barton Mumaw far right.

A reception for the Men Dancers at Maybar, the Mumaw family home in Eustis, Florida, September 28, 1937. Ted Shawn seated right, Barton Mumaw third from left next to his mother.

Barton Mumaw in original costume designed by Mary Kinser for *Funerailles*,
1940.

Above: Barton Mumaw rehearsing *Fetish* for an Army show at Keesler Field, Mississippi, July 1942.

Left: Ted Shawn and Barton Mumaw, Biloxi, Mississippi, 1943.

Below: Sgt. Barton Mumaw in England, 1944.

8

(October 1933–1940)*
Tours, Trials, and Triumphs

Our travel pattern was established that first day as we sought gold beyond the horizon. But our "Argo" moved on tires instead of a keel as we forged ahead on two-lane roads through all kinds of weather over all kinds of terrain—New England hills, southern swamps, Kansas plains, painted deserts, Oregon mountains. We shared overwhelming experiences, such as watching the sun rise at the Grand Canyon and set at Boulder Dam within the same day. We shared the discomfort of crummy hotels, the irritation of impossible theatres, the indigestion of inedible food. We developed, perforce, an energy-saving routine that spared us as much exertion and tension as possible.

Frank and George took turns driving the half-ton truck that bore the name SHAWN in large flowing letters on its sides. Invariably, service-station attendants or drugstore cowboys would ask what "Shawn" meant. At first, Frank would earnestly explain our mission in an effort to convert even an audience of one to the cause of Dance for Men, but these lectures took up so much time that he soon learned to assume his most stolid, Dutch-Indian expression and answer curtly, "Oh, Shawn's a new kind of mayonnaise."

As far as practical, the truck was packed in the order its contents would be needed when it reached its destination. It (later there

*I have condensed the seven years' tours into a single panoramic chapter that records the special kind of company we were: the first dance group to tour by truck and car and the first all-male dance company to face the often hostile cultural wilderness of those times. To avoid repetition, I have omitted our returns to Jacob's Pillow and its routine between each tour.

were two) carried our costume trunks, a special crate for makeup boxes and bundles, a skeleton set of lights, our brown cyclorama, and our floorcloth. Every platform or set piece doubled as a packing box for props and other odds and ends. Space was at such a premium that not even wigs could travel with separate care; each one, to keep its shape, was stuffed with towels, jockstraps, or anything else handy and jammed into the wig carton.

I was usually in charge of packing the car: one personal suitcase for each man, Shawn's "Poisoned Pup" briefcase, and Jess's bag containing his irreplaceable music scores. Into whatever spare crannies we could find, we stuffed our books, souvenirs, food packages, galoshes, and similar miscellanea.

With Mac to spell me when I grew too weary, I also drove the car. Ted acted as navigator from the front seat and the rest of the company took turns in the back seat or in the truck. Jess always rode with Ted so they could discuss new works (until Jess invariably fell asleep).

It was a wonder that we were not constantly at one another's throats, considering the relentlessly close quarters, the strain of driving, the stress of dancing our best under any and all conditions. Somehow, we were not, as Ted wrote to Lucien Price:*

> Money was dangerously scant a couple of times (and will be again) but through it all we ate 15¢ lunches when necessary, changed tires when blowouts occurred in lonely places in the midst of blizzards, unpacked the show, hung the scenery, and lights—gave a *swell* performance, and packed up again—with never a complaint. So with such soldiers as these boys fighting for and with me, how can I help but win?

We did not even have a radio to break the monotony of long jumps. When Juno broke down for the last time and was buried without regret, we induced Ted to permit a radio in the new car. He agreed solely on the understanding that it would be turned off immediately one of us requested.

> I have made a dicker for a new De Soto! They gave me a good allowance on Juno and with the cash down payment it will cost less in monthly installments than Juno is costing in repairs. It is a mid-

*I am grateful to Joseph E. Marks III, a longtime friend and archivist of Jacob's Pillow, for permission to quote from the letters Ted Shawn sent to Lucien Price during the period of the tours. All the excerpts from this correspondence are the words of Shawn himself, unless otherwise noted.

night-metallic-blue-chromium-trimmed-streamlined-beyond-words job. . . . It has the extra width in the front seat which makes for greater riding comfort; it has a heater (which Juno did not have). The name "Pluto" won out (in a vote)—its midnight metallic blue suggesting the King of Hades, and the swiftness with which it passes through the body of the country having other connotations!

Ahead of us went Fern Helscher, our live-wire advance and publicity woman. With unceasing energy, imagination, and devotion, she managed to get stories about the Men Dancers on the front page, in the color rotogravure, in sports interviews, and even in fashion and society blurbs in each city where we were booked. I think we were photographed all over the United States on every local statue and bridge and other points of interest where young athletic dancing men could possibly assume a pose. One unforgettable example of her untiring activity on our behalf is contained in a letter Fern wrote from Montana:

> I've had to travel by bus the last few days and every one on the buses has been talking about your tour out here. One place in between Casper and Billings, the bus stopped at a general store, back of which at about 200 yards a turkey shoot was being held. As we stayed there about 15 minutes, I drifted out to watch the sport. Of course, with my funny hat and getup, the country people asked me who I was. When I told them, they all gathered around and I gave a short talk on Shawn and His Men Dancers! Even these people knew you were to give a recital in Casper. This country is simply a scream!

Despite Fern's Amazonian efforts, we often arrived in a town to find locked doors at the theatre or gym or hall where we were to play. With time always too short before the curtain had to go up, I would deposit Ted at the hotel to catch up on his correspondence and book-keeping or to meet with official greeters, while Frank and George went in search of a caretaker or stage doorman. Once inside the space, we unloaded the truck and hung the cyc from whatever flies the place had. Then we unrolled the heavy floorcloth, which had to be stretched over the stage to protect our bare feet from splinters.

It was even more a necessity when the host management had made us a present of a thoroughly waxed floor, which caused the floorcloth to slide precariously under our feet. One happy day, we discovered a remedy for this hazard: we simply mopped the stage with quarts of Coca-Cola, which somehow dissolved the wax, before we laid the cloth.

As we became expert, laying the floorcloth became choreography, although never an exercise we enjoyed. Armed with hammers, two of us tacked down one side inch by inch as two others preceded us to stretch the edge flat with a kicking, scuffing stamp that pulled the canvas taut even as it wore out our rubber-soled shoes, frayed our tempers, and hurt our feet. The process had to be repeated on the opposite side in order to pull the whole cloth flat. This chore was so detested that we would bellow, "Let's draw lots!" so that no one man's feet would be tortured more than another's.

Into whatever power outlets were available, we next plugged our standing lights and positioned them in the wings. (Many places had no provision for lighting at all. We often danced in gymnasiums without a raised stage, a curtain, or any background décor except the basketball net, the leather horses, and the ropes used for climbing exercises.) Finally we hung our costumes in whatever space served as dressing rooms, one of which Ted and I shared so that I could help him with his changes. That done, we headed back to the hotel or boarding house for a rest, a shower, and a snack.

Ted and I always tried to eat no later than 5:00 P.M. before an 8:30 P.M. curtain. Our supper customarily followed the menu once recommended to us by a basketball coach: buttered whole-wheat toast with honey for nourishment, celery stalks to make us feel we had eaten enough, and a cup of tea to wash it down. We were starved by midnight and loathed having to attend after-theatre parties, where we were obliged to be sociable while we tried desperately to consume some much-needed sustenance. We blessed the rare host or hostess who understood our hunger and took us into a separate room for a decent meal before introducing us to the guests.

Most of the theatres we played hardly deserved the name; we luxuriated in the few exceptions:

> Here [Hershey, Pa.] we have struck unbelievable luxury! We each have a dressing room with private bath (tub and shower) and the building itself outdoes Roxy's. It is all part of this astounding community which surrounds and is built by the Hershey chocolate factories. Everything in the town is owned by Hershey—hotels, stores, theatre, college. The theatre is a huge community building like an Italian palace and in very good taste. Of course we are on with a moving-picture, ventriloquists and Chinese acrobats—doing a forty-five minute program, once tonight and tomorrow, and twice on Saturday. However, it pays well, gives us a chance to sleep four consecutive nights in the same bed, and time for me to get office work done, bookkeeping and business mail, etc.

Among the memorabilia in the archives at Jacob's Pillow are

seven ledgers in which are recorded in Shawn's precise handwriting the place and date of each concert, with every penny of income and expenditure. The scope of the tours becomes evident in his words:

> Our first season, 111 performances, 23,000 miles traveled. Our second season, 115 performances, 25,000 miles traveled. Third season, 125 performances, 38,000 miles traveled. Net income for the first year was $28,000, for the second, $39,000, for the third, $52,000. This represents either our flat fees or our percentage of gross receipts—a reasonable guess at gross would be nearly twice these amounts, as the local manager has to pay his theatre rent, advertising, stagehands, etc. before we get ours.

During the 1933 tour alone, Shawn talked to 150 club or community luncheons, gave 100 newspaper interviews, fifty radio broadcasts, performed ten solo and ensemble numbers, and conducted the niggling but necessary business of managing. In terms of miles, money, and effort, therefore, the record is precise. But in terms of human experiences over seven years, only a kaleidoscopic pattern of major and minor incidents emerges from Shawn's letters and my memory.

——*Accidents and Illnesses*

Crises were inevitable during the course of the thousands of miles we traveled. We suffered illnesses that were serious or psychosomatic, and accidents that were amusing in retrospect or could have been tragic. One such was our performance of the last part of *Kinetic Molpai** at the St. Louis Municipal Auditorium. Called "Apotheosis," it almost proved my demise instead.

We were lying on our backs in a circle, each man's right hand stretched out to grasp the left hand of the man behind him. Shawn sped around the circumference and, just before he seized my hand as the first dancer to be lifted in succession to his feet, I saw overhead an enormous spotlight descending straight for me. The instant Shawn pulled me erect, the spot hit three feet away on the apron of the stage. Seeing in a flash that there were no splinters of glass on the floorcloth, he gripped my hand more tightly, yelled "Come on!" and we finished the dance. We really earned the prolonged applause of an audience that could not have failed to see what had happened.

With this kind of quick thinking and absolute assumption of responsibility, Ted pulled us through many scrapes. Although, un-

*A full description appears in Part Two.

Week beginning Oct. 23 - 1933

	Town & theatre or Call	Income Terms	Gross	Exp	Net.
Oct. ✓ 23	Burlington, Vt. Strong Theatre	65%	367.00		238.55
24	Middlebury, Vt. College Gymnasium Auspices - Le.Ci. U. W. Genevra Lowell	Min. Guar 200 + %	204.43		202.87
25	Barre, Vt. mat. Goddard School for Girls Melita Knowles, Prin.	Spec.			82.00
26	Middletown, Conn Wesleyan Univ - 92 Theatre Auspices - Paint & Powder Club Don Bischoff.	70%	180.50		126.35
✓ 27	Amherst, Mass Amherst College Hall (David Morton)	65%	302.13.		196.38
28	(M) Deerfield, Mass Deerfield Academy	Spec.			100.00
					946.15

Cash on hand to start week 50.00
From sale of books. 18.00
Receipts 946 15
To account for. 1014.15

Disbursements

		Transportation		Living	
		Trucks	Buick		
21	New Tire & Prestone		18.55	Burlington	
	Change oil & grease		2.47	room	30.00
	Bal. on plates	1.26		Meals pd by T.S.	19.00
	Prestone & gas.	9.80		" " Geo Horn.	4.25
23	gas & oil		1.34	Cash to 6 boys	72.00
	" "	1.52		" " 9 Horn	22.00
	" "	2.08		Meals pd by Barton	8.00
24	" "	1.98			
	" "		3.62		
25	gas & oil		6.70		
	" "	1.33			
	Service –	2.35			
26		1.86			
27		1.12			
		~~32.38~~	32.68		155.25
		18.30			32.68
					18.30

C. Stage Hand tip Burlington 5.00
B. Costume & dressing room 2.20)
S. " " – 1.40
Photograph amt. Geo. 9. 15.00
Telegrams, telephones, postage 26.00 | 49.60 | | | 49.60
Commissions:
Gloss. Burlington 47.71
Middlebury 40.57
Barre 16.40
Lyon Middletown 26.00 | 130.68 | | | 130.68

Deposits: E.M.S. acct. 245.37
T.S. acct. 214.38
Barrydale E.M.S. acct. 100.00 | | | | 610.75
| | | | 1036.26 (?)
Cash Bal fwd | | 7.89

| | | | | | 1314.15 |

Pages from Shawn's ledger for the first week of the first Men Dancers tour.

Income
Final Period — Apr. 22 - May 7 - 1940

April	29	Cortland, N.Y. Normal School	all receipts		
		Mary Washington Ball	over expenses	150	00
May	1	Holyoke, Mass — War Memorial	50% gross		
		Norman Thompson	gross 178·00	Pd.	50 00
			50% 89·00		
	4	Pittsfield, Mass. H. S. Aud.	50% of		
		Martha McMahon & Eliz McLaughlin	net.		171.2
	6	Boston, Mass — Symphony Hall	Rental —		
	7	A. W. Handley	own		
		Net after paying all expenses & fee to Handley	management.		872.05
		(see acct.)			
					1243.2
		Deficit fund			94.00
					1149 2
		Fern Helscher - final salary 50⁰⁰ & Exp 25⁰⁰		✓	75.00
					1074.2?
		Deposited Lee Natl Bank. 18.60			
		150.00			
		400.00			
		171.23			739.8
					334 49
		Cashed check on Lee Bank			590.00
					924.49
		Norman Thompson - 3 Weeks Booking exps		✓	165.0
					759.4.

	Transp.	Office Stage Misc.	Sals.
Maher			100 00 ✓
Shawn			100 00 ✓
Co 9 @ 35			315 00 ✓
Franks. S. W. gas, oil, repairs, etc	38 35 ✓		
Mac's " " " "	34 20 ✓		
Buick " " " "	58 85 ✓		
Telegrams, telephones, postage, express, publicity		59.90 ✓	
Final dry-cleaning + laundry of costumes		30.00 ✓	
Repairing hot water heater - fire extinguishers, etc		23.15 ✓	
	131 40	113 05	515 00 —
			113 05
			131 40
		To bal.	759 45

Pages from Shawn's record of the final Men Dancers tour. The May 6 Boston
concert marked their last appearance.

like Denishawners, we never called him Papa, he stood *in loco parentis* for us all.

We were once caught in a vicious blizzard that closed every road by which we could possibly reach our next engagement. Ours were the only vehicles moving through a small town where Ted directed me to the railroad station. While he went to a telephone, we huddled around the potbelly stove, assuming that Shawn was telling the manager that this show sure as hell could not go on. Ted was gone for close to an hour. When he returned, he informed us that he had hired a freight train that would pick us up and deliver us to the town we were to play that night. In order to make our curtain on time, however, we would have to don costumes and makeup en route, presumably in a freezing boxcar. After a stunned group had more or less willingly agreed to the plan, he called the house manager to tell him we would keep our date as scheduled. Luckily for us, that astounded man informed Shawn in no uncertain terms that there would not be any audience in such weather. Our trip by private freight train was cancelled, much to the relief of everyone but Shawn. I have no doubt he would have carried through his plan if he had been held to his contract.

Once, on a perfectly clear day, a car abruptly pulled into the highway ahead of us and swung around into our lane. Neither car was going very fast, and I was sure the driver of the approaching car would move over into his own lane. As I steered farther and farther to the right, he kept coming at us until he hit our car just hard enough to turn it over into a ditch. He then went blithely on his way. Complete silence reigned as we all hung upside down in our seats, Pluto's wheels spinning above our heads. Then Ted called each of us by name. After each had assured him he was not hurt, Shawn very calmly said, "Barton, do you know this dripping oil is ruining my gray suit?"

There were times when one mishap followed brutally close upon the heels of another:

> Mac went swimming and gashed his leg on the edge of the swimming pool so deeply that I had to take him off to the doctor and have several stitches taken in the wound.
> Then that night I had a cell for a dressing room which contained a large radiator that would not turn off, and the result was like a cabinet bath. Finally in desperation, I flung open a window allowing icy cold wind to hit me and in the night I woke up with neuritis, rheumatism, or something in my left shoulder that was agony. The

next day it was worse, and when we got to Columbia, Mo., after some home remedies produced no relief I called an osteopath. I went to the performance entirely on faith, as I couldn't raise my arm above my head without screaming. I did get through the program, however, and attended a reception afterward. How I don't know now. That night it was still worse. While I was writhing, Barton called me, and I went into his room at about 4 a.m. to find him in spasms of pain with a kidney stone attack, which attacks he has had off and on for years. There is no known pain to man that even approaches this. I helped him through the night as best I could.

Got up at 6:30 a.m. and started out for Kansas City. Barton got steadily worse in the car. It took Jess and Foster to hold him down in the back seat. It had snowed heavily during the night, and the roads were bad, but we made the 108 miles in 100 minutes. I got Barton into a room at the Muehlbach [Hotel], called the house doctor, and saw him relieved after a sedative was administered. I left one of the boys with him and set forth, and by this time my own pain had spread all down my back into my chest and neck. I addressed a Chamber of Commerce luncheon after having newspaper interviews; I went on to the Hindu Gallery in the collossal [sic] new Nelson Art Museum and addressed some 300 people on Hindu Art and Religion; I went to a big tea given for me, and talked there, and then to a dinner party, also part of the day's fixed promotion plans.

When I got back to the hotel Barton was in a deep sleep [I passed the offending stone the next afternoon in the ladies' room of the Woman's Club in Topeka. It seemed to me the size of the Kohinoor diamond. I showed it to the boys, who inspected it with proper admiration and some unprintable remarks.] Then I saw the doctor for myself. He sent me out for an electric pad on which I slept all night, gave me a liniment to rub on, then looked at my throat, as I was quite hoarse. He found spots on the tonsils, and said gaily that I should have them out, and then gave me a gargle.

Riding through Idaho one January, Ted wrote in pencil:

All day Sunday we drove—500 miles over these Oregon mountains, roads winding like mad, covered with snow and ice, no fence guards, drops of hundreds of feet to the ravines below—terribly wearing. . . . Reached La Grande in the early afternoon (Monday). At 4:30 I got a wire: TRUCK DEMOLISHED. TELEPHONE BURNS GARAGE, BURNS, ORE. MAC AND DENNY. . . . The two boys were safe, although bruised and shaken, Denny's ankle sprained—but nothing worse. They had gone off a curve, dropped 35 feet, turned over three times, finally lodged against big trees. By the time I got them on the phone they had got a wrecking-car on the job and had got all the contents of the truck safely out, and into the garage. But the truck was still upside down, wedged so tightly amongst the trees they hadn't been able to budge it. . . . By now it was after 5 p.m. and Frank and Ned had not arrived [with the other truck]. I was a lunatic! 5:30 Frank and Ned arrived, having had two flat tires but otherwise all right. I called the President of the Teachers College (where we were to play), told him the story and offered to do a lecture demonstration. After much hemming and hawing, he asked if I would make any reduction in terms on the basis of not giving the contracted program! I referred this back to his sense of justice—agreed to accept anything he saw fit to give us!

Frank's truck carried only curtains, lights, floor cloth. Therefore we did not even have practice shorts with us. Also, all the music was in Mac's truck! We went out to a store which carried athletic goods—and bought seven pairs of grey basketball pants (which later split wide open in the crotch in full view of the audience) and seven jock straps. Then out to the college and rehearsed like mad, limited by what music Jess could play by memory and what dances Mac and Denny were not in. . . .

At midnight I had another talk with Mac [by telephone]. Truck still wedged, but they thought they would have it out today. Boys and baggage are proceeding to Pocatello by train. Truck, when able to run, will be driven on to wherever we are. Estimated cost of this around $300. Both boys, at my orders, had been thoroughly examined by a doctor—no further injuries discovered.

We are now going through the same sort of country and weather. As far as eye can see in all directions, a white world—wild mountain country—snow banked car-high on the roadsides— terrible curves—no protecting fences—very icy roads. We expect to lunch at Boise and I will mail this letter there if we live—for fear we might never reach Pocatello *Morituri te Salutamus!*

[Less than a month later:] After giving a performance in De Kalb, Ill. the night of Feb. 27 we were driving back to Chicago to sleep. Frank's truck was first, then Mac and Denny in the 1½ ton truck, then perhaps 12 blocks behind them, the six of us in the De Soto [Pluto]. It was nearly 2 a.m. when the De Soto reached an intersection where the communities of Chicago, Cicero and Oak Park, Ill. all meet. We saw ahead a crowd and two overturned and horribly smashed cars. As we stopped, appalled at this disaster while not yet knowing who it was—Mac staggered over all bloody and told us that as our truck was crossing this intersection, a Ford V-8 sedan, coming at what seemed 90 miles an hour, hit them broadside and turned them over. The sedan had gone on across the sidewalk, through a plate-glass window, and was almost entirely inside a corner cigar store! By this time, the occupants of the sedan had been taken off to the hospital. It was stated that they had all been drinking . . . seven people of whom three were women. I jumped out and located Dennis who was dripping blood from a cut near his right eye, and got him and Mac into the De Soto, leaving Fred, Bill, Foster and Jess at the scene of the accident, and started for the nearest hospital. Dennis was having hysterics over the sight of the mutilated women: Mac was screaming with pain, and thinking his arm and shoulder were broken. Then Dennis fainted dead away. Finally we got to the hospital, and rushed them into the emergency operating room. We got Mac's coat and shirt off and found a deep cut on the right elbow, the shoulder so painful that nothing but X-ray could tell whether there was a fracture or not, the left hip all lacerated and bloody. One intern and three nurses got to work immediately on him as Dennis seemed now all right except for the cut by the eye which by that time did not look quite so bad.

At this point five Oak Park policemen arrived and crowded into the operating room, wanting information and statements. The intern and I drove them out into the hall. Then while I held Mac's hand, the intern bathed and sewed up the elbow cut. More police— this time from Cicero, arrived, and had to be cleared out. Then the Chicago police arrived, making a total of 15, inasmuch as the accident involved three municipalities—it was very complicated. By this time . . . it was suspected that the sedan which had hit our truck was a stolen car. Also the police were saying that as soon as the boys were fixed up they would have to take them to the station and hold them as material witnesses.

When Mac was resting easy—the further examination of the shoulder giving us much more hope that there was no broken bone—the intern took Dennis on the table and examined his eye. The cut proved to be very deep, and was grimed with black dirt nearly an inch deep. I stood and held Dennis's hand while the intern spent one and a half hours painstakingly picking out each fragment of dirt, so ingrained into the flesh that small particles of flesh had to be lifted with tiny forceps and then cut off. When the eye was thoroughly clean, a deep stitch had to be taken to connect severed muscles—the muscles which control the expression around the eye. Then four stitches were taken to close the wound itself. It was beautifully done and when finally closed, the cut look no bigger than a wrinkle.

Then we got the boys into private rooms, arranged with the head surgeon for complete, thorough examination, and got the hospital authorities to agree that they would not allow the police to get near Mac and Denny, nor anyone but me to communicate with them.

Fred and the rest of the boys meanwhile had turned up. The police would not allow the cars to be touched until flashlight pictures had been taken from every angle. Fred had then had the mangled wreck of our truck towed to a garage; he reported that although one costume trunk had been smashed to matchwood, the rest of the contents seemed all right.

It was after six in the morning when I got to the hotel. I realized from what the police had said that I would need legal advice, and the best. So after coffee, I got my friend Janet Fairbanks on the telephone and she recommended a very fine firm of lawyers. Until I could see a lawyer at nine a.m. I spent the time sending wires, making long distance calls, and getting our insurance papers in order. At nine o'clock I was in the lawyer's office to make a report on the accident to the insurance claim adjuster, also getting reports from the police and from the garage where our truck had been taken. The police had sealed the truck so it couldn't be touched, and warrants were out for the arrest of the two boys when they left the hospital.

Finally at about 12:40 I got reports from the head surgeon that X-rays had revealed no fractures or other injuries, that both boys were in fine condition, and could be removed from the hospital whenever it was legally safe for us to do so. I left these matters in the lawyer's hands, went back to the hotel and called the concert manager under whose auspices we were supposed to appear that night at the Studebaker Theatre. I told her all that happened and asked her to cancel the performance. She insisted that I give whatever program I could with the remaining boys and myself.

I arranged a substitute program [Shawn's *Hopi Eagle Dance,* my *Dyak Spear Dance,** *Singhalese Devil Dance* for three men, Shawn's *Danza Afro-Cubana,* my *Pierrot in the Dead City,** and an abbreviated *Swing Low, Sweet Chariot* from our Negro Spirituals]. By the time I got copy off to the printer for slips to be inserted into the regular programs, it was after 4 P.M. We got the contents of the truck released by the police, and I took them down to the theatre in taxis—and the boys went over to get the show ready and I took a hot bath and drank some Ovaltine. My mind was going around like a pinwheel, so I, too, went down to the theatre to see what I could do there, and stayed on until show time.

I went out before the program started and told the audience my story. They were sympathetic, and all thru the evening gave ecstatic applause. The boys say they have never seen me dance with such an electric quality, although I had not slept for 36 hours nor had solid food for twenty-four. The reviews the next morning were better than any we have had from Chicago critics in the three years we have danced here with the men's group.

[It was after this performance that I received in the Chicago Journal of

---

*A full description appears in Part Two.

Commerce *the following notice written by the Dragon Lady of midwestern critics, Claudia Cassidy: "Mumaw is the only dancer I have seen who seems to suggest what people try to say when they talk about Nijinsky. Extraordinarily light, sexless in an elfin way, the secret of his buoyancy seems to lie in unusual anatomy most remarkable for muscular thighs. He has humour, variety and a sly aloofness that is infinitely charming."]*

After the show and the usual big back-stage crowd, I got some food, went to the hotel and slept as if I had been drugged. Dennis, I forgot to say, had somehow managed to get out of the hospital, and had turned up at the theatre during the program, but had been sent to the hotel and told to go to bed.

At nine the next morning, the lawyer called and said to get everyone out of the state of Illinois at once: since Dennis as the driver of the truck had slipped out of their hands, they (the police) were out to get any of the rest of the company they could. So—wild excitement! We got Dennis onto a train immediately for Gary, Indiana, and shortly after that, six more boys left in the De Soto.

Well, all that day I spent in getting Mac out of the hospital and into a drawing room on a train for Detroit: the truck turned over to the finance company to handle (as they have title to it, so it could not be touched by the police) and the baggage that was still at the theatre packed into new trunks, which I had bought, and shipped by express to Bay City, Mich.—our next date. It was eight o'clock that night when Frank and I drove out of town in his truck for Gary to join the Company.

During this time I was trying to arrange to cancel this week's dates, but Bay City and Battle Creek preferred to have the same curtailed program given in Chicago without Mac and Dennis, rather than cancel. Beyond that I have managed to clear everything so that from Wednesday on for a week we will all lay off in Detroit while Mac and Dennis get well and rested, and I arranged somehow to buy a new truck. What further complications and expense in this whole matter I will have to face, I do not at this moment know. But we are all so grateful that Dennis and Mac are not more seriously injured, and are assured that in a week they will be all right and dancing again.

——Humor

Moments of shared humor made all these rigors endurable. Some of the humor entered our vocabulary. I remember one season when, in order to make connections, we had to drive repeatedly through a New York town named Schenevus. This struck us as so funny that the word became a sort of *nichevo*: "It's *sheneeevus* to me."

Denny, our Romeo, caused one of our most hilarious episodes.

He had met a young girl with whom he maintained a correspondence. (Fern once wrote to Ted that there was scarcely a place we
had played where some girl did not confide that she was "engaged"
to Dennis.) When we returned to play her hometown, Denny drove
his girl in her car from the theatre toward the house where a party
was being given for the company. A few miles along the way:

> A car drove up, crowded them over against a wall; a man jumped
> out, dragged Julie out of the car and began to beat her up! As you
> can imagine, Denny reacted to this in the traditional male manner,
> and started to beat the man up, but got beaten up himself instead!
> The man is a married man whose wife will not divorce him, who has
> been in love with Julie for years, and has paid court to her, and
> apparently has received some encouragement. He is insanely jeal-
> ous, and discovered that the affair with Denny was serious, and
> threatened Julie, and warned her to "lay off" Denny.
>   We had hardly arrived at the party when Denny telephoned,
> asked for me, gave an excited account of what had happened, and
> asked me to bring the whole Shawn gang to his defense. I sounded
> the battle cry and all of us, in three cars, shot forth to the fray. But
> the man had disappeared, Denny had got Julie a ride in a passing
> car, and I brought Denny back with his black eyes, without having to
> do battle for him. . . . I am very glad that Dennis was only beaten
> and not shot, for the man was carrying a gun.

Against all probability, Ted maintained a wry outlook even on
atrocious performing conditions. This is his report of a concert we
gave in the small town of Somerset, Kentucky, where a Dr. Ewers
had talked the local Kiwanis and Parent-Teacher Association into
booking us for $150:

> The theatre dates back to before the Civil War, and had been closed
> for 8 years. Dr. Ewers rented the theatre for $15.00 but he had to get
> it into shape. He arranged for a convict gang to clean it up! When
> we got there it was supposedly clean. Imagination staggers at what it
> must have been before they cleaned it!
>   On the stage bossing the volunteer stagehands was a crippled
> man pushing himself around in a child's "kiddie car"—strapped
> around his chest was a revolver in a holster—he turned out to be the
> Justice of the Peace and the Chief of Police of Somerset! A man came
> up the aisle stuffing soda crackers into his mouth faster than he could
> swallow them, making noises which we unscrambled as "I'm the
> piano tuner. Where's the piano?"
>   The Fire Department decided it was dangerous to have the fur-

nace going in this old firetrap, so at seven p.m. the fire had to be put out, and it was ten degrees below zero! The cold cream in my dressing room froze hard—and when grease freezes you know it's cold. The dressing rooms were filthy. One of the stage hands said they "was never used since a guy shot hisself there!"

With the house half-filled—partly the cultured from five or six other towns, plus the hillbillies and miners—we started the show. They were well-behaved and applauded warmly, except for some little children who ran up and down the aisles and laughed and screamed without apparently annoying anyone but the performers. . . . *John Brown* got to the place where he starts to call for volunteers and at that point the main fuse in the theatre burned out—not a light in the whole building, or another fuse. When someone started out to find if there was another fuse in town, I quieted the now noisy audience, still in complete darkness, and told them Jess would play. Then I talked in the dark about all the rest of the program, describing all the dances in detail. Suddenly the lights came on—A shout went up from the audience. So I walked back into the position I was in when the fuse burned out, Jess started the music, and, as John Brown, I went on calling for volunteers for the Battle of Harper's Ferry!

Whether it was a coincidence or a reaction, as our trucks came from Somerset into Bluefield, West Virginia, through wild mountain country, Mac's truck was shot at—a nice bullet hole through its back door. Mac said he did not know if it was moonshiners, miners, or just social!

With mile after mile of travel, we soon became prone to attacks of what we called "roaditis." Once, shortly after the repeal of Prohibition, we were in a town where we were giving a matinee and a night performance. Between shows, as I walked wearily alone to the hotel to catch a brief rest, I happened to pass a window display of the now-legal wines and liquors with which I had had no experience except the cheap sherry Shawn and I had shared at the Pillow. Seeing a bottle labeled "Invalid Port," I thought it might be just the medicine I needed to get me through the evening concert. I bought it and, with a sandwich, went up to my room.

I returned to the theatre relaxed and refreshed. The program went as usual until I began to get quite warm during the early dances. From then on, the boys took turns guiding my stumbling steps through the numbers. They hauled me up and down the stairs to the dressing room as they helped me with my costume changes. All the while, through my befuddlement, I could hear them giggling like fiends at the drunken antics of the one who had always been under control, the one who had always known to the lift of an eyebrow what was taking place on stage.

I expected the wrath of Jehovah-Shawn to descend upon my head as soon as we returned to the hotel after the show, but when he saw the label on the empty bottle that had caused my disgrace, he burst out laughing. "Hey, dummy!" he exclaimed. "Didn't you know that this is especially potent wine?" Queasy and conscience-stricken, I shook my head and fell on the bed. I had learned my lesson.

Another time it was our all-round athlete Mac who fell victim. We had gone through a particularly long series of one-night stands that had transformed us all into zombies, both on and offstage. One night, four of us were lined up in the wings ready to make our entrance in *Cutting the Sugar Cane*. Mac was leading the group, with me next, followed by the two other dancers. We assumed our correct stooped-over position waiting for Mac to raise his right foot and stamp on the stage, which gave Jess his cue to begin playing the music. Just as Mac picked up his foot, I lifted my eyes to see before me not the white cotton pants of a Cuban cane-cutter but a perfectly bare behind.

I grabbed Mac's ankle in mid-air. "Where's your *costume!*" I hissed. Mac straightened to stare down at his nakedness. Then, coming out of his trance, he made a gigantic leap back to where his costume bundle lay. While a puzzled Jess awaited the delayed signal, we shoved Mac into the pants we had assumed he had put on while the rest of us were making our rapid "skin change." In our self-absorption, none of us had noticed that Mac had got only as far as taking everything off, including his dance belt, and then had not put anything back on.

——Doldrums and Dedication

Traveling under the most rigorous conditions as we most often were, it was impossible for us not to fall into occasional depressions. We tried to keep our blue moods to ourselves and, in general, we succeeded. Yet I, for one, was always acutely aware of Ted's seesaw from elation to dejection. I knew, for example, that he was increasingly depressed by his accumulating years:

> There is a continuous suggestion to meet as to my age. When am I going to retire, is Barton to be my successor, etc. in endless forms. So my mental and spiritual ablutions can never be neglected or I would

sink under a myriad depressions. As it is, for days, I have been frightfully low in mind. And when I get low, I'm like a kerosene lamp nearly out of oil, I splutter and smell bad!

I understood his feelings on the day after his birthday in 1936:

I had the quaintest birthday present from the company: They wrote me a letter saying that they had voted that I was from now on to be paid a salary equal to what Jess has been receiving all along (i.e. $20 a performance, but not more than $100 in any one week) but that I couldn't touch the excess over what I am getting now, but must put it away as saving! I was deeply touched at both the love which prompted it and the lack of faith in my saving powers unless enjoined!

Undaunted as he usually was, not even Ted was immune to the ills of flesh and spirit.

Certain emotional disturbances had been going on in me for days, which reached a crisis there [Wichita, Kansas]. I can bear any amount of physical and mental strain, if my heart is untroubled— but when my emotional deeps are disturbed, something goes "haywire." After *John Brown,* and the bows, I passed out completely back stage, and was unconscious for some time. A long intermission followed, while I was brought to, put into the next costume and got onto the stage. I finished the show all right, but could not sleep all night long. We had to be dressed by 5:15 in the morning, as we had to make Kansas City before noon.

Any reasonable person might well have asked if Shawn's mission was worth such effort and anxiety. With his reputation, he could have settled comfortably in a New York apartment and been content to teach, as so many performing artists eventually resign themselves to doing. But Ted persisted in his determination to present serious dance as an art suitable for one-hundred-percent males. Considering this goal, he and I were always concerned lest a whisper leak out about our emotional involvement. If the men felt a similar concern, they did not talk about it, and they behaved well.

Not even those enemies who took potshots at Shawn during this period insinuated that his Men Dancers were anything but *pukka* athletes. Photographers, members of the press, critics, and others likely to suspect might, by innuendo, have irreparably harmed our crusade. But, remarkably, they did not. Our behavior, offstage as well as on, may have accounted for this.

Some time after we first met, Ted wrote to me about the fey actions of which he thoroughly disapproved: "[It] makes me sick. It's all wrong. That's the kind of thing that brings discredit on what is essentially a noble thing. Our kind of love, as I have often said before, must be lived on a higher plane than the other or it sinks to a lower level." Because we lived on that higher plane, we did not feel we were deceiving our audiences. We knew that they were not ready to accept a relationship of which we were not the least ashamed, any more than they were ready to accept our kind of modern dancing as we carried our message far and wide.

I sometimes secretly questioned if that message was being received. Once, after I had danced several solos that I had choreographed, I myself wrote to Lucien Price in a fit of despondency: "What is the use of all this? How do I know our dancing is having any effect? Am I really touching anyone with my work?" His tough, succinct answer brought me to my senses: I had no right to feel that I should have any recompense from my audience. I was damn well paid just being privileged to dance what I wanted to dance, and I should get down on my knees in thankfulness for anything more.

After receiving that letter, I often did feel like falling on my knees in gratitude for the response of many (though certainly not all) of those audiences.

——Winning Against All Odds

That we were men who danced and presented works of social consciousness offended the sensibilities of many people in different parts of the country. We played for audiences who laughed as well as for those who were outraged.

> If the gods have time to be bothered with us at all—they have had an amusing spectacle [at Kent, Ohio]. A noisy audience assembled, which remained noisy all through the program. They laughed, talked out loud, whistled and threw pennies on the stage. Nothing like it had ever happened in my whole career. [Students who were helping backstage explained to us that the offenders were high-school pupils. They regularly were admitted to concert series and seated in the section reserved for them in the front rows. The adult audience of college enrollees, faculty, and townspeople sat farther back where their supportive applause could barely be heard above the chaos created by the youngsters.]
>
> After the pennies were thrown, I had to restrain Mac by force from going thru the connecting door from the stage to auditorium, as he was determined to beat up whoever had thrown them.

I bore it—even through all the quiet moments of *John Brown* and *St. Francis* that were ruined by the noise of these embryo racketeers. Then I held up my hand, walked forward and waited until I got complete silence, and spoke my mind. I was quiet and behaved like a gentleman. But I said I considered it a disgrace for adults, faculty and those in authority over these youngsters to have allowed their disgraceful behavior to continue. . . . I said that after this talk I would probably never be booked for this college again, and I, in turn, never wanted to give a performance there. It would have been easy for me to just be quiet, but I was making this speech hoping to save future artists from the ordeal we had been put through. Then I stepped back in line with the boys and we danced the *Doxology* and the curtain fell.

Local papers the next day headlined the event and praised Shawn for his talk, saying that action to control the rowdies was long overdue.

Ted demonstrated his courage in another way, one that was far in advance of the civil rights struggles of the sixties: he persisted in dancing his long solo, *John Brown Sees the Glory,* for audiences he knew were bound to be antagonistic if not downright threatening.

It was in Columbus, Miss. that I met the first unpleasant reaction to my dance *John Brown.* The treasurer of the college, when the President brought him back [stage] to give me our check and get a receipt, when introduced, refused to shake hands with me, and in his eyes glowed a venomous hatred. I was taken aback in the midst of an atmosphere of such hysterical adulation as I had received from that student body, to meet this violent contrast. . . . Later, I was describing this incident to the Forbes family in Athens, Ga., and I said "This man thinks of John Brown only as a rascal who came down to invite the Negroes to rise up and murder the whites." The twenty-year-old Forbes son said with deadly seriousness after a pregnant silence in which my "joke" fell flat with the whole family, "And that's all he was, too!". . . . In Tallahassee they did not dare print the program notes to *John Brown!* However, unfailingly the dance itself has had remarkable response, and I think everyone responds to the impersonality and universality of the theme regardless of its local impingements.

At the College of William and Mary [Williamsburg, Virginia] they were afraid to even *print* the words "John Brown" on the program. And yet the committee ladies were fascinated by reports they had heard about it and wanted to see it. So I announced in my [pre-performance] talk that by request I would add my new solo called

The Forerunner and gave a purely abstract, timeless, unlocal scenario for it—and of course the audience loved it—although a strange electric thrill ran through us all when Jess struck the "John Brown's Body" theme in the finale of the music. And an old stage hand, tilted back on the two hind legs of his chair back stage, sat forward, shoved his hat back off his eyes, like an old war horse scenting powder smoke—but settled back again when the theme disappeared again.

[By delightful contrast, at Hampton Institute in Hampton, Virginia:] . . . we were housed in a charming guest house, and our guaranteed fee there being $500, we felt we were in heaven. The Hampton choir sang for us, and I talked to the student body in the afternoon Saturday.

It was a thrilling evening—a packed house—and the atmosphere during *John Brown* was such that my hair stood on end—and the ovation was tremendous. The *Negro Spirituals* they ate up—and after the show I autographed programs for an hour—everybody was happy about it all—they feel I have started something real at Hampton. Williams, the Physical Education Director, is coming up to study with me [at Jacob's Pillow] next summer in order to do similar things with his Negro men. *What* a dance drama *Black Majesty* would make!

It was at Hampton that students of the dance department staged a performance just for us. We were astonished to see them dancing a classical ballet, with the young women dressed in traditional white tutus. Since we had just done *Negro Spirituals* in whiteface, we enthusiastically applauded this standoff. I found it particularly fascinating that ballet was being taught at a Negro college at that time when few white colleges offered any dance courses at all, or, at best, only a smattering given by modern dance teachers.

Then, there were audiences whose stoicism was laudable, if hard to understand.

In Oklahoma City we were booked by the Chamber of Commerce for the Oklahoma State Teachers Convention. The performance was given in the Coliseum, seating some 7,000 people, most of whom were teachers. The Coliseum is used as a skating rink, and has no stage. Frank drove down by night, arrived there in the morning and superintended the building of a temporary stage. The ice of the skating rink was boarded over, and the audience seats placed on these boards, and there was no heat in the building at all. At seven o'clock the place was full, since no seats were reserved, everyone with overcoats on, sitting on one foot until it was warm, and then on the other. At eight o'clock much to everyone's surprise, they introduced speakers, three of them, who held forth on Education until 9:30 while we, in makeup and robes, huddled together for warmth, and the audience slowly but surely congealed.

The stage was of rough boards, none of which met each other evenly—an inch or two difference in height was nothing! Outside the stage space, on which we danced surrounded by our curtains, there was barely six inches to where the edge of the platform dropped off four feet to the real floor of the building. Barton, making an exit after his *Dyak Spear Dance,* slipped off the edge and both legs went down between the edge of the stage and a rafter, and he was imprisoned there until a stagehand and I pried him loose, I thinking he had broken both legs (but they were only cruelly scraped and bruised). The audience kept their hands folded inside their coats and hardly applauded at all until the end of *Molpai.* But that made them forget their cold, and they really broke loose. Then, in intermission, they admitted newsboys who charged down the aisles yelling *"Extra! Murder!"* They stayed on for the next section of the program and continued to sell papers while we were doing our religious dances—this was particularly annoying to me during *St. Francis!* Also peanuts and hot coffee were being sold throughout the evening. We finished the show at 11:30, but not one of the 7,000 had gone home before the end. I don't know of *anything* I would have stayed for under the conditions that audience had to put up with.

This was the same city where, only the previous year, our concert had been reviewed by a wiseacre who began his story:

Either the theater-going public in Oklahoma City does not like dancing of the Ted Shawn variety or else everyone is laid up with the mumps. Otherwise how explain that 400 cash customers, and no more, out of the 200,000 souls living in this cultural center of the southwest, saw Shawn and his men dancers at the Shrine Auditorium Wednesday night?

It was after that performance that I received a gentle comeuppance from a lovely lady who had come backstage. To my complaint about the lack of support for us "in this day and age" in a town the size of Oklahoma City, she gently replied, "Mr. Mumaw, may I tell you that I was the first public schoolteacher in this town, when I was a young girl, and that our first school was a tent? This was not very long ago. *We* were the pioneers then. *You* are the pioneers now. The very fact that you even appeared here has its own message of encouragement."

There were audiences that were special in other ways:

We had to get up at 5 a.m. in order to drive over 200 miles to give a matinee and night show at Tahlequah, Okla. That town is an historic one—there stands the building which was the capitol building of the Cherokee Nation, and later the capitol of the Indian Territory. My memory was refreshed as to the story of "The Trail of Tears," one of the blackest pages in American history. Our audience in the afternoon was mainly Indians, including 200 Indian orphans from a nearby school. It was a little disconcerting, in doing my *Danza Afro-Cubana,* to find that my torrid glances could find no object except 10-year-old Indian girls to flirt with.

In some communities, we sensed that our lives would be threatened as soon as we set foot on stage. In Austin, Texas, we were forewarned that a group of young men had sworn to come to the concert armed with eggs, rotten fruit, or whatever they could throw.

On to Austin, which *was* exciting. The new Hogg Auditorium which is a handsome building with splendid stage and back stage equipment, was sold out, every inch of standing room taken, and 300 turned away. An organization of some fifty wild "West Texas" boys had announced that they were going to break up the show, objecting, in advance without having seen it, "on principle" to men dancers! [With an uncompromising defiance that may well have bordered on madness, we opened our program as usual with *Polonaise,* a work for six men to Edward MacDowell's music. The curtain rose on a dimly lighted stage with Jess in morning coat and striped trousers seated at the concert grand downstage right. Three men facing three at center, we stood against our dark brown "cyke". When the full, gold-tinted lighting flooded up, we appeared to be naked because we wore only our tight-fitting silk trunks dyed the same shade as our suntanned bodies. This number so paralyzed the wild Texans that there was not a peep from them through the whole evening.]

Shawn reported other victories along the route of our crusade:

Performances go on—with thrilling success. Richmond, Kentucky, night before last had an audience of about 900 people—and the *men* who come back stage were legion, wide-eyed, frankly thrilled. Everywhere they say it is the finest thing they had had on their [college] courses for years. Seeds are sown nightly—whose blooming and fruitage we may never see—but this is our real work.
   [From Missoula, Montana:] Response in this "he-man" cowboy and mining country has been amazing. We have been beauti-

fully presented (I enclose one ad. in which a group of men say they present us "with pride"!) They have had extra hard work overcoming the prejudice against men's dancing in this part of the world, but the men who have come have been as sold on it as men in the East and Middle West, which I think we can both agree is a triumph. I have never on any previous tour done so much talking, radio broadcasting etc. Certainly this message is reaching people.

The message came back to us in a variety of forms. Once in a while we learned of an extraordinary reaction to our work, as Lucien Price informed Shawn from Boston in 1936:

This morning, one of my colleagues at the *Boston Globe* said a friend of his wife's had seen your performance. With her husband, this woman keeps an enormous and glorified form of a New England General Store in Salem, such as you would not suppose existed outside of East Doorknob. They go to everything which comes to town, and what she reported was, "The show was wonderful. I tell you it was simply wonderful. Why, the young men had next to nothing on. Next to nothing on. You might say they were naked. *And they sweat like bulls!*"

We were constantly made aware of a more subtle response to our work by young men, students mostly, each of whom confided that his Old Man preferred him to run the risks of injuries in a football game rather than accept the challenge of an art that was equally strenuous, vowing that "I'll see you *dead* before I'll let you be a dancer!" Many of these frustrated boys were proficient in different fields of athletics. Some dared knock on stage doors, or come back to the locker rooms of college gyms to talk to us about dancing. Others approached us on campus or on small-town streets, pathetically pretending a fascination with our streamlined De Soto in an attempt to disguise their real interest. Only a few were furtive. The rare spats I had with Ted during periods on the road were triggered by my meeting someone who became infatuated with me. None of these superficial encounters ever in any way threatened my love for or my commitment to Ted. Nevertheless, they infuriated him so much that he began to read my letters and to cross-examine me relentlessly in his determination to let no one come between us. No one did.

——*The Critics Respond*

Although we believed that the fulfillment of our mission was in the doing and in being permitted to do it, we did study critical reactions to our concerts, odd as these frequently were. Outside New York and Boston in those days, there were no specially trained dance critics. We considered it great good fortune when a drama or music reviewer wrote up a performance. Much more often, the assignment to cover a Shawn recital was given to a sports writer, a news writer, or one of those volunteer ladies who supply newspapers with cultural and social notes.

In the earliest tours, their essays read as if they had been written by garden editors more interested in pansies than in dancing: the critical emphasis was always on "men," rather than on "dancers." SHAWN PROVES THEIR ART ISN'T A BIT SISSY. THEIR PROGRAM IS OF "HAIR ON THE CHEST" VARIETY ran one headline, while other reviews were headed HE-MAN DANCING or WHEN ATHLETES DANCE, SHAWN AND BRAWN ARE THE BIG FACTORS IN REVOLUTIONIZING THE GENTLE (?) ART OF TERPSICHORE or MOST SKEPTICAL CONVINCED MALE DANCING IS NOT EFFEMINATE, and so forth. One preperformance story began, "What! A ballet without women? This idea which Ted Shawn is demonstrating at the Auditorium is just like saying 'Yes, we have no bananas.' Neither makes sense." And a lady reporter headlined her review with SAYS TED SHAWN'S DANCERS CREATE REAL ART; THEY ARE NOT SISSIES! and went on to admit, "They revolutionized my idea of the dance. Before I attended one of their performances, the very idea of male dancers disgusted me. It brought to my mind feminine forms flitting across a stage with effeminate males cavorting after them in leaps and bounds and whirls."

Critical emphasis eventually shifted from our muscles to our message. In 1935, a Dallas critic wrote, "The *Dyak Spear Dance* introduced the young Barton Mumaw, a splendid personality, impressive technician, a sensitive musician." And reviewing the premiere of our *Dance of the Ages* (for which four of us had choreographed a special section), the Montreal critic wrote:

> Through it all the spirit of the dance that is Shawn moves, a commanding figure, the pivot and focus of the whole action. Yet he is invariably one with his men. You have to see such a dance as this to realize fully how far he has gone in the accomplishment of choreographic drama. And I believe he will go farther still: for you cannot restrain such an ardent, determined and inspired artist very long anywhere.

John Martin, dean of dance critics and fervent champion of those secessionists from Denishawn—Graham, Humphrey, and Weidman—reviewed in the *New York Times* our five successive Sunday concerts in 1938 at the Majestic Theatre. Even he had to concede that "The recent season of Ted Shawn and his company of men dancers served to reveal as expert an ensemble as has been seen in many a day." Walter Terry, writing in the *Boston Herald,* claimed that *"O, Libertad!* is in most respects the greatest dance creation that America has yet produced." A far cry from a 1935 headline in a Chicago paper: SHAWN TROUPE PUTS MANLINESS INTO THE DANCE!

Despite the preponderance of accolades over abuse throughout his career, Shawn remained vulnerable to unfavorable criticism. In a poignant moment we shared, he confided to me a true story that exposed this Achilles heel: When Booth Tarkington published his first novel, his hometown critic tore the book to shreds. The young Tarkington confessed his pain to the old William Dean Howells, adding that he was sure such an Olympian man of letters had years ago ceased paying any attention to what the critics said, To which Howells replied, "My dear boy, you will live to learn that long after critics have lost the power to please, they retain the power to hurt!"

To our considerable surprise, we found that even in London, where our earliest dance pioneers had been recognized and acclaimed, we had to overcome strong prejudice against male dancers who ventured to appear without female partners. ALL-MEN BALLET HAS VIGOUR THAT SILENCES THE SCOFFERS ran the heading over a story that began "London's strangest stage show . . . nine male ballet dancers from a remote New England farm: bizarre but arresting."

We opened at His Majesty's Theatre which was, I believe, the largest legitimate house in London at the time. The first number on our program was the ensemble work, *Polonaise.* Jess never struck the first chord until he was certain that the curtain had risen entirely to reveal our seeming nudity. We were used to a moment of complete silence before we began to move. But the London audience, conditioned by ballet, gave a great audible unanimous gasp that startled us off our feet into the dance with unprecedented *ballon.*

Before our three scheduled concerts were over, we had intrigued reviewers into a consideration of dancing for the sake of dancing. Reported the *Yorkshire Evening News:* "To hold the attention for a couple of hours and finally to arouse the intense enthusiasm of a crowd filling an exceptionally large theatre like His Majesty's, with the dancing of nine men, is a unique feat in London." Such success won us an additional week at the Apollo Theatre, where critical acclaim continued.

——Ventures Abroad

We had sailed from New York on May 17, 1935—the first time

abroad for most of the group. London was a lark. It provided our
first introduction to titled society and to England's celebrities of the
theatrical, musical, and literary worlds; our first television program
where, before any of us had so much as seen a flicker on a telly
screen, we danced a full half-hour show; our first appearance on a
Paramount Films newsreel, taken while we pretended, for publicity,
to rehearse in Green Park (for our *Dance of the Dynamo,* we were
wearing our grim, gray costumes with their square, flat, brimless
caps. We overheard one little boy who was watching our strange
antics exclaim to another, "I say! They're *convicts!*").

It was an altogether exhilarating experience, heightened by the
ubiquitous champagne. Somehow, we managed to appear sober,
dance well, resist romantic attractions, generally behave like gentlemen, and not allow our heads to be turned by the adulation. Not
even when the great Anton Dolin of the Sadler's Wells Ballet attended all eleven of our concerts and rushed backstage to congratulate us after each one. He told Shawn that now that England had
seen what men dancers should move like, never again would they be
considered a mere adjunct to ballet; that we had established not only
self-respect but public respect for men in the dance.

In January 1937, we were treated to a taste of another delightful foreign country—Cuba.

As guests of Mr. Alfred Barton at the Miami Beach Surf Club, we
had a very gay New Year's Eve and Day. January 2nd we sailed for
Havana, and on January 4th, 5th and 6th gave performances at the
Teatro Auditorium under the auspices of the Sociedad Pro Arte Musical. [Shawn had last appeared in Havana with the *Ziegfeld Follies* in
January 1928.] Havana seemed to like us as well as we liked Havana, and that was a lot. It seemed to go over very well—even the
Flamenco dances—and you know how Spaniards [sic] feel about
anyone not Spanish, doing Spanish dances. The notices looked
good—I can't read Spanish, but the adjectives I can recognize as
glowing.

Then we sailed back to Miami and danced there January 8th
and 9th to two packed and enthusiastic audiences; between times
doing stunts for press photographers . . . on the beach of the Surf
Club, and at the MacFadden-Deauville, where we lived as the personal guests of Bernarr MacFadden, who watched with evident delight the taking of the news-reels.

——*Plans and an Ending*

The Cuban tour took place in the middle of the first season we had spent in our new winter quarters at Eustis. Quite inadvertantly, I had been the catalyst that moved Shawn to acquire these quarters. On a December morning in 1935 in Casper, Wyoming, the alarm clock woke me at 5:30. We had to leave early so as to reach Billings, Montana, in time for that evening's performance. I pried open my eyes, rolled from the bed, stood up, and passed out cold. The next thing I saw was Ted's white face as he bent over me. As soon as I had recovered from whatever it was that had hit me, he fired off a telegram to our agents, blaming them for my collapse because they had scheduled bookings so far apart we hardly had time to travel from one to another.

It was too late to change the dates for that tour, which lasted an additional five months. Although I quickly recuperated from my little episode, it had convinced Shawn that, if he were to preserve the health and possibly the sanity of his group, he would have to avoid touring through the northern part of the country in the winter.

Even Ted himself—tower of invincibility though he was—was showing the strain of his myriad responsibilities. After my dramatic early-morning blackout, he brought the problem into the open during one of our company "talk outs." Without premeditation, I mentioned that Mazie had recently written that she and Barton Sr., had bought twelve acres bordering a lake, where they hoped to build their own long-dreamed-of home.

Nostalgia took over the meeting as we interrupted one another with memories of the many happy hours we had spent in Eustis whenever we had stopped there on tour. (Our first Florida lay-off had been an enforced one in 1933. After Thanksgiving—a jolly holiday we spent performing for an audience of thirty-five, followed by a dinner of turkey sandwiches, since no one of us had enough money to buy a full dinner—we had no dates scheduled for several weeks.) Why, someone asked, could we not start the next year's tour in the autumn with a route that worked us gradually southward? Someone else suggested, Why not then lay off in Eustis during the worst of the winter and head northward for bookings in milder weather? And why not put up a studio on a piece of the Mumaw land, where we could camp out, rehearse, and create new programs while we were at liberty? added Shawn, the compulsive builder and laborer in the fields of dance.

No sooner said than Ted flew down to Eustis at the end of the 1936 tour, fell in love with the plot Mazie and Barton had bought, and purchased from them the three lakeside acres where he would construct our retreat. Of course, my mother and father were overjoyed at the prospect of our being there for part of every year. Using all their charm, know-how, and contacts among skilled workmen, they made the plans, selected the contractors, and oversaw the building that soon began on their new house, named Maybar, and on our winter domain. Now, the wanderers would be home from the snow and into the sun. No one could have foreseen that this would be Shawn's southern studio and shelter for the next thirty-six years.

Ted had been involved in the plans for his studio but not in the design of the Mumaw house where we would live. Both of us were therefore surprised when we first saw the rooms assigned to us there. They were next to one another, to be sure, but since they had no connecting door, the only way to get from room to room was through the common hallway. We immediately discovered with loving amusement, however, that each of our rooms had a back wall of French doors that opened onto a small covered porch accessible only to us. We never asked Mazie or Barton their reason for this unusual architecture, nor did they ever offer one.

Those French doors, providing a vista of pine trees and live oaks, gave Ted and me the sense of being in a cabin by ourselves, complete with the sounds of woodpeckers, whippoorwills, and mockingbirds, and the scent of citrus groves mingled with the musk of a passing skunk. We sat on our private porch in the maple chairs my father had made for us—a large one with "Ted" painted on its back, a smaller one with "Barton." We talked and read and refreshed our spirits and needed no explanation for the love that had provided us with this sanctuary.

That year, we began our first winter's work in the new thirty-by-fifty-foot barn studio. Almost a duplicate of the original at Jacob's Pillow, it had a good dancing floor, *barres,* mirrors, and electricity, but running water had yet to be installed.

> We started at once a full day's schedule of creative work and training and rehearsals of our newest program. Until the Mumaw house is completed nearby where some of us will live, the studio became a dormitory at night: breakfast, at seven, was got at the studio on a camp stove out of doors: lunch was sent by Mrs. Mumaw and served picnicstyle, and at night we had our dinner with the Mumaws at their home in town. Next year we hope to be able to build cabins and otherwise develop and enlarge our present unit so that it can become a place for teaching and giving weekly performances—in fact, a winter replica of our place at Lee.

This was the pattern established and maintained until war threatened the pattern of the entire world. Ted foresaw the future as early as April 1939:

> What with war scares, business depressions, and the fact that next year will be our 7th consequetive [sic] tour of this country, which has used up more dates than any other dancing attraction in the same

period of time—our agents are having a difficult time booking for next season. I had a four-hour talk with the boys Easter Sunday night. On the carpet is the big issue of the future—not just next season but what we can and should do for years to come. . . . Of course, it may be that after the 7th tour, the cycle will be complete—and the company should disband—and I retire to the security and comfort of a professorship at Peabody. We could still keep the farm going in the summers, for the mens' school, for those who want to teach. And perhaps the summer school will grow until it will support one or two teachers the year round. . . .

The boys and I need something better and higher to work for professionally as well as artistically. Just doing tour after tour of mostly little towns, schools, and small stages, poor fees, is a picture that is disheartening and disintegrating. It does seem that there ought to be financing somewhere in this rich country for us, having demonstrated that we are making a valuable contribution to the art life of America. Outside the season-ticket courses and college student-body audiences, we just do not draw enough of the general public to be self-supporting. But then symphonies and grand opera do not either, nor do any of the "Russian" ballet companies.

[Still without a plan for the future, Shawn wrote in October 1939, one month after Hitler's invasion of Poland:] I started on a series of individual talks with all the members of the company, in order of their seniority, the last of which was finished less than half an hour ago. I presented to them my conviction that it was wise to dissolve the corporation and disband the company at the end of this 7th tour. I said that although we would end in debt, I would borrow to the limit of my life insurance to send each of them out with a fund of several hundred dollars to start each one's new chapter with. I stated my belief that we all of us should take a positive attitude about the ending of our association, and announce now that we had succeeded magnificently and had proved all we had set out to prove; that the individual members of the company would, as it were, receive their "degrees" in May, 1940, and each move out into his own mature career; that I would announce publicly that I was ready and eager to do something still newer and bigger, but that I had to have a year freed from touring and teaching to prepare it and do the creative work on it.

With no exception I met with whole-hearted agreement, and a sense of relief and release. There is a spirit not that anything is ending, but that we are all going on, united in spirit, even though it will mean separation physically. So we have set Monday, the 16th, on which to take the formal vote at company meeting, after which I will make an announcement to the press. . . .

Outward, and to some degree, inward harmony reigns. Their plans the boys do not discuss with me—although I know they all expect to set the world on fire. I do not encourage them to talk to me for this is their life and they must decide and live it. Barton is, of course, another matter. He would stick by me if only I would say the word. But if he is ever to have an individual career he should go after it now. So I have encouraged him to get agents, managers, interested friends to see him at our men's group performances at Carnegie Hall this Spring, and then follow up any leads that come out of that. If he gets a job—it means considerable readjustment in my own life—but I have faced that, too, and it's all right.

Brave words, but it could not be that simple for either of us. Through seven difficult but wonderful years, I had so improved my dancing and choreography that I had become convinced I must attempt to stand on my own bare and calloused feet. The threat of war strengthened my conviction that I must do this before it was too late. This aim conflicted with my devotion to Ted, and I approached the last performance of the Men Dancers with apprehension and sorrow.

That final concert was given in Boston, where Shawn and his Men Dancers had first appeared. The date was May 7, 1940. I danced my Bach *Bourrée*,* and my *God of Lightning*,* and the *Pierrot* that was uniquely Ted's and mine. Price, writing to Shawn the next day, said that never before were our performances so brilliant and so powerful: "From the enthusiasm of the audience even the figleaves of the classic statues, high on the walls of the auditorium, were trembling!". Walter Terry wrote in the *New York Herald Tribune*:

> An immeasurably important cycle in the dance has come to an end. Last Monday and Tuesday evenings in Boston's sedate Symphony Hall, stamping, cheering audiences paid tribute to Ted Shawn and his men dancers on their final performances. . . . Such response from a sophisticated audience is significant. . . . It must be the enduring qualities of fine craftsmanship and stimulating art which would arouse such a demonstration of public approval.

Some who were in that audience tell me that Shawn shook the hand of each member of the group when we took the last of many curtain calls. Others recall that every one of us stood and bowed, and bowed again, with tears in our eyes. I have no words with which to express what I remember of that moment.

*A full description appears in Part Two.

9

(1940)

The World Threatens

After the bittersweet success of our final Boston concert, we returned to the comforting rock of the Pillow, each dancer to puzzle his own future. Secretly, we felt certain that our next steps would be *"Hup, two, three, four!"*: the Nazis had invaded Poland and England had declared war on Germany. Even though the mood of the United States in those days allowed us to hope that we might be able to follow our chosen paths out of uniform, I knew that the years ahead would see the end of everything we had been striving for in the life of the world's peoples as well as in our creative and personal lives.

Shawn's fear reflected mine as we talked late into the September night. Faced with a war he was convinced would involve our country, he confided that he must sell Jacob's Pillow in order to pay off the accumulated debts of our tours which, while successful, had never earned enough to cover all expenses. He told me that Mary Washington Ball (an early sponsor of the Men Dancers, a dance educator, and Physical Education Director at the Cortlandt, New York, State Normal School) had agreed to lease the Pillow with an option to purchase, on condition that Shawn would teach and perform during her first season. He was willing and eager to accept the condition since he had no viable alternative.

When he announced this fait accompli to the rest of the company, he offered each the choice of severance pay or a piece of Jacob's Pillow land. Only Frank Overlees chose the land. Ted borrowed enough money to give a parting cash bonus to the others. Strangely, neither he nor I was unduly distressed by the loss of the

beloved Farm, which had been my artistic home for so long, or by
the disbandment of the performing group that had been Shawn's
greatest artistic achievement to date. This curious resignation, I
think, reflected our adjustments to the many setbacks in our common life. Or perhaps we were numbed by the knowledge that we
would soon endure a greater pain. "Barton would stick by me if only
I would say the word," Shawn had written Price, "but if he is ever
to have an individual career he should go after it now." Easy to
realize intellectually; difficult to accept emotionally.

Ted did encourage me to seek my own way, although he was far
from enthusiastic when that pointed to Broadway—a prospect of
steady work that appealed to me as sheer heaven after the uncertainty of the past seven years. He had never willingly let any of his
protégés enter the arena of "show business" unless *he* had armed
them with their material (as he had with his dances for Florence
O'Denishawn, Ada Forman, Margaret Severn, Marjorie Peterson,
and Martha Graham when they made their debuts in Broadway
revues). I did not want the control this implied, so it was probably
fortunate that none of my many irons in the fire produced an offer of
a job in a musical. The failure to be recognized was particularly
galling when my *Banner Bearer** solo from our *Olympiad* suite was, at
that very moment, inspiring several chorus routines.

In 1936, Shawn had written to Price about Olympiad:

*It had been a mind-scattering week. While I prepared copy for the new circulars,
new window cards and work on the new souvenir program, the boys divided all the
creative hours in the studio [at Jacob's Pillow] and Jess's time between them in
order to finish up their Sports Dances for yesterday's teas. . . .*

*Well, I am so proud, so glowing, radiant, happy that I am fizzling—
inarticulate. They have done a magnificent job. I was called in at the end only for
minor suggestions—to arrange the order in which they came and work on the
joinings and transitions. But each has created a work which stands, is strong,
fresh, original, and holds you on the edge of your seat. . . .*

*There is an artistic unity of style to the whole group which makes it seem the
work of one choreographer. And an extraordinary level of achievement—no one
stood out as best—no one seemed in any way lesser. Jess outdid himself with the
music. The audience cheered and cheered. Miss Ruth was up for this program and
she was delighted. The boys, this being their first big job, nearly tore themselves to
pieces working and rehearsing—and it is all extremely vigorous—today there is a
collection of bruises, blisters, charley-horses such as never before even in their beginning days. And yet very happy hearts with their Papa bursting with pride.*

I had been encouraged by Walter Terry's review in a February

---

*A full description appears in Part Two.

issue of the *New York Herald Tribune* after the Men Dancers' last appearance at Carnegie Hall. He wrote, "Barton Mumaw's *Bourrée* from the [Bach] Second Violin Sonata [sic] was nothing short of brilliant. . . . Mumaw's great romantic fantasy *Pierrot in the Dead City* strengthened the conviction that he is one of the few great dancers of the younger American group." Although I was impatient to discover if I could fulfill the promise implied in this praise, I experienced sadness at the prescience with which Terry ended his critique:

> The program closed with the *Jacob's Pillow Concerto,* a work that captures within its brevity the essence of the seven-year life of the company of men dancers. It is laid in the Shawn Berkshire Hills studio. Shawn opens it with a joyous dance. . . . The boys enter . . . little excerpts from their dances are suggested, temperamental bouts with Shawn appear and then, slowly, each of the boys dances away, leaving Shawn once again to dance his great eclectic creed of religious faith and cleanness, robust romanticism and unfaltering idealism. Then he, too, as he is doing in real life, walks into the future without his dancing sons, leaving a void in the theater of the dance until he once again returns to fill it with the richness of his art.

Through the summer, I assisted Shawn as teacher at the Pillow under the new management of Miss Ball. Imbued with Ted's philosophy that the dance should be all-inclusive, she arranged "The Berkshire Hills Dance Festival" (later to become the Jacob's Pillow Dance Festival). It consisted of ballet, Oriental, Spanish, ballroom, and modern dances by the students, a solo concert by Shawn, a Ruth St. Denis program devoted to the religious dances which had become her prime creative obsession, and a homecoming performance by the Men Dancers, all of whom (except the Delmar twins) returned to the Pillow for this reunion. There was also a program of solos that Ted had devised for me.

It was not unreasonable for me to be nervous about this first program all on my own. Hitherto, my dances had been integrated into the ensemble and solo numbers by Shawn and others, which captured audience interest by their variety. Could I, alone, provide equal contrast? I knew, too, that in addition to programming problems, the solo itself is a risk. To quote Jack Anderson in the *New York Times* of September 23, 1979: "The solo may very well be the most daring of dance forms. Dancers who perform solos must stand alone before an audience and in some way persuade, entertain or amaze that audience. They have no one else to help them; only they can do it. Solos are hazardous; they're gambles."

It was a gamble I would have to take if ever I were to learn whether or not I could stand without Shawn. Fortunately, I could test myself before friendly Pillow patrons who had long been familiar with my work. Their reception of my program was so unexpectedly enthusiastic that I no longer had any doubts about taking the next step toward a New York solo concert.

In the fall, Ted and I drove down to Eustis with little money but a lot of hope. Fern Helscher had promised to be my press agent and manager if my proposed New York performances were successful; Jess Meeker would continue to work with me as he had with Shawn; Frank Overlees, who had performed lighting and staging miracles for the Men Dancers, had agreed to be my stage manager. With Ted to oversee bookings and publicity as well as to create and costume new dances for me, how could I fail? Although I lacked the financial backing that could ensure a Town Hall or similar suitable theatre for my introduction to New York audiences, Shawn assured me that the Carnegie Chamber Music Hall would provide an eminently respectable ambience for my real debut. The die was cast when we booked that house for four dates in April 1941.

Once settled in Florida, where Mazie and Barton opened their home and their hearts to us for a whole season, the work began. We reveled in the luxury of having the studio all to ourselves for daily class and rehearsals. I began the struggle to discover what I wanted to say in dance, for I had learned from Shawn that the "what" was more important than the "how."

This was a priority he had emphasized years earlier and continued to stress. In 1969, for the first time in history, the gala performance of the Northeast Regional Ballet Festival was telecast live. Ted made the curtain speech, saying:
> *You new generation of dancers now have a language that you can use beautifully. But what have you got to say? It should be in some way life enhancing. That doesn't mean it has to preach, it doesn't mean it has to have a religious or serious theme. But it does mean that your audience should leave the theatre feeling that they have been fed. It's not only a question of getting their money's worth for the ticket they bought but that they have been enriched. Somehow or other their vision has been broadened, their vibrations stepped up, and they have been given a feeling that after all life is pretty good and worth living. A great artist performer, a great choreographer, director, producer are needed to create a work of art in Dance, but without great content they give us nothing.*

One solo emerged to reveal my deepest feelings about the world at war. I used as musical inspiration Liszt's *Funerailles*,* which I alternately titled with that name or *War and the Artist* or *War and the Man*. When I showed my dear friend, Mary Kinser, what I was working

*A full description appears in Part Two.

on, that multitalented woman designed the costume that I was to wear for years.

Until she died, I maintained a sort of love affair with this sensitive, intelligent Rapunzel who had played such a meaningful role in my adolescent life. The fact that she had a husband and two daughters never interrupted a relationship that remained vital to both of us, despite our many separations and disparate experiences. When the Men Dancers began to spend winters in Eustis, Mary became a favorite of them all as well. Her parents' home offered us a refuge from our restrictive routine and from Shawn's demanding, dictatorial personality. The Kinsers appreciated the discipline our work required as well as its frustrations. That made us treasure them as friends with whom we could relax and in whom we could confide. Shawn was as fond of them as we were: they remained what he called "loyal" to the end of their days.

Under the most pleasant circumstances imaginable, therefore, Ted and I worked on my program together. Nevertheless, minor friction developed as I, rather than Shawn, became the focus of concentration. My ideas labored to be born without the aid of a midwife. I was often resentful when decisions that should have been mine alone were automatically made by Ted. Although we shared the practical effort to create a program that would hold an audience, I so thoroughly respected Shawn's ability that I acceded to his wishes even when I longed for the freedom to make my own mistakes. Why, then, did I not *demand* that freedom?

I was twenty-eight years old and still found it impossible to rebel openly against the authority of the man who had been the core of my life for nine years. Shawn had shaped my talent, extended my intellectual horizons, become an integral member of my family, determined my sexual fulfillment, and introduced me to the world of the gifted and the famous. If these are not sufficiently convincing reasons to explain my reluctance to assert myself, then I must attempt a clearer picture of the man against whose hold I was beginning to struggle:

Dr. Willard Gaylin, the noted psychiatrist, has observed, "Though a man may not always be what he appears to be, what he appears to be is always a significant part of what he is," a statement that particularly applies to the private and the public Shawn, who embodied so much pure mind, pure emotion, and, of course, pure physical movement. If character is most precisely revealed in action, then much of Ted's behavior was admirable. He would work at the most menial jobs in order to realize his ideal:

On May 6th (1945), which turned out to be the AP V-E day, with

one scholarship boy, I went up to open up Jacob's Pillow. . . . May
10-11 we had a 24-hour blizzard. . . . As usual, besides the dirty
work of scrubbing, cleaning pots and pans, washing windows, airing
mattresses, digging up clogged sewers, patching leaky roofs, painting, cement work, carpentering, etc. I did all the cooking until toward the end of June when our professional cook arrived. . . . I have
pledged myself to keep Jacob's Pillow alive and operating for the
soldier-dancers to come home to, and, so help me God, I will keep
that pledge.

This disarming contradiction of humility and egotism made it
as difficult to be Shawn's enemy as it was to be his friend. I had not
been trained to fight such a formidable opponent because, in all our
years together, we had had only insignificant quarrels. Ted had always treated me with kindness, perception, and generosity. Yet those
years of unremitting closeness had also revealed his negative qualities. I believe now, as I did then, that those qualities derived from
the three most compelling drives in his life: the need to be recognized
for his contribution to dance, the need for a permanent love relationship, and the need to control, to dominate.

When Shawn proclaimed me his successor in American dance,
this created a painful ambivalence within him: if I became an independent dancer, I would inevitably become his rival as well—
something, I suspect, that he dreaded as much as he wanted me to
be famous. Realistically, of course, he need not have feared that
anyone could challenge his place in dance history. He had long been
accorded the recognition for which he hungered, but this never
seemed enough to satisfy his greed for reassurance, a greed that
sometimes drove him to misplaced vindictiveness. For example, one
would think that, despite his bitterness against the "renegades," he
might have felt honored to read in the 1928 announcement of the
first Humphrey-Weidman School how clearly their dance philosophy
had evolved from his: "To be master of one's body: to find a perfect
union between the inner thought and outer form—to draw from this
a radiance and power that makes of life a more glorious and vital
experience—this is to dance." But Ted sneered.

One would think that he might have been gratified to be told
that Charles Weidman, ten years after his break with Denishawn,
still sought "Papa's" approval. When a friend praised his *Thurber
Fables*, Charles's immediate reaction had been, "I hope you told
Ted!" But Ted grinned with malice.

One would think that his hurt pride might have been forever

soothed when, after their reconciliation, Doris Humphrey admitted, "Ted, I'm ashamed that we have forgotten how much we learned from you." But Ted merely nodded.

I am confident there would have been fewer of these petty reactions had Shawn lived to read the verdict on his work handed down by modern-day critics. In a *New York Times* article on March 19, 1978, entitled *The Rise of the Male Ensemble,* Jack Anderson made an observation about Shawn's choreography that had never occurred to me and that would have pleased Ted mightily. After listing the few all-male works by George Balanchine, Jerome Robbins, Murray Louis, Erick Hawkins, and Gerald Arpino's *Olympics* (shades of our *Olympiad!*), Anderson wrote:

> The pioneer in this field, however, was Ted Shawn, whose Men Dancers flourished from 1933 to 1940 and helped propagate ideas about male dancing that are still common. *Yet Shawn's choreography also hints at fresh approaches to male dancing that choreographers are only now starting to explore* [my emphasis]). While he was best known for dances on heroic themes . . . his studies in pure movement now take on new importance as foreshadowing of ways in which choreography for male ensembles may develop in the future if choreographers continue to investigate possibilities of male movement as something that may be enjoyed for its own sake.

Anna Kisselgoff in the August 12, 1979, *New York Times,* quoted Liz Thompson, then newly elected director of Jacob's Pillow: "Shawn's dances in the 1930's were anything but traditional. He was doing outrageous things and he did new dance." Which proves that a prophet is not always without honor in his own country.

Shawn is now credited with having overcome the prejudice against American males as serious dancers. It is not so well known, however, that he was also a pioneer in the struggles against religious and racial prejudices that troubled—and still trouble—our society. He welcomed pupils and staff of all faiths to the Pillow; few either knew or cared who was Jewish or Protestant, Catholic or atheist, least of all Ted. And there were always Negro students. Southern white young women in residence at the school associated with northern black men. Instead of "incidents," there were tributes, one of which in particular I vividly remember: As with all scholarship pupils, a certain black student on a scholarship had been assigned the usual jobs around the school and theatre. These brought him into varied contact with teachers and fellow students, with artists and members of the audiences. At the end of the season, he came to say goodbye to the staff. I was alarmed when this big man, who stood erect before us, suddenly began to cry. When he could finally speak, he said with great dignity, "I do not know how to express my thankfulness for this summer, except to say that never once since I set foot on this place did anyone treat me with anything but friendship and respect."

Shawn was also one of the first American impresarios regularly to engage black artists: the African, Asadata Dafora; Olatunji and the Afro-American Dance Company; Jean-Léon Destiné's Haitian dance group; Arthur Mitchell's Dance Theatre of Harlem; the Alvin Ailey Company; Pearl Primus and her husband, Percival Borde; Matt Turney; Talley Beatty; Morse Donaldson Dance Company; Carmen de Lavallade; Geoffrey Holder; Arthur Hall's Afro-American Dance Ensemble; and the Negro Dance Theatre all appeared during one or more Pillow seasons. So did the National Dancers of Ceylon; the Samoan, Teokila Aasa; the Japanese, Sahomi Tachibana, Yass Hakoshima, and Suzushi Hanayagi; and many East Indian soloists, such as Balasaraswati, Ritha Devi, Nala Najan, Priyagopal, Bhaskar, Shanta Rao, and Ram Gopal.

However, Shawn could not at the same time crusade against a third prevailing prejudice—the one to which homosexuals were exposed. Quite the contrary. If his efforts on behalf of men dancers were to succeed, he had constantly to reconcile his private relationship to me with the *macho* image he unrelentingly had to present to a skeptical public. He did not do this from hypocrisy, but from *necessity*.

It is a mark of the man's integrity that, from the first, Ted never allowed me to feel guilty about our life together. He never hinted that we might be beyond the pale, except according to "popular" mores. This absence of any feeling of guilt left us free to be relaxed and even gay (in the best original sense of the word) in expressions of our love. We took it for granted that we were accepted by people close to us. If they came to know of our relationship, we were never embarrassed. Our only concern was that this knowledge not spread far and wide enough to destroy the image of the Men Dancers as "respectable" artists.

While he was still able to perform—and even later—Ted's horror of encroaching age sometimes shortened his temper. He dreaded the thickening torso, the thinning hair, the loss of teeth, the stiffening limbs. He did try, against all odds, to keep up a façade of insouciance. In February 1952 he wrote:

Ruthie said to me once, "Teddy, the fifties are a very dull period—
you are neither one thing nor the other. But as soon as I passed 60, if
I got my foot 14 inches off the floor everyone thought I was miraculous!" Now that I have passed *my* sixtieth birthday, I realize that a
new life begins at 60! Certainly I feel no diminution of my physical
and mental powers, and life has more zest than ever. I look forward
to at least two more decades of rich, vital, and creative activity and
with joy.

He did enjoy those two decades almost to the exact date of this letter.
When he met an old friend at his birthday gala, he exclaimed to her,
"How the hell did I get to be eighty? Inside, I still feel like nine-
teen."

There were times when he *acted* nineteen, alas. This may well
have been because his deep need for a permanent relationship had
suffered two deprivations before he was fifty-five, the greater of
which was Ruth St. Denis, whom he loved to the day she died (as I
was to love him). Sixteen years after they had parted, in April 1947,
he wrote to her:

Insofar as you and I are truly united with God, we are united with
each other. No passing cloud can do more than temporarily obscure
the sun—it can never stop the sun's shining. This is a cliché and we
say it over and over—but it's still true and still the only thing to say
in the midst of any seeming dark spell: "Love is not love which alters
when it alteration finds" so please know that I am unchanged and
unaltered. Yours, Ted.

Out of his emotional dependence upon the reverence for his
former wife, he incorporated her dances into frequent Pillow programs. They maintained the relationship of two old soldiers who had
shared campaigns that included horror and humor in almost equal
proportions. As he and I grew older together, this same emotional
dependence created an unfounded jealousy that often drove him to
act like a lovesick high-school boy. He monitored my telephone calls
and arranged to have my mail brought to him to "distribute" (although he never read my letters without my permission). Unless one
knew him very, very well, it was difficult to understand this adolescent behavior on the part of an outwardly self-assured, self-
controlled, extremely intelligent, mature man.

He refused to face the fact that, just as *he* had fought to be free
from Miss Ruth's domination so that he could control *his* own life

and career, I must inevitably be free from his authority. I, in turn, long refused to face the fact that achieving my freedom would be no easier for me than it had been for him. I was perhaps blinded by my knowledge that, despite his hot temper, Ted could exhibit surprising forebearance when his domination was challenged. I remembered the report, for example, that after Shawn had at last with great effort raised the money to start building a much-needed additional studio at Jacob's Pillow, he named it the Ruth St. Denis Hall and invited her to speak at its dedication. Introducing her to his assembled staff, teachers, artists, and pupils, he stood proudly aside while she gave a long talk on the history of American dance. She named Loie Fuller, Isadora Duncan, and herself as the founders. Just as in the 1927 curtain speech she had made to a packed Carnegie Hall audience announcing the formation of Greater Denishawn, she never mentioned Shawn. I find it remarkable that on neither occasion did he embarrass listeners by revealing his anguish, humiliation, and anger at such unwarranted treatment by his partner of years.

At a more informal time and place, during lunch with Shawn and his co-workers at the Pillow, Miss Ruth kept eating while Ted boasted of his excellent memory. Abruptly, she looked up to interrupt in a pensive tone of voice, "You know, Teddy, I was just reading the other day that memory is the lowest form of intelligence." I am thankful I was not at that table to witness his forced smile as he accepted yet another public affront without protest.

This, then, was the contradictory, the driven, the beloved Ted. Flawed as he was, I deeply respected the Shawn who could write to Price in 1937:

> I realize keenly my theatricalisms, the egotistic self-assertion, the acidulous resentments of enemies and critics that I show in spite of knowing that I shouldn't. You hold up to me the mirror of truth in which I see God's blueprint of me—the design of the gentleman, scholar and artist I was meant to be and still can be. . . . When you say "hero worship" in regard to your attitude toward me, it makes me ashamed and humble. Which is perhaps a good thing, after all!

When war threatened his world, his closest relationship, and his career, he had the courage to write, "Yes, there is still love and friendship, amidst this present horror, and those will survive, as they have always survived the horrors of the past. Let us keep on loving, even the Germans, as long as we can. Yours, Ted."

It caused me great pain to realize that, in order to be on my own, professionally and personally, I must hurt Shawn in those very areas where he was most vulnerable—in dance, in love, in dominance. Besides, how does one fight such a man?

10

(1941–1942)

On My Own

I was disarmed even before I could strike my first blow for freedom because Ted could not have been more generous in helping me prepare my New York debut. It was an ambitious program, but by the time of dress rehearsal, I was confident that my old dances as well as the new ones had acquired sufficient depth.

On March 21, 1941, Shawn launched me professionally at a cocktail party he gave for the press and for potentially influential guests. Shy as I was, and impressed by the important people who came, I was thoroughly enjoying this event in my honor when I heard Fern Helscher's voice behind me. Turning eagerly to greet her, I found myself face to face with the one man Ted had loved before he met me. His name had not appeared on the guest list, so it was certain that it had been Fern who had invited him. I am sure she had no inkling what effect his presence might have on two who had not seen him for ten years. She must have been puzzled to see me stand staring and speechless. For an instant, I literally experienced what it means to be out of one's mind.

I turned blindly away and bumped into Shawn's good friend, Francis Robinson. In my mindless stress, I introduced him to another friend as "Francis Thompson." Whereupon, smiling, the gentle and courteous man interrupted me to say he was honored but he could not legitimately operate under the great poet's name. (Great in his own way, Mr. Robinson worked in several important capacities at the Metropolitan Opera from 1948 almost to his death in 1980.) As the party continued, I regained my composure, avoiding

149

another confrontation with the guest from the past. It is interesting, I now think, that Ted and I never talked about the appearance of our Banquo's ghost at our little feast.

That was not the only unexpected occurrence. Three days before my debut, dance critic John Martin (whom Ted considered his avowed enemy) had placed in the April 13 *New York Times* a two-column photograph of me with an announcement of my upcoming recitals. Having seen this before I did, Ted spread the paper in front of me with an exultance I failed to interpret correctly. My reaction to the blurb was a simple wish that Martin had given me more than a bald announcement. The wrath of the mighty Shawn immediately descended upon my innocent head.

"Since John Martin has been on the *Times, my* photograph has *never* appeared there!" Ted roared. "He never mentions *my* name unless he is goaded to it by threat of dismissal! And yet *you—you!—* rate a picture smack in the middle of the page!"

I was aghast at his outburst, even though I realized that the emotions aroused by the threat of my independence had triggered it. We did not discuss the incident, but its effect simmered beneath the surface. Then, on the very eve of my first concert, I came down with the worst attack of flu in my life. The God of Wrath vanished at once; the Rock of Gibraltar took his place. Serene, reassuring, patient, Ted fed me countless cups of hot tea laced with lemon as I lay feverish in bed. Neither he nor I so much as whispered the word "cancellation."

Before the performance, however, costumed, made up, and about to proceed on shaky legs into the first dance, I realized I had to have something stronger than Ted's moral support to get me onto the stage. A worried Shawn proffered a flask. I knew from my one past experience that I could not drink and dance, but it was that or not dance at all. I took a large mouthful of brandy. This gave me the strength to do the opening numbers. During the costume change for *Hellas,* I swigged another gulp of the fiery energizer, and continued to do the same before every solo throughout the concert. Thanks to the gods who watch over theatre artists, I finished the program with no staggering, no stumbling, no falling. The only drunkenness I felt was the euphoria of dancing alone for an enthusiastic audience.

Admittedly, I was more fortunate than most young people making their debut because I did not have to paper the house in order to fill it. Not only my own followers, but Shawn's came, while friends in the worlds of modern art and society had literally commanded *their* friends to buy tickets. The throaty tones of Florence Reed (famed star of *The Shanghai Gesture*) could be heard above the piano as she exclaimed during each dance, "Bravo, Barton! Bravo!" Lucien Price was in the audience as were dancers of the calibre of Anton Dolin. Pat (Dolin's real name was Patrick Healey-Kay) was sitting in the row just behind my parents. At one point, he made a remark to his companion that ventured perilously close to criticism. Mazie, ever gracious, ever devoted, turned to him with a smile and said, "Isn't he wonderful? I'm his mother."

The next day's rave reviews were all the medicine I needed to cure my illness. I danced the following three scheduled programs without the assistance of brandy or bravado. If I had been less experienced professionally, my head might have been forever turned by the writeup in the *New York World Telegram,* which began, "With the little Carnegie Music Hall jammed to bursting, Barton Mumaw, rapidly being regarded as the American Nijinsky, gave the first of four dance programs last night." This was the first of many times I was to be compared to the one dancer whom I admired most in the world after Shawn, a comparison that set an artistic standard I would always seek to achieve.

A day or so after my final concert, I overheard Ted, who was monitoring my calls more assiduously than ever, in a telephone conversation with Charles Weidman. From what I was permitted to hear at Shawn's end of the line, I deduced that Charles was asking him if I would be interested in joining either the Humphrey-Weidman company or a Broadway project for which he was doing the choreography. Ted refused with dignified outrage, "But Barton is an *artist!"*—implying that Charles had insulted me by the mere question. This exchange embarrassed me painfully, if only because I was somewhat in awe of Weidman. But my loyalty to Shawn still held me in thrall. To my regret, I lacked the courage, the wit, and the courtesy to call Charles back to thank him for his offer.

The incident, however, sharply reminded me of a piece of advice given to me in private by a person who was a close friend of mine and of Ted: As soon as the Men Dancers had disbanded, she urged me to go to work with Humphrey and Weidman. It is as interesting as it is futile to speculate on what my career might have been had I followed this advice.

When Jack Cole left Shawn in the early thirties, he went directly to Doris and Charles. Some time later, he taught dance for and with Miss Ruth, resuming contact with her Oriental inspiration. After studying authentic Eastern ethnic

BARTON MUMAW

JESS MEEKER, at the piano

PROGRAM

I.

1. Three Dances to Music of Classic Composers:

   (a) "Where'er You Walk"—*Handel*

   (b) Sonata—*Scarlatti*

   (c) Bourrée from the 2nd Violin Sonata—*Bach*

2. Hellas Triumphant (*Meeker*)

   An evzone, not yet at the front, has heard the news of the first Greek victories in Albania. Leaving a village celebration, he enters still in the rhythm of the Kalamatienos and Sirtos. He comes upon an image of the Virgin, and prays; later on, with other soldiers he joins in the Cretan War Dance, and as they hear the Hymn to Freedom, the Greek National Anthem, being played in the distance, they march toward the battle front, knowing that no matter what the temporary outcome, Hellas will always rise again, and be spiritually and materially triumphant.

3. The Mongolian Archer (*Meeker*)

   Inspired by the sculpture of Malvina Hoffman.

4. War and the Artist (Funerailles—*Liszt*)

— *Intermission* —

II.

5. Three Primitive Dances:

   (a) Fetish (*Meeker*) Inspired by primitive African sculpture

   In this interval, Mr. Meeker will play his own composition:
   "Primordial Invocation."

   (b) Dayak Spear Dance (*Meeker*)

   In this interval Mr. Meeker will play his own compositions:
   "Primitive Fire Ritual" and "Hag's Cauldron."

   (c) The God of Lightning (Allegro Barbaro—*Bela Bartok*)

6. The Banner Bearer (*Meeker*)

   From the Sports Suite "Olympiad."

7. Earth Forces (*Meeker*)

   From "Dance of the Ages."

8. Valse Brillante (*Mana Zucca*)

————◆————

Miss Fern Helscher, *Personal Representative and Manager*
(Hotel Winslow, Madison Ave., at 55th St.)

Mr. Frank Overlees, *Stage Manager*

Mr. John Schubert, *Assistant*

Choreography for the following dances is by Mr. Mumaw:
Sonata—*Scarlatti;* Bourrée—*Bach;* War and the Artist;
God of Lightning; The Banner Bearer; Earth Forces.

Choreography for all the other dances is by Shawn.

Costume for "War and the Artist" designed by Mari Eva Kinser.
All other costume designs by Mumaw and Shawn.

Steinway Piano

Program for Barton Mumaw's New York solo concert debut, April 16-19, 1941.

dance with La Meri, he synthesized all these varied techniques into his own
characteristic style, thus changing the shape of nightclub, film, and theatre dance in
his comparatively brief lifetime.

Armed with my reviews, Fern interested one of several managers in booking me on a tour. He insisted, however, that it would be
easier to get engagements if I had a "beautiful partner." The slen-
der, dark-eyed, New York-born Lisa Parnova, whose most notable
dancing was *en pointe*, joined Ted, Jess, and me in Eustis. Shawn
created three duets for us, planned our program, supervised our
costume making, and booked us into Jacob's Pillow for our debut
during the upcoming season.

That summer of 1941, the Pillow had been leased to Reginald
Wright, an English balletomane and friend of Alicia Markova who,
with Anton Dolin, conducted the school. Among other teachers, Ted
taught and I assisted him. With help from the experienced Shawn,
Dame Alicia also ran an "International Dance Festival" that turned
out to be truly gala. Ruth St. Denis opened the season with a program of her East Indian dances, including the famous *Radha*, a ballet
first performed in New York in 1906. (Doris Humphrey and Charles
Weidman came up from the city specifically to honor Miss Ruth on
this occasion. A photograph showing them with her and "Papa"
seemed to signify the healing of old wounds.)

This was followed by Shawn in a solo program featuring his
Cosmic Dance of Siva; Seiko Sarina in Siamese, Javanese, and Balinese
dances; Lisa Parnova and I in a duet performance that disappointed
my followers; a Ballet Theatre program headlining Markova, Dolin,
Lucia Chase, Antony Tudor, and Hugh Laing, with Agnes de Mille
as guest star in her *Degas Studies;* appearances by Nora Kaye and by
Paul Draper; an unexpected solo program by me (upon which
Shawn had insisted to compensate for the failure of my earlier appearance); and a grand finale shared by St. Denis, Shawn,
Markova, and Dolin. Small wonder this season broke all earlier records for attendance.

Participation in that festival was a magnificent experience for
me. The contact I made with those extraordinary talents formed the
basis of my lifelong respect for all dancers. Strange as it may seem,
my familiarity with the work and the personalities of other dance
artists had, until then, been limited to my years at the Pillow and
with the Men Dancers. That summer, a new and richer field opened
for me.

Shawn and I were perfecting my program for the tour Fern had
booked and publicized to begin in October when the New York draft

board sent me an invitation from the President of the United States
to bear arms in defense of my country. To say that consternation
reigned is to understate it. Ted saw my career ending before it had
really begun and was terrified at the thought of our separation,
which could well be forever if I were sent into active service overseas.
To his immense credit, he forswore his control over me in this one
vital instance. As he had with all the Men Dancers who had either
enlisted or been drafted, Shawn refused to suggest what my response
to the examining board should be. He was, in his own nonjingoistic
way, a truly patriotic man. Loathing war with all his heart, he had
served nevertheless in 1917–18. He could not now, with integrity,
dissuade me from doing the same.

Our mutual influential friends were not hampered by similar
scruples. Their well-meaning offers to try to "save this young artist"
confused me. Some hinted that they could go through certain channels to reach politicos who would, in turn, arrange for me to be
assigned to a branch of the service where my "talent would be respected." Others urged me to speak out "the right word" that would
automatically ensure my exemption. Florence Reed lamented in her
beautiful baritone, "You must *tell* them, Barton! We need you *here!*"

I dreaded the thought of killing as much as I dreaded the
thought of being killed, but I resisted these pressures. I felt I could
not with dignity permit others, no matter how loving their advice, to
determine my life. Yet my own ability to determine it was weakened
by conflict. Hatred of all war had been part of my consciousness as
long as I could remember; as a child, I had been taught that one
must always obey the dictates of conscience, no matter what the
price. Now, as a man, I was convinced that the only honorable thing
to do was to become part of what had to happen. I could not see
myself, for the sake of a career, choosing to take the easy way out to
avoid the tremendous drama that was being enacted on the world
stage. On the immediate personal level, I recognized that, if I were
drafted, this would unquestionably be the path to complete freedom
from Ted. Disoriented and alone, I was forced at last to realize how
desperately I had come to rely on him to make all my decisions. And
with this realization, disorientation changed to panic.

I was rescued by a perceptive friend who had never been very
close to me or to Shawn, but who, observing my state, insisted that I
see a psychiatrist—and paid for the visit. Since I had never before
had any reason to seek therapy, I did not know what to expect. Once
seated in a plush office in front of a conventionally dressed, businesslike, youngish man, I wondered (as did the nuns in Byron's *Childe*

Harold) "when the ravishing would begin." The questions the doctor asked *were* a kind of ravishment. My answers had to be pulled inch by painful inch up out of my guts. In the end, those answers revealed to me exactly what had caused my serious confusion. When the doctor dismissed me at the close of the session, saying, "I believe you now know what you want to do," I did.

I reported to the draft board willingly and without bitterness. The only concession I made to my upbringing was a short, ill-advised, extemporaneous speech in which I declared that all war was madness, and I therefore considered myself a conscientious objector. On hearing this, the New York examiners decided they had had enough of me and transferred my "case" to Florida.

As far as I can recall, from the day I moved to the Farm in 1932 until the day I left New York to report to the Florida draft board in 1941, Ted and I had never been separated for a full twenty-four hours.

Miraculously, that draft board allowed me to complete my scheduled tour before I had to report for induction. In gratitude for this concession, I sent the presiding draft-board head a bottle of the best bourbon. I saw nothing unusual in thus expressing my appreciation for the unusual delay. However, Lucille Dean (who was then employed at the Court House and who was to marry Fred Hearn) later reported the consternation caused by my naive gesture. Her boss could not understand how I could present a gift to the man who was presumably condemning me to possible death. But I was simply thankful that my work had been deemed important enough to earn me a reprieve, no matter how brief. I set off with a lighter heart for Worcester, Massachusetts, and my break-in concert on October 21.

The night of October 22 at Boston's Jordan Hall marked my real solo debut. It was a tumultuous occasion. To my amazement, bouquets and wreaths were handed over the footlights at the end of the program. (I was to discover that some of these had gifts hidden in them.) As a final and incredible touch, two ushers staggered on stage, each carrying a basket of flowers as tall as I—a tribute from Mimi's mother, Mrs. Alyce Winslow. Ted had often told me tales of elaborate floral arrangements presented to the Denishawn Dancers in the orchidaceous Orient, but nothing like this had ever happened to me. I was so nonplussed, I could not move. Then, with a strength I did not know I still had after giving a two-hour concert of twelve dances, I lifted one basket on my right hand, the other on my left, and bowed to each, then to the audience. The house came down.

Throughout the tour, the critics were more than kind. From the *Boston Globe,* "Here today is one of America's great dancers. . . . [In

Funerailles] here was a maturity and at times a nobility of style remarkable in a young choreographer." The *Christian Science Monitor*
headlined its story BRILLIANT BARTON MUMAW; in my birthplace, the
Hazleton *Standard Sentinel* reviewer wrote that "The young artist revealed the flawless technique and warmth of interpretation which
has made him the outstanding male dancer in the field of the modern
dance in America today."

Ted replied with encouragement when I mailed him these clippings, but did not respond to those parts of my letters which stressed
how much I had changed—an admission I found easier to make in
writing than it had been during our last "talk out" before I left on
tour. At that time, I had only dared hint that my induction into the
army might serve as a clean and honorable break in our relationship.
Ted had listened with a cool smile that surprised me.

Now I was perturbed when he failed to reply to my first overt
attempts to explain my need for independence because my intuition
suggested that he might be planning to manipulate this crisis as he
had so many others in our lives. Faced with his refusal to acknowl-
edge my need, I could find no way to convince him that I had come
to see myself as a mirror-image, that in the months of preparation
for my concert the weight of his dynamic possessiveness had turned
me into a robot, that only after the disbanding of the men's group
had I become aware of the prison I had permitted to be built around
me for close to ten years.

Of course, I could not reveal, either, the warnings I had received (and ignored) from many mutual friends: Mimi Winslow,
who had predicted that I would never advance to fulfillment as a
dancer as long as I was "tied to Shawn"; darling La Meri, who ever
so diplomatically suggested that I had my own life to live; and even
wonderful Lillian Cox, whom both Ted and I considered our spiritual guide. This dear friend had once taken me for a long walk at the
Pillow, during which she intimated that when one becomes strong
enough, one breaks strangling bonds even at the cost of great tor-
ment and grief. I never, in all the years to come, told Ted of these
"disloyalties," even when I came to recognize how right those
friends had been.

As I continued to write to him from the tour, I could not bring
myself to be more explicit, especially when his letters emphasized his
tremendous pride in my work. Did he, though, protest too much?
Were his excessive expressions of pride tinged with envy of his
protégé, with regret for his own lost youth? Perhaps. But there was
not the slightest doubt that he felt genuine alarm for me on Decem-

ber 7, 1941. (On the night of the sixth, I had been feted into the dawn at an after-concert party in New Orleans. Since I slept through most of the following day, I was probably one of the last persons in the United States to learn of the attack on Pearl Harbor.) With the country now at war, my contracted tour concluded with a recital at Washington Irving High School in New York on April 18. After spending a troubled few days with Ted, then some time in the South with Mazie and Barton, May 22, 1942, saw me embarked upon my military destiny.

I blithely smiled into the camera for a local newspaperman when I climbed aboard the bus that was to carry me and sixteen other candidates into the war machine. I was sure that I would only be a civilian playacting as a soldier for a short time, that I would not be deflected from my chosen path by this brief charade, that I would remain untouched by the experience. Even after initiation into boot camp, I only came to my senses after I looked about me and saw to what an incredible extent lives were being profoundly changed. My companions were frightened and insecure beneath their expressions of raunchy humor, braggadocio, bitching, and cursing. Most of them had seldom been away from their birthplace. They could not even remember to take a toothbrush with them to the latrine because back home it had always been right there in the bathroom. Minor inconveniences and discomforts thoroughly upset these untraveled youngsters, compared to whom I was a man of the world. I was thankful that my touring experience had equipped me, far better than my fellow recruits, to take anything the army might decide to hand out. The regimentation, the hours crowded into filthy trains, the claustrophobic barracks living, the primitive plumbing, the uniform I wore as if it were just another costume, the inedible food (how many times I remembered Ted's indignant bellow, "This coffee tastes like slop!")—all differed little from life on the road. This gave me the confidence that I would survive my present tour of duty as I had those in the past, never suspecting how drastically my attitude would alter in the years ahead.

Camp Blanding was a bleak, hot processing assembly line along which we moved to bleak, hot training assembly lines. I was labeled "Entertainment Specialist 442" after the examining M.D. discovered I had "the heart of a mule," which seemed to be just what they were looking for. The psychiatrist neither asked me any leading questions nor probed beneath the surface of my psyche. Since these medical sessions were held in tents, everything had a circus sideshow quality that made what was happening to me unreal. It became real enough when I was suddenly ordered to report to Headquarters. I double-stepped in that direction on legs that began to tremble. What part of the sky was going to fall on my head? Of what had I been guilty? Or could it be, of all things, some kind of reprieve? It was. Ted had wangled an unheard-of early furlough for me. Acutely conscious of the many pairs of raised eyebrows in the Orderly Room, I accepted my pass, attempted a salute, and got the hell out of there as fast as I could stumble in my heavy G.I. boots. Repacking my duffelbag, I returned by hook and by crook to the Pillow. I had been in the Army only two days. I was apprehensive about Shawn's reception since, in my mind, our last parting was to have been final.

The staff welcomed me with open arms, as an excerpt from the diary of that season's dear cook and mother-confessor, Esther Miller, shows:

> May 25th.   Barton arrived—very handsome in his uniform, but the same reticent person and the same sweet smile.

Neither reticent nor sweet when Ted and I at last confronted one another in private. I protested his daring to invade even the Army in order to keep me at his beck and call, exclaiming that this assertion of his dominance over me was a perfect example of why I had to be free of him. He refused to believe that there was not "someone else" who had shattered our "divine love." To lure me from his nonexistent rival, he then proceeded to sound every chord we had composed together: the glories and hardships we had endured, the triumph of our emotional commitment, our common artistic achievements, our virtue in having maintained high personal standards, our responsibility to those who knew of our ideal love and took heart from its existence. It was a struggle to deny the melody of this siren song, "But," I said, "I had to . . ."

"For *whom* are you giving all this up?" Ted interrupted.

"There *is* no one!" I cried vehemently. I demanded that he believe me. I reminded him that I had never lied to him in my life. In vain.

He put on a performance that would have won him an Oscar; Shawn, the actor, was as formidable as Shawn, the dancer. His anger dissolved in tears. He was "heart stricken," he was "wounded in body and soul," I *must* "return" to him so that our relationship could flower into something even finer and stronger in the future we would share.

I gave up and gave in because I could find no words to convince him once and for all that his only rival was myself and my need to escape his influence. I also knew that he would not even consider any plan of continued association on a different level which would be acceptable to me. We had reached the impasse of a truce. For the rest of my furlough, we resumed our Pillow routine in an effort to lessen the hurt we had inflicted on one another. Esther recorded those days:

May 28th.   Barton and Shawn unpacked trunks of costumes.
May 30th.   Barton and I went out to a wonderful dinner.
May 31st.   I carried rocks for Barty who was building a rock edge
              along the road.
June 1st.   Shawn and Barty finished the rock edging.
June 2nd.   Barty left today—we all wanted to howl but managed
              to smile. Shawn and Fern drove him to N.Y.

When I received my regular leave in August, I again returned to the Berkshires. This time, I made the pilgrimage not in response to a summons but because, as an associate director of Jacob's Pillow, I felt an obligation to seize what might be my last opportunity for a long time to function in that capacity. Also, wily Ted had promised me a solo concert in the new Ted Shawn Theatre—which might be my last chance to dance for a long time.

In October 1941, after the option to buy the Pillow had not been taken up, a group of local dignitaries had met with Reginald Wright and Shawn to propose that a new, nonprofit, educational corporation be formed to buy the Pillow and put up a dance theatre in which visiting and resident artists could see their works properly presented and audiences could be comfortably seated. They asked Shawn if they could engage him as managing director of the school and the festivals for a minimum of five years. After he agreed, they applied for a charter which was granted by the Commonwealth of Massachusetts to the Jacob's Pillow Dance Festival. A Board of Directors was named, the members of which raised the funds to buy the property from Ted and construct the theatre that had already been designed by Joseph Franz, the architect of the Music Shed at Tanglewood.

Community pride in this project was shared by the many skilled neighborhood workmen who participated in the building. Warren Davis, a seventy-four-year-old Black woodsman, for example, felled one hundred great trees from which he hewed by hand the seven perfect and enormous beams that span the auditorium. Despite war priorities, Mr. Franz managed to assemble the materials needed to complete construction in time for the 1942 season. He even made with his own hands the cast-iron weathervane to be placed on the cupola of the theatre—an exultant figure shaped after a photograph of me in a step from my Bach Bourrée.

Esther Miller wrote of my latest visit:

Aug. 2nd.   La Meri left and Barton came. He looks wonderful.

Aug. 3rd.   Baked Barty a chocolate cake. Asadata and his boys arrived. Mac and his bride also arrived.

Aug. 5th.   Dress rehearsal tonight. Shawn and Barton's dances are
so beautiful.

I was now a featured performer, a member of the Board of
Directors, and a soldier in the United States Army. I no longer participated in the Pillow life that had included everyday domestic duties for Ted, yet I wrote a note one evening that read, "Dear Esther,
Shawn would like his tray at five minutes to eight tomorrow morning. Why five minutes, I do not know." Such is the power of devotion and habit!

Aug. 6th.   Jess came today—and what a day. We had no water in
the house. Rehearsal at 8, and a cocktail party and no water—a
real mess. Barty helped with the dishes.

Aug. 7th.   An evening to remember. Barton danced just for us and
Jess was here to play for him.

Aug. 8th.   This Sat. performances were all of Barton's dances.
They are all beautiful and effective.

I think I was inspired to new heights of dancing by my first
appearance in the magnificent theatre. I remembered that Ted had
prepared for its design by restudying Gilbert Murray's *Classical Tradition in Poetry*,* reading aloud one particularly moving passage:

"And there rose up the chorus of the chosen public umpires, nine in
all, and they made smooth the dancing ground and wide the meeting
place. And the herald brought the harp to Demodocus and he went
into the middle; and on either side of him rose youths in their prime,
skilled in dancing, and they beat the divine floor with their feet." It
is all intelligible enough except perhaps why the floor should be
called "divine." Perhaps it was divine in the sense of "inspired" or
"inspiring." Because when you came to that floor . . . you felt that
you were bound to dance. There was music in it or, as the Greeks
said, some divine power.

And so it came to be that the stage of the first theatre in modern
times that had ever been built especially for dance was constructed of
hard, splinterless maple laid over stout wooden beams, giving it a
resiliency that did, indeed, seem divine to those who danced upon it.

*Cambridge, Mass.: Harvard University Press, 1927, pp. 30-31.

Aug. 9th.   Gave Barty and Jess breakfast in the kitchen. They
dread to go back [to the army]. Cocktails in Shawn's room. The
kids [students] showed Shawn, Barton and me their show. It
was good and I am proud of them.

That night, on the eve of still another farewell, I was compelled
once again to raise the question with Ted of our future relationship.
He responded this time with pleading, tenderness, reason, and love.
I would, he promised, remain a member of the Pillow directorate as
long as the war lasted, while he, Shawn, would keep Jacob's Pillow
and my place in the dance world alive for my return. He did not
remind me of my indebtedness to him as man, as dancer, as teacher,
as lover. He did not need to. Beneath the scene we both knew he was
playing, I sensed a terrible and frightening sincerity. Perhaps without intent, Ted made me believe that he would die if I broke from
him with finality. Because of my terror of this, and because great
physical attraction still existed between us, I once again succumbed.
We sealed our private adieux with a pledge of absolute integrity, no
matter how long our separation might be.

Aug. 10th.   Barton left today and the sky wept, too. He belongs
here.

11

War and the Dancer

I was to keep my promise to Ted throughout my years of war service, not so much because, like Brutus, I was an honorable man as because I was thoroughly intimidated by the threat of army repercussions. If I remained true, it was not for lack of opportunity, even within the upper echelons of that very army I feared. Exemplary as my behavior was at all times, there were those who saw through my soldier disguise. I particularly remember an attractive, girlish grandmother who had opened her home and her heart to G.I.s and whom they, in turn, adored. She knew Shawn's work and always asked me for the latest news of him. Once, in the kindly accent of a southern belle, she murmured, "You really love him, don't you, Barton?" I was speechless for a moment, but so certain of this lady's regard for me that I managed to answer, "Yes, I do."

When Ted allowed the armed services to have me back again, I was posted by military train from Jacksonville, Florida, to Keesler Field at Biloxi, Mississippi. This fairly short journey took two nights and a day as our train was shunted onto sidings for hours to accommodate the regular passenger schedule. Not enough sleeping cars had been commandeered for the troops, so we had to cramp together two to a berth, sleeping in our uniforms. Fortunately, I had as my bunkmate a youngster fresh from the Iowa cornfields and unimaginative to boot, or I might have yielded to temptation despite the army's attitude toward such goings-on.

Keesler Field was a major unit of the Air Corps Technical Command. Its principal purpose was to train men in all phases of repair

161

and maintenance of Consolidated B-24 Liberator bombers. In my lowly rank of private, I had no time during basic training to draw a breath I could call my own. However, I did manage to incur the fateful resentment of another private. In the course of a physical training session, we were ordered to do as many situps as we could. When all the others dropped out, a contest developed between me and the one remaining rookie, a handsome, muscular young man whom I shall call Robbie. After I had managed to do a few more situps than he could, he flashed me a brilliant Mephistophelean smile with menace I failed to recognize.

There was nothing of Mephistopheles about the post Commanding Officer, Col. Robert E.M. Goolrick. He was an imposing Virginia gentleman, over six feet tall, broad of shoulder, with carved features finer than those of ordinary mortals. The fairness of his beautiful wife contrasted strikingly with his swarthy coloring. Marjorie Goolrick enjoyed her role as the Colonel's Lady, but she was determined not to let its demands cut her off from the world beyond our military boundaries. Well-read, informed on current art, theatre, and musical events, interested in the lives of the men on the base, she was a mellowing influence upon her austere husband.

When I later came to know the C.O. as a friend, I asked him how he maintained such a high level of morale among so many men. "First of all," he replied, "a well-fed soldier wins me half the battle. If he also has entertainment provided for his off-duty hours, the other half is almost won. These guys are living under unfamiliar, confining circumstances that make it difficult to train them. But I run my post in the belief that good food plus good entertainment will keep them as happy as possible." He had one naive P.R. officer who, in the cause of boosting morale, declared a "Find-Your-Buddy-Week." Except for writing of this to Ted, I had no one with whom I could share my secret laughter.

The weeks spent in basic training under the torrid sun of a Mississippi summer seemed endless. At midday on the drill field, men fainted right and left. In the unrelenting humidity of early autumn, we moved like automatons whenever we were free to stumble along the beaches by the Gulf's brown waters or under the pale violet moss that drifted down from the cypress trees. I felt like a character in Faulkner's miasmic-mythic Yoknapatawpha County, and it was in this state of mindlessness that I obeyed orders to report to Special Services. I had no idea what Special Services meant, but the classification sounded ominously like cloak-and-dagger operations, for which I had no talent and less appetite. What I was told instead realized a prediction that had been made earlier.

Just before I left Eustis to be inducted, sensible Mazie—who had never before evinced the slightest interest in the occult—surprised me by asking if I would consult a highly recommended palm reader who lived out in the boondocks. To please her, I agreed. When we entered the one-room shack, I was invited to sit before an imposing man who seemed carved, like Daniel Chester French's Lincoln, into a straight-backed chair with wide armrests. On the table in front of him he wordlessly dealt out some cards, then announced in a broad country accent that I was soon to go into the army. Since this was the fate hanging over the heads of young men all over the country, I was scarcely impressed by this bit of "divination." Then he took my hand, studied its palm, and stated, "You will be surrounded by machines and machinery, but you will be doing your own work." As I was on the verge of abandoning my own work to go into the service, this contradictory assertion made so little sense I promptly forgot it.

Special Services headquarters now informed me that I had been assigned to help entertain the many squadrons in the command—dancing for them! When the realization hit me that, surrounded by behemoth bombing machines, I would indeed be doing my own work, I conveyed my deepest apologies to the Florida fortune-teller by mental telepathy. I collected my gear and moved to my new quarters, where the sergeant welcomed me as if I were Nijinsky (although I doubt if he had ever heard of the great Vaslav). I was startled when he ventured to join the class I soon organized for my company.

Earlier on, I had had a crack at leading a class. The physical education instructor failed to show up one bright morning and I, as the handiest substitute, was given his assignment. I proceeded to lead the men in the kind of Shawn stretching and limbering that would prepare their bodies to move without risk of injury into the strenuous regulation exercises that would follow. After the session, I was called to report to the Captain, who wanted to know what the hell I thought I was supposed to have been doing. Didn't I know that not a single exercise I led had resembled anything in the training manual?

I explained that, because the men were roused from sound sleep, hurried out onto the grounds, and forced to do rigorous exercises without previous warmup, the great strain placed on their muscles could cause heart attack, hernia, or other complications. The Captain allowed as how sure, he knew that, but the Army did not. Besides, if a man was going to have a heart attack, better to have it in training than in combat! I was relieved of even temporary duty as a physical education instructor.

One of the men in the company was fellow dancer, Daniel Nagrin, who had also been rescued from the ranks to do his bit for post morale. He was very popular with the soldiers when he performed his down-to-earth kind of modern dances touched with elements of folk and jazz. But he was miserable at being separated from his wife, Helen Tamiris, and mine soon became a sympathetic shoulder upon which he could cry.

I must have possessed some unique quality that encouraged lonesome soldiers to confide their sorrows to me, for Danny's were not the only tears to dampen my G.I. shirt. I almost fell in love with one sad recruit. Years later, when he brought his wife to see me dance at Jacob's Pillow, I was so surprised to see him that, all unthinkingly, I embraced and kissed him. I never heard from him again.

The schedule assigned to our outfit of singers, dancers, comics, magicians, and musicians was tough. We regularly entertained every squadron, gave shows at the Officers' and Enlisted Men's Clubs, and performed in the enormous Field Theatre. It was heartening to work at a one-night-stand pace again, but because there was neither the time nor the opportunity to develop new dances, I felt as if I had slipped into the groove of a badly worn phonograph record. I was saved from utter boredom only by the challenge inherent in every appearance before an audience made up exclusively of soldiers. I knew perfectly well that my kind of dancing was outside the experience of almost every man watching me and, since we frequently performed on rickety platforms with no scenery or lighting, the exposure was bare in more than one sense. Unlike the other entertainers, with their more conventional acts, each time I stepped on stage, I drew a deep breath in anticipation of hearing the brutal sound of a collective raspberry. To my amazement, that ugly response to my performance was rare.

Perhaps I should have expected that Ted would inevitably come down to see me in Biloxi (he had often danced there with Ruth St. Denis and their company and later with the Men Dancers). Perhaps I should have resented this intrusion into my life, but I accepted it with equanimity and no little pleasure. As a visiting celebrity, Ted was entertained by the town's social leaders and I was invited to accompany him on every occasion. I even dined en famille with the Goolricks, not understanding why they immediately banished me to an upstairs bedroom if a member of the Colonel's staff happened to call while I was there: officers, I came to learn, did not associate socially with soldiers.

Marjorie Goolrick skirted this protocol as often and as skillfully as she could. Shortly after I arrived at the camp, and was still unaware of segregation by rank, I went to a dance for the G.I.s sponsored by the ladies of Biloxi. When I asked the hostess who "that beautiful woman" was, I was told she was the wife of the Commanding Officer. Although I had not yet been introduced to her, I promptly

asked Mrs. Goolrick to dance with me. She flicked a glance at her startled escort,
then said with an enchanting smile, "Of course!" We moved out onto the floor
together, and immediately became, as it is described in period novels, "the cynosure
of all eyes." From that moment, Mrs. G. and I began a friendship that developed
throughout the two years I was under Col. Goolrick's command.

When we staged our Army Air Corps extravaganza, *High Flight,* Shawn donated his services as choreographer and was so listed in the program, although he contributed only two numbers: I got together four of my dance-student soldiers, whom we shaped into a version of the Machine Section from the Men Dancers' *Labor Symphony.* I also transformed my old Mana-Zucca *Valse Brilliante* into a *Victory Waltz* by the simple addition of a rope of rhinestones that crossed my costume from shoulder to waist as a dazzling decoration.

I basked in reflected glory when I introduced Shawn to other members of the Special Services, including Robbie, the soldier I had bested in the situp competition. He had also been classified an entertainment specialist by virtue of his first-class musical training and angelic voice. We appeared on many programs together, swam together, had drinks together, rehearsed together, and were generally so compatible that I suspected he felt a physical attraction for me, even though I knew he was a husband and a father—a fact that never seemed to interfere with his compulsive womanizing. It was known all over the base that he came from a wealthy family with political clout in Washington, where Evalyn Walsh McLean (then owner of the Hope diamond) was his close friend. Since, in addition to having such high-and-mighty connections, Robbie was handsome, amusing, and a fine singer, he, too, became a favorite of Col. and Mrs. Goolrick.

With their unusual sensitivity for the welfare of their men, the C.O. and his wife had long regretted that there was no secluded place where a soldier could enjoy some privacy to greet or say good-bye to his family, wife, or friends. When Marjorie Goolrick mentioned the problem to Shawn, this architect *manqué* immediately suggested that they construct a special small building where emotions could be expressed without embarrassment. He further suggested that he would present concerts in and around Keesler Field to raise the money needed to put up such a structure. For added publicity, he insisted that I, as a "soldier-dancer," appear with him. Ted was not about to let go of me lightly.

With the enthusiastic support of the Women's Club of the Field, we evolved a program that must have been unique in the history of the United States Army as well as in the history of dance:

Star Ted Shawn and Corporal Barton Mumaw alternately presented solos, culminating in Ted's bring-down-the-house *Flamenco Dances*. We deliberately chose numbers that emphasized the ethnic and/or the muscular (my *Fetish* and *Mongolian Archer*, Ted's *Thunderbird* and *Mevlevi Dervish*), but also dared to present Shawn's *St. Francis* and my *Pierrot* (for which Robbie sang the accompanying aria from Korngold's *Die Tote Stadt*). This was hardly fare to offer appetites addicted to tap dancers and high-kicking chorus girls, yet the audience of soldiers, Biloxi civilians, and girl students at Gulf Park College ate it up. The admission charged was twenty-five cents for enlisted men and fifty cents for officers, but we raised enough money to build a charming Reception Cottage that was decorated by Mrs. G. herself. Above the fireplace, she hung a plaque that Ted had carved in wood to represent the Air Force symbol, complete with its motto, *Sustineo Alas* (which means "I sustain the wings," but which I always translated in my mind as "Alas for the carnage of war.")

In 1943, our outfit staged an Easter Parade show for the benefit of the Red Cross. I danced my *War and the Artist*, Danny Nagrin his *Finlandia* to the Sibelius music, and Robbie sang Bizet's *Agnus Dei*. At the postperformance party, I was puzzled that Robbie kept away from me. Ever since Ted's visits to the Field, with the resultant publicity from our program together, the bonhomie between Robbie and me had cooled. I failed to recognize the hurt-ego-at-work sign, thinking only that it was strange when he sometimes avoided me to the point of rudeness. He was granted an exceptional three-day pass to go to Washington soon after the show, and I had no reason to believe it was for any purpose other than to see his family.

Three days later, I—alone of my squadron—was told that I was being shipped overseas to join a combat unit, for which I had been given no training whatsoever. Ted was frantic when I phoned him the news. He at once called Col. Goolrick to demand that he right this terrible wrong, reminding him of the citation he had awarded me as Entertainment Specialist 442. The C.O. admitted that he was as astounded by the unusual orders as I was, but he informed Shawn sadly that they had come from such a "High Command," there was not a damned thing he could do about them. Ted raved about "Nazi tactics" and threatened to go to his own influential friends in Washington to have this "grave injustice" corrected.

Col. Goolrick held out no hope of success for this maneuver. The best he could do was immediately raise my rank to Staff Sergeant in an attempt to ease my way along the tough road he knew lay ahead. On every step of that road from Keesler Field to the embarcation point at Fort Dix, New Jersey, my weird classification, my lack of assignment to a definite battalion, and my puzzling destination were all questioned by every clerk and officer who examined my papers. As I zigzagged from repple-depple [replacement depot] to repple-depple, I stirred up waves of consternation in the bureaucratic soul of anyone who had to figure out what to do with me.

This zigzag course continued on the English transport that carried me across the Atlantic with hundreds of G.I.s. Only during KP duty one day did I realize why and how I happened to be on this overcrowded, foul-smelling little ship. Then I gagged on a fury against Robbie that was as powerful as the stench of the kippers I was cleaning. Throughout the long, miserable voyage I remained odd man out among a shipload of buddies who had trained together for months. Whenever I could squeeze through the mob on deck, I stood at the rails and stared at the horizon and raged bitterly against my fate.

After what seemed an eon, we docked one dawn in bombed Liverpool, where we disembarked to march over damp cobblestones to an unknown destination. As we absorbed our first sights, sounds, and smells of war, the shock muted our expletives to a muttered "Christ!" or "Dear God!"

I had barely settled into our Quonset barracks when my zigzag course resumed. As various commands tried to decide where to send a dancer who hardly knew how to hold a rifle, I was literally carted all around the west of England. At last, the C.O. of one base concluded that the only practical use to make of an Entertainment Specialist 442 was—as an entertainment specialist. When informed of this unexpectedly percipient decision, I thanked my lucky stars that I had had the foresight to disobey Stateside orders to leave all personal belongings ashore upon embarcation. As if I had been an experienced smuggler, I had sewn under the lining of my woolen G.I. overcoat some of my sheet music, a few illustrated souvenir programs, and press reviews of my concerts. Although I knew, even as I stitched away, that I was damned, I had refused to face the abyss before me without my true credentials. This unusual defiance of authority might now, I hoped, save my life.

Still shunted from base to base, I began to dance again under incredible conditions. At one camp, because there was no piano, I decided to present *Osage-Pawnee* done to drumbeats. I had neither drum nor costume, so I filched an empty one-gallon lard can from the mess kitchen and, turning it upside down, I taught my buddies how to do the beats with wooden hammer handles. Then I stole two

gunny sacks and put them together with safety pins to contrive a
costume that more or less covered the essentials. With red poster
paint smeared over my exposed body, I was ready to go on. Under
similar conditions, I painfully collected costumes one by one so that I
could perform more dances.

One day, my name appeared on a list of men to be shipped out
of England to no one knew where. I was appalled by the suspicion
that my evil genie was forcing me into the front lines, only to be
rescued from the blunder by a Lt. Winn. He had been looking for
new talent for his entertainment company when he spotted my name
on the list of those assigned overseas and issued orders for me to join
his outfit. Here I discovered that my fellow-entertainers were skeptical about how my numbers could be introduced into their long-run
show—a typical soldier production with comedy skits, pop songs,
lampoons of army life, a buck-and-winger, and G.I.s dressed as chorus girls kicking in a ragged line. They were proud of their little
revue's success and did not want it spoiled. To my amazement, they
asked me to audition for them. They assigned me a first-class pianist
and allowed me plenty of time to rehearse with him, but I danced
my solos with unusual apprehension. While the group consulted, I
changed from costume back into uniform to await their fateful decision. At last, their spokesman announced that they had voted unanimously for me to do my *War and the Artist.* I got such a lump in my
throat I could not speak for a full minute.

"Are you *sure?*"

"Yeah," the soldier replied," and we want the Indian dance
and that Cuban thing and those Negro spirituals, too."

Is it any wonder I lost my heart to Lt. Winn and his men?

By the time we had made a tour in Ireland and returned to
Britain, Shawn had made the lieutenant's acquaintance by correspondence and invited him and his wife to visit the Pillow after the
war. I was not told of this, but it was not long before my C.O. did
tell me something dire: Ted was pulling every possible string in
Washington to have me sent back to the States. As a result, Lt.
Winn's superior officer had ordered, "You tell Mumaw if he doesn't
see to it his friends at home stop their shenanigans, it will be the
worse for him." I was terrified by the implication of this warning—
and helpless and baffled—because I knew there was not a damned
thing I could do to control Shawn.

I cannot prove a connection between Ted's activities and my
subsequent removal from Winn's company, but shortly after I had
received my warning, I was sent out—with a baritone and a

pianist—on a tour of Air Force bases. I had thought that I had already danced under every possible circumstance. But no. Now I was condemned to perform in the middle of muddy football fields and stony parade grounds, in mess halls, tents, and Quonset huts. With lights in blacked-out buildings, without lights in the open. We only set foot in a real theatre on those rare times when we played cities near a field. Since the rule was that even a concert group like ours had to be assigned to a regular military company, I got to know several enlisted men. From their scuttlebutt, I learned that we were going to be shipped out in a few weeks. It seemed all too likely that Robbie would at last realize his aim for me, unless I could somehow again propitiate Fate.

One day, walking through a village with a soldier from our company, I saw a sign that advertised tea-leaf readings. I recalled the accuracy of my Florida seer and persuaded my companion to join me for a look into the cup of the future. The only prediction I heard the kindly English lady make was, "Your friend will be sent overseas. You will remain here." She was right. Because I was attached to the outfit under the special services "umbrella," not as a regular member, I remained in England when the others left.

In my relief at this second reprieve, I went through the routine of my days in a relaxed, almost childish mood—which is the only reason I can now imagine for participating in a plan concocted by sentimental Shawn to celebrate my birthday and Margerie Lyon's, which fell on the same date. He instructed us by mail to drink a toast to one another at the same moment on August 20. Knowing that midnight was the only time I might manage such a thing on the base, he calculated the exact corresponding hour in California (where Margerie was) and in Massachusetts (where he was) to ensure we three would be united in thought and action. Then, to be certain I had the proper drink with which to join them, he smuggled a medicine bottle full of brandy in a food package to me. I felt pretty foolish that night as I stumbled through the black and past the sentries, my little bottle in hand. Climbing to the top of a hill within the camp, I heard the drone of planes, then bombs exploding on nearby fiery London. Against this obscene background, I drank my toast to Margerie and Ted on the dot of twelve.

This was only one of many silly incidents that helped make tolerable an intolerable situation. When on leave in London, I was at one and the same time horrified by its destruction and exhilarated by its spirit. To attend a performance in a packed theatre—to hear Dame Myra Hess at a free luncheon concert in the National

Gallery—to learn that Margot Foneyn and Robert Helpmann were mounting new ballets—to read everywhere bright posters announcing the premiere of Benjamin Britten's opera, *Peter Grimes*,—all this absolutely stunned me. It was incredible to see cold, hungry, threadbare, threatened Londoners participating in every kind of cultural activity provided by a Government besieged by insuperable problems. Once, at the Old Vic, I was immersed in the production of a Shakespeare play even as I could hear the earthshaking V-2 bombs falling in a distant part of the city. During intermission, as I marveled to myself at how wonderfully the English stage and act their Bard's works, I realized that the handsome lady on my right was trying to catch my attention. I turned to her with a smile. She looked down at my sergeant's stripes and murmured, "One did not suppose you went in for this kind of thing in America." I felt my face redden at the apparent affront, but knew from experience this was really only another British attempt to be "friendly toward the Allied forces." I also knew it was not the moment to mention William Faversham or Edwin Booth.

Another time in London, I was bunked down in the unheated dormitory of a Red Cross hostelry on a night when bombs were falling too close for comfort. For the first time, I resorted to a practice I knew was well established among American soldiers billeted in barracks heated only by a small iron stove: when a man could no longer endure the cold, he would climb into the bunk of another so they might share not only their blankets but the heat of their bodies. This night, swaddled as I was in two sweaters pulled over my woolen underwear and two pairs of thick socks on my feet, I still shivered under my one thin blanket. In desperation, I finally rolled over to the cot next to mine, shook the shoulder of the soldier sleeping there, and begged, "Can I get in with you? I'm so *cold*." Without hesitation, the man raised his blanket and shifted to the far side of his narrow bed. "Right you are, mate," he mumbled in a cockney accent. "Climb in. Make yourself comfy." He turned his back to me and promptly resumed his snoring. He was gone when I awoke the next morning. We had never even seen one another's faces.

All adventures in culture, all amusing contretemps, came to a dead stop on June 5, 1944. I was ordered to dance as usual that night, knowing that the camp was on a four-hour alert. I did not know, of course, that the long-awaited invasion of France was about to begin. Sensing that it would be tasteless and futile to try to distract the men with a light-hearted work, I decided to do my *War and the Artist*. Mary Kinser's costume had been replaced by the ragged, filthy shirt and torn trousers of a front-line soldier, and a bloodied bandage was tied around my head. I feared my picture of delirium might cut too close to the emotions of real soldiers going into real battle, but I had no better homage to offer them.

In the blackout, I climbed up onto the twelve-by-sixteen-foot wooden platform that had been erected at one end of an enormous tent. As soon as I assumed my opening pose, the only permitted lighting flashed on: a single unshaded bulb hanging over center stage. At one side, my accompanist started the *Funerailles* music, playing on an upright piano with hammers worn of felt, and strings so rusted they emitted eerie, tinny tones. When I raised my head to begin the dance, I saw before me a mass of uniformed men that spread into the farthest shadows. They were squatting on gun crates, their rifles and helmets at their sides, their shapes grotesque with the bulk of combat equipment. As Liszt's melody resounded through the gloom with an off-key poignancy the composer could never have conceived, audience attention enveloped me like a fog through which I moved on legs as heavy as my heart. These men knew, and I knew, they were going to face death.

I ended the dance with one small gesture on one quiet note, collapsing into a distorted sitting position as I stared straight ahead. No applause. I got awkwardly to my feet, bowed my head to the men, and walked off. Then the grim silence was shattered by shouts and whistles and loud clapping that told me those men knew what I had tried to say.

I never afterward performed this solo without first dedicating it to those soldiers on the eve of D-Day, to Johnny Schubert, the youngest of the Men Dancers, and to an end of the cursed waste of war.

After that June night, everything that happened in "my" war was anticlimactic. I often felt like a clown as I continued to obey orders to dance despite the horrors and suspense, the victories and defeats of the next months. How much worse I would have felt had I known then that Johnny had been shot down over Germany, that Mac had been wounded, and that Jess had barely survived the Battle of the Bulge. Sometime in August, my morale got a sorely needed boost when I received a letter from Walter Terry, serving in Egypt:

> Just the other night I heard John Charles Thomas, on the radio, sing "Where'er You Walk," and I could just see you dance. [I had used this Handel music for the opening number of my solo concerts.] It was strange, in a way, for I didn't actually visualize the dance you did to that music, but rather your whole dance with *Bourrée, War and*

the Artist, Pierrot, Molpai, and Shawn's great works. Being away from it all and having a chance to look in retrospect, suddenly made me realize how truly great and cleansing has been Shawn's dance and yours and those who have come from him. As you know, some dances I haven't liked and you probably haven't either, but cumulatively the dance contribution has stood for the very best in America, has revealed our physical prowess, our spiritual heritage, our vision, and something that I can describe only as the clean freshness of the New World. Such dances being as they are distillations of America, are worth living and fighting for and I realized it deeply with the song "Where'er You Walk" sounding in my ears.

When I copied this to send in a letter to Shawn, I added:

Isn't that marvelous, Ted—to be able to see in your own life-time, as you are doing, the cumulative effect of your life's work? Not to many dancers has come that satisfaction which is beyond any personal success that can be achieved. I think it's very hard to gauge a dancer's effect on his own period for it is so evanescent a thing.

V-E Day found me in London on courier service from my base to an English installation. To be part of that great city's elation was to drown in a sea of joy and grief. But until the war with Japan also ended, the Americans in England faced the possibility of being shipped to the Pacific. Tension and discipline relaxed as we waited, at loose ends, to learn our fate. The Army, however—recalling the chaos after the 1918 Armistice, when thousands of doughboys went berserk as transport home was delayed—had plans to keep us occupied. In one of the many G.I. educational centers that sprang up, I was trained as a librarian. After that, I was sent to study acting at London's Central School of Dramatic Art. I was there on September 2, 1945, V-J Day.

Almost at once, like steam building in a pressure cooker, the demands of the G.I.s to be returned home rose above the danger point. Every available ship was commandeered for trans-Atlantic duty, loaded to the gunwales with wounded, weary, homesick men. But plenty of us remained behind to carp and curse and count the days until we, too, could sail. It was an interminable period of ennui and anxiety. Because the men in my outfit had the illusion that I might exert some pull back home on their behalf, they persuaded me—much against my better judgment—to fire off cables to John Martin of *The New York Times* and to Lucien Price of the *Boston Globe,* begging them to do anything in their power to secure our quick return. As the days dragged on with no response to my pleas, I knew that they would have no effect. Our turn would come when it came; that was all.

When it did come, we were not permitted to notify anyone Stateside. One day in January 1946, I ran up the gangplank of a Liberty ship headed for New York. Although there were no more U-boats to fear, we had all heard that these particular vessels had a penchant for splitting apart in mid-ocean. I, for one, made sure to keep my life belt always at hand throughout the long crossing.

In 1946, Shawn wrote to his Pillow friends:

> On the night of January 14th, I received a cable from a mutual friend in London that Barton Mumaw had sailed that day from England, for home and discharge. So I waited until he landed on January 25th. After four days at Ft. Dix, he joined me in New York, January 29th, a civilian again, after three years, eight months and eight days in the Army Air Forces.

My exit from Fort Dix duplicated the scene from a B movie in which a released criminal walks out of prison: the gates open; I emerge; there stands Ted awaiting me, erect as a four-star general, under his arm a cardboard box containing a suit of civvies for me. The only thing lacking was an offstage chorus singing Beethoven's *Ode to Joy.*

When we were alone in Shawn's hotel room (heightened by my indescribable euphoria at being safely home, my tremendous relief at being out of the army) our reunion was ecstatic. There was no sense of strangeness. There was simply the release of the long-held breath of our physical delight in one another. Ted had such a young, lean, and appetizing look that I teased him about the particularly invigorating solace he must have found during my absence. At this, he protested with infinite detail that the thousands of Jacob's Pillow problems had demanded their pounds of flesh. Faced with my skeptical smile, however, he finally confessed that the moment he had received the cable from the United Kingdom announcing the departure of my troop ship, he had put himself on a rigorous diet and a routine of strenuous exercises in order to look his best for me.

We spent several blissful days in New York, during which Ted went with me on a clothes-buying spree and filled me in on the events and the gossip I had missed while overseas. I also had two encounters that were so ironic I could never, in my wildest nightmares, have imagined them.

Long ago, I had confided to Ted my fear, while in the service, that the army might penetrate my "disguise." Now I could boast that I had acted my part so well that I had never been "unmasked." At a cocktail party one day, I ran into an ex-soldier named Bill whom I had known at Keesler Field. We greeted each other with the enthusiasm of the newly demobbed, and began to reminisce about the "old days." Bill was feeling no pain from all the drinks he had imbibed. In the middle of a rambling, semicoherent sentence, he suddenly grinned and stared me right in the eye.

"Hey, there, ol' buddy. I know all about you, ol' buddy Barton.'" He punched me on the arm with a friendly fist. "But *you* never knew, did ya, that when I was workin' in the C.O.'s office I read every fuckin' word you and Ted Shawn wrote to each other all the time you were at Keesler. You didn't know *that*, did you, ol' buddy?"

"Old buddy" sure as hell had not known. I felt my knees dissolve when I understood that, ever since I had declared myself a conscientious objector, I had been a soldier under surveillance.

Then I met my nemesis. I was taking a shortcut through Central Park one afternoon when I saw a man approaching me. He moved with a self-important stride that I immediately recognized. I stopped dead in his path. He kept walking toward me. Hesitated. Stopped. The sun was in my eyes. I saw that Robbie was not smiling. He blushed scarlet as he awaited my first move.

I was so full of sudden, murderous rage that I could have smashed his beautiful nose to a bloody pulp and stomped his beautiful body into the sidewalk. And, thanks entirely to this thing standing before me, I had been trained to do just that. My muscles remembered the power, my mind the conditioning, although I had escaped the necessity of having to kill another human being. Until now. Now I knew I was capable of doing so. Now I *wanted* to.

This realization paralyzed me. Robbie gave a great sigh. His fists, which he had raised to defend himself, fell to his sides. He began to sob. I watched him without a word. When he could speak, he muttered, "Let's go someplace where we can talk." I led him to the nearest bar. Shaken by the insight into my darkest self, I gulped my first brandy, then continued to drink while Robbie poured out the words he must have memorized to speak if ever we should meet.

He admitted that at Keesler his envy of me had arisen from an unrecognized personal frustration, an unfocused anger at his life. I had just happened to be the unfortunate target. After falling in love with another soldier and going through the hell of losing him, Robbie had at last learned the cause of his frustration. Had come to understand—why he had done what he had done to me.

One of the toughest things I ever did in my life was to sit there and listen to the guilt-ridden creature. I did not even revile him with the words I, too, had memorized for this encounter. How, having heard his story and putting myself in his place, could I not try to forgive, even if I could never forget, the harm he had done me?

I did not report these two extraordinary episodes to Ted because I did not want anything to mar his happiness. Supremely content to have me back under his control, he wrote to his friends:

> After some days of shopping and seeing friends, Barton and I went to Pittsfield, got our station wagon out of the shop where it had had a thorough job of face-lifting done, and drove on down here to Eustis.
>
> Barton's parents and I had decided that we just could not celebrate Christmas on December 25th without him, and this is one reason I sent no gifts or cards as we three tried to avoid doing anything that would indicate that Dec. 25th was any different from any other day. So on February 5th, when Barton entered his home again as a civilian, we had our Christmas—Christmas dinner, and the presents opened (still piled beneath the Christmas tree). That was "M-Day" at Maybar!

The fetters of security and love closed around my wrists.

12

(1946–1948)

The Bough Breaks

Ted lost no time getting me back on my dancing feet, as he wrote:

> There had been a demand for Barton to dance in Texas on the Jacob's Pillow benefit program. . . . Therefore, the day after we arrived here in Eustis I started to work "rehabilitating" him, hours of technical workouts in the studio every day since. And from the soreness of my own muscles, I think the process is going to be harder on me than on him! But he is dancing as beautifully as ever, and needs only to build up strength and endurance.
>
> [Ironically, as matters were to develop between us, he closed with a reference to the end of the war.] But peace is not a static thing, achieved by mere military victories. And in my own little way, I intend to dedicate myself from now on to making such contributions as I can to a real, lasting true peace—beginning in my own heart and relationships, believing that if each one does this . . . Peace will come for the whole world, to stay.

For my part, I was not so sure. The rehabilitation exercises were exhausting and disheartening. While waiting all those months in England to return home, there had been no opportunity to keep in condition. To start over again now was worse than if I were a raw beginner and, although I anticipated making the brief tour that Ted had arranged, I also dreaded it. I was happy that La Meri would join us to introduce her new "Gesture Songs": classic Hindu technique danced to occidental music. It was an honor to appear on the same stage with this delightful person and fine artist-dancer-scholar.

177

When the tour ended, we returned to the Pillow to start the usual work on the new season and the usual repairs of winter damage.; It was as if I had never been away.

As Ted reported in his Third Annual News Letter:*

> We were joined by one scholarship boy and for the first three weeks the three of us, mostly in pouring rain, worked from dawn until after dark 7 days a week. George Horn came up from Springfield weekends, and his help was invaluable. . . . The outside platform, in the "tea yard" had rotted and buckled until it was entirely unusable; this we tore up and carted away (in three days of ceaseless rain) and then with new stringers and heavy cedar planks, we built an entirely new platform. Also we doubled the size of the students' shower room and built cubicles for four new toilets.

With only a few more hands to help us, we then put up an eighteen-foot-high tower to support a water tank which, because of a drought, remained empty all summer. It was all too, too familiar, and somewhat joyless.

With other teachers, Ted taught his own classes, José Limón taught modern technique, and I was given the dubious pleasure of directing that division of the school we had decided to devote to returned G.I.s. Shawn had contracted to add opera to the summer's schedule, on the understanding that Margharita Wallmann would act as choreographer and director of the selections. But Wallmann ran into visa red tape that prevented her coming to the United States, so, in addition to all his other impresario responsibilities, Ted had to assume this one as well. (The appearance of the great singer-actress, Marie Powers, proved an unexpected bonus. Later famous for her performance as Madame Flora in Gian-Carlo Menotti's opera, *The Medium,* she and I were friends from the moment of our introduction until her untimely death.) By the end of this 1946 season, Shawn had lost twenty-three pounds and was closer to being seriously ill than I had ever seen him. "If Barton Mumaw had not been there to be Joshua to my Moses," he wrote, "I do not believe I would have lived through it all." Since he had fulfilled his five-year contract, he demanded that the Board of Directors grant him a sorely needed sabbatical year in which he might regain his health, and sanity.

---

*The News Letters appeared every year on February 22 from 1945 to 1971 and covered the events of the previous year.

It was during this hectic period that Del Arden, a singer in our entertainment unit at Keesler Field, visited me at the Pillow to ask if I would join him in a few New York recitals that, he hoped, would revive public interest in our names. I had so little free time that I could not leave the Pillow even for a dinner in town to discuss the idea with him. I assured Del I would give him my answer in the fall.

When I did have a chance to consider the plan, it seemed a good way to resume the career that war had interrupted. I was never bitter about this interruption: for the first time since I was eighteen, I had been compelled to move among "real" people out in the world beyond the tight little circle of concert dance. I had been thrust from that circle to encounter fear and to test my courage when faced with the possibility of death. I had known soldiers and civilians who were in misery and pain, stripped of all the accustomed comforts of living. I had been forced to escape from myself to share their suffering, and I was proud that I had earned their respect.

When I told Ted that I had decided to appear with Del, he at once offered to do anything he could to help. I worked at the chores of closing the Pillow, so that I might make my exit as soon as was decently and honorably possible, leaving Ted to finish up his business and bookkeeping duties. No matter how normal the relationship between us may have appeared to others, it had begun to ravel at the edges during the summer. We took a last walk together on a golden October afternoon and I remembered that epochal race we had run down the same path when I had been as young as my universe. Our voices came back through the cathedral arches of the trees, and our laughter—

"But you must never call me Ted in public!"

"Oh, no, 'Papa'!"

Now our dialogue rang a leaden bell as I explained as gently as I could that my concerts would mark a separation for us—that the old pattern no longer fit the new me—that I had to break from the routine of tour-Pillow-Florida which he seemed to take for granted I would be forever thankful to follow. Ted suspected Arden, of course, despite the evidence of his own senses that this suspicion was completely baseless. The frustration of knowing that he could not and would not understand what I was saying was unbearable. After we returned to the house, I put my arms around his upright, unyielding body to tell him without a word goodbye. But he knew. When I got into the car and drove down the road, I saw that, for some unaccountable reason, he was standing in the open door that led to the marble terrace we had built together. On his face I read an expression, not of farewell, but of "All right, if that's the way you want it. . . ."

Shawn returned to Eustis; I stayed in New York to rehearse with Del. Our nine concerts in Carnegie Recital Hall (where I had made my debut in a different era, a different world) were successful. I received excellent critical notices, and Ted, who had come up from Florida just to see me, reported to his friends, "He danced magnificently and had added depth, strength, maturity and richness. He created several new numbers, proving again that his superb genius as a dancer is matched by his power as a choreographer."

For the sake of my parents, I went home with Shawn to spend our first real December 25 Christmas in five years. In spite of the currents beneath the surface of the festivities, it was a happy, restful time. Inevitably, on the eve of my return to New York, I had to tell Ted once again that I could no longer remain with him. By now, we could both play out the ensuing scene as professionally as the Divine Sarah had enacted her many "farewell" performances: that did not make it any easier. Ted rejected all my cogent reasons, insisting that I was "abandoning" him for "another," protesting my "disloyalty" with tears. As before, nothing I said could convince him of his error. This time, however, I was sure that Ted knew the break was final. I returned to New York both relieved and heavyhearted for now I was truly adrift without my pilot to steer me into the next port.

I cannot remember how such an unlikely thing happened, but on February 1, 1947, Ted and I gave a joint concert of solos, under the auspices of the Baltimore Department of Recreation, in the city Art Museum. We enjoyed, as Ted put it, "unprecedented success." It was after this performance that he told me he had accepted an offer to lecture, teach, and perform in Australia for the coming season. When I asked him if he felt strong enough for an adventure that might prove strenuous and would last for months, he looked at me and sighed. "I am going there to forget," he replied and left the room.

I was so distressed by those words that I almost offered to go with him. Some time later, I had to subdue an ugly surge of guilt when I read that Shawn had written to a friend, "I feel that this trip to Australia will give me perspective; I will get far enough away to see the forest—and not just the immediate tree that I had bloodied my nose against!" I well knew I was that immediate tree.

I was bruised, too, even if by my own choice. I badly needed the comfort I found in a query from Helen Tamiris. She wanted me to be the principal dancer in an outdoor pageant she was staging for the Mormons' celebration of their settlement of Salt Lake City. Planned for this music-and-dance history was a spectacular Indian solo for me. With Alfred Drake as singing-acting star, the Salt Lake City Symphony Orchestra in the pit, and the famed Tabernacle Choir as chorus, the pageant proved to be an exciting experience, thanks in great part to Helen herself.

Tamiris—with her thick mane of reddish-gold hair, her strong features, her body that sang of well-being—was the picture of vigorous American womanhood. Her character was generous, enthusiastic, and vibrant. To me, her intense concern for man's physical state allied her to Isadora; her philosophic approach to dance spoke of Miss Ruth; her use of Indian, Negro, and folk themes seemed to derive from Shawn. She had won acclaim for her choreography of Irving Berlin's *Annie Get Your Gun*, which had opened while I was still overseas and in which her husband and my friend, Danny Nagrin, appeared as her lead dancer. From the very beginning of our association, I worked more easily with Tamiris than I had with Ted. I never doubted that I could do anything she asked of me, even during some weeks when I could only walk through rehearsals while I fought my old enemy, another kidney stone.

When the Utah pageant closed, Helen asked me if I would accept the role of Wild Horse* in the Mary Martin national company of *Annie Get Your Gun*, which was to start its tour in the fall. I agreed, confident that I would be approved by the producers and would emerge from the inevitable haggling with a decent contract. I was elated to have been given so quickly a sign that I had been right to decide to go it alone.

I needed to experience again the tension of performing regularly before an audience. Studio work and rehearsals, no matter how rigorous, cannot raise a dancer's endurance to concert pitch. (I was to discover how true this was in the early months on the road with *Annie*. I was so exhausted after every performance that I went straight from the theatre to my hotel room and stayed in bed until I either had to catch a train or do the next show. Yet my *Wild Horse* Indian solo was not inordinately long or tiring. It was, however, the one moment when I alone was responsible for what went on on stage, the one moment when I alone could register with the audience. The energy one expends in a two-hour recital has to be compressed into just a few minutes in a musical if a solo spot is to make its full impact. I must have met this challenge because, everywhere

*A full description appears in Part Two.

we played, my *Wild Horse* dance was singled out as a high point of the show.)

When I began rehearsing for *Annie,* I lived in a Lower East Side cold-water flat that I had rented with John Watts Stoakley III. John had been one of our pupils at the Pillow in the early days of the Men Dancers. He was a Virginia gentleman whose insistence on the use of his full name and number tended to keep one at arm's length. But he was a charming person, a talented decorator, and a painter who became a lifelong friend. When we discovered that we each needed a New York pied-à-terre from which to relaunch our respective careers after the war, we went apartment hunting together. In those days, any search for housing at a low rent was almost inevitably doomed to failure. John and I considered ourselves very lucky to find a hole-in-the-wall barely fit for human habitation. With my elbow grease and John's eye for picking secondhand furniture he could refurbish, it soon acquired a comfortable Southern air of aristocratic shabbiness. Since our rooms were directly over an outdoor fruit and vegetable market, they resounded with the cries of pushcart vendors and reeked of the odors of overripe greenstuff.

Although I now had a job I could respect, I was discovering the truth of the thesis that a slave, suddenly set free, is not prepared to cope with freedom. Without Ted's emotional support, his élan, and his ambitious planning, I wavered in my new direction even as I struggled toward it. The more firmly I carved my niche in *Annie Get Your Gun,* however, the more my dancing seemed like a routine that I could rationalize only as a sabbatical leave to ready myself for my real work.

Then my world changed, and I changed with it. I met John Christian. At twenty-four, he was beginning to make a name in the theatre for his set and costume designs, skills he had developed in the course of his work with John Fredericks, the famous millinery designer known as "The Hat Man." Christian had the head and physique of a Greek warrior in an ancient bas-relief. He had the magnetism that I had learned from Ted to value when the character within a perfect body was also perfect, as I quickly learned was true of Chris. In him, I found an irresistible combination of physical beauty and brains, of many abilities and much charm, of culture and common sense, of ambition and energy. I was swept off my feet for the first time since meeting Shawn. When I learned that the attraction was mutual, I felt unbelievably fortunate and a little humble.

I had never dreamed that I could love—and be loved by—

another person with the same force and fidelity Ted and I had known. Now I realized this was possible because it had happened. Now I knew how wrong were those who claimed that anyone who thinks he has loved more than once has simply never really loved at all. And now I knew how right Ted had been in the philosophy we had explored together and that had become mine: what is called "animality" and what is called "spirituality" exist simultaneously and co-equally in a loving sexual relationship because the prime satisfactions of human beings are to be found in sex, food, and shelter—in that order.

With the elation of shared emotions, Chris and I vied in exchanging confidences, expressing arcane ideas, and enjoying each other with such intensity that I was certain our feelings could never change. I was also enjoying my unfamiliar role as mentor to a younger love. Those days I flew uptown to rehearsals on winged feet, danced *Wild Horse* as it had never been danced before, and worked through the boring hours in a blissful, tireless trance until I was free to be with Chris again.

Immersed as I was in my new work and my new love, Ted's frequent letters from Australia jarred me like distant earthquake tremors. Each envelope bearing an exotic stamp reminded me of the guilt I felt for the pain I had caused him. I knew every word must have been as difficult for him to write as it was for me to read.

Sidney [sic] Australia, Sept. 18, 1947. . . . I was terribly ill when I got here. I have been ill one way or another ever since. I have been going through probably the worst ordeal emotionally of my whole life; and this has been the most strenuous tour of my life. . . . How I have lived through it is a miracle. . . . I must get some rest somewhere, somehow—even if my heart still goes on dying.

About "Annie" . . . It will give you money. . . . It will keep you out of my clutches (you *are* out, but apparently you still fear that). So it must be right. It was not my picture of what the great Barton Mumaw should do—but then my picture is no longer of value—it is Barton's own picture, only, that counts. You must have your own experiences and learn from them. . . . Now that I have made connection with the richest and most powerful firm in Australia, the idea of a tour here next year with a small company grows more solid. . . . Would you consider touring with me next year on *any* basis, or is it just completely *out*? Right now I know of no one else that I would care to bother about, if you turn it down. . . .

By the way, the Aborigine dance ceremonies I saw at Delissaville were, in themselves, well worth going half way round the world to see.

I recalled this statement some years later when I read *Adam in
Ochre** by the Australian writer, Colin Simpson. The author, address-
ing Mosek, a gardener at the Aboriginal Settlement, wrote:

"Mosek, you show that paper, what Mr. Shawn he write about
you." Mosek came out of his hut with a copy of *The Dance*, the American magazine, with an article by Ted Shawn. Mosek could not read
what Shawn had written. I read: "At Delissaville I have seen some of
the finest dancers in the world. This has been one of the most remarkable experiences of my life. . . . The individual quality of Mosek and Beeanamu put them in world class. They have the ability, to
an amazing degree, of expressing themselves with style and dignity
and projecting their personalities through the dance. This is found
only in great artists." Shawn, who had seen and studied dances
among the American Indians, in North Africa, in India, Tibet,
China, Japan and Java, added: "I can say without hesitation that, of
all the primitive dancing I have seen, the dancing I saw at Delissaville is the best."

[Ted's letter continued:]

If I return via the Pacific, I could see you, stopping off in San Francisco or Chicago for a week on the way back to N.Y. But I am not
letting that have any weight in my decision, especially since I have
had no expression from you yet that you would like to have me visit
you. I realize I must go on making my decisions on other lines—and
no longer with regard to you. Until or unless you make a decision
which rules me into your life in a vital and important way again. . . .
Suffice it to say that what I have for you is finer, richer, deeper than
ever, and it leaves you absolutely free. I would like to hear what you
have arrived at about me, but must be patient and let that come
when *you* feel impelled to put it into words.

[Later that same month, Ted wrote:]

Your last letter dated Aug. 16th from NY ended "Don't forget that
no matter what we are going through, you are always in my heart in
love and prayer—I know I am in yours. Nothing can destroy this
mutuality or whatever it is." Perhaps you don't realize it but this is
the first statement of anything like this since I left New York over five
months ago. You wanted, and I believe needed, to be "free." To free
you, I had to free myself. That has been done . . . I am honestly now

*Sydney & London: Angus and Robertson, 1951, pp. 171-72.

at a point where I cannot ever again be affected by what you do or do not do, as I have been in the past. I believe you will be making a tragic mistake if you, through will or perverted judgment, wipe out of our life the richness of our friendship, tried and tested through 16 long years of stress and strain. But if you do so, I will go on with a rich and happy life, knowing that as Emerson says, when the angel departs he makes room for an archangel to come in. I hope it will be the archangel in you that will replace the lesser Barton. . . . Obviously . . . since this separation was not of my choosing, but yours, I cannot make any positive move. I will go on about my life not counting on you in any way. Any more will have to come from you. . . . It can never be the same again, that we both know. But I believe it can be finer, freer, and more fulfilling, and all sense of limitation on both sides be dropped forever. If you are not up to that, then that is your problem. . . . Please feel honestly free from worry about me. I have fought my battle and won. Completely. If there is never again any close relationship between us, you will always be a very dear memory, and one with no bitterness in it. If you choose to avail yourself of my love for you in all its fullness, I will be happy—but my happiness no longer depends on your decision. This should be a great relief to you. . . .

If you feel association with me again, in a close and intimate personal and professional relationship, will hinder your growth and freedom, then you must decide according to your own lights, and I will respect that decision, and as I have said, without any resentment or bitterness. . . .

Well, my best beloved, fear not, and *be happy,* for you *are* free and I am free, and all is well. God governs the whole situation, and His will is being done. Yours, Ted.

I do not remember what I wrote in response to these pleas, explicit and implied. I walked a tightrope between rejecting Ted and raising his false hopes as I tried, across the miles, to keep us both on balance. I did promptly refuse the proposed Australian tour. As for Chris, I knew I would have to tell Ted, but certainly not by letter.

Despite the tug-of-war between old loyalty and new love, and the pain of being separated from Chris when I went on tour, my immediate work was enjoyable. After many years, I again had a crush on a girl—a big, colorful, vibrant gal named Annie Oakley. Producers Rodgers and Hammerstein had not stinted on the national road show; the costumes and scenery were, if anything, more lavish than those in the Broadway production. My *Wild Horse* headdress alone, they told me, cost more than a thousand dollars.

We opened in Dallas on October 3, 1947, and played across the

United States for months, eighteen of which I remained with the company. At the opening, the inhabitants of Mary Martin's hometown of Weatherford, Texas, turned out en masse to see their local girl make good. It seemed as if the population of the whole state, from the Governor on down, was there, too. I think that Mary, and other members of the cast, were surprised when I received an ovation on making my entrance. They may not have known that I had appeared in Dallas so many times, I had an audience of my own there. When the critics singled me out for special mention in their reviews the next day, that may also have been a surprise. Instead of being upset or jealous, however, Mary Martin went out of her way to congratulate me. I knew that many other stars would have had me removed from the cast, but such was not the style of this real show lady. Instead, she rearranged the conclusion of the comic "I'm an Indian, Too!" dance, in which she is initiated into the tribe. Originally, I exited to leave her alone on stage at the end of the number. Mary now set the ending with a pose that both of us held together for the applause. It was a rare and generous professional courtesy, which I have never forgotten. (Director Joshua Logan must have okayed this change. Since I was not an actor with lines, I had had little contact with him during rehearsals. On the train, en route to the Dallas opening, he passed me in the corridor and remarked, with a grin, "Barton Mumaw in a musical comedy? I don't believe it!")

Ted could not believe it either when he saw me in October. I had written to him in Sydney, offering the use of my apartment while I was on the road and assuring him that John Stoakley would be delighted to share his "digs" with such a famous man.

Shawn's version of the renting of this apartment is interesting in its distortion. He had written, in his Annual News Letter of February 1947:

Barton, John Stoakley and I took a "cold-water flat" here in New York which the two of them will keep on in my absence [in Australia] and which will be a pied-a-terre for me to come home to. [In his Letter of February 1948:] our "cold-water flat" here at 519 Second Avenue was a joy to come home to—Barton and John had made many improvements. . . .

Both letters bore the return address of my apartment.

Ted accepted my offer, writing that he would come to see me on his way East from San Francisco. In Kansas City, the company was staying at the Muehlbach Hotel, where the Men Dancers had also stayed, and nostalgia provided warmth that melted the self-conscious frost of my meeting with Ted. He seemed genuinely glad to see me and expressed his eagerness to attend the show that night. Much as I dreaded the prospect of telling him about Chris, I was happy to see him again. He looked fit, but tired, and for the first time I noticed definite signs of his age—the hair thinner and grayer, the lines more deeply carved in his face. Since he had always seemed eternally young to me, I found these signs startling. So, too, were the number of cigarettes he smoked and the number of cocktails he drank.

During the Denishawn era, no one, from Miss Ruth and Ted to the youngest member of the company, was allowed to drink or smoke at all. Shawn had acquired both habits, in a temperate way, during the course of the Ziegfeld Follies *tour, when his marital relationship with St. Denis had at last become untenable.*

Mary Martin, who had begun her theatrical life as a dancer, welcomed Shawn with open admiration, as did the rest of the company. After he had seen the performance, Ted—typically, compulsively—came backstage at once, got hold of the stage manager, and began to correct the lighting of my dance as he pointed out certain moments that were insufficiently emphasized. Blushing with embarrassment beneath my body paint, I stood by in my costume. For an outsider to presume to change the lighting plot of the original expert was like a Philistine daring to change the wording of the Ten Commandments. Oh, oh, I thought, this is one time, Ted, you have overstepped your authority. Then I heard the almighty stage manager ask, "Do you think so, Mr. Shawn? What do you suggest we do?" From Kansas City to the end of the tour, *Wild Horse* was danced in Ted's light—because our stage manager had worked Denishawn shows in former years, and Shawn was one of the few theatre gods from whom he would take a direction.

On the last night of Ted's brief stay, we joined Mary and her husband-manager, Richard Halliday, for an after-show supper in their hotel room. Since Ted was leaving early the next morning, I went with him to his room after the little party to say goodbye. I had postponed telling him about Chris because I had not wanted to spoil the pleasure he seemed to be having in our visit. But now I knew that the last possible honorable moment to speak had come.

I began by thanking him for stopping over on his way to New York. Before I could say another word, the genial companion of the past few days—the man I thought I knew better than myself—this friend of my heart changed into a giant of uncontrolled rage. The transformation was so unexpected that it took me several minutes to comprehend the words he was roaring.

A "friend" had written to Shawn in Australia about John Christian and Barton Mumaw.

I was so numbed by the cruelty of that act that for an instant I thought I would faint. Yet all the while I could hear Ted's voice, vibrant with the jealousy of an Othello, accusing me of deceit, hypocrisy, and disloyalty.

When I could speak, I begged him to listen to me. With a scream, he seized my shoulders and forced me backward across the bed. He choked my throat with iron hands, cutting off all breath. I stared up at him in agony and disbelief. He looked straight down into my staring eyes as I began to lose consciousness. Then suddenly he relaxed his grip. His expression deflated from fury into impotent bewilderment. He straightened, still looking down at me as he muttered, "I could have killed you . . . I could have killed . . ."

He stumbled to a chair and fell into it, his hands over his face. I lay gasping and swallowing, limp with the realization that he could, indeed, have killed me because I had not made a single automatic move to protect myself.

When I was finally able to get up, I went to a chair facing Ted's. There we sat through a long, terrible silence. At last, in a hoarse whisper, I tried to tell him how sad and angry I was that he had learned about Chris from another, when he was alone and so far from friends. How I had thought, by not writing him, only to spare him such solitary pain. How I had determined that I must be with him to tell him of my new love myself. How I hoped that, in spite of Chris and what had happened this night, we could remain friends.

Ted leaped to his feet in frenzy. "Don't you *dare* use that word to me! *You* have dragged friendship into the mire!" Then he loosed a tirade of such filth and profanity as I had never heard from him, or from anyone. In despair and disgust, I ran toward the door to escape. "Yes! Yes!" he screamed. "Get out! Get out!"

I kept running down the empty hall until I reached the elevators. There I stood, my forehead pressed against the wall. When I could control my nausea, my trembling, I put my hand on the elevator button. Before I could push it, I found myself turning compulsively back to the half-open door of Shawn's room. I closed it behind me to face the man who crouched beside the savaged bed, his head sunk between his shoulders, his eyes closed, unaware that I had returned.

"Ted," I began, "I cannot leave you like this. I cannot let you leave *me* like this." A stricken, aging Prometheus, he gave no sign that he had heard me. "You cannot let this be the end for us."

When I placed a hand on his shoulder, he moved away from me, sighing, "I suppose you are right. I will try. I will try to. . . ." I waited to hear what he might add, but he simply stared at the floor.

"Goodnight, then," I mumbled.

Ted looked up at me briefly, lowered his head, and answered, "Goodbye."

I knew I would struggle for years to obliterate this scene from my memory. I swore I would never speak of it to the one who had, in all innocence, been its cause. Chris wrote after the company had left Kansas City to tell me that he was fed up with his commercial job and planned to take a vacation before seeking another. Could he come see me when we played Chicago? This filled me with such joy that I almost succeeded in forgetting that I had had no word from Ted since his return to New York. I thought that I was healing from the emotional blows he had dealt me, and resolutely put him out of my mind in anticipation of seeing Chris again.

Meanwhile, my dance life went on. When we opened in Chicago, I wondered if my presence in the show would be noted by Claudia Cassidy, whose reviews of the Men Dancers concerts had always been perceptive. She was noted for demanding such high standards for "her" city that she kept a sharp eye on the quality of a road show to see if it measured up to the Broadway production. We were all relieved when she gave *Annie* a rave notice. As the only member of the company other than Mary Martin to be singled out, I was delighted to read, "The Indian ceremonial is considerably better because no less a dancer than Barton Mumaw is its star. He is brilliant at his job, but you should see him, too, when Miss Martin joins him. A dancer with a sense of humor belongs in this show." In the list of cast names at the head of her column, Miss Cassidy placed my name right after Mary's. This was a most unusual honor for one with no speaking part. The honor did not go unremarked. When I reported to the theatre for the next matinee, I was brought up abruptly at the stage door by a voice shouting for all to hear, "Hey! Who's the star of this show anyway?" Mary Martin was laughing as she commented on my "promotion."

The night that Chris arrived in Chicago to see the show, I experienced that very special thrill of performing for one particular person in the audience. He had never seen me dance on stage and, as Ted had long ago done his *Flamenco* just for me, so I now danced *Wild horse* just for Chris.

There were many exquisite firsts. We crossed sleety Michigan Boulevard to the Art Museum. There, I looked at paintings through Chris's discriminating eyes and we stood, quite overwhelmed, before Michelangelo's Dawn and Evening, Day and Night, copies though they were. We vowed that someday we would go to Florence to see the originals on the Medici tombs. Although the Windy City was at its wintry worst, we made a pilgrimage to the Field Museum to search out Malvina Hoffman's statue of the "Mongolian Archer" in the Hall of Man. Chris had yet to see the solo inspired by this work which Shawn had choreographed for me, but we hoped that someday he would.

On a more mundane level, we explored Marshall Field department store where, with uncharacteristic extravagance, I indulged myself in buying presents of cashmere and silk for Chris. (Money had never before meant anything to me except as a means of subsistence, of buying costumes, of helping Mazie and Barton when they needed help. Life with Shawn, on our meager income, had been Spartan, and our gifts to one another had nearly always, perforce, been utilitarian.) I discovered other pleasures I could give a loved one: our room in a fine hotel, with a view of the ice-rimmed lake— dinners at fine restaurants, always with a bottle of good wine— breakfasts of melting butter on hot potato-flour muffins, luscious strawberry jam, and pots of coffee whose rich flavor even Ted would have approved. For this frugal, hard-working Dutchman, the days were sybaritic—a Baudelairean episode of *"Luxe, calme, et volupté"* that opened sensuous vistas I had never imagined and knew I would never forget. I was desolate when Chris had to leave.

The monotonous tour went on. Everything was dull except for that one electrifying moment alone on stage each night (and twice a week on matinees). Otherwise, I only came to life when I held a letter from Chris in my hands. Then I got the first letter from Ted since our dreadful parting in Kansas City. He made no mention of that horror. Instead, he sent a sign which indicated, beyond anything I could have hoped, that we might some day be reconciled: after meeting him through John Stoakley, Shawn had asked Chris to be personal manager for his concerts and stage manager-designer for the upcoming Jacob's Pillow season. This fortuitous arrangement seemed to me a godsend for both of them. I posted a letter to Shawn at once, telling him that I knew how much he needed the help of someone with Chris's varied theatrical abilities. The letter to Chris in the same mail told him how glad I was that he had found such an invaluable opportunity to escape from the Broadway-Seventh Avenue rut. I added that I recognized his need to develop his talents to their fullest and that I wanted this for him more than anything in the world and would do anything I could to help him.

Chris detailed his new responsibilities in frequent letters, and Ted soon began reporting on the usual difficulties of scheduling the Pillow summer. I answered Chris with all the love and encouragement I could express. At the same time, I resumed my habitual scrawls* to Ted as if nothing had happened to interrupt them:

> . . . Thanks for your letter and circular which is a knockout. Chris is Genius #1—a beautiful job. . . . I am glad you feel the summer at J.P. is going to be *new* and fun this time and with so many *chores* off your shoulders and mind it should be.

> . . . Chris also wrote about his virus and said how wonderfully you'd nursed and taken care of him—how thrilled he is with your dancing—and seems generally pleased and enthusiastic . . . loved the Pillow and the Berkshires and even thot [my habitual spelling of this word] he'd be able to do a good job on the drums. So you see how wise you were, human and psychologically [to take on Chris as a working partner]. I am also pleased at the general tone of *your* letter and your refusal to worry and fret. There will always be these difficulties and you always deal with them very well. If you can cut out the wear and tear on yourself from worry or impatience I know it is all going to be much easier and you may *even* have some *fun* out of it.

> . . . Thanks for your letter from Eustis. So glad Chris could be with you. I'm sure it has made all the difference, bless him. How do the folks look? Dad's birthday is April 1st so look out. He's sure to pull an April Fool's trick on you, if I know him. And he is so innocent about it you *always* get fooled. . . . Now do have fun. Everything always works out as it should anyway. My heart sends love out and all good as always. It makes me happy to have you say your heart is happy, too.

> [Des Moines, Iowa] It was here we found the material for *Pierrot*, remember? I am going back to see if I can find it again. Faint hope but worth a try for nothing has been so good as that ever.

> . . . I *hadn't* realized it's over a year since you started to Australia and I'm very thankful that you feel as you do and that all is well between us. Our wishes and hopes for each other are the same, and fulfillment for one is by the other equally.

That spring, on his way north from Eustis where he and Ted had been working out plans and budgets and publicity for the upcoming Pillow season, Chris wrote that he could stop over and see me again, this time in Richmond, Virginia. I was overjoyed.

> Dear Ted, Thanks for your letter. I am anxiously awaiting Chris.

---

*These letters of mine survived because Shawn never threw anyting away. They were returned to me after his death, and, although they are all undated and mostly unlocated, excerpts from them give an accurate picture of my feelings then for Ted and for Chris.

. . . Thank you, dear Ted, for this visit with Chris. I love you for it and for all that you are as always.

This time, my visit with Chris had the added dimension of good talk about the hectic performing and managerial life with Shawn that I knew so well and that Chris was just learning. I was happy to see him looking so healthy, to detect new self-assurance in his bearing, and to sense the rapture he shared with me in our re-union. By now, however, I knew he found it difficult to come to a firm decision; I went out of my way to convince him that he was on the right path to his future. He left, with my blessings, to rejoin Shawn in the Berkshires.

It was wonderful to see Chris and he looks wonderful and tan and healthy and so healing. It's a great boom and joy and I know you rejoice with me. . . . Tons of love, and thanks for making this oasis possible.

On opening night of the 1948 season at the Pillow, I sent presents to Ted and to Chris with a telegram that read, HOPE YOUR SUMMER IS A GREAT SUCCESS AND A HAPPY ONE, MY DEAREST ONES. LOVE, BARTON.

As soon as Ted learned that I was to have a week's vacation from *Annie,* he wrote to ask if he could count on me to appear at the Pillow during that time. I accepted at once, so eager to be with Chris again after our months of separation that I would have gone there even without the chance to do my own dances once again. Through letters, Shawn and I began to plan my program. But the personal struggle—which I had thought resolved—persisted, and I responded to Ted's complaints with barely controlled resentment.

You confuse me. I thot you were happy and content, that we were at last friends again tho no longer lovers, and that you "go on loving me no matter how hatefully I behave to you" I don't get. For I haven't behaved hatefully toward you. I have spread your praises wherever I've been and whenever an opportunity occurs. My com-munications to you have been frequent and not on the basis of "if you write, I'll answer," as yours have been, for I don't operate on that basis. As a matter of fact it has been weeks since I've heard from Chris, and tho I miss the pleasure his letters give me, I know he is busy, and when he has an opportunity he'll write, but I don't con-sider our (i.e., Chris and my) relationship has been damaged. As a matter of fact the natural thing for me to conclude is that he's work-

ing so hard he doesn't have time, which I should take out on you in
resentment if I were inclined to behave hatefully toward you. Please
don't mention this last to Chris for I don't want him to write except
at his own compulsion. . . . You have a great dissatisfaction with me
and I wish you'd tell me what it is. . . .

There were the expected upsets during the Pillow season, after
one of which, a very distressed Shawn telephoned me in Chicago. I
answered the next day:

It was good to hear your voice and talk to you again. I'm sorry for
the "williwaw" but surely you know that it's going to happen.
Which doesn't make it any less difficult, I know. You ask *me* what is
the answer to Shawn? I don't know. I doubt if there is anyone who
loves and understands and values you more than I but I don't know
the answer. I don't think there needs to *be* one. You operate as you
have to operate and damned good operation it is, too, so don't fret
about it or doubt yourself.

You *are* an egomaniac for your Plan, for your Work, for your
Ideals, for your Vision, else all would be swallowed up by the great
levelling forces that are against these Great Things. I sometimes
think that your will and force and fighting for these things defeat
your purpose to some extent, for if people don't *"get"* you, you often
don't *"get"* them but that is universally true. . . . Often you will not
deal with people in the way they *wish* to be dealt with. You say "Well,
there's no reason why I should. We made an agreement, a contract,
and I expect *him* to live up to it as *I* do." But is the important thing to
get him to live up to his contract, or to get the thing accomplished? I
don't know. There are all sorts of values involved. Knowing you and
the Pillow, there is nothing I would give you but praise. It probably
can be run in a different way, but not by you. You do a magnificent
job. The head of any institution, if he *is* the governing power, has all
your problems except that yours are *dynamite* since you deal with
dance and adolescence and general screwiness.

I know this is the season when you say "I'm doing my best but
I guess I'm not fit for the job." Pish and twaddle! You're brilliantly
successful and the overtones prove it, not the cacophony at the cen-
tre. With much love, Barton.

In a better mood, Ted wrote of plans for the coming year and of
how much he was beginning to count on the support and help Chris
was giving him; to which I replied:

I am so glad for Chris and for you. I know his effect, and how I miss

it! How long can this separation go on? I try not to think of it or the
future for it looks as if he'll be all season with you next year, and for
that, if we *have* to be separated, I couldn't be happier. But I don't like
it at all, at all.

With my program planned, it only remained for me to get my
vacation release date from *Annie*. Whereupon, I at once wired Ted:
HAVE LEAVE TO BE WITH YOU WEEK OF SEPTEMBER FIFTH SENDING MU-
SIC AIR MAIL LOVE BARTON.

As that date neared, I wrote to Ted:

> I'll leave our living arrangement at the Pillow to you. I *was* thinking
> of you, but please arrange it as you think best for all of us. [And
> later:] How smart you are! I thot I had to go thru N.Y. to get to the
> Farm but the same train stops at Pittsfield on the *way* to N.Y. So I
> arrive Pittsfield 5:25 Daylight on Sunday the 5th and I can leave
> from Pittsfield the next Sunday afternoon (September 12th).

As I stepped off the train, I saw Chris standing before me in
white shirt and jeans, tanned as he had never been before, his magnetic presence blotting out everything else around me as I took his
outstretched hand in both of mine. When my sight returned to normal, I saw Ted. Although I well knew that the season's wear-and-
tear could take a toll, I was distressed by his appearance. He was not
only haggard, but preoccupied and tense. The visible strain might, I
thought, be caused by this first meeting of the three of us because I,
too, was tense. To put us all more at ease, Chris maintained a flow of
chatter while he carried my bags to the waiting car.

At the Pillow, I was greeted by the beloved sounds of pianos
and teaching voices, the scents of pine and perspiration, the sights of
young men and girls in leotards, moving from studio to studio—all
those integral elements of my environment for so many years. Even
my old room in the house, where a pair of twin beds had replaced
the huge burl-walnut one I remembered, revived nostalgic memories.

Drinks and dinner followed the familiar routine as I shared with
Ted, Chris and old Pillow friends the same table in the dining room
that the Men Dancers had built. Shortly after dinner, I rose to retire
early, pleading weariness from my long train journey. Ted and Chris
followed me into the hall, where I overheard a whispered, "You *must*
tell him." I sighed. I was in no mood to listen to a recital of Pillow
programming disasters or another tale of woe about the plumbing.

To avoid this, I quickly said goodnight to Ted at the door of my room and, as Chris entered, began to undress at once, hoping to forestall the saga of distress he had been instructed to relate to me. He placed his hands on my shoulders and I turned swiftly, eagerly to him just as he started to speak.

There must be a split second when the one to be executed hears the slashing descent of the guillotine's blade. That is what I heard in the words, "There is something I have to say to you."

What Chris then told me would have long been obvious to anyone but an idealist as blind as I. While my eyes were being opened, I stood totally unfeeling, as if my head had indeed been severed from my body. Then I said, "All right, Chris. I have to give a performance tomorrow. I have to go to sleep now." Incredibly, I did sleep.

The next morning, I went through class. That afternoon, I went through dress rehearsal in the theatre under Ted's direction. From the stage, I interrupted a dance in progress to announce in a loud, firm voice that I would not do *Pierrot* as programmed. Jess Meeker, at the piano, flashed me a startled, worried look, but Shawn calmly suggested a substitute solo.

In the dressing room that night before the concert, the anesthesia of shock suddenly wore off. I started to cry. Strangers and friends alike stared while I sobbed through the company warmup, caring neither that they saw my grief nor what they made of it. The instant I stepped into the spotlight for my first dance, the tears stopped. After the bows and throughout my costume changes, I wept again. So it went through the entire program. Back alone in my bedroom afterward, the weeping never ceased until, around dawn, exhaustion brought my *noche triste* to an end.

As the remaining days passed—for of course I would not run away and thereby disrupt a Pillow schedule—I came to know that Chris's deception would leave a permanent scar. I faced the truth that Ted's perfidy was a blow to the solar plexus from which I would never recover. Still, I had to know the "*why*". It was Chris alone I questioned, when at last I found the strength and courage.

"*How?*" I demanded. Chris explained the first meeting: as soon as Ted had reached New York from Kansas City, he had insisted that John Stoakley arrange the introduction.

"*When?*" Last winter.

"*Before* you came out to visit me in Chicago?" Yes.

"*While* you came to stay with me in Richmond?" Yes.

"*Where?*" I insisted, adding intolerable pain to intolerable pain. "In *my* apartment?" Yes. "In *my* studio at Eustis?" Yes. "In *my* room at the Pillow?" Yes! Yes! *Yes!*

I was bludgeoned by the cruelty and stunned by the failure of this beautiful person to live up to the ideals I had assumed we shared, even as Ted and I had shared them. This realization inflicted the deepest hurt of all. Shawn was the man who had told me, "Our kind of love must be lived on a higher plane than the other or it sinks to a lower level." Shawn was the man who had proudly proclaimed to press representatives at Keesler Field that "Mumaw is my right arm—my right leg!" Shawn was also the man, I remembered with the sting of alum in my mouth, who had once exclaimed with a laugh, "Oh, Barton, you can be so damned dumb sometimes!"

Well, appalled by twin duplicity, Barton was no longer "dumb." "Gullible" Barton, experiencing his first shattered illusions, now knew he had not been loved by Chris as deeply as he had believed. "Sheltered" Barton fought the cynical suspicion that Shawn had taken Chris from him—not out of love, but out of deliberate vengeance. If this were true, it could only mean that Ted still loved *me*.

I could not face the implication of that insight, but I knew the situation had to be resolved. The day before I left the Pillow, I told Chris, in Ted's presence, that he must decide immediately which of us he chose to stay with. Shawn and I stood in front of him like duelists poised back to back. Then, as if advancing the prescribed number of paces away from one another, we went upstairs, each to his own room. At our separate windows, we looked down on the road in front of the house where Chris, with long, stumbling strides, walked back and forth, back and forth, his head bent to avoid our watching eyes. The longer he took to return with his decision, the more certain I was of what I had known it would be. He needed someone who could help him in his career far better than I could, and this would outweigh whatever feelings he still had for me.

While I was packing the next morning, a former associate at the school asked if I would dance something for her that she could film with her movie camera. I put on my leotard and went down into the sunlight that filled the old barn studio. There, drained of all emotions except those I could express through physical movement, I danced full out as never before—improvising, losing myself in a release of self-pity and sorrow, a release I had to have to see me through the rest of the day.

That afternoon, Ted insisted upon holding one of his therapeutic "talk outs." In the formal Victorian house parlor—before the very fireplace where Ted and I had once slept in blankets on the floor—Shawn and Chris and I sat and discussed matters like gentlemen taking tea together. I tried to be as generous in defeat as Ted was in victory, saying I hoped they would both be happy, that I would make a real effort to think of them as my friends. Shawn responded by calling my attitude "saintly," "heroic," and declaring that I had thereby placed upon him and Chris "a duty to conduct our love on a plane commensurate with your nobility." I lacked the energy to beg Ted not to endanger his new relationship in this manner. Chris said nothing. I walked out of the room.

The two of them later drove me to the station, where I caught the train headed toward that inevitable moment when anger, like lava, would erupt through the crust of pain.

Barton Mumaw posing for a Shawn wood sculpture, Eustis, Florida, 1946.

Below: Bas-relief wood sculpture of Barton Mumaw by Ted Shawn, 1946.

Barton Mumaw removing *Wild Horse* body paint in a tin tub during South African tour of *Annie Get Your Gun,* 1950.

John Christian.

Barton Mumaw with his parents, twenty-fifth anniversary reunion of the Men Dancers, Jacob's Pillow, 1957.

Barton Mumaw wearing wreath of dollar bills presented to him by the cast at his final performance after five years with *My Fair Lady.*

Barton Mumaw with Hanya Holm, choreographer of *My Fair Lady,* on a New York street.

Ruth St. Denis and Ted Shawn in their final duet, *Siddhas of the Upper Air,* Jacob's Pillow, Golden Wedding Anniversary, August 14, 1964.

Barton Mumaw and Ted Shawn teaching during the last season before Shawn's death, Jacob's Pillow, summer 1971.

Reunion of the "Class of '31" during Ted Shawn's last season, Jacob's Pillow, 1971. L to R: Barton Mumaw, Mary Campbell, Ted Shawn, Jack Cole.

Last studio portrait of Ted Shawn, 1971.

Last photograph of Ruth St. Denis, eighty-nine years old, 1968.

Last photograph taken
of Barton Mumaw and
Ted Shawn together,
August 1971, following
Shawn's address to the
Dance Masters of
America convention.

Above: Barton Mumaw, wearing Shawn's original skirt, in *Mevlevi Dervish*, taken during performance at Jacob's Pillow on a memorial program to Ted Shawn, 1972.

Below: Ted Shawn in *Mevlevi Dervish*, choreographed in 1929. Program note read, "270 revolutions in 4½ minutes are made within a space 12 inches in diameter."

Barton Mumaw in performance at Jacob's Pillow during the season dedicated to the memory of Ted Shawn, 1972.

Above: In Shawn's *Negro Spirituals.*

Upper left: In Shawn's *Divine Idiot.*

Left: In Shawn's *Four American Dances.*

Barton Mumaw in Ted Shawn's study of St. Francis: *O Brother Sun and Sister Moon,* taken in performance at Jacob's Pillow, August 20, 1981.

Above: Members of the Men Dancers after a cold, hard day's work on the Farm (Jacob's Pillow), fall 1934. L to R: Ned Coupland, Wilbur McCormack, Fred Hearn, Frank Overlees, George Horn, William Howell, Dennis Landers, Barton Mumaw, Foster Fitz-Simons.

Below: At the rock that is Jacob's Pillow, reunion of the Men Dancers to celebrate their fiftieth anniversary, August 7, 1982. L to R (front): Frank Overlees, Foster Fitz-Simons, Barton Mumaw, Wilbur McCormack, Fred Hearn, John Delmar. L to R (back): Frank Delmar, Jess Meeker.

Above: Barton Mumaw demonstrating for students during "Denishawn Week," April, 1984, at The Forida State University, Tallahassee.

Below: Nancy Smith Award plaque to Barton Mumaw, June 1984.

13

New Worlds to Conquer

I had hoped and prayed that anger would cauterize my wounds—but no. Once the bomb of rage had exploded within me (of course, a Mumaw does not allow his emotions to "show"), I was left with the war between my jealous, bitter self and the understanding, forgiving self I most earnestly wanted to be. I could not know if that war would end in victory or defeat for the better Barton, but I did know that I would have to keep fighting it for a long, long time. For a first victory, I determined that *I* would not be the one to cut off contact with Ted and Chris, no matter how high the price of continuing it. As soon as I rejoined the *Annie* company, I wired Shawn to let him know that I was safe and well.

I was welcomed back by the cast with a heartiness that soothed my bruised psyche. In *Wild Horse,* I expressed the hostility for which I could find no other outlet. One night, after the show, Ted telephoned. I wrote an answer the following day.

> It was good of you to call me. It helped a bleak return to be less devastating, and it was good to hear Chris. . . . Of course I feel nothing about the future except dread at the moment, so I guess it's lucky I have a job and one that has become pretty much routine. . . . Now the cord is cut between us I hope you don't tie it to Chris. I noticed a change in him that I don't think was due entirely to the situation. There was less Chris and more Shawn which is, I suppose, inevitable when two people are so close but it showed, I think, domination. Or would you like me to shut up and leave you alone? Pray for me. Your Barton.

So the correspondence between Shawn and me resumed, but on a different level as we compulsively explored new areas of feelings.

> Dear Ted, I won't go into anything for it couldn't be pleasant for you to go on dragging out this emotional thing. I want to tell you that I have asked Mary Kinser not to indicate to Mother and Dad anything about this, for much as they love you and your home is there in Eustis it couldn't but make it a bit unpleasant for all concerned, which is needless. . . . Don't be proud of me as a person but I am happy if you are proud of me as a dancer for the rose-colored glasses must be off by now, as you have said, and I have always admired your judgment of dancers and dances because you have always seemed able to be impersonal about them no matter your relationship to the person or work involved.
>
> If writing me or me to you at this time is too much, say the word. Unlike you, I believe there are times when silence should reign. . . . But there is also physical love involved in this and you might find it easier not to have to write or hear from me. For me it's as hard one way as the other for the same reasons, so please do what is right for you. . . . With love, Barton.

The struggle between the good and evil in me continued through weeks of touring made bearable only by the support of compassionate friends. On October 21, 1948, I sent Ted a gift with a card reading, "Happy Birthday to you—and to 519 [Second Avenue]. With love, Barton."

Shawn's letters stressed the financial plight of the Pillow, after the final summer accounting, and the consequent uncertainty of his plans. I responded:

> I'd like to say that while I haven't got *much* money in the bank, it is enough for an emergency use for you and/or Chris or me and it is yours to use at any time. I don't know how much longer I can *stick* Annie and (rather than make a gift to the Pillow) I'd prefer to have some protection for the three of us. I have every confidence in your tour as an artistic success but we both know what can happen to dates and expenses, etc. If I suddenly need money I shall not hesitate to come to you, as I never have. Please do me the same honour.
>
> Thank you a thousand times for the Leo pin and your message. I fall very short of being brave and kingly, but it's nice of you to say so! You ask why you are always in your present financial situation. It's because, dear Ted, and bless you, you will not lower your standards. Many people will pay heavily for entertainment but few peo-

ple will pay even moderately for Art. You could have a hell of a successful commercial dancing school if you wanted it. So what? You'd hate it—you'd never even *start* it.

I don't want you to doubt true values. I don't think you do really, but you do think there ought to be *enough* response to relieve you of having to fight so hard. Believe me I think so, too, and wish it were so. It is *possible,* I'm sure, but the odds are against us. At least you are doing what you want to do and I guess for that there is a price. I'm not, really, and still there is a price. . . .

Haven't heard from you yet about whether it's easier for you to write or not write. I'll do whatever is easiest for you. Horrible exhaustion has set in for I've been going pretty much on nerves and tension so I'm relieved to some extent that it has broken. You are not to worry about me. I know you both love me and that means everything. Barton.

[A year after our infamous scene, I wrote:] Dear Ted, I couldn't write from Kansas City as I'm sure you will understand. . . . *Underneath all,* dear Ted, is my wish for your happiness, and for Chris's. Do not doubt this or me, or "handle" it. There are things I do not understand and may never but I don't *need* to or want to.

[As the endless winter warmed toward spring, I was still trying to find my path.] I'm in a very strange position. To you as my friend I want to pour my heart out but to you as Chris's lover it would not be fair. So while I would like to talk it out I think it is better to talk about it very little for it is now after all my own problem to work out and be glad that you and Chris are happy. Which I am—and thankful for, too—and our very special friendship of the three of us will come to be, I'm sure. What life holds for me I'm sure I don't know and am beyond caring at the moment but that, too, I must pass thru. Love, Barton.

What life held for me was a cable from South Africa, asking if I would repeat my role as Wild Horse in a company that was forming there. Just as Ted had seized upon his Australian tour in order "to forget," I seized upon this God-given opportunity. I gave ample notice to my American *Annie* because I wanted sufficient time to rehearse my understudy. I left for New York only when I was convinced that he could give a creditable performance. I found, to my surprise, that I was leaving with some reluctance: the "known" had been my security and I had become very fond of the members of the cast. They must have reciprocated because they gave me a farewell present of a beautiful Mark Cross leather attaché-makeup case, inside the cover of which was affixed a small silver plaque bearing the words, "To Barton from his friends in *Annie.* 1949."

Ted did not see me off when I sailed on my spick-and-span,
first-class passenger freighter, but he sent me a large *bon voyage* basket
of fruit and flowers that filled my cabin more with bitterness than
fragrance. There were only sixteen passengers on board, most of
them missionaries going out to Africa. On one of the early nights at
sea, as I stood at the deck's rail gloomily contemplating the black,
oily waves, a ship's officer joined me with the opening remark, "I
enjoyed reading the pamphlet you distributed."

"*What* pamphlet?"

"Oh, aren't you one of the missionary fellers?"

"Lord, *no!*" The idea was so hilarious that I laughed aloud for
the first time in weeks.

"Well, thank God! Come and have a drink, then."

The missionaries were, however, very friendly. The purser and
I even persuaded a few of them to play bridge with us. These innocent pursuits—and the fresh salt air, excellent food, freedom from
the stress of performing—proved to be the best medicine any doctor
or psychiatrist could have prescribed for me. Every morning of the
three-week crossing, I did my daily one or two dozen on the topmost
open deck. Once, I overconfidently challenged the Chief Engineer to
a wrestling match, which he won hands down. As I was soon to
discover, South Africans are mightily sports-minded, mightily concerned with physical fitness.

Near the end of the voyage, I was beginning truly to *think* and
to *feel* the way I believed I ought. In my compulsive pondering of
whys and wherefores while walking the deck alone, I was brought up
sharp by the realization of an uncanny parallel between Shawn's life
and my own: he and Miss Ruth had been married seventeen years
before they broke up over a man whom they both loved; Ted and I
had been together seventeen years before we broke up over a man
whom we both loved. Another time, in the ship's library, I felt impelled to leaf through a certain book until I came upon a poem by
Yeats that I had never read before. Although written in another context, it spoke directly to me:

TO A FRIEND WHOSE WORK
HAS COME TO NOTHING

Now all the truth is out,
Be secret and take defeat
From any brazen throat,
For how can you compete,
Being honour bred, with one

Who, were it proved he lies,
Were neither shamed in his own
Nor in his neighbor's eyes?
Bred to a harder thing
Than Triumph, turn away
And like a laughing string
Whereon mad fingers play
Amid a place of stone,
Be secret and exult,
Because of all things known
That is most difficult.

I felt rearmed in spirit and refreshed in body by the time we reached the great blue Capetown bay. When I disembarked on wobbly legs, I was greeted with genuine warmth by members of the *Annie* company and the director of African Theatres, Ltd. He almost immediately informed me that, not only was I to dance, I was to be the director-without-portfolio of the entire production! I accepted this challenge of a new world to conquer with an outward display of confidence because I really did know the show backward and forward. But before the actual staging work began, I suffered more than a few moments of nervousness at the prospect of assuming such a responsibility.

Once settled in a large and lovely hotel room, I was taken to His Majesty's Theatre where *Annie* would be playing. There, I was shown my equally large and lovely dressing room (I suppressed a grin, remembering the dingy cells of Men Dancers days). I dropped my attaché case on the dressing table to follow the director on a tour of the excellent stage facilities. When we returned to my room, my treasured case had disappeared. The director commiserated with me, advising me that theft was a usual occurence and, at the same time, giving me the distinct impression that it was my fault for having left the case unguarded.

Within my first few hours in South Africa, I thus experienced not only the impact of a different professional status but of a different society—one in which I would learn not to blame a local have-not for snatching at a crumb. Coming as I did from a land where beauty is rarely a top governmental priority, I was entranced by the local coins, which bore exquisite low bas-reliefs of the most exotic animals on earth. The obverse, I soon discovered, represented a nation that held captive its human native life by means of a subtle terror that even an innocent visitor could sense.

My education began with the appointment as my personal

manager of an efficient, small, feisty, attractive woman named
Jeanette Zion. (She became a friend with whom I exchanged poetic
as well as practical ideas. I called her, in private, "my little Pekingese" because she had the intense protectiveness of that breed, which
traditionally had guarded the Emperors of China.) Jeanette gently
but firmly instructed me in her country's sad history and sadder
politics. I had known, of course, that a minority of British and Afri-
kaner whites ruled a huge majority of black Africans and what was
called "coloreds," of mixed descent, as well as East Indians who had
originally been brought to South Africa to work the sugar plantations before gold was mined. Vile as the racial situation had been
under General Jan Smuts, Jeanette warned me that it had seriously
worsened under the present Nationalist regime. She therefore im-
plored me not to voice my opinions to press, public, or even friends.
She did not have to implore too vigorously. I knew my own country
was just beginning, state by state, to remove its WHITES ONLY signs
from rest rooms and drinking fountains: I would have choked with
hypocrisy if I had expressed my indignation at the FOR EUROPEANS
ONLY signs on Johannesburg public park benches. Nevertheless, I
loathed the indignity those signs represented as fiercely as I loathed
the police state that enforced it. Later, when I was less a stranger to
the country, I offered to help a group that was trying to break down
the segregation of theatre audiences. More than once, I asked if I
might dance for all-"native" audiences. Jeanette, who sympathized
with my attitude, declared that these or any similar actions would be
cause for the immediate cancellation of my contract and that, without work, I would be unceremoniously kicked out of South Africa.
Since I desperately needed both the work and the distance from
America, I permitted myself to be seduced but not corrupted.

Even though I was disturbed by the society in which I had to
function, I determined to do my best for my profession. I closed my
eyes to injustice and lost myself in the staging of *Annie*. The choreography developed as smoothly as I had expected, although I had to
work with some raw material. The surprise and the reward lay in
discovering how successfully I could direct singers and actors. It was
stimulating fun to add my own creative touches to the familiar dramatic scenes, to the humorous bits, and even to the lighting. (I
smiled to imagine how Josh Logan might have reacted to these "improvements" upon his original work.)

One of the most moving moments in my theatrical life occurred
during a late rehearsal. I had been so preoccupied with perfecting
the ensembles that I had merely marked my own solo for the cast.

On this day, I thought it was time we ran through the show as it would actually be done. When my cue came, I danced *Wild Horse* full out. The chorus broke from their assigned poses to turn and gape at my antics. When I ended my solo, they and the principals begged me to repeat it so they might watch from out front. As the Johannesburg *Sunday Express* reported in a feature story, "He danced and there was a deadly silence. For some time after he had finished the cast remained still, completely in the grip of the spell he had cast over them. Then they began applauding excitedly." As every pro knows, this kind of approval from one's fellow workers is precious.

Of course, I sent the clipping to Ted in one of my infrequent letters, adding, "The dancers have worked hard and are so eager to learn. My training of them has been a real joy and they do magnificently in spite of having had (*most* of them) no other training than classic ballet. *All* the men are now learning my solo although technically I have only one understudy."

My ego, which had barely survived its battering of the past year, was rejuvenated by the show's reception. I hastened to write Shawn, with understated smugness, that "The opening night was a terrific personal success for me. The tribute paid me at the final curtain would have done your heart good. The applause started at my entrance in *Wild Horse* and continued intermittently throughout, with an ovation at the end." I did not exaggerate. Overnight, I became a local phenomenon. The critic of the *Rand Daily Mail* wrote, "One of the great moments is provided by Barton Mumaw in his Red Indian Dance, one of the most astonishing performances I have seen on any stage. It is not too difficult to understand why he is one of the world's foremost dancers, with an ease and grace that would put the nimblest of gazelles to shame." This review flew off to Shawn airmail the next day.

Everyone in the "white" world of the Union of South Africa knew everyone else, it was said, and the internal network was promptly buzzing. For the first time, I experienced the delight of being a superstar: sought after for interviews, asked to speak at hospitals and girls' schools, invited to appear at the Museum of Art as guest of honor of a theatrical group, often photographed in the parks and palaces of notables—in short, running the gamut of lionization. I lapped it up.

> It must be similar to your Australian reception [I wrote Ted], for I feel I am the glamorous foreign star and am treated as such—only to return to America and fight for recognition at the end of this, I sup-

pose. . . . This town is not yet sixty-three years old . . . just out of the "Wild West" era so to speak tho of course it is modern in every respect. But culturally they are just beginning, and yet there are two amateur ballet companies as well as [dance] activity at the University. I have had requests like mad to give classes but I shall start with the dancers in the company only, at first.

I did lecture on Delsarte at Witwatersrand University, but all was not work. It seemed that every hostess in the city was bent on inviting me to a tea, a garden party, an after-theatre soirée— flattering attention that reminded me of Shawn's stories of the Denishawn Orient Tour. I reported to Ted:

> The social whirl is unbelievable but so far I've been able to skip most of it. But certain parties I've had to appear at and they are fabulous. It's a bit like Texas—the gigantic fortunes, etc. and all it entails. The country is in rather a political and economic turmoil at the moment, but what country isn't? And the color problem is more complicated than ours. Hope all goes well with you and your season at the Pillow. Love to you both, Barton.

My salary allowed a few small luxuries. For example, before a performance I had always liked to have my simple dinner early and alone. Now it was graciously served to me in my hotel room by an Indian waiter. He never spoke unless necessary, but he steadfastly regarded me with sorrowful black eyes. Jeanette later told me that he had asked her, "Is the Mr. Mumaw not permitted to eat in the dining room, memsahib?" He had assumed, sympathetically, that— because of my dark coloring, my high cheekbones, my reputation as an "Indian" dancer—I, too, was a target of racism.

Many a night after the show the dancers, particularly the Americans, gathered in my hotel at a milk-bar that featured delicious thick shakes flavored with tropical fruits. We indulged in these treats, figuring that after our strenuous dancing, calories could well be damned. Jeanette once whispered to me that this same bar was also visited by members of an oppressed "white" minority—the homosexuals who lived in the closed and precarious world of South African gays.

In one of the few, if not the only, letters on which I ever put a date (perhaps I remembered this first anniversary of my departure from Jacob's Pillow), I wrote on September 12, 1949:

> All goes well. Still don't know the length of our run here. . . . Much

talk of my doing recitals. Nothing definite. . . . From your last letter
I think I can congratulate you on a successful season, *including* financial this time? I hope so. With love, Barton.

Unfortunately, I did not save Ted's replies, but his Annual
News Letters were revealing as much for what they did not report as
for what they did. In Johannesburg, I received a belated copy of his
1949 letter, in which I noted wryly how he described one of the most
significant events in our lives:

> Barton Mumaw, taking a week's vacation from "Annie Get Your
> Gun," came on and danced many of his famous concert dances on
> the final program [of the 1948 Jacob's Pillow season]—and danced
> magnificently—retaining all the technique and projection of former
> years, with added power, richness and depth. [With a calm I had not
> thought I could achieve, I went on to read:] Chris has become one of
> the finest and most valued friends in my life—a man of noble charac-
> ter, a gracious companion.
>
> [A year later, I read:] John Christian remains my wonderful
> "Poo Bah" filling the manifold jobs of booking dates, stage manag-
> ing, designing costumes and scenes, on tour driving the station
> wagon, running the sound equipment, helping me change
> costumes—in fact my "without which nothing" for whom I am pro-
> foundly grateful.

Well this was what I had wanted for them, was it not? Why, then, did
the words blur before my eyes as I read them?

Because of *Annie*'s success in Johannesburg, it was decided to
tour the provinces, at each stop alternating one week of *Annie* and
one week of *Oklahoma!*. I had never seen this musical, but my balle-
rina in the dream sequence, Louisa Fornaca, had been in the original New York production. She taught me my role as Curly, and
staged the other dances. *Oklahoma!* also became a love of mine; now I
had de Mille's as well as Tamiris's choreography under my belt.

Since we stayed at least two weeks in each city, the tour was not
hard. It allowed us time to see the thrilling countryside. There was
Cape Point, the southernmost tip of the African continent, where I
stared beyond the expanse of ocean to the very edge of the world.
There was Cape Province, with its vistas of enormous fruit, vegetable, and sugar-cane plantations, where I felt drunk with the rich,
green perfume. There was the visual, aural, and visceral impact of
Victoria Falls, where I trembled as, so it seemed, all the water of the
planet thrust from the towering gorge down upon the earth. It was

here, remembering pictures of Denishawn's *Egyptian Ballet,* that I saw in the mist Hapi, androgynous god of the Nile, with Ted's energy in the force of the falling river and Miss Ruth's beauty in its iridescent spray.

Even before our tour ended, I was asked to do a series of one-night-stand concerts in small, isolated towns, with longer runs at Durban and Capetown. I began to plan my programs, amused at the thought of following the route of my friends, Alicia Markova and Anton Dolin, who had appeared on a similar tour the previous season to solid acclaim.

Back in Johannesburg, I returned to His Majesty's Theatre to start rehearsing my dances for the solo tour. In my absence, African Theatres, Ltd., had laid down a new stage floor because, during the run of *Annie,* I had complained about the old flooring. I was deeply impressed by this act of generous courtesy. It made me realize, more than anything else, what a big star South Africa considered me.

But I failed to examine this new stage surface closely and to recognize the material of which it was made. After Jeanette Zion had settled herself in the balcony to watch my rehearsal, I signaled the accompanist to begin the music for my *French Sailor* solo. On the first notes, I started out confidently with the opening long, forceful slide of my right foot over the floor. A pistol-shot echoed through the empty auditorium as I fell on my face. Jeanette, thinking I had been murdered, screamed "Police!" and rushed down to the stage. By the time she reached my side, it was obvious that I had not been wounded by a bullet; I had been felled by a flooring of cork. My foot had stuck to this surface, turned completely over, and fractured a metatarsal bone. As I lay there, I could see the swelling begin and with it the abandonment of my projected tour. With cries now of "Ambulance! Doctor!" reverberating through my head, I was carried off to the city hospital. There, thank God, I was placed in the hands of a doctor who had seen me dance and therefore appreciated the tragedy of what had happened to me.

Bright and early the next morning, before the extent of my injury had even been diagnosed, a representative of African Theatres, Ltd., visited me. With no syllable of sympathy, no consoling gift of flowers or fruit, he launched breathlessly into the details of a proposition. If I could be ready to dance within three weeks, his firm would star me with the Bodenweiser Ballet of Australia for its appearances in Johannesburg and for the rest of its tour of the country—a tour, he was frank to admit, that had not been doing well. By featuring me as the principal attraction on the programs, the management was confident they could kill two birds with one stone: make up the Bodenweiser losses and salvage my canceled solo tour.

This was an attractive offer for many reasons. The stay in each town would be longer than the one-night stands originally scheduled for my solo tour, and, even though I would have to perform eight times a week, my fees would be commensurately larger. I would at last be earning what I thought I was worth. Furthermore, I would be spared the expense, strain, and nuisance of being my own manager. Everything would be arranged for me: advertising, press coverage and interviews, travel schedules, and bookings. In short, I would be freed from those necessary but unpleasant details that plague the life of the solo artist in the United States. Best of all, Jeanette would travel with me as personal manager, secretary, and bodyguard.

Hardly had I agreed to this plan, contingent upon the rapid healing of my injured foot, than in waltzed Madame Bodenweiser herself to discuss the all-important matter of billing. A comic battle in two accents raged above the bed of one who was not yet sure he would ever again dance another step. I may have been down on my back, but I was far from out. I proved more than a match for the stubborn lady when I came up with a unique idea: a back-to-back program book. One cover featured a full-page photograph of me, with my dances listed immediately inside. Turn the program over and upside down, and this cover featured an equally large photograph of La Belle Bodenweiser, followed by pages listing *her* dances. I felt King Solomon himself could not have devised a more satisfactory solution.

My good doctor also solved my foot problem. Without benefit of plaster cast, he used instead constant diathermy and massage, and I did my own exercises on the floor, but without placing any weight on the mending foot. I was able to open as scheduled—and to do thirteen performances in a row without complications. The injury even provided newspaper publicity for the concerts because, oddly enough, it was also in Johannesburg that Anna Pavlova had suffered the identical injury many years earlier, after which it became known as "ballet dancer's fracture."

The cure held through the strenuous tour of eight recitals a week. Despite the Bodenweiser contributions to the program, I danced as many solos as if I had been the whole show. By the time our bookings ended in Pretoria, I was weary in body and in spirit. I was also homesick. I had been away from my own land almost exactly a year and suddenly wanted to get on a ship headed north. My doctor came to Capetown to see me off, as did a tearful "little Pekingese." Then, my pockets filled with hard-earned, resolutely saved gold, my scrapbook filled with laudatory clippings, I sailed back to America to "fight for recognition".

I was thirty-eight years old that August of 1950 (the same age Shawn had been when I first saw him dance) and the struggle for recognition was to assume unpredictable forms, some interesting and rewarding, some boring and fruitless. I leaped on the merry-go-round of the summer theatre circuit, dancing in the well-worn *Chocolate Soldier,* the old, familiar *Annie,* and similar repertory, outdoors and in, from Dallas to Kansas City to the St. Louis Municipal Opera. These jobs were routine, but they paid well. Sadly, I was beginning to realize that it was to this level my dreams might have to descend.

More challenging and therefore more satisfying was an engagement for winter stock in St. Petersburg, Florida, where I did the choreography for and performed as leading dancer in ten different shows in ten consecutive weeks—productions of *The Red Mill,* twenties musical comedies, *Brigadoon,* and even a *Carmen* in English. My schedule allowed me only five hours in which to work with the dancers for each show. Rehearsing and choreographing took place in the foyer, the aisles, the rest rooms, and even the sidewalks behind the roller-skating rink that had been converted into a Theatre-in-the-Round.

The series proved so popular that we had to add another week, in which we did *The Song of Norway.* This is a very dancy show, climaxing in a ballet set to Grieg's *Piano Concerto in A minor.* Its *pas de deux,* which I danced with Dorothy Duschak, produced such a moment of emotional rapport with audiences that many people were moved to tears. I was especially gratified by this reaction, considering the minimal time allotted to prepare the production. As long as the choreography was appropriate to the mood and filled the assigned span of music, it stayed in. Facing such constraints and the exhaustingly demanding responsibilities of the season, I swore never again to accept a job that required me to double in brass at such a breakneck pace.

After a recuperative stay with Mazie and Barton, I returned to New York. I continued to exchange casual letters with Shawn, although I was not to return to Jacob's Pillow for another seven years. Thinking I might catch the eye of a very successful Agnes de Mille, I enrolled in one of her classes. We had met long ago when she had appeared at the Pillow, where she had seen me dance. We had never become close friends, but I was surprised when she failed to recognize me at all. Through the *barre* and center practice of the first lesson, she watched me work as if I were a total stranger. When we moved across the floor in freer exercises, she called out, "You there, the boy in the white leotard. Do it again. You have an interesting quality." I repeated the combination and stood, smiling at the puzzled expression on her face. "Who *are* you?" she asked. Reproachfully, an assistant turned to her ballet mistress and exclaimed, "Why, Miss de Mille, it's *Barton!*"

Miss de Mille was visibly upset at this public exposure of her nearsightedness. No doubt she was also still angry over a recent spat with Ted, about which he had written me. Whatever her reason, she did not deem it essential that Mumaw join her upcoming production.

Reduced by now to seizing whatever opportunity came along, I joined the Amato Theatre Company down in Greenwich Village. One night, Hanya Holm came backstage after a performance and I asked if I might visit her. She had a reputation for being not only a fine choreographer, but a kind and wise lady. I found this to be true in her response to my indecision about abandoning the honorable, but unreliable, concert field in favor of steady work in "show biz": "At this moment in your life, you do not have time to sit and invite the Muse, Barton," she advised gently. In my reluctant heart, I knew she was right. Not long after this talk, Hanya engaged me to dance in Cole Porter's *Out of This World*, directed by de Mille but choreographed by Holm. I again worked for Holm in *The Golden Apple*, the Johnny LaTouche-Jerome Moross musical that played originally at the Phoenix Theatre before it moved uptown.

Now that I was more or less permanently stationed in New York, I began to give thought to ways and means of ensuring a more practical future than my unpredictable profession seemed likely to provide. Typically, I plunged into the most *im*practical venture that could be imagined by a rational man: with my South African savings, I bought a tenement in Harlem. My plan was to transform it into a corner of paradise for at least a few inhabitants of that hell. I knew this utopian impulse arose from my experience of South Africa racism. What I did not know was that my real-estate adviser-agent was also a visionary who had as little idea as I that we would be attempting the impossible. I did not learn until too late that one cannot do anything effective for "the good of humanity" without a thorough knowledge of the workings of mobs, politicians, bureaucrats, and other corrupt elements determined to prevent the slightest change in the ways they operate. The payoffs demanded, the murky channels through which we had to swim, the sleazy employees in city departments—these required far more capital, expertise, and chicanery than either of us possessed. After losing several thousand dollars, I lost the building and with it, my dream.

Yet some clouds truly do have a silver lining. It was during this quixotic episode that I met M., an attorney who steered me through what could have been a disastrous financial whirlpool to a shoal of security. A tall, handsome, intelligent young man, his integrity shone as clearly as his brilliance. For the past few years, I had armored myself against just this kind of assault, so I was surprised to find that I was once again vulnerable to loving and to being loved. Trust in this man's character developed almost at once into reliance upon him, not only in practical matters, but in every area of the life we were to share in the ensuing years. (And, I hope, for as long as we shall live.)

Whatever misfortunes we might experience in the future, we came to hold one another in such high regard, with such deep respect for "things as they should be" (as Shawn had said), that nothing could threaten us. As if cleansed by a needle shower of purest water, I no longer had any feeling for Ted or Chris except friendship. With this came the confidence that I could return to Jacob's Pillow. I could even enjoy going back because I had earned my place there and because I still believed in Shawn's artistic aims. Although Ted had never expressed this to me, I sensed that during our years of separation he, too, had reconciled our relationship to reality. It was, therefore, almost as if I had anticipated his words when he informed me that I must consider the Pillow as "home," that I must perform, teach, or visit there whenever I wanted to.

But, being Shawn, he would not make this too easy for me to do. In 1955, two years after M. and I had met, I read that Ted was to appear at the Brooklyn Academy of Music in *Sundered Majesty*, Myra Kinch's version of *King Lear,* in which she danced Cordelia. I decided that M. and I should go, principally because M. had never seen Shawn dance. As Ted recorded the event in his 1956 Annual News Letter:

> . . . a big and distinguished audience. The critics said I danced even better than at the Pillow, and I was given a most heartening ovation. The backstage crowd was huge and there were representatives from every chapter of my career present, including Barton Mumaw.

True, as far as it went. What really happened was that I led M.

backstage to the star dressing room, where we joined the well-wishers around Shawn. Chris was nowhere in sight. I was warmly greeted by dancers and other people whom I had not seen since Pillow days. Only when I noticed a strange expression on several faces did I recall the rumor that Ted had spread a story of my "perfidy" among our mutual friends. The longer I was compelled to wait for him to recognize my presence, the more certain I was that this rumor was correct. I knew that Ted had seen me. I knew he had seen M. at my side. And I knew that he had deliberately, vindictively avoided speaking to me. Instead, as I had learned to do myself, he maneuvered to welcome lesser courtiers among those gathered around his dressing table. Some of these were obviously embarrassed to be cordially acknowledged by the king while his ex-favorite stood in Coventry.

Suddenly M.'s voice resounded above the hubbub: "I think we had better go." At once, Ted bounded to his feet, reached out his hand over the heads of three people, and called, "Barton!" in fake surprise. I introduced him to M. and we both expressed a cool appreciation of his performance. Before we could leave, Shawn held us in a conversation full of graciousness and wit and smiling affability. When he went out of his way to exclaim, for no reason at all, "There's life in the old boy yet!" the point was not lost upon many who heard him.

I had no wish to see Shawn for some time after that encounter, a time unexpectedly rich in varied experiences. M. and I, in addition to decorating our new home, went into several profitable (and *non*utopian) real-estate ventures. And I fell in love with still another theatrical lady—the cockney flower-seller who was to blossom into *My Fair Lady*. It was a love affair that was to last through the five-and-a-half years I appeared in it. Under the direction of Moss Hart, rehearsals were phenomenal for their smoothness. My friend Hanya Holm's choreography was pure delight and the feeling among company members was unusually noncompetitive. All the elements of this theatrical creation meshed so beautifully that I never thought of it as a musical comedy but only as the perfect play it was.

After we opened on March 15, 1956, I seldom missed watching as much as I could of Rex Harrison's performance. He once exclaimed, "Who *is* that strange young man who watches me like a hawk from the wings? Really *extraordinary!*" Thereafter, so as not to disturb him, I selected a less obvious observation post. I never ceased to marvel at his skill and consummate professionalism. Throughout the five years that he played Professor Higgins, once a

month he could be seen restudying the script to refresh his memory
of the original interpretation. (This always reminded me of the end
of a Men Dancers tour when, back again in our Berkshire studio,
Ted would drag out his "Fundamental Charts" and announce,
"Well, now we start again.")

Hanya had wanted Harrison to dance in one sequence. Good
sport that he was, he watched us do the scene, then joined as best he
could. But he quickly decided his public would have to be content
with his burlesque tango with Liza and Col. Pickering to *The Rain in
Spain,* corybantic shenanigans that brought down the house night
after night.

When *Lady* showed every sign of running forever, my first real
sense of security permitted me to relax and even to indulge in studies. Eight performances a week and occasional rehearsals left me the
time and energy to take singing lessons with Richard Malaby, a
three-year acting course with Osna Palmer, Yoga with Moya Devi,
and ballet with Nenette Charisse.

When I received Shawn's unexpected invitation to participate
in the twenty-fifth Anniversary Program at the Pillow in 1957, I did
not hesitate to accept it. From my rich personal life, I had by that
time achieved a mature plateau of friendly feelings for Ted, which I
had reason to believe he reciprocated. When I saw an advance copy
of the souvenir program for the Silver Jubilee, I knew I was right.
Under a pose from our *Pierrot* (which Shawn had insisted that I perform), he had written the caption, "Barton Mumaw is here seen in
his greatest solo dance, *Pierrot in the Dead City,* as he danced it at
Jacob's Pillow every year from 1933 through 1939." Next to this
picture he had placed a studio portrait of me as Pierrot that had been
taken in South Africa. It was rare indeed that two photographs of the
same performer were published in the same souvenir program—
something Shawn was quick to point out to me as soon as I arrived
at the Pillow.

I greeted Ted and Chris without self-consciousness. From Ted's
letters, I knew that Chris was established as an invaluable partner in
many aspects of the annual season. I was to see during that week
with what skill, proficiency, and taste he accomplished his multivari-
ous tasks to help Shawn make this anniversary summer truly gala.
Programmed for the season were Erik Bruhn and members of the
Royal Danish Ballet, Maria Tallchief, the National Ballet of Canada, Carola Goya, Matteo, Lotte Goslar, and many distinguished
ethnic dancers. Climaxing these appearances, the Men Dancers

would be honored in the final week, during which Alicia Markova and Hugh Laing were to recreate their *L'Après-midi d'un Faune.*

Perhaps because Ted had never had a normal family life filled with normal festivities, he always relished every opportunity to make a situation into an occasion. Master alchemist that he was, he transformed many an occasion into a celebration—particularly if he could combine sentiment with publicity and thereby make a bit more money. As he wrote: "I would like to make this 25th year a homecoming for all of the Men Dancers whose fine programs launched the Pillow on its way to becoming what is universally acknowledged today as 'the world's greatest dance festival.' Barton Mumaw, now dancing in *My Fair Lady,* will come to dance again at the Pillow whatever week he can wangle his vacation."

I was housed for that week with other artists in a posh hunting-lodge-style motel some distance from the theatre. It was complete with swimming pool and barbecue dinners—a far cry from my quarters at the Farm twenty-five years earlier. Markova and Laing were nearby, as was dear Fern Helscher (grayer, stouter, but still energetic, still sporting an assortment of her "crazy" hats). Except for Denny Landers, whom Shawn had been unable to locate, all the original 1933 company of Men Dancers showed up: George Horn from Springfield, Fred Hearn on a one-day leave from the New York musical, *Damn Yankees,* Frank Overlees all the way from California, Harry Coble and Foster Fitz-Simons up from North Carolina, and Major Wilbur McCormack, who had flown in from his post at Fort Leavenworth, Kansas.

In addition to the festivities Shawn had planned, he was completely surprised by another and very real cause for celebration:

> Fifteen minutes before opening night, July 9th, I was handed a letter from the Danish information Office in New York City which read, "It gives me great pleasure to let you know that His Majesty, the King of Denmark, on June 20th, conferred upon you the Cross of the Knight of Dannebrog, as an appreciation of your valuable work in the cultural field—an achievement that has been very much appreciated in Denmark."!
>
> Well, if ever I made a mess of my opening speech, it was that night! I went before that audience trembling and not knowing what I was saying! This is just about the nicest thing that ever happened to me in my life! And so entirely unexpected. . . . But they timed it perfectly—to precede immediately the opening performance of the Eight Soloists of the Royal Danish Ballet at Jacob's Pillow!

Along with the notification came a large cross to be worn only at state functions, a miniature cross to be worn with evening dress, and a rosette that one was permitted to wear in the buttonhole of daytime garb. It was Chris who remarked on seeing this, "I bet Shawn wears that in his navel while he's taking a shower!"

Shawn had introduced Bournonville to America when, in 1955, he programmed ten leading dancers of the Royal Danish Ballet. As the noted Bournonville scholar and European dance critic, Erik Aschengreen, has said, "When one small part of the [Royal Danish Ballet] company went to Jacob's Pillow, it was this style, this new light dancing that was a revelation." Shawn ever afterward cherished "his" Danes and their work; without knowing much of anything about Bournonville, he shared many aspects of the great choreographer's philosophy of the dance as expressed, for example, in the following paragraph from Bournonville's autobiography, My Theatre Life:*

Like all the fine arts, the dance has its origin in nature. It comes from a warm heart, from a healthy imagination; its action expresses joy and pleasure. The body becomes eloquent and says precisely that which words cannot express. The effect is beneficial and the mind is inclined to poetry. . . . It is not the fact that he [the dancer] is applauded in a real theatre . . . that ranks him among artists, but, rather, that he recognizes the origin and destiny of the Dance. All of the arts demand a great deal of technique. Let us, then, bring art into the craft, but never allow the craft to appear in the art.

Continuing his report on the Jubilee, Ted wrote:

The real peak week was the week Markova danced her immortal solos [Prelude from *Les Sylphides* and *The Dying Swan*] and *The Afternoon of a Faun* with Hugh Laing. On that program, Barton Mumaw, on his first week's vacation after more than a year's run in *My Fair Lady*, danced four of his most famous solos—and all our oldest patrons were astounded at the fact that in body and technique he had demolished time—and it could have been the Barton who danced on the very first program at Jacob's Pillow 24 years before. And besides he had a greater depth, maturity, warmth and communication than ever before—his performances were truly great and unforgettable. It was a challenge for anyone to appear on the same program with Markova and Mumaw. . . . Four days before that week even started every seat in the theatre for the whole week was sold out; all standing room was sold. Each performance hundreds were turned away.

That Friday night, Ted arranged a small "family" celebration for Fern and for the Men Dancers in the dining room where we had

---

*August Bournonville, *My Theatre Life*, translated by Patricia McAndrew (Middletown, Conn.: Wesleyan University Press, 1979), p. 11.

had our meals for many historic years. Ted reported: "One of the boys [sic] said, 'Shawn, I came reluctantly, fearing and dreading the experience—almost with a morbid curiosity.' But it was all as natural and as much fun as it had ever been. And I am very proud of these wonderful 'sons' of mine—they have grown into fine, solid citizens, every one of them."

This was not, however, to be the real reunion. Although M. had driven up to see the final performance and take me back to New York the following day, I did not invite him or Ted or Chris to the party I gave in my room that night. This was, I felt, a moment for the "survivors" to be together alone and independent, joined only by our faithful Jess Meeker and our beloved Fern. With our first drink, we toasted absent friends—Margerie Lyon, Mary Campbell, Denny, and John Schubert. After a moment's silence, we refilled our glasses to compete in proposing the pithiest toasts to Ted Himself. Over many more brandies, and with lots of laughter, we relived our past triumphs and terrors, recounted our present lives, and confided our hopes for the future. Fern's outrageous stories and George Horn's antics saved us from becoming maudlin. With God's great gift of humor, we looked at one another, and were pleased.

I was quiet, remembering, when M. drove us away from the Pillow the next morning. Suddenly, with the ESP we often mutually experienced, he asked the very question that was going through my mind: "Why did they stay with Ted? Go through those years of backbreaking work for no money and only a little glory? To meet them now, nobody would dream any one of them had ever been a dancer, or had ever wanted to be."

"That's true. I think I was the only one who was bound and determined to dance."

"Then why did they do it?"

"Funny. That's just what Mac asked me when he stayed on after the others left last night. 'God, how did we do it? The tours, the teaching, the performing, the rehearsals, the endless driving. Or, I guess I really mean, *why* did we do it?' " I tried to repeat the exact words he had used to explore a question neither of us had asked the other before. " 'When you gave your curtain speech tonight, Barton, thanking Shawn and the audience for our homecoming, I remembered the hundreds of times we all stood in back of Shawn while he made similar speeches. And you know, the whole period went through my mind like when you're going to have an accident and can't prevent it, and your life flashes through your consciousness.' "

The familiar countryside unrolled beside the car as we moved south toward home and I thought about Mac and the others. "He went on to say that he guessed he put up with everything because he loved the physical demands dancing made on him, because he had learned from Ted's classes at Springfield that there was more to movement than fun and games. But he admitted it was all a damned sight harder than the army."

"What about Fern? She had a tough job, too. What motivated her?"

"Fern was special. I think she set out to plaster our names and pictures of our half-naked bodies from coast to coast because she fell in love with Ted when he and Miss Ruth played Corpus Christi on the *Follies* tour. Didn't I ever tell you the old story how she followed him to the beach in front of his hotel one day, stood on her head in front of him, then flipped upright and boasted, 'I bet *you* can't do that!'? Shawn never forgot that bit of showmanship, and that's why he hired her."

We laughed at the mental picture of the stoutish lady we had been with last night doing a headstand. "But you know," I went on, "she really and truly believed in Ted's crusade. She couldn't have got us an inch of publicity if she hadn't, that's for sure! She told me once that her Texas publisher had yelled, 'Great balls of fire, Fern, you goin' to give up a good job to advance a bunch of men hoofers? They'll laugh you outa every newspaper office in the country, girl!' But they didn't. And I think the challenge, and her achievements, made her stick it out."

"And that tall, rather silent fellow?"

"Foster? Like Mac, he loved the physicality of motion, of playing in character. But at heart he was a poet and he became frustrated, I suspect, at not being able to express himself fully in dance, although he did admit to me yesterday that he wouldn't have missed the Men Dancers experience for all the tea in China."

"You think they all felt the same way?"

"To different degrees. I believe Horn liked the theatrical excitement of costuming and stage managing. He didn't have much patience with what he called the 'art-dancy stuff.' Fred enjoyed the adventure, the freedom of the life, and so did Frank. Denny, of course, loved the action, on stage and off. And you know, in spite of the labor, it was glamorous for all of them—the reporters and the photographers in every strange town, and then the theatre full of people, and the applause. I think it made them feel that they compelled respect."

I hesitated self-consciously. "And it's really true, Shawn convinced each man that in his own way he was making a contribution to the dance and that it was important for him to do so, come hell or high water."

"You have to admit, Barton, that is pretty damned hard to believe in this cynical day and age."

"I know it is. But I'll tell you something that's even harder. What I value most, in looking back, is how absolutely sure each of us was of the others. We were like aerialists in the circus—we *knew* that everyone would always be in his correct place in relation to everyone else, that we could count on this interdependence. And this was true in our daily lives as well as in the theatre. I am certain this trust was reflected in our dancing. I know it helped make those seven years magical."

That very day, after we returned to New York, I wrote to Ted: "I can't speak of the homecoming week yet. I only want to say that it was one of the great experiences of my life. These experiences are the true bread of life, the thing which sustains us when *everything falls down*. That's why we *plod*—the moments of enlightenment erase all the tortures and fatigues of the road."

That evening, I received a telegram: MAY ETERNAL YOUTH SUCH AS YOU DEMONSTRATED HERE THIS SUMMER BE YOURS ALWAYS. LOVE FROM CHRIS AND TED.

14

Goodbye to All That

After my return to the Pillow as the Prodigal Son, it was some time before I saw Ted again. My life was filled with studies and new friends, appearances in *My Fair Lady,* learning the subtleties of real estate from M., and attending New York cultural events that I had never before been able to experience. A special joy was to go to Sunday night concerts given by the many young choreographers who were just then emerging. When I read that Glen Tetley was to present some new works, I made particularly sure to get a ticket for his recital because he and I had been members of the *Out of This World* company.

As I walked down the right aisle of the lighted theatre to my seat, I happened to look across the house and saw Shawn striding down the left aisle. Our eyes met. Without a flicker of hesitation, we both stopped in our tracks to gesture an identical greeting of open arms and smiling faces, a sincere and spontaneous pantomime of public reconciliation which I am sure a goodly number of people in that audience correctly interpreted.

The letters Ted and I exchanged soon reverted to their earlier easy intimacy. For the first time, I told him that Doris Humphrey had once telephoned to ask me if I would join her and Limón. I knew that Shawn had never entirely overcome his bitterness about Humphrey's "defection," but now I no longer feared to admit to him how proud I was that she wanted me to work with her. (Because she could not guarantee the regular salary I then needed to survive, I had most regretfully been forced to reject her offer.) In 1958, Ted wrote that "Late on the night of December 29th, a friend phoned me that Doris Humphrey had died—this was a shock as I had not realized the serious nature of her illness. A real loss, personal as well as to the whole dance world." I grieved with him.

I continued to receive Ted's reports on the woes and wonders of Jacob's Pillow: Grace Badorek, who had joined the staff as general factotum, "does everything so efficiently yet so easily and unobtrusively that I now wonder how I ever got along without her," while Chris "is now taking more and more of the directional burden off my shoulders." He made sure to notify me of the "Graven Images of the New York Stage" exhibit at the Museum of the City of New York, where not only was Allan Clark's bronze of Shawn's *Thunderbird* on display, but also three of Ted's own mahogany bas-reliefs of me that he had carved right after I returned from the war. He attended the Ninth Annual Capezio Award luncheon in 1960, where Martha Graham received a citation, and reported to me, "I was deeply touched when Martha in the opening sentence of her acceptance speech paid tribute to Louis Horst and to me as the two men who had most helped her in the start of her career."

The year 1961 proved a turning point for me as well as for Shawn. I resigned from *My Fair Lady*, but lacked the heart, the will, or the desire to search for more stimulating work on Broadway. Perhaps, I thought, at age fifty it was time to put my performing uniform in mothballs and don nontheatrical mufti. The real estate partnership with M. became a full-time challenging job. We moved from apartment or house so frequently that Grace Badorek warned, "I'm going to take you off the Pillow mailing list, Barton!" This peripatetic life was not without its creative aspects: I developed skill in remodeling, in redecorating, and even in gourmet cooking—all of which I reported to Shawn.

His letters in reply hinted at preoccupation with age. (Erik Bruhn has written that turning forty is a moment of crisis in the life of a male dancer. Shawn was in his seventies.) He hated the limitations imposed upon him by the years, but he was proud of the public image he managed to maintain. In each of his Annual News Letters, he began to include a snapshot that exposed as much of his firmly muscled, well-tanned body as the United States postal laws would allow. In one letter he wrote:

I have kidded about my "Narcissus complex" and here I am throwing another nude photo at you. But to a dancer, his body is something from which he cannot depart, and like a painter viewing his painting, or a sculptor his carving, a writer his book, a composer hearing his works played—we are undetachable from our bodies. . . . So I have always had a birthday picture taken every year as a record of how the instrument stands up under increasing years. So here it is—taken just before my 74th birthday!

Shawn's letters were full of interesting observations about people. When Miss Ruth accepted the Tenth Annual Capezio Award, he wrote that in her speech, "She was witty, she was wise, she got a lump in your throat and tears in your eyes and then socked you with a belly laugh! What a girl!" When he talked to Eleanor Roosevelt at a small private party, he noted that "You have to meet her face to face to get the colossal greatness of this woman—she has warmth, humanity, radiant charm, great wisdom and all with a simple, gracious unconscious-of-her-greatness manner that wins all hearts." When he wrote a eulogy to Mary Kinser, who died in Eustis (he and Chris were pallbearers at her funeral), he expressed my own deep sorrow in better words than I could summon: "She has left a void not only in our lives but in the lives of hundreds of others. When she decided that a person was basically worthwhile she could take in the whole man without being disturbed by any nonconformist behavior that might offend the small-minded provincial." To which I could only add, "Amen, my dearest Rapunzel."

On July 12, 1961, Shawn had his first heart attack. I was not to learn of this until later, when he sent me the details:

School had started, I was teaching my class in Principles of Movement and Rhythm, was already rehearsing my role as King Lear, and doing all the usual things that go with directing the whole enterprise of Jacob's Pillow. But I began to feel more and more exhausted, and LOUSY! The night after my opening speech, I couldn't stay for the performance but went to bed where I sat up fighting to get my breath. It was a nightmare. In the morning, I was coughing so terribly and constantly that Grace dashed me off in the car to the Pittsfield General Hospital where I was put right to bed under an oxygen tent. "Acute congestive heart failure," I was told. Bed rest for many weeks was prescribed and, seeing the inevitable, I relaxed and enjoyed it! I was so very tired, and had been tired for so long, that once my conscience was cleared of any responsibility in the decision, I was so grateful for this period of absolute rest and quiet that I could have cried with joy. And I *love* an oxygen tent—I would like to have one of my own to crawl into on hot, muggy days—for it is like suddenly being transferred to a mountain top where the air is pure and cool and delightful.

I was dismayed by this intimation of mortality in a man I had always regarded as immortal, but I was not surprised: for too many years Shawn had driven himself, body and spirit, with hardly a pause in which to restore or strengthen either. Now, under the care of an excellent doctor—who immediately ordered Ted to stop smoking and prescribed one or two highballs a night at bedtime—Shawn was forewarned and would, I hoped, slow down.

I should have known better. No sooner was he on his feet again than he resumed making plans for the future with the same *joie de vivre* as always, although he complained to me about the no-smoking edict. Among these plans was a celebration to mark the thirtieth anniversary of the Pillow, which would be coming up in 1963. "May I persuade you," he wrote, "to work with me on reviving some of the most successful of the Men Dancers' choreographic works, such as *Kinetic Molpai*, to present at the Pillow on this occasion? Can I persuade you to dance my roles in them?"

How could I refuse, even had I wanted to? From the moment of my acceptance of that invitation, Shawn once again shared with me in letters his innermost thoughts, his dreams and schemes, his honors and disappointments as if he were talking to me. Now he saw me whenever he came to New York, honoring my present life and my companion in it, whom he soon came to respect. For the next two years, I was fulfilled in all things, my good fortune marred only by the shock of Mazie's sudden death.

My lovely mother had been dressing for a Mother's Day celebration with Barton, Sr., when an aneurysm caused her heart to fail. She simply fainted away from life. I telephoned Ted to tell him that I was flying down to Florida to be with my incredulous, bereaved father. (Dad never recovered from this loss. He lived on for some years with dignity and even enjoyment. But the light had gone out of his days. At the end, he longed to be relieved of the burden of trying to live.)

In his Annual News Letter reviewing 1963, Ted wrote of Mazie's death: "What a big change this makes in our life and atmosphere—for it was due to Barton Mumaw's parents living in Eustis that I first came to this town. This gradually became my real home, so from 1936 on, Mazie and I had been next-door neighbors—Her absence makes a gap that nothing can ever fill."

During my sad, brief stay in Eustis, the seeds of the idea to live again in Florida were planted. But for the immediate present, I had to fly back to the Pillow to begin work on the Anniversary Program.

Shawn had assembled—God knows with what ingenuity, skill,

persuasiveness, and persistence—a season of artists supreme in the ballet, modern, and ethnic fields: The Ximenez Vargas Ballet Español; the American premiere of England's Western Ballet Theatre; Carola Goya and Matteo; classical ballet stars Violette Verdy, Edward Villella, Marjorie Tallchief, and Inge Sand; moderns Pauline Koner, Norman Walker, Cora Cahan, and Myra Kinch; East Indian Shanta Rao; and—of particular interest in demonstrating the sensational advance of serious black dance that Shawn had helped initiate—the Alvin Ailey Dance Theatre, Geoffrey Holder, Carmen de Lavallade, and Donald McKayle's company.

That season's souvenir program bore, on the black background of its cover, a John Lindquist photograph of me in white, with banner flying, from *Olympiad*. Shawn had planned this, I suspected, to assure me that my appearance would be a central attraction of this glamorous summer because he believed the highlight of all the programs would be the one on July 14—precisely thirty years after the first performance of the Men Dancers at the Pillow. He delayed his traditional opening talk until that Sunday night. He did dances he had done those thirty years earlier, and so did I. Exactly as at that premiere, Mary Campbell and Jess Meeker accompanied us on the two pianos.

At the cheering end of the concert, I made a curtain speech in which I said that I felt as if I had been welcomed as a Crown Prince of the Realm (a reference that mightily pleased the royalty-loving Shawn). Then, down from the overhead center flies, a large basket of red roses descended. It was adorned with bottles of champagne, satin ribbons, scrolls, and other items of décor that Chris had added to this fantasy of his creation. The gala was written up in many newspapers, both at home and abroad. The Hon. Silvio Conte, Representative from Western Massachusetts, even congratulated Shawn on the anniversary from the floor of Congress, saying, "Jacob's Pillow is certainly one of the great cultural centers of this country." Ted was especially proud to learn that Mr. Conte's speech was printed in the Congressional Record, "Appendix of July 30, 1963, pages A4831 and A4832" (a fact he noted for future historians).

That fall, I taught a sixteen-week dance course at the University of Oregon. Then I flew to Eustis to be with my father for Christmas—his first one without Mazie after fifty-two years of marriage. M. came down to stay with us at Maybar for the holidays. On the twenty-fifth, we three joined Ted and Chris and other guests in Shawn's home-studio for apertifis and appetizers, starting a progressive dinner party that continued with the turkey and dessert courses at the homes of mutual friends. It was a happy, relaxed occasion, despite its undertone of sorrow.

There were to be other sorrows in the new year of 1964. As Ted wrote me: "I am now outliving my contemporaries, and that is the worst part of growing old." First, Lucien Price died. Shawn's tribute to him was published in the *Boston Globe* under the headline, THE GREATEST MAN I EVER KNEW, and concluded, ". . . without his constant help for seven years the most important chapter of my own career would not have been written. Through his books he has guided, illumined and ennobled the lives of countless thousands. . . . The sum of his contributions to his time and humanity will not be fully realized for a hundred years." Then George Horn was gone. Ted wrote, "His fantastic sense of humor left laughter behind him in the hearts of thousands who love him." Next, the novelist-photographer, Carl Van Vechten, ". . . whom I have known, admired and loved for many years—he helped me find my first real authentic Flamenco teacher." And Joe Franz, architect of the Ted Shawn Theatre. And the irreplaceable music director for Denishawn (as later for Martha Graham), that distinguished man of American modern dance, Louis Horst.

Ted did not show that he felt personally threatened by these losses. Nevertheless, as he continued to struggle against ill health, I suspected he feared death no matter how valiantly he hid it. Perhaps this unacknowledged fear stimulated his celebration of so many "occasions," as if each were a talisman warding off the inevitable. Perhaps his sentimentality, which could approach Teutonic proportions, blossomed whenever he sensed an opportunity to make a box-office hit out of a gala. What, then, more logical than a Golden Anniversary summer to honor fifty years of Shawn's marriage to Ruth St. Denis? This seemed a brilliant idea because past Pillow anniversary seasons had proved profitable. When an intermediary asked Miss Ruth if she would come East to participate in this event, she grinned, shrugged, and remarked wryly, "Well, if Teddy wants to make an occasion of it, I suppose it's all right."

Teddy not only wanted to, he thought that August 13, 1964, deserved to be declared a national holiday. I—who knew the happy couple had not been bedded for more than three decades—was thoroughly skeptical of this "occasion." I remembered too many times when the press had predicted their divorce; when "Ruthie," in a restless mood or in the throes of yet another romantic attachment, had asked Ted for one.

Each time she made this request, Shawn told me, he invariably replied, "I tell her to feel free. She doesn't like that. She has hysterics until she settles down with Mary Baker Eddy or Kahlil Gibran or Tagore or Krishnamurti or whoever is her spiritual guru of the moment. Then, in two years or so, we go through the same scene again." Which may explain why they stayed married.

I was disturbed by the hypocritical aspect of the celebration which, I feared, might cause unintended publicity fireworks. My fear was confirmed when the public relations director at the Pillow confided that he despaired of getting national coverage for the event because newspaper and magazine editors regarded it as a big joke. When I wrote asking Ted if he were not apprehensive about possible press reactions, he answered in genuine surprise: What reason was there for apprehension? Fifty years *had* passed, had they not? He and Miss Ruth *were* still married, were they not? Disregarding my doubts, he invited me to appear on programs that included the Paul Taylor Dance Company, Patricia McBride and Edward Villella, Erick Hawkins, Sonia Arova, Maria Tallchief, the Royal Winnipeg Ballet, and others. He took it completely for granted that I would participate in the festivities scheduled for The Date.

I did appear for one week that summer. If I remember aright, I danced, among other numbers, Ted's *Divine Idiot*—rather appropriately, I thought. But I refused to stay at the Pillow for the brouhaha on the thirteenth. I knew, of course, that I should go through with it. But I did not choose to swim against so many and such strong crosscurrents, convinced it would be less embarrassing for everyone involved if I were not present. From New York, I sent "Mr. and Mrs. Ted Shawn" an elaborate card of congratulations that bore a delicate drawing of a man and woman dancing (a reference to their last Denishawn duet, *Idyll*). Although there was a touch of malice in my choice of card, I need not have worried that it would be sensed: both Ted and Miss Ruth rationalized my thought of them as a man and woman *still* dancing.

Ted never let me know that he had missed me among the 800 guests at the party hosted by Chris, but he lost no time sending me a colorful detailed description of the celebration—the special programs printed, the food and drink supplied, the "onslaught of press, radio, and TV handled with diplomacy. . . . the crew coming on from Hollywood to film the new duet which Ruth and I premiered for a documentary on Ruth's life which is soon to be shown," adding, "I am deeply grateful, touched and humble before the flood of congratulations from all over the world."

The duet to which he referred was one he had choreographed, with music composed by Jess Meeker, based on Miss Ruth's poem

inspired by an East Indian miniature, "Siddhas of the Upper Air":
> In the blue spaces between the stars,
> The siddhas stand together,
> Blown by the lifting winds of the whirling worlds
> They move side by side with the effortless motion of
> A divine dance.
>
> Gazing ahead, their hearts beat to the
> Unearthly rhythm of perfected Love.
>
> They are going towards the light of an unimaginable sun!
> Their garments are blown behind them
> Like a comet's saffron tail.

From Shawn's description, it must have been vintage Denishawn: she in saffron sari (the octogenarian lines in her face concealed by perfect makeup) and he in saffron dhoti and turban (his face gaunt from illness and overwork). They moved minimally in their flowing, inimitable style, the whole reaching a beautifully lighted climax in a slow, two-as-one dramatic walk up an inclined ramp into the wings, their heads high, their eyes fixed on the "light of an unimaginable sun."

I could vividly imagine the whispered dialogue that might have gone on throughout the dance:

Ted: *Put out your right foot first.*
Miss R.:   *I have always meant to do that, Teddy.*
Ted: *I know, Ruthie. Take four steps with me, then pose.*
Miss R.:   *Thank God for the pose.*
Ted: *You're doing fine. Now head for the ramp.*
Miss R.:   *Where is it, Teddy? You know I can't see a thing without my glasses!*
Ted: *Neither can I. But it seems to be right here.*
Miss R.:   *Well, then, here we go—up into Heaven, with luck!*

Some time later, Ted spoke the commentary for a film, Fifty Years of Dance, *in which he described this final duet with the customary Denishawn hyperbole: "The two of us were going up and up and up, remembering all the love of the earth but still lovers in infinite distance and infinite space, and still always up, going up."*

After the performance, Ted enthroned his bride on a dais at center stage, where he and Brother St. Denis stood by her side as she sat regally in her pale chiffonery, greeting notables and "dug-ups" with equal charm ("dug-ups" was Miss Ruth's name for those people she had not seen for years but who invariably appeared at such functions). With Walter Terry acting as major domo *par excellence,* José Limón, Martha Hill, Pauline Koner, La Meri, Marjorie Tallchief,

George Skibine, and other dancers and members of the audience filed past to kiss Miss Ruth's cheek and shake Ted's hand. The scents of flowers from many enormous baskets and the murmurs of adulation from many voices filled the air to make the "occasion" as joyous as even Ted could have wanted. To my astonishment and delight, the press treated it all with only a few raised eyebrows and a rare *double entendre*, as writers, too, paid homage to the survivors.

I was particularly happy about this in retrospect because it was the last time Miss Ruth appeared at the Pillow. She had danced there in the course of nearly every season between 1940 and 1964, always a special attraction. Her personal magic made her a star at the box office long after her dancing had become academic. Ted never lost his admiration for her art: her death in 1968 ended a fifty-four-year era that represented the most important years of his life. He wrote to his friends:

> *The one news event of the past year that overshadows all else is the death of Ruth St. Denis on July 21. . . . What she was to me as a person I am still too close to, to say, or what that loss means to me. . . . Word came that she had had a massive stroke, had gone into coma, and that her whole left side was paralyzed. I prayed she did not become conscious of this, because with her ideals of Beauty this condition would have outraged her.*

When Brother St. Denis phoned him that Miss Ruth had died, Shawn flew out to Los Angeles for the simple funeral services. As well as pain, I think Ted felt relief at her going, and so did I. We both loathed the thought that this magnificent woman of great grace and courage and spirit might linger on in a humiliating deterioration after so long and active a life.

On July 20, 1969, in the Ted Shawn Theatre, Walter Terry arranged and spoke at a special evening devoted to her memory. The only memoriam a visibly moved Shawn asked of the audience was their help in completing the Ruth St. Denis Studio at the Pillow.

In 1965, M. and I transferred our home and our business to Florida, where I could keep a close eye on my lonely, ailing father. Wilbur McCormack and his wife, both retired army colonels, had built a house on the shore of Lake Dorr, about ten miles north of Eustis. The two McCormacks and the two Bartons spent New Year's Eve with Shawn and Chris in their home. Ted reported on this party, remarking, "I am so grateful for the nearness of these two stalwarts [Mac and Mumaw], who from the very beginning of my men dancers crusade in 1933 have been my closest friends."

Every summer for the next seven years, I was to perform and/or teach through each Jacob's Pillow season—no longer relegated to being just a weathervane above the theatre, but back on earth as an integral part of the revered establishment. Ever since Ted had been ordered by his doctor to cut his work load to zero until he

regained some weight and more fully recovered from his heart attack, Chris and Grace had assumed the major burdens of running
the Pillow. The Board of Directors unanimously voted me a member of the staff to assist.

With my South African experience in training dancers and
staging choreography and my teaching experience at the University
of Oregon, I felt confident that I could honestly communicate to
young students not only what I had learned from Shawn, but my
own mature ideas of space and body movement. In 1967, I was
promoted to Associate Director of Jacob's Pillow. (This was the
same title with which Shawn had honored me after my induction
into the Army, and which I still carried. After the Pillow changed
hands, it was the new Board of Directors that bestowed the title
officially.) I lectured on "The Twin Arts—Dance and Architecture"
as part of the Dance Appreciation Course. I regularly taught a class
in "Principles of Movement and Rhythm" and one in "Kinesiol-
ogy." I danced on many programs, and automatically fell back into
the old habit of doing anything with my hands and head that had to
be done around the place. Despite the myriad additions, improvements, and modernizations of the Pillow since the early days, a
breakdown of one thing or another, of one schedule or another, invariably demanded prompt attention. My spare time was spent in
the privacy of my own primitive cabin in the woods, the one that had
been built by Fred Hearn.

As Ted saw it:

> It was a joy to all of us to have Barton Mumaw in residence the
> entire summer. . . . He had felt it was not wise to schedule him as a
> performer, due to various injuries that had plagued him in the last
> few years. But on the last program, when one of the scheduled ballet
> soloists had to go into hospital, Barton jumped in and danced in
> these spots, and magnificently!

It pleased me that Ted went out of his way to quote some critical
reactions to my unpremeditated performance:

> From the Boston *Herald-Traveler*: The works were simple and clear in
> style, and they were elevated to significant expressive impact
> through Mr. Mumaw's contained strength and sensuous projection.
> Here is a quality too rarely seen on the contemporary stage—a depth
> of feeling galvanized through physical technique into a force of com-
> munication. Isn't that what modern dance should be all about?
>   From the *Christian Science Monitor*: His dancing was feeling made

visible. All his movements came from inner quietness, and all were carried to their ultimate conclusion without anything superficial or forced. He won his audience completely!

It also pleased me that, at age fifty-five, such things could be said of my work.

I always enjoyed teaching at the Pillow, in spite of the expected annoyances of the pedagogic profession. What I thoroughly did *not* enjoy was my new responsibility as watchdog over student "morals" in this period of sexual freedom. Ever since the earliest days of the school, with the numerous clandestine escapades involving girl pupils and members of the Men Dancers, I had been aware of the Pillow problem that girls will be girls and boys will be boys and always the twain shall manage to meet. I was thankful that I had learned from Shawn when to avert eyes and when to assert authority.

I had also learned by his example how to coax a reluctant pupil into doing what was required: Once, a bright young man refused to attend ballet class which, with modern and ethnic, was obligatory for every student. It seems he thought ballet was effeminate; he felt foolish trying to do its steps. I knew that it was useless to attempt to *argue* away this prejudice. Instead, having noticed in his file that this young man had studied acting, I urged him to consider the ballet lessons as if he were a world-famous actor preparing for a role. My ruse worked better than I could imagine. Many years later, I was in New York to coach Dennis Wayne in Shawn's *Divine Idiot*. As I was walking through one of his studios, I saw dancers at work on a new ballet in the classical tradition. The movement and design were so beautiful that I asked the name of the choreographer—it was my former student who had once found ballet reprehensible.

Norman Walker remembers that I got along with the students very well and that they liked me. Certainly, I liked *them*. I was most uncomfortable when Chris, as Director, shifted his disciplinary responsibilities onto my shoulders, making me the devil who meted out punishment or ordered dismissal. Perhaps he had no choice because he found it difficult to work with people. Chris liked things done only his way, an adamancy that often led to serious misunderstandings. For one so sensitive in so many ways, he could be curiously insensitive, sometimes to the point of discourtesy. I particularly remember one morning when La Meri arrived unannounced. I happened to see her wandering around, looking a bit lost. I asked Chris if he had invited her to lunch. Not only had the idea never occurred to him, he had no intention of doing so even after I suggested it. La Meri stayed as my guest—the least I could do for an artist who had given her heart's blood to the Pillow.

When Ted returned after a second heart attack in 1968 as *impresario assoluto* (wondrously recovered and full of the old love and vinegar), he resumed his chores as controlling engineer, teacher, and lecturer. Now, however, he had emphysema to contend with; his energy was often sapped by coughing spells and shortness of breath. This did not always prevent his participation in screaming matches with Chris, quarrels that must have been heard far and wide. During a sudden lull in one of these tantrum displays, I shook my head sadly and remarked to Grace, "Ach! So *childish!*" Only to be answered by a sharp-eared Chris from upstairs at the other end of the house, "Oh, so it's childish, is it?" I never interfered again.

Except once. From the thirties Farm days—with our cheap domestic sherry and our Pink Ladies for Margerie and Mary—the gathering of the "family" for a predinner drink had been a ritual. When better spirits were affordable, the ritual was transformed into a tradition. The cocktail hour had become a command appearance before the Master, the purpose of which was ostensibly to enable the staff to discuss the day's problems without tension. Imperceptibly, what I had first noticed in 1948 had grown: Shawn took more and stronger drink on these afternoons, followed by his doctor's prescribed bedtime highballs. I had not realized the extent of this indulgence until Ted's opening speech to the first audience of one season. As I stood in the wings, I was horrified to hear uncharacteristically blurred words and stumbled phrases.

Immediately after the concert that night, I cornered Chris and Grace in the office and demanded to be told how long Ted had been drinking so much. They looked at one another sheepishly. Neither could remember when it had first become obvious that Shawn was improving on his doctor's orders.

"Didn't you try to stop him? Didn't you tell him what he was doing to himself?"

"Well, no. It wouldn't have done any good. *You* know how stubborn he can be."

I knew. I knew the Ted who had yelled in agony every night for a week while I ripped off the adhesive that held his displaced sacroiliac in place so that he could dance. I knew the Shawn who had stopped smoking on the day his physician ordered him to. I knew the giant who had hired a freight train to haul his company through a blizzard to keep a performance date.

I turned on my heel and left the office to run upstairs. Bursting through the door of Shawn's room without knocking, I went to his bedside, where he lay reading. I took the book from him and looked down into his startled, bemused eyes.

"Barton? What's happened?"

"*This* happened, Ted." I picked up the half-empty highball glass from the table, held it before him, then put it down.

"The doctor . . ."

"I know all about the doctor. What *you* don't know is that it appeared you had too much to drink tonight. I could not believe it was *Shawn* I was hearing out on that stage."

"Well, maybe I was a little tipsy, but nothing anyone but you would notice, I'm sure."

As I had had to face him after our terrible scene in Kansas City, I knew I now had to confront him with words that would penetrate his pride. I answered him angrily.

"You are *wrong,* Ted, and you must listen to me. You are destroying your own image—in front of your own audiences—in your own theatre! How can you do this to the kids who look up to you? To the Pillow friends? To yourself? To me, if I matter?"

Shawn's eyes were closed. The silence weighed unbearably. Then, at last, he reached out to grip my hands. "Thank you, Barty. Thank you," he whispered. I knew a promise had been made. No one ever again saw Ted Shawn under the influence of alcohol in public.

His will was formidable. Even though his physical condition had continued to deteriorate, he forced himself to remain active. I well remember that, to mark the twenty-fifth anniversary of the Ted Shawn Theatre on July 9, 1967, he had shown a film of the dancers with Walter Terry and John Martin, taken the night the theatre opened in 1942, told stories of those days and closed the program by dancing his St. Francis. *Terry wrote about this in the* Springfield Union:

> As the curtains drew together at its close there was silence [Shawn had requested that there be no applause], and then a choir of young men, all Jacob's Pillow students, sang "The Doxology." A deeply moving occasion it surely was, and an historic one in the annals of dance in America.

Perhaps because he always felt that they came too late, Shawn went to great lengths to write about the honors he received. He was particularly proud to have his name carved into the Benefactor's Column in the foyer of New York Public Library's main building, in recognition of his donations to the Dance Collection. Ever a bit of a name-dropper, he reported all the many notables present to watch him pull the cord that removed the curtain covering his name in gold incised into the pinkish-brown marble. As he remarked to "my dearly beloved friend Francis Robinson of the Metropolitan Opera Association," it was the nicest thing that had happened to him since the King of Denmark received him in private audience, especially since this honor came from his own country.

In the last Annual News Letter, dated February 22, 1971, he described every detail of the party given at the Plaza Hotel after he, Carolyn Brown, and Sir Frederic Ashton were each given a silver bowl inscribed with their names and the words, "Dance Magazine Award, 1971." In that same letter, he wrote of his upcoming eightieth birthday:

> Just forty years ago this summer after having produced *Job—a Masque for Dancing* at the Lewisohn Stadium, I came up to Jacob's Pillow with two men dancers from *Job*—one was Barton Mumaw and the other Jack Cole. . . . Later we were joined by the other members of my last mixed company [both men and women]. We rehearsed in the newly remodelled barn-studio and took off on tour from the Pillow, fall of 1931. . . . Here [in Eustis] now it is 90 degrees and humid, which makes it heavy going for my emphysema. Barton is here again "Papa-sitting," and he is suffering from an abscessed tooth—and also directing *Rain* for the Ice House Players in Mt. Dora. But in spite of such handicaps, we have managed to get out a press release on the 1971 Faculty and Courses [at the Pillow] and the printed-illustrated faculty folder to a student list of over 2,200. Now envelopes are being addressed for this newsletter . . . that will soon be in the mail. Then next comes an advance letter about the festival itself.

The summer of 1971 was to be the last that Ted would spend at Jacob's Pillow. Although he was losing his battle with emphysema, he had not lost his obsessive drive to teach. I assisted in his Delsarte classes, not one of which he missed. Each morning, when we walked from the house to the studio, he had to lean on my arm for support. But, once standing before his students, he leaned on no one while he delineated his basic principles of dance. He also often enjoyed observing classes taught by Jack Cole. In 1966, Ted had written of Jack, "He is amazing! He has the slim, wiry body of a 20-year old, moves more excitingly than ever before in his life, and is a fabulous teacher!" Now Shawn secretly applauded each time he heard Jack puncture the balloon of a lazy pupil's complacency.

At the height of that summer's heat, Ted asked me to drive him to Boston where, "In a weak moment," he had agreed to speak to

the Dance Masters of America convention. I vehemently protested
the folly of this exertion, but once Shawn had given a promise, Ma-
chiavelli himself could not tempt him to break it. So I packed Ted's
evening clothes and we set off on a blazing Sunday afternoon in the
unairconditioned car. He insisted that the back roads were quicker
than the turnpike. Maybe so. But they were also dustier. By the time
we reached the Statler Hotel convention site, Shawn could not stop
coughing. I got him into bed in a cool room, where he grew calmer
as he breathed more easily. But when the time neared for his talk that
night, he was in no condition to make it.

I alerted Bill and Edith Royal, devoted friends of Ted. Bill, as
president of the Dance Masters of America, assured me he would
rearrange the program so that Shawn could appear if he recovered
sufficiently. Some time later, when Ted said he felt better, I announced, jokingly, "Half hour, then!" Trouper that he was, his eyes
brightened. "Do you really think you can make a speech?" I asked.

With a surge of energy, he pulled himself into a sitting position.
"Oh, God, I don't know, Barton."

"All right, all right," I said hurriedly. "Stay in bed. I'll call the
Royals and tell them to cancel."

At that word, he pushed aside the coverlet and rose to his feet.
"No! I don't want you to do that! You just help me get dressed,
please."

Putting on his dinner clothes was a slow process, interrupted by
severe attacks of coughing. When I tied the bow tie, he clutched my
shoulder for support. When he sat down so that I could put on his
shoes, it was right foot first as he had taught me many years ago.
With a deep sigh, he groaned, "Oh, Barty, I don't think I can do
it."

I answered a soft knock on the door to admit Edith and Bill.
They went right to Ted, saying, "Please, dear friend, if you do not
feel up to it, you must *not* go on."

Shawn got up and held out a hand to each. "It's all right
(cough, cough). Let's just go slow."

With Edith on one side of him, I on the other, and Bill preceding us to open doors and hold elevators, we made a funereal procession to the ballroom, where sounds of the orchestra brought a smile
to Ted's white face. His stride became longer, his back and shoulders
straightened, a twinkle appeared in his eyes as he announced firmly,
"Once more unto the breach, dear friends."

When the applause died down following Bill's introduction of
Shawn, he walked as erect as always onto the stage, gave as witty a

talk as always, then turned to the orchestra behind him and asked the leader to play a waltz. Descending the steps from the platform to the ballroom floor, he swept Edith Royal into his arms, saying, "If I am to die, let it be in three-quarter time!"

Alone, they circled the huge ballroom to continuous and rapturous applause, Ted leading his partner in the perfect steps he had championed all his life. And I remembered how he had once told me, "My idea of heaven is having eternally Viennese waltzes played, and me dancing to the glory of God to this heavenly music!"

Shawn stopped at the table where Bill and I were sitting and gallantly bowed and kissed Edith's hand. Then he sat down, very heavily. I had a stiff brandy ready for him. After he had swallowed it and caught his breath, Bill and I inconspicuously led him to an exit through the kitchen in order to hide his true and miserable condition from the dancing conventioneers. In a pantry, he collapsed on a chair and, although not a single cough had interrupted his talk or his exhibition of the waltz, the dreadful wracking began again. Somehow, a news photographer had discovered his whereabouts. I was on the verge of throwing him out by the scruff of his neck when Ted spoke up, "O.K., O.K., go ahead." Between spasms of coughing, he posed for pictures.

At the end of the season, Ted asked if I would look after him in Eustis while Grace and Chris closed the Pillow. To do this, I brought my father up from our home where he had been staying with M., opened Maybar, installed Dad in his old bedroom, and stowed my gear in mine. Then I went over to Ted's house to help him unpack and settle in for the coming winter. He loved being back among his gardenias. He loved walking around his "estate," pointing out to me the cement work and the plantings and the house improvements he had put in over the past forty years.

Most of all, he loved being again among his wood sculptures, which I took out of storage and placed in the rooms where he could study them from every angle or run his hands over their familiar polished surfaces. Close to twenty years had passed since I had posed for some of those bas-reliefs and statues. I still marveled how Shawn, with no schooling, had transferred his knowledge of the way the human body moved into recognizable forms, taking advantage of the grain of the particular wood to create motion and muscle in what otherwise would have been a static pose. He did not consider this hobby great art, but he was terribly proud whenever it was exhibited at professional galleries.

Ted could hardly keep a straight face when, at an exhibit, he saw that every one of his male figures had been discreetly placed so that its back was turned to the viewers. Out of the side of his mouth, he quipped to me, "Is it then more respectable to show the ass in public?" Another time, he was working in New York at a community studio, when a lady visitor stopped by his bench to watch him chisel at a block of wood that had not yet taken shape. Finally, she asked, "Pardon me, sir, but what is that for?" Without lifting his head from his chipping, Shawn replied, "That, madam, isn't for anything. It has no use. It is a work of art."

Now, however, he could no longer sculpt or garden. He rested most of the day, rationing his strength to carry on his correspondence, his business, and his plans for next year's Jacob's Pillow season, as he sat at his typewriter in the office he called the "pout house." I kept the place clean and cooked meals for the three of us in the Maybar kitchen. At dinnertime, I would pack hot food in thermal containers and bicycle with it over to Ted. Then I returned to eat my own dinner with Dad who, unknown to him, was slowly dying from an inoperable cancer.

That year, Ted showed less interest than usual in preparing for the Christmas holidays, which had always meant so much to him. He seemed intent only on achieving his eightieth birthday on October 21, when a mammoth party in his honor was to be held at The New York Public Library Performing Arts Research Center in Lincoln Center. This event had been planned by Genevieve Oswald, curator of the Dance Collection, to whom Ted was devoted and whose work he greatly admired. Notorious for saving anything and everything, he had recently donated his vast collection of Men Dancers material to the Library.

He urged me to accompany him, but I felt I would be out of place at this birthday "occasion." Besides, I had to take care of Dad. Two weeks before the party, I saw Ted off on a plane for New York, where he would be met by Chris. Concerned friends there had brought Shawn's medical problem to the attention of Carl Stough, who was known as "Dr. Breath." His specialized breathing expertise had helped bronchial and emphysema patients as well as singers and athletes. He rearranged his schedule to include ten training sessions for Ted that would prepare him for the stress of the celebration. When Ted returned to Eustis, he reported how spectacularly well the breathing exercises had worked, and went on to describe for me in exuberant detail every aspect of the gala birthday party.

He said that, seated as he was on a tall stool, he felt like a Roman emperor (minus toga and laurel wreath) receiving his subjects as hundreds of well-wishers filed past him through the exhibit room. Its walls were hung with photographs and posters covering every phase of his career; its display cases contained costumes and other memorabilia. The whole dance world was there, it seemed, as well as socialite friends and patrons of many years, theatre and film stars, newspaper, radio, and television reporters and, of course, photographers. "Gigi" Oswald, Carolyn Brown, Dame Alicia Markova, and Gloria Swanson made congratulatory speeches praising Shawn's sixty years of contributions to the art of dance.

The tiny, still beautiful Miss Swanson provided the surprising highlight of the gala: she recalled that in the first moving picture in which she was starred, a young, unknown Ted Shawn had been her partner in a fantasy bacchanale, during which he chased her, caught her, squeezed the juice from a bunch of grapes into her open mouth, then kissed her. When the laughter at this little story had died down, Miss Swanson suddenly produced from behind her back a large bunch of ripe California grapes and held them over her head. As flashlights popped, photographers captured for posterity the picture of the eighty-year-old Shawn once again kissing the glamorous Gloria. Knowing nothing could follow this act, Francis Robinson swiftly brought the official ceremonies to a close by leading Shawn to a huge birthday cake and handing him a knife with which to cut the first slice.

The physical strain of the party had been dreadful, but Ted pulled through beautifully. I knew he would not have missed the event had his life depended upon it (as well it might have). With a truly Delsartian gesture of "At last, he admits it," he handed me Walter Terry's retrospective article on Shawn's life that appeared in the October 23 issue of the *Saturday Review of Literature*. The piece concluded by quoting Ted's pointed questions, "Do you think it [the American dance] is entirely a matriarchy? Do you think it is possible that I am the father of American dance?" To which Terry added, "On his eightieth birthday, Shawn not only deserves the affectionate 'Papa' but also warrants, as the pieces of the vast dance puzzle settle themselves, the dignity of the term 'Father.'"

Pleased as he was by this accolade, Ted admitted to me that the sweetness of his birthday celebration was seasoned with a dash of bitterness because he remembered how long the recognition had been in coming, how difficult and lonely had been the climb, and how unending the effort to find enough money.

"Do you know how much help some of the others got?" he asked me querulously. "Why, one year—I think it was when I was seventy-five—Martha Graham not only got the $35,000 Aspen

Award but a Federal grant for $181,000. Limón received $23,000, Anna Sokolow $10,000, Antony Tudor $10,000, and Ailey, Cunningham, Alwin Nikolais, and Paul Taylor $5,000 apiece!''

I was not surprised that his bookkeeping memory had retained all these figures, but there was little I could say to console him.

"I don't begrudge them this, you know, Barton. But wouldn't you think by now that I've struggled enough so that a grant would not weaken *my* moral fibre? Or maybe," he joked with a pained smile, "maybe, like body odor or halitosis, I emit something that repels money, hey?"

Whatever the cause, he certainly never *attracted* funds. I continued to look after him and my father ("We must work out some plan by which you can be twins!" Ted exclaimed) until Grace and Chris could get down to Eustis. Dad, who had been Ted's friend and volunteer caretaker for close to forty years, visited him daily. After the stress of the birthday party, Shawn declined alarmingly. It was as if, having achieved the summit of Mount Everest, he could, at last, allow himself to slide down its slopes to rest. Much as his condition distressed me, it was a relief when Grace arrived to stay in the cottage Barton had built near Maybar, and I could take my father back to M., where he could be near his own doctor. I was feeling the strain of caring for two invalids at the same time.

Dad and I planned to return to celebrate Christmas with Shawn, but on December 23, Chris telephoned to tell me that Ted had been rushed to the hospital with what had been diagnosed as flu and a slight stroke. I brought Barton right up to Eustis, where he wanted to see Ted immediately. I feared this might be too much for him, but he insisted that he must go to his "dear old friend." We were immensely relieved to see an alert Shawn sitting up in his bed like a king at a levée. Throughout the visit, Dad was strong and cheerful; I was the weakling. I had to leave the room precipitately when my two fathers laughed together over incidents they recalled from their past, when Shawn began to demonstrate the exercises designed to help him regain the use of his right hand. Neither man would have believed, if told, that this was to be the last time they would see one another.

Every time I went to the hospital, I marveled anew at Ted's spirit. He discussed his plans for the upcoming Jacob's Pillow season with his usual creative, managerial verve. He regally proclaimed which of his many visitors he would consent to see, enjoying long talks with the chosen few. But, no doubt owing to the sedatives he was given, his thoughts often wandered from a specific subject to unrelated recollections. Once, out of the blue, he demanded, "Whatever happened to that coat I gave you?"

"Coat? I don't remember . . ."

"Yes, yes," he interrupted testily. "The full-length suede one that was so expensive. You saw it out in Oregon or someplace on that horrible winter tour, and you loved it. So I bought it for you. God knows *where* I found the money!"

It seemed a strange memory for him to have dredged up from our deep well of shared experiences. Or was this another of the imagined "ingratitudes" he had entered against me in his ledger?

Then again, in the middle of describing an idea for one of the 1972 Pillow weeks, Ted suddenly stopped talking to look beyond me out the window. "You understand, Barton, that I am leaving the Eustis place to Chris," he said casually. "And those stocks that someone gave me a long time ago—I forget who it was—they're going to Grace."

"I understand, Ted," I assured him.

As if he had not heard me, he at once resumed the discussion of program plans. Why had he felt compelled to tell me about his will? Surely, at this stage of our relationship, he must have known that I expected nothing from him.

On New Year's Day, Shawn suffered a major heart attack and was placed in the special Cardiac Care Unit. Some time later, a tracheotomy had to be performed. On January 9, 1972, he died.

My shock was surpassed only by my ache at the loss. Through great joy and pain, Ted had opened many worlds to me and, even if inadvertently, had equipped me to stand on my own two feet. Through great joy and pain, I respected, loved, and finally understood him. My deepest regret for him as a person was that, right through the last days of our friendship, he continued to resent, to be hurt by my break for independence twenty-four years earlier. My deepest sorrow for him as an artist was best expressed in his own words (quoted from his obituary on the front page of *The New York Times*): "I have been burdened all the time with the simple fight for survival." Who can say what miracles this man of many miracles might have worked had this not been true? As it was, he earned epitaphs that could be applied to no other American male dancer. From Clive Barnes, "There is not a modern dancer in the world today who cannot trace his pedagogical heritage to Shawn." Another, "Every little boy who goes to dance class today has had a battle fought for him by Ted Shawn."

Ted had requested cremation, the return of his ashes to Jacob's Pillow, and some memorial there. All of us close to him immediately conceived the whole 1972 season as that most fitting memorial. Chris, however, did not want it known exactly where, beside the famous rock from which the Pillow got its name, he had buried the ashes. Neither did he want anything to mark the spot. Only upon the insistence of members of the Board of Directors was a simple bronze plaque affixed to the granite, bearing the words, "Ted Shawn, Founder of the Jacob's Pillow Dance Festival" and the dates 1891–1972.

When Ted's will was made public, the bequests to Chris and Grace did not surprise me. However, I was disturbed by the oddly brusque tone of this document prepared by a man, most of whose writings seemed intended for the eyes of future historians. I was shocked to read no word for his lifelong friends—Margerie Lyon, Mary Campbell, Jess Meeker, Fern Helscher, Mazie and Barton— or any of the many other members of his "family" whose devotion deserved some recognition. And there was no syllable for me.

I believe it is the custom in Japan to leave a letter to those one wishes to remember—a word of farewell, a summing up. This, I felt, was the least Ted might have done. It seemed completely out of character that he had not. His rejection of old and trusted companions was inexplicable, but I was not bitter for myself. I, at least, had the solace of knowing that I had been remembered earlier. On the eve of his long and possibly perilous flight to Australia, Ted had made a will in which I was mentioned. (Years later, I came across a letter to him from his attorney, dated March 6, 1947, which verified this.) I was touched by his thought of me in that period of emotional turmoil. The memory of this consoled me for his later change of mind, even though I was told by those who claimed to know that Ted had originally left me everything.

In truth, he *had* left me everything. I was to express my gratitude for his bequest by appearing at the memorial festival. The opening week (the first without Shawn there to greet his guests and make his preperformance curtain speech), I danced on a program commemorating Denishawn, with the Marion Rice Dancers, Carolyn Brown, and Carmen de Lavallade, who revived some of Miss Ruth's works. Jess Meeker was at one of the two pianos. It was a program that the critic, Anna Kisselgoff, said ". . . was marked by taste, dignity and artistry." Her review in the *New York Times* of June 23, 1972, concluded, ". . . Mr. Shawn's creativity was confirmed by Barton Mumaw's spellbinding performance in two solos previously danced only by Mr. Shawn. In *The Divine Idiot,* Mr. Mumaw, through incredible muscular control and intensity, created a piercing portrait of the archetypal holy man who speaks the truth others do not hear. His whirling *Mevlevi Dervish* quite simply approached ecstasy itself." I treasured these words as the best present I could possibly have received for my sixtieth birthday that August.

That fall, I revived *Kinetic Molpai* for the Alvin Ailey Company. (Shawn had been an early admirer of Ailey. When he programmed Ailey's company at the Pillow in 1953, he was one of the first producers to present it to the public. Ted had told me then that, if ever the *Molpai* were done again, this was the group to do it. He was right. The Ailey dancers worked with tireless dedication to recreate Shawn's masterpiece as perfectly as possible.)

By eerie coincidence, my revival of this dance took place on Ted's birthday, October 21, in Boston, the city that had seen both the first and the last concerts of the Men Dancers. As I stood in the wings watching the nine dancers prepare to go on, I thought how extraordinary it was that this work could still be meaningful. Thirty-seven years earlier, it had asserted the right of American men to participate in serious dance. Now, through an integrated company, it was declaring the right of any man to dance on stage with any other man.

At that moment, I wished to God that Ted were out front to see this realization of his aims, to accept this birthday gift from me. Above all else—after the *Molpai*'s electrifying climax—over the tumultuous applause for these young men taking the curtain calls he and I had so often taken together—I wished I could hear his strong voice crying, "Bravo, Barton! Bravo!"

PART TWO:
LIFE IN DANCE

*DANCES DESCRIBED IN CHRONOLOGICAL ORDER
OF FIRST PERFORMANCE BY BARTON MUMAW*

Introductory Note
by Barton Mumaw

I entered this country's river of dance at the moment it was separating from the headwaters of Denishawn into the divergent currents of Martha Graham, Doris Humphrey, and Charles Weidman. It was a moment when many other dancers—Agnes de Mille, Ruth Page, Helen Tamiris, Hanya Holm, La Meri to name a few—were also seeking new ways to express themselves. I have been fortunate to see the confluence of these streams form a deep, sparkling ocean now known worldwide as American modern dance.

To the end of his days, Ted Shawn disliked the term "modern." He believed that dance should not be arbitrarily labeled old-fashioned or up-to-date, classical or avant-garde. He was convinced that no school of movement should be allowed to degenerate into a fad. With the new dance that was developing from the seminal Denishawn influence and the increasing imposition of European standards on our ballet schools, he foresaw the emerging totality purely as "American dance." Luckily, dancers are a peculiar breed: given a whiff of a fresh idea or the sniff of an original concept of motion, and off we gallop like pastured firehorses leaping a fence when they scent smoke beyond the horizon. Today's choreographers and performers are no longer hobbled by any single school or philosophy, as were partisans of the War Between Dancers in the thirties.

It was choreography of the kind described in the following pages that established a secure place for males in the varied techniques with which large dance audiences were to become familiar. Some of these works were created by Shawn, some by me. They

were all pioneering dances for their day. I therefore believe that they
merit the attention of anyone who wishes to trace the stream of
American dance back to one of its most important sources. The
works follow chronologically the events of my life related in Part
One.

IDYLL (MAN AND WOMAN DANCING)
Choreography: Ted Shawn, 1929
Music: R.S. Stoughton, *Idyll* (specially composed)
First Performance: October 17, 1929 by Ruth St. Denis and Ted Shawn; New Brunswick, N.J., Roosevelt Junior High School
First Performance by Barton Mumaw and Ada McLean: 1931, Eustis, Fla.

The lush quality of this duet would seem to demand the scenery of a rococo garden, complete with vine-covered marble columns. In truth, the only background was a plain, black-velvet cyc; the only lighting, a faint, warm glow. The Man appeared to be nude because his tan-painted body closely matched the tan silk *lungoort* he wore. (This article of clothing is to an East Indian what a jockstrap is to a Westerner, but much more aesthetic: a length of material is wound tightly around the lower hips, gathered in front, and tied with tapes to form a flattened pouch.) The Woman wore the thinnest of flesh-colored chiffon shifts over a silk leotard. With her white body paint, she, too, appeared almost nude.

The couple enters from stage left, the Man slightly ahead of the Woman as they move with long, slow steps to center stage. On his right hip, he holds a large, round, traylike basket heaped with green leaves and white flowers. His left arm encircles his partner as she leans against him. Her right arm, extended parallel to his right arm, reaches into the garlands. Their dignified advance indicates that, despite the sensuous music, the seminudity, and the luxuriant flowers, this duet is to be more a ritual than a bacchanale. When they reach center stage, the Woman moves to the opposite side of the basket, and together they lower it to the floor.

Freed of this burden, the couple then begin a series of fluid, sculptured movements that were known, in Denishawn vernacular, as "plastique." (A plastique resembles a slow-motion film in which each movement develops into the next with a flow that never quite comes to a final conclusion. Such controlled succession is compelling because it conveys emotion without recourse to overly specific gesture.) The two dancers first move in parallel, then react moving apart, only to come together again in a held pose of frank physicality not often seen on the stage at that time. (Although this was most sensual to watch—and to perform, as I was to discover—it neverthe-

less gave an impression of total innocence, as if one were watching Man and Woman in Eden before the Fall.)

Now, both return to the basket and each takes up an end of one of the garlands that had been carefully coiled so that they could be unwound in the progress of the dance. (As with props used in many Denishawn works, the basket and the garlands were not mere theatrical gimmicks but were, instead, essential to the meaning of the dance.) The Man moves to the right of the stage, the Woman to the left, both handling with reverence the trailing ropes of flowers. They raise these overhead. They turn back toward one another, as if to assert that freedom in love is only possible through recognition of the chains that bind lovers together. Moving apart again, each holds the end of a garland against the waist as they slowly turn within its encirclement back to one another, ending as two made one.

With reluctance, they unwind from the garlands, replacing them on the basket which the Man picks up and holds high above his head. The Woman stops an instant before him, facing forward, twining her arms back into his while she looks up at him with an expression of absolute acceptance. Maintaining this position, step by slow step they exit downstage right.

Idyll was last performed by St. Denis and Shawn at Lewisohn Stadium in 1931. Although both then knew that this was the final public demonstration of the "perfect partnership" and the "perfect marriage," there was no hint in their dancing of anything except mutual love.

Ted Shawn and Ruth St. Denis in *Idyll*, the last Denishawn duet they danced together, 1931.

Above: Ted Shawn in *Gnossienne*.

Below: Barton Mumaw in *Gnossienne*, the first solo he performed.

GNOSSIENNE (A PRIEST OF KNOSSOS)
Choreography: Ted Shawn, 1919
Music: Erik Satie, *Gnossienne No. 1*
First Performance: December 17, 1919 by Ted Shawn; Egan
Little Theatre, Los Angeles, Cal.
First Performance by Barton Mumaw: March 21, 1933; Boston
(Mass.) Repertory Theatre

Gnossienne was originally created by Shawn in 1917 as a classroom
exercise to help pupils achieve disciplined body control. It remained
in his repertory for thirty years after its first public performance in
1919. In *One Thousand and One Night Stands*,* Shawn tells how it became one of his most famous solos:

> [It was] a dance in flat two-dimensional style movement that didn't
> come off when the class tried to do it for Ruth who dropped by the
> practice studio. I jumped in and did the exercise, solo. . . . When I
> finished I turned to the class and then to Ruth saying, "There. *That's*
> the way it's supposed to look."

St. Denis urged him to include the dance on a program, and
that was the way it looked for the next nineteen years. According to
Shawn, Doris Humphrey maintained that the solo was "unteach-
able." By that, of course, she did not mean the steps but the inimitable quality, the unique presence, with which Ted imbued the work.

He had found his inspiration for the dance in The Cup Bearer
fresco (one of the few that remain on the walls of the ancient Cretan
capital of Knossos) and in the music of a then obscure composer,
Erik Satie. In 1917, as Cocteau expressed it, Satie "was well known
only to public and critics who had a particular liking for what
seemed very advanced music." His *Gnossienne No. 1* bears no time
signature, contains no bars, and has none of the conventional mark-
ings, such as allegro, lento, or crescendo. Instead, Satie's musical
instructions read, "With absolutely unchanging rhythm throughout.
Monotonous and white," "Far away," "Step by Step," and even
"On the Tongue." These suggested a quality difficult enough to
translate from page to instrument, let alone from melody into move-

---

*Ted Shawn and Gray Poole, *One Thousand and One Night Stands* (Garden City, N.Y.: Doubleday, 1960), p. 70.

ment. But Shawn was able quite amazingly to sense the sly, ironic intent of the music and to incorporate it into a Cretan ritual of distinct originality.

The dancer was costumed in tight-fitting shorts of a dull gold color patterned with large, black, snail-like circles. A thick roll of gold-colored tubing encircled the waist, and similar thinner tubing edged the legs of the shorts, twined around the upper arms of the dancer, and formed a band around his flat-combed hair. These odd, rather graceless rolls of fabric represented the snakes of the goddess whom the priest was honoring.

Throughout all the movements of the solo, arms, legs, body, and head are restricted as much as possible to a flat profile. The entrance steps are made with bent knees, arms squarely angled up at the elbows, hands held at right angles, fingers stiffly pointed, head facing the opposite wings. On the first of the abrupt, staccato chords with which the melodic line is consistently interrupted, the body twists sharply from one side to the other. At the same instant, the arms, always bent, reverse at the elbows so that the hands point down. This movement is done with swift precision and an absolutely expressionless face, as are all similar steps throughout the dance.

In a variation of this movement, there is a sharp, exact rising from flat-foot to half-toe, falling to flat-foot again, knees always bent. At a pause, the dancer poses with flexed knees, body and head in profile, arms bent at an angle overhead with fingers touching. On the following declining phrase of music, he slowly leans down to the floor until his head touches it, all the while balancing on one leg with bent knee, the other leg raised high in back, also with bent knee. This deliberate "fall" is repeated in the opposite direction. In another pause, the dancer faces the rear, at stage center, flexes both knees widely, poises on half-toe, and arches his body as far as possible to the right, both arms angled at the shoulders with fingers just touching overhead. The opening walk, with its stops, reversed positions, abrupt rises to half-toe and drops to flat-foot, is repeated. The solo comes to an end with the dancer posed at center stage on high half-toe, arms angled and head facing forward as the lights immediately black out.

This brief dance appeared deceptively easy to do. In reality, the strict geometrical body positions, the persistent bent-knee steps on half-toe, and the precise control of balance demanded tension in every muscle as well as an exact rhythmic response to the accented grace notes and chords of Satie's weird melody. Although it was danced with a straight face, there was more than a hint throughout that the priest and his Snake Goddess were secretly amused by a ritual in which they no longer found deep significance.

In my experience, audience reaction to *Gnossienne* varied. Children, more quickly than adults, recognized the suggestion of fun in the unusual movements. They often giggled freely, while grownups seemed unsure if they should enjoy the laugh hidden in the dance or treat it with the reverence due a serious work of art. Not until the dancer took his first bow in character did they realize that it was "safe" to be amused. Then, an encore was inevitable.

When he first saw *Gnossienne,* Dr. Arnold Genthe, the noted photographer and sage critic of the arts, remarked to Shawn, "It is very difficult to add anything really new to the vocabulary of the dance, but I think you have done it with your *Gnossienne.* It's a genuine contribution." When Joyce Trisler's Danscompany revived several Denishawn dances in the winter of 1976, Deborah Jowitt wrote in the *Village Voice,* "Denishawn pieces remain more than just charming by virtue of their clear, simple designs and their structural presence of mind. I can't imagine that many other choreographers in 1920 were interested in . . . the kind of unfussy, hypnotically repetitive choreography displayed in Shawn's *Gnossienne.*"

Barton Mumaw in *The French Sailor,* the first solo he performed with the Men Dancers, 1933.

THE FRENCH SAILOR
Choreography: Ted Shawn, 1933
Music: Darius Milhaud, from *Le Train Bleu*
First Performance: August 14, 1933 by Barton Mumaw; Beach
Theatre, West Falmouth, Mass.

The French Sailor was a solo extracted from what could be called a
miniature ballet, *Kankakee at Cannes,* in which Shawn choreographed
an American businessman, his wife, and his daughter as they encountered the bedazzling life of the French Riviera. (It was also a
satirical hail-and-farewell to a former friend from Kankakee who, St.
Denis and Shawn felt, had used them as steps on a climb up the
social ladder from Illinois to New York.)

The music had originally been composed by Milhaud for a
Diaghilev ballet with choreography by Bronislava Nijinska. Although Milhaud was Satie's contemporary in the avant-garde musical era of the twenties, where Satie's compositions were cool and
distant, Milhaud's were bright and straightforward. In *Le Train Bleu,*
he captured the warmth and vivacity, with its suggestion of deca-
dence, of the golden Mediterranean resort of Cannes.

In Shawn's scenario, the straitlaced but socially ambitious midwestern parents do their utmost to protect their innocent teen-age
daughter from any lower-class enticements she encounters as they
sight-see in the city. Father does a dance. Mother does a dance.
Then the young girl's eye is caught by a dashing sailor in his formfit-
ting trousers, blue-and-white-striped basque shirt, and red-
pompommed beret. They dance a duet despite parental protests.
The whole is climaxed by an exultant solo for the sailor, which
proved to be the most popular dance in the piece and was, therefore,
subsequently taken out of the suite and added to the repertory of the
touring Men Dancers.

It was one of the most strenuous dances I ever attempted to do.
Although composed of seemingly simple balletic movements combined with pantomime that reflected aspects of a sailor's life, from
start to finish the solo demanded that the feet touch earth only to rise
immediately, a *"tour (en l'air) de force"* similar to male variations in
traditional ballet. I literally had to skim over the stage as if I were a
gull flying over water, with nary a pause for breath.

Fortunately, in recognition of human frailty, Shawn had devised some slow-motion combinations in the middle of the dance.

These were lyric steps done to a tricky ⁵/₄ rhythm, on the fourth count of which I had to be high in the air and on the fifth, back down again. Of course, that fifth always suffered because what you steal from one count has to be compensated for on the next. The result was that this section, intended to provide a brief respite from exertion, was not all that restful. Then back again I went to covering the stage with the widest of leaps and the highest of jumps, as if epitomizing the free, wild sea itself.

Often, to my dismay, I had to encore this tiring solo, which flattered my ego but was tough on my lungs and legs. In order not to seem too breathless a *matelot,* therefore, I always started the encore with the slow middle part in order to gather enough strength and wind to sail through the finale. The critic of *The Schenectady (N. Y.) Star* wrote in 1934 about this work, "Barton Mumaw pleased with the sophisticated quality of his humor and the almost indescribable lightness of his handling of the difficult technical requirements of this solo." It is interesting to note that Nijinska's choreography for her sailor, Anton Dolin, made extensive use of his spectacular acrobatic feats, while Shawn independently reverted to a rather classic ballet style in his interpretation of the same dance.

When it came time to take publicity photographs for the upcoming tour of the Men Dancers, we were in the Berkshire Hills at Jacob's Pillow. Many a wise head was scratched as we tried to think of a background that might suggest Cannes. Then some bright someone made the connection—sailor, seawall. Since New England is abundantly supplied with stone walls, I was posed dramatically against the nearest one for a sunlit shot aimed upward so that the sailor seemed to be standing above the Mediterranean itself. "Where there's a will, there's a way" was the slogan under which we had to operate in those early days at the Pillow.

FETISH

Choreography: Barton Mumaw, 1933
Music: Jess Meeker (specially composed)
First Performance: October 23, 1933 by Barton Mumaw; Strong
Theatre, Burlington, Vt.

As with all other forms of creation, some dances have an easy birth,
others come into being after long, painful labor, and still others re-
quire something like a Caesarean to bring them into the world. My
first attempt at choreography, *Fetish*, emerged into the spotlight only
after trials, errors, and happenstances.

On the way to San Antonio in April 1933, Shawn, Mary
Campbell, and I stopped at a roadside stand in Oklahoma. There I
caught sight of a drum that was made of animal skin the color of
honey. This was stretched over a round form and held in place by a
skeletal network of bones laced with rawhide. I must have stared at it
like a needy child because, on impulse, Shawn bought it for me.
Through the rest of the trip, if I was not driving, I handled that
drum in every imaginable way that might help me make a dance.

Posing with a drum and moving with it meaningfully are two
different things, as I quickly discovered when I began to work out a
choreographic plan after we returned to Jacob's Pillow. I placed the
frustrating thing at every angle on every part of my anatomy. I beat
it, of course. I rolled it around the floor. I leaped with it. I even
balanced it on my head. Finally, reluctantly, I abandoned it.

The disappointing drum had served a purpose, however, for I
had written to ask Jess Meeker if he could compose a piece of primitive music for me. When he arrived to join Shawn as permanent
pianist and musical director for the Men Dancers, he brought me a
finished piano score. Richly orchestral in quality, it evoked such
deep, dark, earth-magic that no drum was needed. Fate, or Mumaw
luck, next led me to an illustrated book of African tribal statues. In it
I found a color photograph of a witch doctor, and I knew I had found
my first dance. Primitive it would still be, but on the highly developed level of medicine-man culture, in which the beating of feet
against the ground created a resonance that was itself a drum.

Shawn, having already guided his novice choreographer in
many ways, went on to help me put together a costume. An expert
at utilizing old scraps, rags, tatters, and fragments for new purposes,
he delved into one of the Denishawn trunks that had been rescued

Barton Mumaw in *Fetish*, the first dance he choreographed.

from incineration. Like two witch doctors pawing over the tools of their trade, he and I made a pile of this and a heap of that from which to concoct our magic. The result was a mixture of Denishawn costume bits and souvenirs from many tours: a handwoven Mexican fabric became a G-string with long tabs that almost touched the floor fore and aft; an embroidered Philippine belt held this together; from Borneo, a Dyak network of tiny, multicolored beads necklaced my throat and upper torso; bands of feathers circled below my knees, silver and brass bracelets circled my arms. As the supreme touch, I seized upon a pair of deer hooves to tie around my right wrist. Their strange appearance and the weird sounds they produced when rattled together created the eerie effect of a fetish made by a real witch doctor. And there was the name for my dance.

Since we still lacked the dramatic headdress shown in the photograph—a mass of red, black, yellow, and white feathers—Shawn and I made a trip to New York to the emporium of Kate Shea. She was famous for supplying the thousands of avian accessories that were demanded by the costumes for the *Ziegfeld Follies,* Broadway musicals, and nightclub shows of the day. She presided over an enormous loft filled with tables on which stood bins overflowing with feathers from all parts of the world and in all shades of the rainbow. A large, imposing, expressionless woman, she seemed to brood in an almost malevolent way over her collection. When Shawn asked her cheerily, "Anything new in feathers today?" I was not the least surprised to hear her deep, raspy voice reply, "Vultures." The way she pronounced that word sent chills up my spine as it evoked a vivid picture of the loathsome bird. I determined then and there that my headdress would be made solely of that creature's glistening feathers sprouting from my head like evil incarnate.

Mistress Shea sold a fine quality of merchandise. That headdress has survived years of one-night stands, with constant packing and repacking, and, although a bit motheaten today, could still be worn. It must also have been of classic design because, when I was performing in South Africa more than twenty years later, I was astonished to see rickshaw-pullers in the streets of Durban who were in costume and wearing replicas of my Fetish *headgear. I refused, on principle, to be pulled in a vehicle by a fellow human being, but I questioned one of the men about his outfit. He told me that it was worn as a tourist attraction. How hath the mighty fallen!*

At last, *Fetish* was choreographed and ready to make its debut. The curtain opens on my motionless figure poised in an angular position at center stage. Dark blue from one wing and dull red from the opposite wing provide the overall lighting. From the junglelike gloom thus created, my head with its soaring feathers emerges menacingly in the focus of a small, white, footlight spot. The effect must have been startling because there was always an instant of shocked silence before the audience broke into applause.

At first, I move with extreme slowness, drawing into myself potent forces from the air. Next I attack the stage floor with dignified stomps to call up earth energy. Then, joining these two elements but still with slow, controlled movements, I advance from one pose to the next (each based on African sculptures) as if I were praying to my gods. Once inspired and strengthened, I suddenly erupt into a frenzy of incantation, with vibrantly-pounding feet and the ghostly clacking of deer-hooves bracelet. My nearly naked body flashes before the purplish background; the towering vulture feathers seem to take flight.

At the climax of one particularly exultant movement, as I pose high on left half-toe with the right knee bent up at an acute angle and the head and body arched backward, the right arm thrusts straight out into the infinity of air and the left arm draws back with palm down to the earth. When the end of the dance approaches, I return to my opening pose. This I hold with head and extremities motionless but with a slight continuing movement of the torso to suggest that the ritual will go on long after the curtain closes.

Fetish was always fun to do, probably because, quiet as I am in private, I enjoyed making a ruckus. At each performance, the music excited me as much as it had on first hearing, while the rhythmic foot-pounding, the extravagant gestures, the glaring eyes, and the gnashing teeth all provided a most satisfying catharsis for me (and, I hope, for the audience). I believe that everyone should do a savage dance at some time in his/her life.

It never occurred to Shawn or me that this solo could in any way be considered lascivious, but, when advance photographs of *Fetish* arrived at a girls' school where we were booked for a concert, the sponsors were outraged. Did I not realize that under the long back tab of my costume, my bare behind was visible? I was tempted to reply (as would Rhett Butler later), "Frankly, my dear, I don't give a damn!" but I restrained myself. Being young and full of my "rights as an artist," I was furious when told I could not do the dance. Shawn let me blow off steam for a moment, then calmly suggested to the censors that I might wear a pair of flesh-colored trunks under the costume. I agreed, and so did they. When they left the dressing room, Ted and I burst out laughing. How much more provocative the dance would seem to the innocent females when done in what would surely look like underwear showing beneath the G-string!

At another performance, however, I risked a real and no doubt illegal pubic display. At the end of *Fetish* that night, I posed as usual in a deep *plié,* legs spread wide, arms out to sides. Suddenly, I felt something give in the belt that supported the G-string, underneath which there was only me. All at once, the belt loosened entirely and started to fall. I froze in character, making no move to save myself from disastrous exposure, and for one instant the belt caught in a fold of flesh at the top of my hip. I made a very awkward bow and retreated offstage, clutching the two ends of the *verdammter* belt in both hands and murmuring, "*Merci! Merci, le Bon Dieu* of the Voodoo jungle."

Barton Mumaw in solo version of *Cutting the Sugar Cane,* revived for the Ted Shawn memorial season at Jacob's Pillow, 1972.

CUTTING THE SUGAR CANE
Choreography: Ted Shawn, 1933
Music: Ernesto Lecuona, "Danza Lucumi" from *Danzas Afro-Cubanas Suite*
First Performance: March 21, 1933 by Jack Cole, Sterling Stamford, Wilbur McCormack, and Barton Mumaw; Boston, Mass. Repertory Theatre
Later Performance by Barton Mumaw: 1941–42, United States solo concert tour

Shawn never missed an opportunity to add to his knowledge of dance or to participate in a situation that might inspire him to new movement, whether by intention or by chance. His appearances in Havana in January 1928, when he, Ruth St. Denis, and the Denishawn Dancers were the stars of the *Ziegfeld Follies,* provided him with several such opportunities.

One of these occurred when he was taken to various "hot spots" where the authentic rumba—a dance that purported to show the passionate coupling of a man and a woman—was performed. Shawn extracted from this experience steps, costumes, and atmosphere for his own version, which he later danced on Denishawn tours with the beautiful Ernestine Day.

He told a good story when he described this "unfettered" Havana exhibition, but admitted to me that he had been secretly disappointed by the performance, which he sensed had been corrupted into a tourist attraction. His rumba was considered by American audiences and press alike as authentic and erotic, although it was only slightly "hotter" than the popular ballroom caricature of the dance that soon followed on the heels of his interpretation. He was reminded that the same thing had happened in the early years of his career, before he met Ruth St. Denis, when he supported his serious study of dance by doing exhibition ballroom dancing that included his adaptation of the Argentine tango.

Another Cuban dance inspiration came as a result of a drive through the countryside, where Shawn saw examples of movement by workers in a sugarcane field that could have come straight from murals by Rivera or Orozco. The workers cut the tall stalks with gleaming machetes, moving with a design and rhythm accompanied by chants or shouts that together created a natural dance form.

Shawn's way of looking at, understanding, and digesting all movement lent a certain texture peculiar to his own work-derived movement ideas, to which he gave a quality larger than life or mere imitation. I think he conceived such movement as akin to the continuous progress, the rise and fall, the regularity and dynamics of the cosmos, even as he recognized the vagaries of human life. I particularly remember his attention riveted on the ceremonial dances we saw American Indians perform at the pueblo of San Ildefonso, and his brooding over seeming inconsistencies. He soon discovered that the unending and unintelligible chants, which became monotonous to the untutored, bore within them a subtle, subliminal complexity that could be explained only when one understood that the words of the chant determined the minute changes in the rhythms and execution of the steps. It could be said that the American Indians invented Music Visualization.

I can imagine how, in Cuba, Shawn absorbed the shape of a machete's light swing as it is raised high in a clutching brown hand. I can see him studying the movement of body and legs as muscles respond to the sharp downthrust of the cut into the base of the cane. These sun-drenched memories surfaced in the cold dampness of a late New England winter when Shawn began to arrange the dance he called *Cutting the Sugar Cane*. This was originally designed for the four men who were to premiere it at the historic first all-male dance concert in 1933. It then became a part of the regular repertory of the Men Dancers. A work stark in line and technique, it nevertheless contained the literal acting that is taboo in some dance areas today. On October 9, 1936, however, the critic of the *Montreal Daily Star* was to write appreciatively, "*Cutting the Sugar Cane* is a masterpiece of pantomime."

The dance developed such great audience appeal and had so much inherent strength that Shawn recreated it as a solo for himself, and I later danced it in concert in this country as well as during my stint in the Air Force in England throughout the war. It was very popular with soldier audiences because it was undeniably "masculine" and easily understood. Its syncopated rumba beat made it musically appealing. Although it was a simple dance, it was always a challenge to the group to keep in correct form the straight, long lines of its choreography. When I reconstructed it as a solo, even though the last section was in essence a repetition of the first, I changed it to harder, stronger, cleaner, and heavier movements to make up for the absence of the three other dancers.

Our costumes consisted only of red neckerchiefs and full, white cotton Cuban work pants tied with a red belt. The four workers are portrayed under the unrelenting heat of an equatorial sun while they slash, carry, and stack the sugar cane. When the overseer's back is turned, they interrupt this work pattern in relief and laughter to compete in executing different patterns of village dance steps. Then the overseer bursts upon this moment of levity to whip the men back to work. At the end of the day, they are seen wearily carrying bundles of cut cane on their backs as they start offstage. But the leader exits with a final, cavorting leap of defiance that seems to cry, "Curses to you! Our spirits are high!"

Barton Mumaw in *Dyak Spear Dance*, photographed with stroboscopic light at 1/30,000 sec.

DYAK SPEAR DANCE
Choreography: Barton Mumaw, 1934
Music: Jess Meeker (specially composed)
First Performance: October 4, 1934 by Barton Mumaw; Hawley
Armory, Storrs, Conn.

Christena L. Schlundt, in her excellent chronology, *The Professional Appearances of Ted Shawn and his Men Dancers*,* credits the choreography of this dance to Shawn. But Ted, in going over her manuscript, may have forgotten the actual circumstances of its creation: while he contributed inspiration, encouragement, and advice, the movements were mine.

Much of the material for the second tour of the Men Dancers was tried out on those who attended our summer "Teas." With only that one performance a week, we were free to devote most of our energies to technique (at that time, some of us were barely one jump ahead of our audience) and to creating dances for the next season's program. Each Friday afternoon, Shawn talked to the faithful on such subjects as "The Training of a Dancer," "Labor Rhythms and Themes," "The Primitive Dance," and "The Eternal Dance and the Modern Dance." There, in the studio, we used the people sitting at stage level as sounding boards for new works. Shawn always claimed that "If a dance in the studio—in almost skeletal form, without theatrical lighting, makeup or costume—proves to be successful, then it deserves to be dressed and lighted and presented in a theatre." Props as well as fabrics had often provided the stimulus for many Denishawn dances, however, although each work had to prove worthy of repetition in public before it was added to the repertory.

Ted and I were reminiscing one day as we unpacked crates that had been sent up to the Pillow from Denishawn House, when we came upon the wooden box that housed the spear for Shawn's *Danse Japonaise.* (I had first seen him perform this exciting solo in Boston the previous year.) Opening the container, Shawn took up the weapon, hefted its familiar weight, and wondered aloud if he might include the dance in the coming tour. Would there be room enough in the truck for the spear's packing crate and for the specially designed box that carried his samurai wig? As he returned the spear to its case, his hand fell upon a smaller spear. This was long and black, with a small necklace of feathers near the blade tip and colored

*New York: The New York Public Library, 1967.

strands of cord wound around the handgrip. "Look at this, Barton!" Ted exclaimed. "It is made from ironwood, if I remember correctly, because that material is exceptionally hard and straight. The blade is deadly sharp. Be careful." He handed me the weapon, which I seized and, with a light, almost flippant gesture, aimed at an imaginary target. "No!" Shawn shouted. "Not like *that*! You have to remember that until recently the Dyaks were headhunters. Their style was close to the earth in more ways than one." I think the idea for a Dyak dance came to both of us at that moment.

We had been working in the studio on a Maori War Haka and a Ponca Indian ensemble. Shawn began to visualize an entire section of our next program devoted to Primitive Dances. He brought out books and pictures about the Dyaks. Among these, he found a snapshot taken during a brief side trip into Borneo during the Orient tour. He was wearing a cap and plus fours and stood next to a diminutive Dyak warrior in full regalia. I had my costume.

The warrior's headdress featured feathers that looked like plain turkey feathers to me, but Ted pointed out the five white "eyes" at the end of each plume. These, he told me, came from the Argus pheasant and were as iridescent as the eyes in a peacock's tail. Since Argus pheasant feathers were in short supply in our area of the globe, we used the turkey feathers that resembled them, carefully painting the "eyes" in their proper space on each feather. A flat, turbanlike headdress, made from handloomed material, held the feathers in place at the back, so that they fanned out on each side.

For the rest of the brief costume, Ted fished out of his Orient collection a very wide belt made of stiffly woven cloth. From this, he fashioned a high-waisted G-string to which we attached strings of colored wooden beads that hung on each side of the pouch in front and trailed down in back over the considerably exposed rear. This nod to modesty also proved very decorative and interesting in movement. Strips of cloth the color of red earth crossed my chest like bandoliers, but instead of cartridges they displayed "gold" pieces, the warrior-hunter's entire fortune. These strips were held tightly to each hip. My wrists were braceletted with the same material, my upper arms were encircled by cowrie shells, and a beaded choker was tied around my neck.

Spear in hand and costume accomplished, Jess Meeker was brought on to the scene to help us realize a hunting dance. With his invaluable collaboration, I translated the rhythms he created on the piano into movements that it would have been impossible for me to compose out of thin air. My hunting story thus began with leaping strides, as if I as the hunter were traveling through high grasses, at the same time manipulating the spear to get a sense of its weight and balance. I next do a series of off-center jumps, ending with a thrust to test my skill and show off my dexterity to my companions. Then—suddenly—I am alone in the forest on the trail of my prey. (I always imagined I was stalking a great, beautiful, striped tiger.) I slowly and silently creep closer to him with long, crouching, slithering steps. But all at once, the animal turns on me and I have to attack. He springs around to my other side and I attack again. This time, he stands his ground for an instant, then comes at me so swiftly that I am compelled to jump straight up into the air and strike at him from above as he streaks beneath me. I follow him like an arrow and, with a great leap, bury the spear in his jugular.

As was the custom of the Dyaks, I perform the ritual of thanking the tiger and telling him I was sorry to have had to kill him. Also, according to Dyak culture, I have to propitiate the gods with gestures to the four quarters of the earth. Only after that has been done am I free to celebrate my victory with a series of fast, intricate, weaving steps, twirling the spear as I advance toward the audience. Heavy stamp-thrusts, a swift whirl with the spear circling me in spirals, and a crash of the spear to the ground as I jump high with arms outflung and up in exultation brings the dance to its end.

It was all over in a matter of minutes, but I have been told that no one who ever saw this solo could forget it. It was without "padding," it was full of "pictures," it was vigorous and suspenseful, it was theatrical in the tradition of Denishawn, and it had roots that audiences could recognize.

A word about props: In theatre language, a "practical" prop is one that can be handled as if in everyday life. This handling is an art in itself. Suzanne Shelton notes in her biography of Ruth St. Denis, "The unvarnished practicality of her movements—the way she hoisted her flower-chain in _Radha_, the way she set down her tray in _Incense_, as any housemaid would do—was a powerful antidote to the farfetched exoticism of her dances."*

This is an interesting observation, because props have a life of their own that must be respected, even when they are used symbolically. To the audience, my hold on the Dyak spear may have seemed light and easy throughout the dance. In fact, the muscles of my right hand, fingers, and arm were achingly aware that they must never relax their control of this potentially lethal practical prop.

*Suzanne Shelton, _Divine Dancer_ (Garden City, N.Y.: Doubleday, 1981), p. 64.

Men Dancers rehearsing *Kinetic Molpai* at Jacob's Pillow. Ted Shawn right,
Barton Mumaw third from left.

KINETIC MOLPAI

Choreography: Ted Shawn, 1935
Music: Jess Meeker (specially composed)
First Performance: October 5, 1935 by Ted Shawn and his Men Dancers; Clark School, Goshen, N.Y.
Later Performance by Norman Walker and Group: July 1962; Ted Shawn Theatre, Jacob's Pillow, Mass.
Performance by Alvin Ailey City Center Dance Theatre, as restaged by Barton Mumaw: November 16, 1972; City Center Theater, New York

Kinetic Molpai was, I believe, Shawn's crowning achievement for his Men Dancers. Originally a separate dance, it was later titled *The Future* and became the closing segment of *O, Libertad!,* the first full-evening production of a contemporary dance work.

Shawn began to set the work on us with no definite theatrical idea beyond experimenting haphazardly with forms he developed from his knowledge of Delsarte—oppositions, successions, parallelisms, tension and relaxation, rising and falling, response to natural forces, movements of water, of air, of resolution, the motion of a single body in relation to the group, architectonic forms resulting from bodies that moved in unison or fell in succession or simultaneously. Together with more formal gymnastic and balletic combinations, these were all grist for his mill long before he knew what kind of flour they would make.

Shawn considered the concept "abstract" to be as inexact as "modern," contending that all movement had meaning because it depended upon the human body. *Kinetic Molpai* proved his contention because, within the compositional structure he evolved, his choreography projected dramatic immediacy directly from the dancers to those watching them.

But Shawn did not want to leave his audiences helplessly trying to guess what we were doing, despite their gut reaction to what they saw. He sought an explanation for the powerful, programless dance strophes he had created. His old friend, Lucien Price, provided the perfect answer when he explained, "To utter in dance that for which no other language exists is the Molpê." He gave Ted a copy of Gilbert Murray's *The Classical Tradition in Poetry,* wherein the great teacher used the word Molpê to designate one of the earliest marriages of movement and song-poetry. It was, as *New York Times* dance

critic, Anna Kisselgoff, was later to note, the root of Greek drama
that preceded the dithyramb.

Molpai were the primitive beginnings of dance, music, and
song used for secular and religious celebration; sowing, reaping, and
harvesting as well as magic rites.

> In its essence [wrote Murray] it is only the yearning of the whole
> dumb body to express that emotion—the Greeks would say that
> longing—for which words and harp and singing are not enough
> (p. 34). . . . Love, Strife, Death, and that which is beyond Death.
> These are definitely the four themes about which our earliest bards
> sang, and, when singing was not enough to express all their stress of
> emotion, yearned and reached out their arms amid the dancers
> (p. 40).

We did feel the arms of the audience yearning and reaching out
"amid the dancers" for, at every performance of *Kinetic Molpai*, applause came long before the final movement. This always gave us
great joy, no matter how weary or depressed we might have been,
because such response lifted us to the ecstasy that Gilbert Murray
asserted was often part of the molpai's effect.

For those who never saw this work, I regret I must rely on
ineffectual words to describe it. Shawn and the eight Men Dancers
were dressed alike in long brown pants made of a handwoven raw
silk that hung heavily on the legs. Cut to fit tightly at waist and hips,
these trousers graduated to very wide bottoms that flared with a
sculptural effect in moments of exultation and tension. They were
held to our bare torsos by leather belts, and around our wrists we
wore wide leather bands. From its inception, Jess Meeker's music
was an integral part of the choreography: what was extraordinary
was that the dance done without music and the music done without
dance were equally powerful. Together, they made an invincible impact upon performers and audiences alike. The finished suite was in
eleven parts, each flowing without a break into the next and each
appropriately titled in the program as an aid to audience understanding of this novel "abstract" choreography.

The work opened with "Strife," in which Shawn, as the epit-
ome of a hero, strides from center stage in a large circle with a tread
that signifies he could walk over corpses without a qualm. He gestures to the four corners of the earth, calling out the eight dancers
who become his followers in a display of warlike movement.
Clenched fists and contracted muscles indicate brute strength barely
under control; heavy-footed tramping suggests military drill. This

comes to a climax when Dennis, as a sacrifical figure, throws himself
flat on his back downstage center. The other men stride forward,
kneel, and, lifting his rigid body on their hands, throw him straight
up over their heads as they rise swiftly to catch his descending weight
on the backs of their bent necks. It was a breathtaking moment until
the men, each holding Dennis by an arm and a leg, throw him flat to
the floor again where he turns and turns as if he has been drawn and
quartered. When all the other dancers exit, he rises to his feet as I reenter to participate in "Oppositions."

From opposite sides of the stage, we do a stylized baseball
pitcher's windup figuration, at the end of which three dancers enter
to form a file before each of us, as if in response to our pulling-in
movements of tension. The two center figures lead thrusts and parries, one line making a thrust while the other parries. The whole
weaves into an intricate design on a loom of movement. This develops into a swaying backward and forward of one against two. The
"twos" fall backward in an interlacing pattern, then sit up forcibly
to face the "ones" standing opposite them. Suddenly, the music
changes to harmonious chords as the fallen men rise to join the others and, in seeming brotherhood, all leave the stage in pairs, walking
with a soft, measured tread.

The solemn exit introduces "Solvent." Signifying Divine
Love, "that universal all-embracing love which unites nations and
divers peoples in harmony" (as Ted wrote in the program note), this
was a Shawn solo in lyric movement centered upon the Denishawn
pas de basque. * There were also sustained low turns, turns *en arabesque*
(modified from the classic form), and those spiral turns that were a
particularly innovative part of Denishawn technique. Combined
with slow walking patterns, the whole conveyed an impression of
infinite peace, its deceptive simplicity and calm disguising the immense control required for its performance.

This is interrupted by "Dynamic Contrasts," in which one
dancer bursts onto the stage with an explosive turning figuration as
he crouches close to the floor, arms wrapped around his body. Three
more dancers follow him in the same progression. Shawn responds
to their energy and tension with gestures of comfort, facing the men
with his arms outheld as if he yearned to help but realized it was
useless. When at last he leaves the stage, the dancers are joined by

---

*Patterned on the standard *pas de basque,* but with the feet close to the floor and the arms held
high and parallel overhead as the body arches sideways toward the leading foot. For more
detail, see Barton Mumaw with Jane Sherman, "Ted Shawn, Teacher and Choreographer,"
Dance Chronicle, IV:2, 1981.

the other four, and the section builds to a dynamic, bravura pattern of bodies turning at different levels, contrasting with pulsing, "breathing" moments. In a series of low, individually spaced turns, all but three of the dancers disappear. Those three walk upstage left, where the section called "Resilience" begins.

Since Mac, Dennis, and I were the "light" ones of the group, Shawn had composed this trio especially for us. He used us as if we were one, keeping us on the same level throughout, even when we moved in sequence. Every step was quick and off the floor; most of the time one's elbow or finger or foot touched that of another's to maintain our entity. The effect of lightness and precision depended on our buoyancy as a unit, particularly in a passage of *ciseaux-coupé-assemblé*. We repeated this combination three times. These and other joyous variations, following the somber opening sections, always struck audiences as pleasingly humorous. The trio ends with low *sauté* turns that allow the other five dancers of the group to feed in, one after the other, until we form one large circle. Our movements then subside into a plain walk of two groups of four, one downstage right, one down left. This walk establishes the motif for the next section, "Successions."

Here was a study developed from Delsarte's concept of the division of movement itself into three categories: oppositions, parallelisms, and successions. Successive movement is that which passes through a hand, a limb, a body, a group in a smooth, unbroken, wavelike progression. This section, therefore, developed an architectural successive form as one group follows after another in duplicated combinations. With flowing movements, our torsos reach toward one another or outward and away in varying relationships that contrast with the walking patterns. These are sometimes in circles, sometimes in files, demonstrating different styles of walks—long and low, fast and light, smooth and staccato. (Audiences were intrigued as they tried to follow the different "voices" in this canon structure. It was always a challenge for each interpenetrating group to hold its own "voice" because parts of this section were so rapid that it was difficult for all four dancers of one "voice" to arrive at the correct spot at the musical cue—and in correct formation.) As we cross one another at the end of this movement, Shawn arranged it so that, although there were only eight of us to cover the space, he could slip in unnoticed, upstage center to begin his solo, "Unfolding and Folding."

The audience discovers his crouched figure only after we walk slowly off downstage right and left. His first motion of unfolding seems to come from the earth itself as he rises by degrees to suggest the struggle of growth. The dance is another study in succession, now with dramatic overtones. There are moments when he tries to overcome adversity, only to be struck down and then to try again. As he explores every variation of unfolding and folding movements, the theme of birth, maturation, and death becomes obvious. "Dirge" logically follows.

Here emotion is expressed as an ensemble experience after I, as leader of the group, discover the warrior-leader, Shawn, lying dead. I call the men together with realistic, if hieratic gestures, and we move in sequences that resemble a frieze of Greek soldiers. During these figurations, we shield Shawn's figure so that, again unseen by the audience, he can exit.

We move like bas-reliefs as we file across the rear of the stage in a progression that strikes a brooding, bitter note. Then, gathering together upstage left, the group suddenly seems free of all earthly attachment when some of us begin to walk in a swift, smooth, almost floating manner, as if borne on the wind and moved by its vagaries. The second group is caught up in this. The dancers cover the stage in expanding and contracting shapes, sometimes following one another, sometimes intermingling then separating into spiral formations. These formations convey the impression of characters influenced by outside forces and lost in "Limbo"—which was the title of this section.

The section "Surge" follows, a combination that creates the illusion of violent storm waves. Here all movements are vigorous, swift, done full out. (As Anna Kisselgoff wrote in a December 1972 *New York Times* review of my recreation for the Alvin Ailey company, "Its patterns can be magnificent and its cascade of men rising and falling in the *Surge* section is nothing short of compelling.") These patterns consist of a low swinging forward and backward, followed by a complete circle of the body and a reaching out to the fullest extent, followed in turn by a high straight jump into the air, into a backward fall, a roll-over on the floor, a full body circle, then a repeat of all. Since these formations are done repeatedly one after the other, our overlapping movements as we progress across the stage fool the eye into believing there are many more dancers than there really are. This effect invariably brought applause. It was a section that was also particularly enhanced by Jess Meeker's score, which rumbled and splashed up and down the scale in polyrhythmic style.

The end of "Surge" finds us all lying in a circle on our backs, head to toe, with the right arm (inside the circle) stretching backward on the floor to join the left hand of the dancer who is lying just behind. We are linked together in a single tight grip when Shawn enters in a running walk to circle the group. He reaches down to take hold of my hand, and runs clockwise, thus pulling each dancer to his feet in succession until we seem to fling around his head. This action always raised audience expectations as to what might happen by the time the last reclining man in the circle soared into the air at the end of the "crack the whip."

What did happen was "Apotheosis"—Shawn's dream of heaven in a waltz movement that showed us off in a free ballet fashion. First, the ensemble dances. Then every man does a solo which he had composed himself. As each phrase finishes, the next immediately follows, even at times overlapping, to create a mounting excitement that invariably set off an explosion of applause long before the conclusion of the work. Never one to understate his convictions, Shawn's program note on this final section calls it a "dynamic, exhilarating, radiant climax of life deified and glorified."

Shawn reported from Jacob's Pillow in 1935:

> When *Molpai* was finished, the audience at the Tea rose and yelled until they were hoarse. This audience has never been vocal before, even though always genuinely enthusiastic. Afterwards dozens came up with actual tears streaming down their cheeks. One hardboiled man who came for the first time (one of the unwilling males dragged there by his wife) said he was so unprepared for what happened that he ranked it among the five or six experiences of his life. Letters have piled up from those who said they were too moved even to speak to me after the performance.

Writing about *Kinetic Molpai* in the *Boston Herald* of March 11, 1936, and again on October 15, Walter Terry said:

> One can look at the *Molpai* as a series of masterful and exciting movement sequences ending in a group of virtuosic solos. But there is a great deal more there if one wants to see it. These elemental truths concern every man, and as Shawn dances them they are truly abstract, for the beholder may receive them in terms of his own knowledge and experience of strife and love and death. . . . This new work of Shawn's has triumphed over the restraining hands of antagonistic dance schools—it isn't modern, it isn't ballet, it isn't Denishawn. It is, rather, the dance in its essence and at its fullest. . . . We should be proud of Shawn, the choreographer, the dancer, the director and educator, for he has united the clean and vital ath-

letics of modern America with the profundity of ageless art, giving us
a truly great American dance.

In the *New York Herald Tribune* of that same year, Mr. Terry wrote
that "Ted Shawn's *Kinetic Molpai* is to my mind not only one of the
greatest dance works I have ever seen, but an art work that is as
great in form, as rich in emotional content, and as titanic in theme as
the greatest of Wagner's music dramas."

PIERROT IN THE DEAD CITY
Choreography: Ted Shawn, 1931
Music: Erich Korngold, "Mein Sehnen, Mein Wahnen" from *Die Tote Stadt*
First Performance: October 5, 1935 by Barton Mumaw; Clark School, Goshen, N.Y.

During his 1931 tour of Germany, Shawn heard Erich Korngold's opera, *Die Tote Stadt.* He was deeply moved by the baritone aria, "Mein Sehnen, Mein Wahnen" which, in a rough summary, reads:

> My longing, my dreaming, reach into the past
> Dancing means happiness, found and lost,
> Want and need, love and hate
> Such is the dancer's fate.
> My longing, my dreaming, reach into the past
> Again . . . again . . . again. . . .

It was on this theme and to this melody that Shawn created his first solo for me in the earliest days of our relationship. This dance has always had a special place in my heart for that reason: it was to become the symbol of my career. Brief and evanescent as it was, it contained those elements that comprise the stuff of life—the yearnings, hopes, joys, sorrows, fulfillments, and frustrations that are personified in the mythical clown.

In 1921, Shawn had choreographed *Pierrot Forlorn* as his first solo for the young Charles Weidman. It was, I am told, a cliché of a rose-colored dance to undistinguished music, of which Charles made a Chaplinesque gem of wit and poignancy. Ten years later, Ted developed a stronger, sadder character to the haunting, modern Korngold waltz. On the Men Dancers tours, the dance was accompanied by piano; for my solo concert at Carnegie Recital Hall, by voice and piano; on my South African tour, by full orchestra.

Shawn garbed me in Pierrot's traditional pleated neck ruff and flowing tunic with long, full sleeves worn with pyjamalike pants. These he wanted made from material that would suggest a figure moving through mist. The search for the right fabric began long before the dance was created. While on tour, Ted and I prowled the aisles of the yard-goods sections of department stores, big and little, whenever we had a free hour. One day, we were rushing through a store in the maligned Middle West (whose inhabitants we found to be much more au courant than their reputation had led us to be-

Above: Charles Weidman in *Pierrot Forlorn,* choreographed in 1921, at the Imperial Theatre, Tokyo, September 1925.

Below: Barton Mumaw in *Pierrot in the Dead City.*

lieve), when Shawn caught sight of a bolt of exactly the desired hue
of ghostly material. Immediately unwinding yards and yards of the
cloth, we waved them through the air to test the drift and drape.
Salesladies assembled to gape at us, too astonished to attempt to stop
our antics before we had decided the fabric was just what we had
been looking for. Alas, funds as always being short, we bought only
enough yardage for one Pierrot.

I still have the costume that was made of that material. It became discolored and ragged with use, but no subsequent costume
was ever as successful.

*Miss Ruth once succinctly revealed to me the importance of a tried and
trusted costume, no matter what its age and condition: During a rehearsal of her*
Legend of the Peacock, *I happened to look closely at the long, glittering train
that represented the bird's tail. It was so bedraggled and filthy that I blurted aloud,
"Why, in heaven's name, doesn't she have that cleaned?" To which, without
missing a peacock's strut, Miss Ruth answered in a penetrating tone, "Because,
dear, in heaven's name it would fall apart!"*

At the Pillow, Shawn supervised the design and making of my
costume. He himself manipulated the fabric in a dye pot so that a
deep Concord grape color remained at the unhemmed edges of the
sleeves, pants, and ruff, shading into the gray body of blouse and
trousers. Then he devised the scenario for our love-child. The leg-
endary Pierrot returns by moonlight to the city where, in his youth,
he had loved and lost Pierrette. He is now a wraith and the city is
deserted. Confused though he is, he nevertheless discovers a few
signs of the past which beguile him into believing that he is back in
the time when he used to serenade his beloved. With his customary
attention to theatrical detail, Shawn used a combination of steel-blue
overall lighting, with a lavender follow spot from the wings at one
side of the stage and one of purple from the other, thus achieving the
desired eerie effect.

For the choreography of *Pierrot,* Shawn devised a floor pattern
of circles, spirals, diagonals, and straight lines. The dancer, entering, seems to be *pulled* toward center stage and then into a circle as he
tries to orient himself in the dimly lighted space. In a spiral turn, he
breaks through the barrier of gloom for an instant, only to be drawn
back into the circular pattern of despair. Suddenly, a light appears in
Pierrette's window, high above him offstage right. Pierrot's surprise
repels him diagonally back and away from it. When he "sees" her
come out onto the balcony, his ecstasy propels the phantomlike figure diagonally toward and away from her, in repeated retreat and
advance that express his passionate longing. At the height of his joy,

the light in the "window" fades. He refuses to believe that he has lost Pierrette again. In a small diagonal pattern moving to the left away from the "balcony," he executes a series of Volinine beats (so called in honor of Anna Pavlova's great partner, whose tour de force they were). These hesitate and falter, as if the dancer's heart were fluttering near death. Pierrot makes one last forward progression to convince himself that his love has indeed vanished. Then he retreats to disappear into the mists from which he had come.

There were few technical fireworks in the solo, each movement having been contrived to make the most immediate dramatic effect, but the work was full of *luft* pauses that permitted held-breath suspensions.

To me, a suspension in dance resembles a singer's voice descending from a high to a low note in a single, delicate, smooth phrase. There comes a moment of balance, when the dance movement is clearly etched in space until, like a breaking wave, it overflows and falls into a resolution. Nijinsky is reputed to have had this quality—a "floating" at the apogee of a leap. The emphasis on quality of movement characterized Denishawn training, in contrast with many of today's techniques where the dance titles may change but the movement quality too often remains the same.

Other basic steps in *Pierrot* were a turn in *arabesque,* sustained *arabesques,* spiral turns, a *grand battement en l'air, pas de basque,* a *renversé,* and *chaîné* turn. These made up the vocabulary of the work. But only the manner in which the "words" were arranged by the choreographer and spoken by the performer created the "*life*" of this dance. It existed as a brief remembrance of things past that had strong audience appeal.

Shawn did not permit me to perform *Pierrot* in public for four years after he had created it, feeling the work demanded certain emotional depths that I, at age nineteen, had not yet explored, certain nuances that I was not ready to project. When I first did dance it, people said how marvelous it was that one so young could portray the emotion it called for. When I was older, they would say that I must have lived through a similar experience in order to be able to project it so convincingly. Yet no movement of the dance changed to any noticeable degree in all the years I performed it. I learned from Shawn that in youth—simply from the gifts of sheer litheness and agility—one gets credit for more than is really there. Next comes the hard, discriminating labor when the machine must be trained physically, mentally, and emotionally. At last, if you are lucky, you acquire the technique, the confidence, and the courage to dare to dance as you wish.

This is what produces those few moments in a dancer's career when everything goes superbly. The audience is receptive, the music is in perfect accord with you, the lighting cues are precise, the costume seems part of your body, you do not drop any props, you do not fall flat on your face on a slippery stage, and you move through space like an angel. Such moments can be counted on the fingers of one-and-a-half hands over a lifetime. But they are what keeps a dancer going—what kept Shawn going for sixty of his eighty years—despite the bittersweet knowledge that the Celestial Pub-Keeper may at any moment announce, "Time, please, gentlemen."

Audiences and critics alike refused for years after the premiere of this dance to let me retire Pierrot. Walter Terry was to write in the *New York Herald Tribune* of April 19, 1941, "One of the finest things in American dance—Mumaw's great romantic fantasy *Pierrot in the Dead City* strengthened the conviction that he is one of the few great dancers of the younger American group." Almost thirty years later, the critic for the *Berkshire Eagle* noted about my 1970 performance of *Pierrot* at Jacob's Pillow, "The decades disappear under his nimble feet and soaring body. Having seen the original performance in the 1930's, we can detect no hint of fading vigor or faltering artistry. It's uncanny and delightful."

But the summation of *Pierrot* I most treasure was written by Lucien Price in a 1937 letter to Shawn:

> It is anybody's lost youth, including, alas! some day Barton's own. . . . The beauty, the wistfulness, the yearning, the gaiety and tenderness, the grace and the fleeting joy that are packed into those brief moments of the dance are great lyric poetry and I don't wonder that it can make people weep. It is the pathos of human life that it is so beautiful, and so brief. Which is exactly what the dance itself is.

THE BANNER BEARER (From *Olympiad,* a suite of sports
dances forming part of Ted Shawn's full-evening production, *O,
Libertad!*)
Choreography: Barton Mumaw, 1936
Music: Jess Meeker (specially composed)
First Performance: October 7, 1936 by Barton Mumaw; Cherry
Valley School, Garden City, N.Y.

In the summer of 1936, Shawn gave his Men Dancers instructions to
create a section of the new program for the upcoming season. He
wanted us to base this on different sports because so often when
watching football or basketball, he had observed that the motions of
the players were akin to dance movement, and the formations resembled choreographic patterns.

*Since he had been deprived of the use of his legs by temporary paralysis as a
young man, Shawn was always aware of the value of strong, healthy muscular
development, as distinct from that required essentially for dance. This was so
important to him that, whenever we were in New York, Ted and I would take a
class with Joseph Pilates, a trainer whose original system was championed by
Shawn, St. Denis, and other dancers whom they had brought to his studio. As
often as it could be arranged, Pilates taught at Jacob's Pillow for Shawn felt that,
in order to achieve technical perfection, the dancer should be given exercises purely to
strengthen and control the body. Indeed, his most quoted definition of grace was
"efficiency of movement."*

*In the years following his death, the use of Pilates's unique technique de-
clined somewhat, but was revitalized by the recent publication,* The Pilates
Method of Physical and Mental Conditioning *by Philip Friedman and
Gail Eisen.* * *This is an update of Pilates's 1960* Return to Life Through
Contrology, *which had been published by the Christopher Publishing House in
Boston. St. Denis, Shawn, Margaret H'Doubler, and other figures prominent in
dance and physical education wrote blurbs for its jacket.*

The Men Dancers held a private powwow to decide which
sports we would include in our allotted section, and who would choreograph what. Wilbur McCormack opted for "Boxing," based on
his experiences as a boxer and wrestler at Springfield College. Frank
Overlees chose to do "The Cheer Leaders" with Dennis Landers
and Mac. Foster Fitz-Simons, he of many talents, elected the
multifaceted "Decathlon." Fred Hearn asked Dennis to oppose him

---

*Garden City, N.Y.: Doubleday, 1980; paperbound, New York: Warner Books, 1981.

Barton Mumaw in performance in *The Banner Bearer.*

in "Fencing," while Denny drafted the team of Mumaw, Hearn, McCormack, Overlees, and himself for "Basketball."

This left choreographer Mumaw up in the air for, unlike the others, I had never excelled in any one particular sport. I had played basketball only when I could not avoid it, and participated in some soccer. Living in Florida on a lake for most of my early life, I swam, of course, and at Rollins I had gone out for crew, but neither watery activity seemed danceable. I did not discover the solution to my dilemma until I saw, of all things, a Soviet poster of a man waving a red banner. The Russian script could have been promoting the merits of Coca-Cola for all I knew or cared because, just as Ruth St. Denis long ago had been inspired by a poster advertising Egyptian cigarettes, I knew at once that I had found my sports solo. In my mind's eye, I superimposed the five circles of the Olympics insignia upon a banner that symbolized the sacred flame from Mount Olympus, and I would be "The Banner Bearer." It was not until years later, when I finally saw it in performance that I realized the poster had advertised the ballet *The Red Poppy*, and that the dancer, in reality, used a very thin ribbon attached to a short wand. In contrast to my concept, both ribbon and wand had to be manipulated close to the body.

My banner turned out to be nine yards long and nine inches wide, fixed to a wand that was four feet in length. The white China silk of which it was made was bound in orange and bore the five varicolored, interlocked Olympic circles. I wore a white silk long-sleeved leotard with the same insignia on my chest. It was only when I began to work with the unwieldy length of my banner that I fully appreciated and respected the skill and artistry of Denishawn scarf technique, performed by seemingly delicate young ladies. I quickly discovered that, in order to keep in motion a lifeless twenty-seven feet of fabric, I had to have the arm and body strength of an Olympic athlete, for sure. Often close to despair, I learned that I must measure energy precisely to be transmitted through the entire length of the banner, or its end would not lift and I would either trip on it in the next step or end up wrapped in a cocoon from which I must foolishly unwind, much to the disgust or amusement of an audience.

In the long run, my "Banner Bearer" was choreographed by the banner itself. My intentions as well as my inspiration were at the mercy of what it would do, given its teasing impulses. I found that I could jump with it in open *sauté* turns without landing on its tail. I found that I could whirl it in spirals about my body while standing still or while turning myself. I could make it undulate in snakelike patterns, or I could stand motionless, after giving the scarf impetus, and watch it arch over my head, then catch it just before it lost its power and repeat the action. I made figure eights both high in the air and close to the floor. These demanded great strength but their effect made the effort worthwhile. And I ended the dance in a series of diagonal jumping turns with the banner held aloft like a following flame.

The day finally came when we tried out our sports suite before an audience at the Pillow studio (the Ted Shawn Theatre had not yet been built). Shawn explained the section, stressing how proud he was to show the first individual work of "the boys." Since my solo was the prelude to the games that were to follow, I was particularly nervous, even though Jess Meeker and I had rehearsed without incident just before the performance. But hardly had I made my entrance when the infernal banner caught around the staff, and within two seconds I was frozen midstage, swaddled like a babe in arms.

"Jesus!" I yelled.

Jess stopped playing. The audience sat in stunned silence while I disentangled myself from the grip of the silken boa constrictor. Then I signaled Jess to start again from the beginning.

This time I made it and, of course, the audience responded with exceptional enthusiasm, as when a juggler misses an "impossible" trick then does it perfectly. I had not planned this miss, however, and learned bitterly from the experience that I must pay strict attention to that banner's every impulse, no matter how exhausted I might be.

After my "exciting performance" (as a newspaper review was to describe it), I rushed to find Shawn and apologize for my inexcusable and irreverent expletive. I knew he would be tolerant of my tangled "Olympic flame," but I was apprehensive because I also knew that his relationship to God was deep, personal, and familiar to his audiences. When I had finished my apology, Ted put his arm around my shoulders and said, simply, "Who better to call upon for help?"

The *Olympiad* became a most popular series of dances. In "The Cheer Leaders" that followed my "Banner Bearer," Overlees had created a happy trio with its participants mirroring one another in their white corduroy trousers and white sweat shirts, with a large orange S on the chest. Fitz-Simons's "Decathlon" brought pictures of the ancient Olympics to mind: his body, in short white trunks which allowed a display of muscles not often seen on the stage at that time, could have been an inspiration for Praxiteles. Hearn and

Landers proved superb in "Fencing," their foils seeming actual extensions of their finely attenuated body lines. McCormack, as
"Boxer," gave as good as he got. One could almost see his opponent
as Mac went down for a count. But he recovered to win the bout.
Denny's "Basketball" was so thrillingly realistic that basketball fans
and coaches alike frequently came backstage to advise us, "But you
can't do such-and-such," as if we were really their home team.

     Yet, of all of us, I think composer-pianist Jess Meeker was the
real star of our Olympics. I doubt if Jess had ever pitched a baseball
or dribbled a basketball or kicked a football in his life. But he worked
closely with each of us as he composed for our dance, making perti-
nent suggestions and tailoring his music to the rhythms of the thrust-
ing foil, the bouncing ball, or the billowing banner.

     Shawn always remained proud of our work in this piece. He
remembered it one night in 1966 when he took Isadora Bennett to
see the Joffrey Ballet at New York City Center, where they performed an all-male ballet called *Olympics*. Ted was careful to note that
Clive Barnes wrote in his review that Shawn's Men Dancers had
produced *Olympiad* on the same theme thirty years earlier.

Barton Mumaw in the "weathervane" pose from *Bourrée*.

BOURRÉE (from Section I of Shawn's full-evening production, *The Dome*)
Choreography: Barton Mumaw, 1939
Music: Johann Sebastian Bach, *Partita No. 1 in B minor for Violin*
First Performance: January 24, 1940 by Barton Mumaw; Surf Club, Miami, Fla.

The *Bourrée* was the first abstract dance I created—abstract in the sense that it had no story and required no program notes. Without my realizing it at the time, it was very like a Denishawn Music Visualization. Perhaps that was inevitable, given my brief Denishawn schooling and the fact that it had been natural since childhood for me to turn to music for movement inspiration. And what music this was! Vigorous, sharply accented, with a definite unceasing, "running" (i.e., *bourrée*) rhythm throughout, the accents softened momentarily with the secondary theme, only to reassert their authority to the conclusion.

It was truly music to give life to a moving body, and that was undoubtedly why choreographing to it proved to be one of those miraculous experiences where inspiration and execution merged immediately one into the other. As if it were a ticker tape, which I could read and interpret at once, the dance evolved without my having to rework its movements or forms.

I chose a costume as abstract as the music: a white silk, long-sleeved, brief-legged leotard. Although I used ballet steps and positions in the free style Shawn had developed, their execution did not follow a strictly classic discipline. Turns grew out of the passage preceding them rather than from preparations. *Attitudes* were achieved from a bent-over or even a kneeling position. *Pas de bourrées* flowed as smoothly and swiftly as a mountain stream. Extensions, sustained by the beat of feet on the floor, became distorted by extreme back-bends and outflung limbs. The arms moved with classic *port de bras* assurance but never froze into a recognizable ballet position. And because a *bourrée* bespoke a certain courtly dance period, at appropriate moments I deliberately flourished my hands as if lace cuffs encircled their wrists.

These hand gestures were to cause me some disappointment and even anger. At the time when the Men Dancers were to be disbanded and I was considering the next step in my career, Shawn received a letter from the noted dancer, Paul Draper, in which he said that he knew much about me but had never had the opportunity to see me dance. From what he had heard, he surmised it might be possible for us to work together, although I no longer remember in what particular venture. Came the day when Mr. Draper saw me dance the Bourrée, *among other solos—he did not so much as come back afterward to meet me. Instead, he reported to Ted that he found my hand movements in the* Bourrée *"too effeminate." What an ironic blow when the Men Dancers had been lauded for the masculinity of our dances!*

But mine was not the only comeuppance resulting from the conversation between Draper and Shawn. Draper confessed that he was hurt because his own original work of balletic tap dance to classical music was not considered serious art. Why, he asked, should this be? To which Ted answered succinctly that as long as Draper had taps on his shoes, his feet would be tied to a limited expression.

Shawn never thought to tell me that, in the twenties, Doris Humphrey had created her own *Bourrée* to the same music. It would have been fascinating to see the two versions on the same program. Where Humphrey wore a red satin tunic and entered with a powerful downbeat gesture and step, I was all in white and interpreted the opening notes as wings to lift me almost into a *sauté*. Both abstractions must have differed in similarly significant ways throughout the entire dance.

In my solo programs, I wore the same white leotard for what I called my "white ballets": the three opening dances of *The Banner Bearer* (with its streaming white scarf), a Scarlatti *Serenade* (with its hint of lute-playing and emphasis on *épaulement*), and the *Bourrée*. This last short but radiant dance was immortalized when Joseph Franz selected a pose from it to forge into the weathervane that still responds to the winds that blow over the Ted Shawn Theatre at Jacob's Pillow.

Claudia Cassidy, writing in the *Chicago Journal of Commerce*, said of this work, "Mumaw is a brilliant dancer—with great lightness and spectacular technique, and he has audience magnetism. He can mold the classic form into something bodily his own—he proved that with the plastic steel-spring strength of his Bach *Bourrée*, choreographed by himself, and the high point of the whole program of the Men Dancers."

THE GOD OF LIGHTNING (from the suite of dances entitled
Remembrances of Things Past, part of Shawn's full-evening
production, *The Dome*)
Choreography: Barton Mumaw, 1939
Music: Béla Bartok, *Allegro Barbaro*
First Performance: January 24, 1940 by Barton Mumaw;
Temple Theatre, Miami, Fla.

To be a student of Ted Shawn, or a member of his company, considerably broadened one's interests. By the time I came to create my
God of Lightning solo, I had danced and read my way through cultures
Aztec, Amerind, Cuban, Spanish, Japanese, Cretan, ancient and
modern Greek, Maori, African, Afro-American, Singhalese, Dyak,
and American folk. Small wonder it seemed no insurmountable ob-
stacle to imagine a dance inspired by a black-and-white illustration
of the God of Lightning that I had found in Shawn's dog-eared copy
of Prescott's *Conquest of Mexico.* *

   As I have said before, it does appear that when one sets out on a
creative course, one discovers essential elements as if by magic.
Hardly had the picture determined me to become the God of Lightning than I heard Jess Meeker toiling over an unfamiliar composition. Its thumping rhythm, with flashes of brilliant, lightning-like
sound, struck me as a terrifying expression of a god's rage. From
this Bartok music, the choreographic patterns developed easily.

   I knew I would have to dance at an elevation above audience
eye-level if I were to give the illusion of bolts of lightning hurling
down from on high. I also knew that I would have to accommodate
the space and weight of my set to the touring facilities of the Men
Dancers. Therefore, I traced out on the studio floor the size of a
structure that would fit into our company truck and that could serve
both as a platform and as a packing case for props and costumes. I
was irked by this limitation placed on my ''inspiration'' for the
dance. (I have since concluded that it is a benefit for choreographers
to have to cooperate with scenic artists, costumers, composers, and
directors, as in a musical comedy, because this collaboration can test
the calibre of one's craftsmanship.)

   I next had to imagine a costume from the black-and-white hints
of the Prescott illustration. Eventually, I had one made that consisted

---

*William Hickling Prescott, *A History of the Conquest of Mexico* (1843).

Barton Mumaw in *The God of Lightning*.

mainly of a belt of red corduroy with a saw-toothed hem that was outlined in gold and black braid to represent lightning. The fabric was backed by stiff canvas that held the forked shapes. These hung down at regular intervals over a red-black-and-gold G-string fastened low in front with a large, ornate, "golden" East Indian buckle inlaid with coral. Corduroy encircling the wrists fell in jagged points over the backs of the hands like lightning flashes.

The illustration gave no indication of what material might be appropriate for the headdress. I thought of one made from a flat length of wood about three-by-one-half feet, cut into notched edges and having a crownlike center superstructure. With cries of "Help!" I cornered George Horn, the designer of many a wig, headpiece, or prop for the Men Dancers. He said I was crazy to try to dance with such a heavy contraption on my head, but he proceeded to build, paint, and fit it to me. His objections were all too correct: It was like trying to run against the wind with an immovable windmill for a hat—my neck muscles bulged in protest at the effort not to let the thing overbalance me when I danced—I looked like a royal drunk stumbling across the stage.

Since this design was clearly impractical, I searched out an edition of *The Conquest of Mexico* that was illustrated in color. There I saw the frequent use of feathered headdresses, and these reminded me of Shawn's *Noche Triste de Moctezuma,* which we had danced on an earlier tour and for which our costumes were made of every kind of feather, from egret to ostrich. When I handed George a multitude of varicolored feathers, he was able to construct from them a wingèd cupola that seemed gossamer in contrast to the board.

The dance opens as I pose in a spotlight on the platform, my feet wide apart in second position with sharply flexed knees, my arms bent at the elbows, and my hands, with fingers held together, crossed over my chest. As if taking a breath in preparation, I rise slowly to high half-toe in silence. With the crash of my heels on the floor, Jess strikes the first chords of music. Shooting arms out in sharp lightning gestures, the god pounds loud rhythms on the platform as he travels its periphery in a series of stabbing movements, warning the world that he will not be opposed or appeased. In a state of fury, he leaps to Earth, landing on both feet in a vertical spreadeagle position. With a succession of jabbing hand movements, he covers the stage diagonally to right, left, and front. The movements change to the teasing, tentative strikes and withdrawals of a cat playing with a mouse, gestures that represent flickers of heat lightning. He next circles to the back of the platform, mounts it, points skyward toward the zenith, then sinks slowly to his knees to sit on his heels. By locking the fingers of both hands over his eyes, elbows held out high on each side, he gives the impression that he has hidden behind a cloud to conceal his rage. There he stays, watchful.

Soon his knees begin to beat out a rhythm as if on a great drum, in simulation of distant thunder. His body remains erect and motionless while, one after another, an arm flashes out and back as the god uncovers an eye, then retires behind his cloud. The knees maintain their barbaric beating as the hands shoot ever stronger lightning bolts aimed at the Earth: right, left, center, up and over the head until a climax of speed and intensity is reached that drives the god to jump from his thundering knees and land on the floor with both feet.

The cat-and-mouse theme is here repeated, now extended in long diagonals across the stage until the god ceases this game. He shoots out shafts of destruction that culminate in a turning-beating motif in place at center, his hands slapping and snapping like sparks. A final drop to both knees, arms extended downward and out at the sides, appears to be the end of the dance. But the knees resume two measures of threatening beats without any music. Then, on a last sharp chord, the god is galvanized into his original opening pose.

My beating of the knees on the floor of the platform and stage made every dancer who ever saw it cringe. Fortunately, I have un-usually flat kneecaps and never suffered discomfort or injury despite the predictions of my friends and the expectations of my enemies.

Theatrical this work certainly was, but critics and audiences alike did not hold that against me. I really do not know why the term "theatrical" has become pejorative in dance circles. Theatre is arti-fice: the moment a dancer steps out in any space before an audience, the result is theatre and what he or she does is, willy-nilly, theatrical. One can only create "good theatre" or "bad theatre." I like to think my god of lightning created good theatre, and John Martin seems to have thought it was when he wrote in the *New York Times*:

> Barton Mumaw is one of the best young dancers of the day by any-body's standards. He dances with that instinctive flair which cannot be simulated or acquired but belongs only to the born dancer. His technique is brilliant and unstrained, and there is an admirable defi-nition to his movements and his phrasing. There are also depths of feeling behind his movements. It is in part this latent quality which gives him his command of an audience's attention.

FUNERAILLES (WAR AND THE ARTIST or WAR AND THE MAN)
Choreography: Barton Mumaw, 1940
Music: Franz Liszt, *Funerailles*
First Performance; April 16, 1941 by Barton Mumaw; Carnegie Chamber Music Hall, N.Y.

On September 3, 1939, England entered World War II. I do not remember how I learned this foreboding news, but I do remember that it was a brilliant Indian-summer day with a touch of crispness when I walked alone down Carter Road, Jacob's Pillow's still unpaved country lane.

As I passed the house, our dear friend, Lillian Cox, came out to join my vigil. Hers was the one presence I could tolerate as I mumbled through tears about the senseless destruction of honorable and ancient buildings, the carnage of beautiful and wonderful people. A touch of her hand on my arm signaled a stop.

"Barton dear, we don't need the buildings. It was their creation that was important. What is important now is our creation of an environment in which the beautiful and wonderful people who survive can exist."

Lifting me from the indulgence of self-pity, she thus gave me both solace and direction. That winter in Eustis, I began, in the only way I knew, to follow that direction. Moved by Liszt's music, *Funerailles,* I went to work on a dance about two soldiers lost in battle and the effect of their deaths on an artist (me). After weeks of fumble, I knew I had to show my rough outline to someone. I did not seek Ted's opinion at this stage of the solo's development because I feared his suggestions might deflect my tentative approach to the subject I had chosen. Instead, I asked the only one whose opinion of my work I knew would provide insight without distorting my aim, my dearest friend, Mary Kinser.

When she arrived at the studio in response to my invitation, I broke the ice by putting on a record of Richard Tauber singing *Dein ist Mein ganzes Herz,* which had long been a favorite of ours, and we danced together to it as we had done so often. Only then did we sit down as I began to explain my war solo, seeking her ideas for a costume as I postponed my "audition." From her feeling for color and line, as demonstrated in her art work, Mary had discovered a real talent for clothing a dance and for knowing how a costume must

Barton Mumaw in *Funerailles,* danced for soldiers on the eve of D-day in Britain, June 5, 1944.

"work" on a moving body. (I always kept in mind Ruth St. Denis's dictum that "Costumes are not designed, they are suffered.")

But the moment of truth could no longer be put off and Liszt replaced Lehar on the phonograph. Although I was still very unsure of technical bits and subtleties, of beginnings and endings, joinings, pauses, dynamics, and delineation of movement, I presented to Mary's discriminating eyes the dance as it had so far been explored. This first exposure of a work, this trial by fire, corresponded to the period in a kiln that a clay vessel must endure until its colors are fixed. The final glaze is only achieved later in performances that emphasize those patterns which never lose the underlying strength of the original form.

Because my communication with Mary had always been beyond words, I felt none of the tension that might be expected as I awaited her verdict at the end of the dance.

"All I know," she said, "is that what you have done is very moving. The whole body must be seen in motion—its lines must not be obscured. And I know what you are saying. Is that good enough?"

It was good enough for me. I returned with confidence to complete work on the solo. Mary designed and made a costume that was a stylized, impersonal uniform. Its brief, oyster-white, ribbed trunks, trimmed with narrow brown-and-white stripes, derived from no specific nation or era. An arrangement of brown cord, coiled like rope around the waist and over the shoulders, vaguely suggested military dress. This was my costume for the premiere of the work on my first solo concert, and I danced barefoot. But when I performed *Funerailles* overseas for real soldiers on the eve of real battle, I wore a torn, dirty, khaki uniform and boots, with a bloodied bandage tied around my forehead. This was what I always wore subsequently.

The work opens with brittle, nervous movements, the dancer's body turning from profile to profile when he moves warily across the stage as if over a smoke-filled field of rubble that could hide an attacker. Then, suddenly, the soldier relives the conflict he has just survived. Wounded and delirious, he reenacts the loss of two comrades. Through movements depicting the approach of battle and the encounter with the enemy, the audience sees first one, then the other of the soldier's friends shot down. The dancer goes berserk with grief and rage, killing, killing, killing in his turn until he falls exhausted. He manages to rise unsteadily and to gesture a euology over the bodies of his comrades. This culminates in a slow retreat from the front to the rear of the stage. Turning there, the soldier gathers his forces to march straight back toward the footlights, where he halts to stare out at the audience as if to demand, "And what are *you* going to do about this?"

A review in the *New York Herald Tribune* of my concert in April 1941 stated, "In *War and the Man,* theme and technique fused uniquely in a composition of tense power. Taken solely as design, it grew naturally from a core of formal logic. With the thesis of war's havoc on art woven in, it took on the poignant overtones of stunned feeling." This recognition of what I had tried to do raised my spirits when they most needed a lift.

It was not until years later, when I read Findley's *The Wars,* that I realized to my depths what had driven me to create this dance:

> The war was part of it. . . . You live when you live. No one else can ever live your life and no one else will ever know what you know. . . . The thing is . . . not to take refuge in tragedy—but to clarify who you are through your responses to when you lived. If you can't do that, then you haven't made your contribution to the future (p. 115).

WILD HORSE
Choreography: Helen Tamiris, 1946
Music: Irving Berlin, from *Annie Get Your Gun*
First Performance: May 16, 1946 by Daniel Nagrin; New York production
First Performance by Barton Mumaw: October 3, 1947; National company production, Dallas (Texas) State Fair Grounds

During my basic training days in the army, I had been surprised and delighted to discover that Daniel Nagrin was in my outfit. There had never been any rivalry between us. Danny was fully as accomplished a dancer as I, yet he seemed to have real respect for my work. This, of course, made him a friend for life.

I could have no idea at the time that he would be instrumental in bringing me to *Annie Get Your Gun*. After his wife, Helen Tamiris, signed me on for the national company, Danny taught me the Indian dance, which he was performing nightly in Ethel Merman's New York company. The scene that featured the dance was a spectacle based, to a great extent, on the cliché musical comedy concept of American Indians. But Tamiris, by insisting upon some authenticity of costume and steps, gave it the veracity of a real tribal rite.

As the spirit, Wild Horse, I wore a G-string that was minimal even by Shawn standards. This, a sort of breast-plate, and my arm bands had been embroidered in gold thread by a titled lady who had fled the Russian Revolution and supported herself by her fine handwork. The expensive feather headdress was a miracle of design. It ended in a black horsetail that hung down my bare back. Its base was a skullcap that simulated the shaven head of a brave. This cap supported a flaring row of foot-long, vividly colored feathers that curved down the center of the head from front to back, reaching as low as my shoulder blades. The placement of these feathers was a marvel of engineering: they always remained upright but they were also movable, falling forward or backward as my dance movements dictated. Delicate as this headdress appeared, it had to be sufficiently durable to withstand daily wear, tear, perspiration, handling, and packing. My body was covered with a red-tan paint, and my facial makeup took a long time to master: it depicted a horse's head with teeth bared, in a style worthy of Picasso. When costumed and made up, I came as close to epitomizing the spirit of a wild horse as a human could get.

Barton Mumaw as Wild Horse in *Annie Get Your Gun*.

Men and women chorus members open the scene with a ritual dance. At a certain point, the group freezes in apprehension as I appear from nowhere, upstage right, with three spectacular leaps. (I always thought of these as bow-and-arrow-*sautés* because the right leg had to carry the body into the air and, as it reached its straight forward position, draw back in a line to the rear while the left leg bent sharply at the knee and was drawn up under the body. It was as if the bow were strung by the right leg and the body and arm movements shot the arrow at the moment the string was released.)

A struggle at once begins between the men of the chorus and Wild Horse, with the women forming the background of a painted frieze that changes from time to time. Near the climax of the conflict, I perform what I am sure was then a completely new dance movement (I later saw it used by other dancers). This was a creation of Nagrin. While he was coaching me, my jaw dropped when I first saw him straighten from a crouching position to stand on the very tips of his toes with one wonderful flourish of the arms in a circle about his torso as he rose like a bird leaving the earth. "You can do it," Danny assured me. So I did it. The sensation of balancing for just an instant on toe-tips was exhilarating, no matter how often I danced this movement.

Unable to subdue or bridle Wild Horse, the men, in pantomime, try to kill him with bows and arrows. The Spirit outwits them for some time, but he is eventually wounded and falls dead. The victors lift his rigid body high, one leg pointed straight up as if rigor mortis had already turned him into a statue that they carry off the stage.

If a show gets into your blood, it never becomes dull, and I never felt bored while performing throughout the long run of *Annie.* In addition, *Wild Horse* became a dance I treasured, and it even had fans of its own. In one city, we noticed that the same group of young women occupied the same orchestra seats every Saturday matinee. They finally got up their courage to invite me to lunch with them. When I accepted, they presented me with a biography of Nijinsky. During the tour, two oil paintings of Wild Horse were sent to me, although I never met their creators. And one young lady used to come regularly throughout our long Chicago run to sit by herself in a box. This excited so much curiosity among the members of the company that one of them took the trouble to observe that she stayed only long enough to see the Wild Horse scene, then left.

Barton Mumaw in *I'll Make Me a World*, performance at Jacob's Pillow, August 1981.

I'LL MAKE ME A WORLD
Choreography: Barton Mumaw, 1975
Music: Claude Debussy, *La Mer* (first section)
First Performance: 1975 by Barton Mumaw; Temple of the
Living God, St. Petersburg, Fla.
Later Performance by Barton Mumaw: August 1981; Ted
Shawn Theatre, Jacob's Pillow, Mass.

St. Petersburg, Florida, where I now live, has long been a center for
believers in spiritualism and metaphysics. They probably descend
from followers of the theosophists, Annie Besant and Madame
Blavatsky. The Temple of the Living God is a fine example of
present-day studies and practices in these fields. Since the pastor, the
Reverend LeRoy Zemke believes all religious pursuits merit study,
classes for church members and nonmembers are held in yoga, as-
trology, metaphysics, and healing. I had been closely associated with
churches only in my early years and felt no attraction to any particular denomination. I did not care to be told what to believe, but here,
where everyone was welcome no matter what his profession or persuasion, I found the opportunity to study more deeply those forms of
belief to which I had been introduced by the esoteric talks of Ruth
St. Denis and the discussions that formed part of the training Ted
Shawn gave his students.

Given the free atmosphere of the Temple, I was not too surprised when the pastor asked me if I would dance there. He assured
me that I could choose the theme and that it need not have any
religious connotations. I was intrigued by the idea but, alas, the so-
called stage was about the size of a postage stamp and, what was
even worse, it had recently been covered with a much-admired,
sculptured, thick blue carpet. When I considered what seemed to be
this insurmountable problem, I thought aloud, "If there is no space,
what can take the place of space?" I remembered reading somewhere that the Divine Sarah Bernhardt had claimed that if she lost
both arms and legs, but her head and torso remained intact, she
would still be able to act—with her voice, of course. *Voilà!* I must
speak, and I must use my torso (fortunately, with legs and arms
attached).

It has been my experience that the title of a play, one poem
among hundreds in a book, a photograph or painting, a phrase of
music, the observed leap of an animal, a whiff of burning logs on a

frosty morning, the perfume from a passing woman—any one of
these can inspire the creative process. So it was that my latest pot
was set a-boiling when I came across James Weldon Johnson's classic poem, *The Creation,* now titled *I'll Make Me a World.** I recalled
having seen Carmen de Lavallade's superb interpretation of this
poem, in which she spoke the lines as she moved. It did not enter my
head that I, too, might dance the same poem because the work
seemed so exclusively hers.

At home that same day, I was listening to a recording of Debussy's *La Mer* when, as the first movement unfolded, I found myself
automatically speaking aloud the opening words of the Johnson
poem:

>And God stepped out on space
>And he looked around and said:
>I'm lonely ——
>I'll make me a world.

I had my dance. I put aside for the moment the problem of
having such limited space in which to express such an enormous
theme as the creation of the world. Instead, I concentrated on the
problem of dancing to one's own spoken words. I had often done this
as a child, but I knew the difficulty of a public performance. If the
dance is vigorous, breath can be exhausted. If the voice is weak or
untrained, projection can be lost. If the recited lines are too poetic,
too subtle, or too philosophical, the attention of the audience is always divided between hearing and seeing: a thought or image expressed verbally demands more time to digest than the dancer's
movements can allow.

Even realizing this, I nevertheless went to work with book and
record. The poem provided the scenario for the dance, but I had to
discover how to tailor each syllable to each musical phrase; how to
obey and fill the pauses in both; how to move with their crescendos
and decrescendos; how to be soft, hard, gentle, thunderous. I also
had to think in terms of almost purely horizontal space because the
"stage" had little depth. Furthermore, I had to determine what costume and lighting would be appropriate. The project was a gigantic
puzzle. Only after some 500 hours of shaping, tinkering, sore muscles, aching back, screaming knees, hoarse throat, and sleepless
nights did my creation begin to come to life.

Only then could I allow myself a mite of satisfaction. Whether
the work would be successful had become irrelevant. I could love it,

*James Weldon Johnson, *God's Trombones* (New York: Viking Press, Inc., 1927).

hate it, destroy it, preserve it as teaching material, or put it out of my conscious mind forever. But it had become a part of my reason for being, and I was pleased that my baby had been born whole. Its voice was lusty enough to be heard and the words understood. Its limbs moved in strong, wide, controlled abstract patterns that suggested the dramatic immediacy of the poem's development and the music's emotion. I dressed this infant in plain brown close-fitting shirt and slacks, the only nod to the Deity being a halo-like roll of gold cloth encircling a black skullcap.

During my performance, I sensed that although my movements were restricted to the torso and to extensions of legs and arms (mostly from side to side and with gestures of the hands), they were at one with the words which at some moments I intoned, at others spoke softly, or almost sang in exultance. (I was sharply reminded by a gouge from the large cross hanging behind me that my corresponding *movements* should not be that exultant.) It was a strange sensation to dance a religious work in a house of God and not be bound to a specific sect. I realized that whenever I danced for charity, as indeed I was doing, I experienced a kind of release, as if a special freedom comes from the doing of a thing for itself alone.

I was touched by the audience's understanding and acceptance of what I had tried to create. In that audience happened to be Edna Johnson, the publisher of *The Churchman,* a national journal devoted to "a humanistic approach to Religion, Ethics and Education." She asked me if I would repeat this dance for the 1976 annual United Nations luncheon. (I was later to be particularly glad that I accepted this invitation because in the audience at that celebration was a friend of Jane Sherman who knew of our mutual Denishawn background and brought us together—"something Strange and Wonderful.")

This time, the dance was presented in the ballroom of a local hotel on a bare, square platform surrounded by dining tables. There was no lighting except the sun that streamed down from tall windows. I felt as if I were again back in the army entertaining the troops, with the usual lack of theatrical amenities and precious little room in which to move. As then, most of my audience had never seen anything like my kind of dancing, and certainly not as part of luncheon entertainment. Also as then, I was apprehensive about the kind of reception my work would get under the peculiar circumstances. But from the first note of music, the first gesture, the first word, the attention was phenomenal. No one swallowed a mouthful of food or sip of coffee. Not a tinkle of silverware or glasses came from impatient waiters. Not a pan crashed in the nearby kitchen. Sunlight poured down on me as if from a heavenly spotlight. The acoustics favored my delicate tape-recorded Debussy while lending my voice the resonance of Almighty Authority. I managed to restrain my more exuberant movements within the confines of the platform. With bowed head, I spoke the final words, "Amen, Amen," and walked off.

The silence was a held breath. Then that response was transformed into acclaim as the audience realized they were allowed to applaud. My baby, having been properly baptized in a church, had now taken its first steps in public on its way to a theatre debut at Jacob's Pillow five years later.

I remembered what Shawn had written after watching on television a human being step on the moon: "I wish we could see the first historical step of man having learned to live harmoniously and lovingly with all Mankind!" and knew he would have been pleased with the dance-grandchild that expressed these feelings on an occasion honoring the United Nations. For had he not also written in his *Credo*:

> I believe that dance is the universal language, and as such, has the power to promote One World.

So be it, dear Ted.

Postscript

In retirement, I continued to teach dance at various schools, colleges, and universities and to coach revivals of Shawn's works. I faithfully did my daily *barre* at home to tapes made from old Denishawn records, with Ted's own voice announcing the exercises. Except for infrequent local appearances, however, it seemed that my professional life might be over, and I missed it.

Then, unexpectedly, I was invited to teach Denishawn and Shawn techniques, and to dance Shawn solos, at a conference called *The Early Years: American Modern Dance from 1900 through the 1930's* held in April 1981 at the State University of New York in Purchase, under the auspices of SUNY's University-Wide Program in the Arts. My friend and co-author, Jane Sherman, was also invited to participate, with two papers on Denishawn.

I have often been astonished as I watched a dancer in full maturity when performance is no longer possible. As she or he gestures or illustrates a movement, I suddenly glimpse a vivid picture of that person at youthful career's height. Although I had never seen Jane dance, I sensed on this 1981 occasion how enchanting she must have been in her Denishawn roles. As she spoke, the lilt of the voice, the quality of the carriage, the expressiveness of the eyes belied the years to show me the Jane of the twenties.

That summer, I also taught and danced again at Jacob's Pillow, performing Shawn's cherished solo, *O Brother Sun and Sister Moon,* and my composition, *I'll Make Me a World.* (This appearance marked, almost to the day, my debut as a professional dancer in Shawn's ballet *Job,* presented at Lewisohn Stadium in August 1931.)

On the same program at the Pillow, the Vanaver Caravan dancers brought to life Jane Sherman's reconstruction of Shawn's *Boston Fancy: 1854,* in which she had danced throughout the Orient and United States tours of the Denishawn Dancers in the mid-twenties, and in which I had appeared in the 1931–32 revival. During this week, Jane and I also assisted with early planning for the Jacob's Pillow fiftieth anniversary celebration, scheduled to continue through the following season.

Health problems prevented me from dancing in these 1982 festival programs, but I did have the pleasure of coaching Mark Morris in Shawn's *Mevlevi Dervish* and David Brown in my *Banner Bearer.* The week of August 3 saw a very specialized program on the stage of the Ted Shawn Theatre. The Vanaver Caravan presented Jane's revival of Shawn's *Five American Sketches (Danse Americaine, Around the Hall in Texas, A Gringo Tango, Pasquinade,* and *Boston Fancy),* a suite that had not been seen in its entirety by the general public since the Denishawn concert at Carnegie Hall on April 6, 1927.

Richard Cragun of the Stuttgart Ballet danced *Pierrot in the Dead City* and *Fetish.* (I worked with Mr. Cragun until I sensed that he had absorbed the original intent of the pieces, then said to him, "You're a great dancer. I respect your sensitivity and understanding, your school and your technical accomplishment. Will you please dance these solos as if they were your own, without reference to how I danced them?" He did. As a result, the works seemed new, free from that deadening weight of accuracy that so often restricts the quality of revivals.) Cynthia Gregory of American Ballet Theatre evoked Ruth St. Denis in an interpretation of her 1922 *Brahms Waltz-Liebestraum.*

Programmed with these reconstructions of Denishawn-Men Dancers works were dances from the genres of classical ballet, modern choreography, jazz, and clogging. As a powerful affirmation of Shawn's belief that dance should include all forms of movement, the performers in their varied disciplines thus paid fitting homage to the man on this anniversary of his founding Jacob's Pillow.

On the final night of the program, director Liz Thompson followed her opening curtain talk by projecting slides of the original Men Dancers in poses from their most famous dances. Then, one by one, she introduced from their seats in the audience the seven Men Dancers who had come from all parts of the country to celebrate this place of dance that they had helped build with their own hands and their own artistry. I stood beside them again for the first time in twenty-five years or more: Foster Fitz-Simons, Fred Hearn, Wilbur

McCormack, Frank Overless, and our twins, John and Frank Delmar, (later to be joined by Jess Meeker, who was accompanying Cragun and Gregory). Jane watched tearfully from the wings.

Interrupting his bows at the end of *Fetish,* Cragun brought me out on stage to share the applause. I took that moment to voice my tribute to Shawn and his ideals, which had found ultimate fulfillment in this landmark of American dance. Not wanting to end the festivities on a somber note from the past, however, I concluded my brief talk by asking the audience to join me in three cheers for Jacob's Pillow and its future. The shouted "Hip, hip, hooray!" set to vibrating my weathervane atop the theatre and almost raised the roof on which it perches.

May such applause for the next generations of dancers, who will appear on the stage of Shawn's theatre, echo among those mighty hand-hewn rafters for at least another fifty years.

Editor's note:
On June 16, 1984, following a weekend of dance festivities in his honor at Florida State University in Tallahassee, Barton Mumaw was presented a merit award for his lifetime contribution to dance by the State Dance Association of Florida.

Asides

―*A Word on Lighting*

Martha Graham has said, "Dance is another way of putting things. It isn't a lyrical or literary thing, but everything that a dancer does, even in the most lyrical thing, has a very definite and prescribed meaning. If it could be said in words, it would be: but outside of words, outside of painting, outside of sculpture, *inside* the body is an interior landscape which is revealed in movement." I believe that in order to reveal this interior landscape, choreographers need to study the use of theatrical tools—costume, music, and lighting—as thoroughly as they study the dynamics of motion and design.

Imaginative lighting in particular can contribute depths of meaning to any dance work, as the greats from Loie Fuller to Graham herself have always known. Young dancers might well study Fuller's original experiments with fabrics, chemicals and lights. Or refer to Diaghilev, who once kept an audience waiting for hours while he rehearsed the lights. Or look to Ruth St. Denis, a true lighting innovator in her day, who maintained that "You cannot *talk* lighting. You have to *do* it." (Working with and learning from her, Shawn often complained that she had no conscience about expense when it came to that department.)

―*Three Performers to Remember*

I always enjoyed visiting stars backstage, and I particularly remember when Shawn took me to see his old friends, Gilda Grey and

311

Julian Eltinge, who were then appearing at Billy Rose's Diamond
Horseshoe. Long ago, in Hollywood, Gilda had been sent to Shawn
for coaching. Although she was already famous for her notorious
"shimmy", she admitted that she had never had a dance lesson in
her life.

"What," Ted asked her, "do you do when you get on stage,
Miss Grey?"

"Oh, I just go out there and express myself," she replied.

With this story in mind, and with only the vaguest memory of
having seen Grey in the movies of my youth, I did not expect to
witness much of an illuminating nature. But from where Shawn and
I sat in the theatre, this maturely contoured woman looked pretty
good. To a piece of nostalgic twenties music, she began to move
slowly, almost unnoticeably, then faster and faster until her entire
body was vibrating. It was a neat technical trick, but it was more
than that. It projected the quality of a religious trance right across
the footlights into the audience, exactly as I had seen in Shawn's
Mevlevi Dervish. Art, obviously, takes many forms.

I was equally astonished by the artistry of Julian Eltinge, who
appeared utterly and beautifully feminine on stage. Ted told me that
Eltinge had originally starred in drawingroom comedies—as an ac-
tress. This was years before he and Shawn toured vaudeville circuits,
often appearing on the same bills.

When Ted and I went backstage at the conclusion of his Diamond Horseshoe act, a gruff voice yelled "Come in!" in response to
Shawn's knock on his dressingroom door. As soon as we entered and
Eltinge recognized Ted, he grabbed him in his arms, babbling a
string of four-letter words that would have brought blushes to the
cheeks of a top sergeant. He forced us into chairs, then sat down
himself—a dumpy, pot-bellied, elderly man in underwear shorts
who thrust his big, slippered feet up on the dressing-table amid the
jars and powders, the falsies and wigs of his trade. Jamming a
smelly, much-chewed cigar in his mouth, he launched into bizarre
reminiscences of other times, other places. Not a hint of the stage
vision of lovely womanliness could be detected.

Mae West's was the only autograph for which I ever stood in
line. Where Julian Eltinge seduced the audience into believing he
really was a woman, the overtly sexy Miss West gave the impression
of being a man in drag. After one of her rare appearances in a
Broadway play, I was curious to see her close up. I joined the line of
fans who had been instructed to wait at the stage door for Miss West
to exit.

And what an exit! One could almost hear trumpets blare when, with a gesture worthy of Richard Mansfield himself, the doorman flung open the iron barrier. Out marched a liveried chauffeur, erect and expressionless as a storm trooper. Following him, Mae West sauntered past us with her inimitable hip-swaying walk as she bowed right and left with the stiff-necked dignity of Britain's old Queen Mary. Behind her stalked a handsome, beefy man who protected the star from any approach by the hoi polloi. Once safely installed in her limousine—its lighting skillfully adjusted to focus on her million-dollar face—the great West graciously leaned forward and indicated through the open window that she would now sign autographs. This performance was staged in regal silence. No one of the little crowd moved until the car at last slowly advanced into the traffic and disappeared, bearing its spotlighted vision away from our entranced eyes.

Denishawn Technique
and Greater Denishawn

Many misconceptions about Denishawn technique still persist, but I well remember the combination of ballet, Delsarte, Dalcroze, and ethnic movements that Shawn had devised and that I learned at Greater Denishawn. From the interaction of these techniques emerged Denishawn dancing, which freed ballet from rigid bonds and westernized Oriental traditional dance to adapt to our sturdier, less pliable American bodies. For example, in the thirties an observor watching St. Denis dance her solo *Cathédrale Engloutie*, to the Debussy music, exclaimed, "Why, her movement is as modern as any I have seen Martha Graham use!". To which Shawn replied with a grin, "Miss Ruth did modern before modern was invented."

Denishawn classes were customarily three hours long. They began with stretching, *barre*, and open floor exercises to perfect *arabesques, attitudes, developpés en tournant, grands jétés,* and *fouéttes*. Then each pupil alone did a series of Spanish, Hungarian, and Denishawn *pas de basques*.

Next we danced a sequence called "Arms and Body", done to the *Briar Rose Waltz* from Tchaikovsky's "Sleeping Beauty." This was a forerunner of the technical warmups now used in some modern dance schools. It started with feet placed widely apart, flat on the floor. A slow, loose swinging of the body developed into ever larger circles. Then came head, shoulder, and torso rolls, arms sweeping from floor to overhead; side extensions; and at the end, a relaxed running around the studio, culminating in a back fall. We would then sit in a circle and practice hand stretches to force the fingers as far back as they could go, in imitation of Cambodian or Balinese flexibility. Or we would strain to copy the East Indian cobra side-to-side head movements above motionless shoulders.

Class always concluded with learning a dance that could be costumed and presented on stage. Some of these—*Serenata Morisca, Gnossienne, Invocation to the Thunderbird,* among others—found their way into the Denishawn performing repertory. Most of them never left the studio, such as a solo to Chopin's *Waltz in A-flat minor,* a *Tunisienne* taught to acquaint us with the use of those small brass finger cymbals Shawn called *krotali,* a *Sevillanas* for two couples playing castanets, a simple nautch, a gypsy dance, a sculpture plastique. Our courses also included German *modern Tanz* as taught by Margharita Wallmann.

As Shawn wrote, "We were never *exclusive.* We gave our students the richest and most varied fare possible—old, new, domestic, foreign, and anything we felt would enlarge their knowledge of dance that had any value (we did *not* include tap dancing!")

Greater Denishawn evolved from the original Los Angeles and New York Denishawn schools. In 1915, the first classes given in California lasted all day and cost $1.00 each. This fee, which each pupil dropped into a cigar box at the entrance, also included lunch. For years thereafter, Denishawn schools proliferated from coast to coast. At the New York schools located, in the twenties, in Carnegie Hall and on West Twenty-eight Street, Doris Humphrey and Charles Weidman acted as Shawn's assistants for advanced classes. Hazel Krans and Paul Mathis taught beginners. Shawn determined the curriculum each season, and also taught. Teachers who headed Denishawn schools in other parts of the country came to New York during the summer to study with him. He also prepared choreographic notes of exercises and dances to mail to those who could not come to the city.

Most of the best-known schools outside New York were later headed by former Denishawn Dancers: Ernestine Day in Arkansas City, Estelle Dennis in Baltimore, Betty Horst in Los Angeles, and Edith James in Dallas. At least one Denishawn school is still functioning after more than fifty years. Located in Fitchburg, Mass., it is headed by Marion Rice, a former pupil of the Braggiotti sisters at the Boston school. In an era when "going on the stage" was still considered not "nice", the American public regarded as impeccable the private lives of the happily-married Ruth St. Denis and Ted Shawn, and the "respectable" image of their Dancers. (Miss Ruth had long fostered that image by letting it be known through the media that she lived according to the highest personal ideals—in unspoken but clearly implied contrast to the "scandalous" Isadora Duncan.)

As the Denishawn schools grew in number, it therefore soon became fashionable to enroll one's child in their classes, as if in a finishing school. This "moral" reputation carried over to Jacob's Pillow, to which parents, with complete peace of mind, sent daughters as young as fifteen to live for weeks in rather primitive dormitories under very strict housemothers.

St. Denis and Shawn were always deeply concerned about the total education of their pupils. Ted often told me with pride that every school was supplied with books on many different subjects, which the students were encouraged to read. In the planning of Denishawn House, the architect was instructed to include a library. I remember that its shelves were filled with the books Shawn and St. Denis had collected over many years, and that later, the main house at Jacob's Pillow also included a library that was accessible to everyone.

For a long time Shawn, with the support of a more or less enthusiastic St. Denis, had envisioned every aspect of the Van Cortlandt Denishawn House. After the long years of touring, always having to lug with them not only their lares and penates—notes, books, music, photographs—but also the scenery, costumes, and all the other essentials of a professional theatrical company and of the school from which the members of that company must come—here at last they hoped to establish a permanent base. Here were housed resident teachers, students, a costume department, the storage warehouse for scenery and props, music files, and the library, to comprise a dance university as well as a home for its founders. Nothing like it had been seen before in this country. There were even plans to add a Theatre of the Dance, for which Claude Bragdon had prepared blueprints and which, in the always optimistic minds of St. Denis and Shawn, they saw already built and functioning.

They did achieve this beginning of Greater Denishawn, but they never realized its complete conception. And they certainly had not foreseen its premature end.

Dances Performed by
Barton Mumaw 1933–1981

WORKS CHOREOGRAPHED BY TED SHAWN FOR
HIMSELF; LATER PERFORMED BY BARTON MUMAW

1919 **Gnossienne (A Priest of Knossos).** A full
description appears in Part Two.

1929 **Mevlevi Dervish.** Solo. Music by Anis Fuleihan.
First performance by Shawn: Carnegie Hall, New
York, April 15, 1929. First performance by Mumaw:
Ted Shawn Theatre, Jacob's Pillow, Mass., summer
1972.

1930 **Osage-Pawnee Dance of Greeting.** Music by
Homer Grunn. First performance by Shawn (solo):
Bachsaal, Berlin, Germany, March 15, 1930. First
performance as group dance (Mumaw, Cole, Griggs,
Shafer): Chapin Hall, Williamstown, Mass.,
December 4, **1931.** First performance by Mumaw
(solo): Program for troops stationed in England
during World War II, **1942.**
The Divine Idiot. Solo. Music by Alexander
Scriabin. First performance by Shawn: Washington
Irving High School, New York, October 17, 1930.
First performance by Mumaw: Ted Shawn Theatre,
Jacob's Pillow, Mass., summer **1972.**
Four Dances Based on American Folk Music: *Old
Fiddler's Breakdown,* music by David Guion; *Nobody*

*Knows the Trouble I've Seen, Gimme That Ol' Time
Religion,* and *Battle Hymn of the Republic,*
traditional.   Solos. First performance by Shawn:
Opera House, Providence, R.I., January 8, 1931.
First performance by Mumaw: Ted Shawn Theatre,
Jacob's Pillow, Mass., summer **1972.**

1931   **O Brother Sun and Sister Moon (A Study of
St. Francis).**   Solo. Music by Ottorino Respighi.
First performance by Shawn: Chapin Hall,
Williamstown, Mass., December 4, 1931. First
performance by Mumaw: Ted Shawn Theatre,
Jacob's Pillow, Mass., summer **1981.**

1933   **Cutting the Sugar Cane.** A full description appears
in Part Two.

WORKS CHOREOGRAPHED BY TED SHAWN
FOR BARTON MUMAW: MEN DANCERS CONCERTS

1933   **The French Sailor.**   A full description appears in
Part Two.

1934   **Pleasantly Satiric Comment.**   Solo. Music by
Sergei Prokofiev. First performance by Mumaw:
Hawley Armory, Storrs, Conn., January 4, **1934.**

1935   **Pierrot in the Dead City.**   A full description
appears in Part Two.

1936   **Blues–1929.**   Solo in *The Jazz Decade,* from Shawn's
full-evening production, *O, Libertad!* (Act II: "The
Present"). Music by Jess Meeker. First performance
by Mumaw: Cherry Valley School, Garden City,
N.Y., October 7, **1936.**

WORKS CHOREOGRAPHED BY BARTON MUMAW:
MEN DANCERS CONCERTS

1933   **Fetish.**   A full description appears in Part Two.
Dyak Spear Dance.   A full description appears in
Part Two.

1936   **The Banner Bearer.**   A full description appears in
Part Two.

1938   **Spirits of the Earth.**   Solo from Shawn's
full-evening production, *Dance of the Ages* (Section III).
Music by Jess Meeker. First performance by

Mumaw: Massachusetts State College, Amherst, Mass., October 7, 1938.

High Priest and Initiate.   Duet for Shawn and Mumaw from *Dance of the Ages* (Section I). Music by Jess Meeker. First performance: Massachusetts State College, Amherst, Mass., October 7, 1938.

1940   **Bourrée.**   A full description appears in Part Two.

The God of Lightning.   A full description appears in Part Two.

WORKS CHOREOGRAPHED BY TED SHAWN FOR BARTON MUMAW: MUMAW CONCERT TOURS AND ELSEWHERE

1941   **Where'er You Walk.**   Solo. Music by George Frederick Handel (from *Semele*). Sung and danced by Mumaw, concert debut program: Carnegie Chamber Music Hall, New York, April 16, 1941.

Hellas Triumphant.   Solo. Music by Jess Meeker. First performance: Carnegie Chamber Music Hall, New York, April 16, 1941.

The Mongolian Archer.   Solo. (Inspired by Malvina Hoffman's sculpture.) Music by Jess Meeker. First performance: Carnegie Chamber Music Hall, New York, April 16, 1941.

Valse Brilliante.   Solo. Music by Mana-Zucca. First performance: Carnegie Chamber Music Hall, New York, April 16, 1941.

Morning, Noon and Night.   Solo. (Inspired by three bas-reliefs of Mumaw carved in wood by Shawn.) First performance: Jacob's Pillow, Mass., summer 1941.

1942   **The Banner Bearer.**   Solo. Rechoreographed by Shawn; danced by Mumaw in the Air Force production, *High Flight.* Music by Sergei Rachmaninov. First performance: Keesler Field, Miss., 1942.

Polka.   Solo. Music by Glahe. Danced by Mumaw in the Air Force production, *High Flight.* First performance: Keesler Field, Miss., 1942.

Mechanical Ballet.   Ensemble. Music unknown. First performance by Mumaw, leading a group of soldier-dancers: Keesler Field, Miss., 1942.

1946   **Polka Italienne.**   Solo. Music by Sergei
Rachmaninov. First performance: Carnegie
Chamber Music Hall, New York, November 24,
1946.

WORKS CHOREOGRAPHED BY BARTON MUMAW: MUMAW CONCERT TOURS AND ELSEWHERE

1941   **Sonata.**   Solo. Music by Domenico Scarlatti. First
performance, concert debut program: Carnegie
Chamber Music Hall, New York, April 16, 1941.
Funerailles (War and the Artist).   A full description
appears in Part Two.

1942   **Holy Roller.**   Solo. Music by David Guion.
Choreographed for Army performances in the
United States and England, 1942.
Two Spirituals: *Get on Board L'il Children* and *Sometimes
I Feel Like a Motherless Child.*   Solos. Traditional music
arranged by Henry O'Neill. Choreographed for
Army performances in the United States and
England, 1942.
Lover.   Solo waltz to popular music.
Choreographed for Army performances in the
United States and England, 1942.
Alborado del Gracioso.   Solo. Music by Maurice
Ravel. Choreographed for an Army performance:
Keesler Field, Miss., 1942.

1946   **La Puerta del Vino.**   Solo. Music by Claude
Debussy. First performance: Carnegie Chamber
Music Hall, New York, November 24, 1946.
La Cathédrale Engloutie.   Solo. Music by Claude
Debussy. First performance: Carnegie Chamber
Music Hall, New York, November 24, 1946.

1952   Mumaw was also leading dancer for the season's
eleven productions by the St. Petersburg (Fla.)
Operetta Company. Each of the following musicals
was scheduled for one week of performances: *New
Moon, Bittersweet, Sally, Music in the Air, The Merry
Widow, Sweethearts, Showboat, The Red Mill, Brigadoon,
Carmen* (sung in English), and *The Song of Norway*

(with a ballet danced to Edvard Grieg's *Piano Concerto in A minor*).

1953   **Florida Aflame.**   A historical pageant based on the Seminole Indian wars. Mumaw was also solo dancer for the production. First performance: The Amphitheatre, Lake Wales, Fla., summer 1953.

1963   **Lady in the Dark.**   Music by Kurt Weill. College production of the Broadway musical. First performance: University of Oregon, Eugene, Ore., November 15, 1963.

1967   **When Johnny Comes Marching Home.**   Solo. First performance: Ted Shawn Theatre, Jacob's Pillow, Mass., summer 1967.

1975   **I'll Make Me a World.**   A full description appears in Part Two. Performed at Jacob's Pillow, Mass., 1981.

1977   **Royal Hunt of the Sun.**   A pageant to celebrate the fiftieth anniversary of St. Petersburg (Fla.) Junior College. Mumaw was also solo dancer. First performance: St. Petersburg, Fla., April 14, 1977.

WORKS CHOREOGRAPHED BY OTHERS: PERFORMED BY MUMAW

1947   **Indian Dance.**   Solo. Choreographed by Helen Tamiris for a pageant, *The Promised Valley.* First performance: Salt Lake City, Utah, April 21, 1947.
       Wild Horse.   A full description appears in Part Two.

1950   **Oklahoma!.**   Agnes de Mille choreography reconstructed by Louisa Fornaca (original company) for African Theatre Productions. Music by Richard Rodgers. Mumaw danced premier role of Curly in the *Dream Ballet.* First performance: Johannesburg, South Africa, 1950.
       Out of This World.   Choreographed by Hanya Holm. Directed by Agnes de Mille. Music by Cole Porter. First performance: New York, December 21, 1950.

1954   **The Golden Apple.**   Choreographed by Hanya Holm. Music by Jerome Moross. Mumaw danced

solo and duet with Nelle Fisher, understudied role of
Paris. First performance: Phoenix Theatre, New
York, March 11, 1954.

1955   **Tales of Hoffmann.**   Music by Jacques
Offenbach.   **The Merry Widow.**   Music by Franz
Lehar. Choreographed by Willam Christensen.
Mumaw was leading dancer in both operettas. First
performance: Salt Lake City, Utah, summer 1955.

1956–61   **My Fair Lady.**   Choreographed by Hanya Holm.
Music by Frederick Loewe. First performance:
March 15, 1956.

Index